TERROR AND DEMOCRACY IN THE AGE OF STALIN

Terror and Democracy in the Age of Stalin is the first comprehensive study of popular participation in the "Great Terror," a period in which millions of people were arrested, interrogated, shot, and sent to labor camps. The book shifts attention from the machinations of top party leaders to the mechanisms by which repression engulfed Soviet society. In the unions and the factories, repression was accompanied by a mass campaign for democracy. Party leaders urged workers to criticize and remove corrupt and negligent officials. Workers, shop foremen, local party members, and union leaders adopted the slogans of repression and used them, often against each other, to redress long-standing grievances, shift blame for intractable problems in production, and advance personal agendas. Repression quickly became a mass phenomenon, not only in the number of victims it claimed, but also in the number of perpetrators it spawned. Using new, formerly secret, archival sources, *Terror and Democracy in the Age of Stalin* takes us into the unions and the factories to observe how ordinary people moved through clear stages toward madness and self-destruction.

Wendy Z. Goldman is a professor of history at Carnegie Mellon University. She is author of *Women, the State and Revolution: Soviet Family Policy and Social Life, 1917–1936* (Cambridge, 1993), winner of the Berkshire Conference Book Award, as well as *Women at the Gates: Gender and Industry in Stalin's Russia* (Cambridge, 2002).

Terror and Democracy in the Age of Stalin

The Social Dynamics of Repression

WENDY Z. GOLDMAN

Carnegie Mellon University

CAMBRIDGE
UNIVERSITY PRESS

CAMBRIDGE UNIVERSITY PRESS
Cambridge, New York, Melbourne, Madrid, Cape Town, Singapore, São Paulo, Delhi

Cambridge University Press
32 Avenue of the Americas, New York, NY 10013-2473, USA

www.cambridge.org
Information on this title: www.cambridge.org/9780521866149

First published 2007

Printed in the United States of America

A catalog record for this publication is available from the British Library.

Library of Congress Cataloging in Publication Data
Goldman, Wendy Z.
Terror and democracy in the age of Stalin : the social dynamics
of repression / Wendy Z. Goldman.
p. cm.
Includes bibliographical references and index.
ISBN 978-0-521-86614-9 (hardback) – ISBN 978-0-521-68509-2 (pbk.)
1. Soviet Union – History – 1925–1953.   2. Political persecution – Soviet Union.
3. Political purges – Soviet Union.   4. Soviet Union – Social conditions.
5. Soviet Union – Economic conditions.   I. Title.
DK267.G639   2007
947.084'2 – dc22   2006037701

ISBN   978-0-521-86614-9 hardback
ISBN   978-0-521-68509-2 paperback

This book is dedicated to my children
Eva Jane Rediker
and
Ezekiel Kalman Rediker
in the hope that the past will prove useful to them in building a
better future.

Contents

Photos   *page* viii

Acknowledgments   ix

   Introduction: Toward a Social History of the Terror   1

1 The Social Crisis of Industrialization   11

2 From Murder to Mass Conspiracy   55

3 Mobilizing Mass Support for Repression   95

4 The Campaign for Union Democracy   133

5 Victims and Perpetrators   163

6 Rituals of Repression in the Factories   204

   Conclusion   252

Index   263

Photos

1 Serp i Molot (Hammer and Sickle) factory, 1935   *page* 52
2 Serp i Molot, 1935   53
3 Krasnyi Proletarii (Red Proletarian) factory, 1935   54
4 Funeral of Sergei M. Kirov with Stalin by the coffin   93
5 Nikolai I. Ezhov, head of the People's Commissariat of Internal Affairs   93
6 Nikolai I. Ezhov   94
7 Meeting of workers in Serp i Molot's open hearth furnace, 1936   131
8 Meeting of workers in Trekhgornaia Manufaktura   132
9 Women workers in the Kauchuk Rubber Factory at an election meeting, June 1937   162
10 Workers cast secret ballots in multicandidate elections for the factory committee in the Chicherin Machine Building factory, Moscow, June 1937   162
11 Aleksandra V. Artiukhina, head of the Union of Cotton Textile Workers in Moscow and Leningrad   202
12 Nikolai M. Shvernik, head of the All Union Central Council of Unions   203
13 P. F. Stepanov, director of Serp i Molot, 1933   248
14 Workers in the Likernovodochnyi (Spirits and Vodka) factory pouring vodka into bottles, 1937   249
15 Workers in Krasnyi Proletarii listen to a speech by a party organizer, 1939   250
16 Meeting of workers in Serp i Molot, 1939   251

Acknowledgments

I am grateful to many people and institutions for their help. The National Council for Eurasian and East European Research and the American Council of Learned Societies/Social Science Research Council/National Endowment for the Humanities International and Area Studies Fellowship provided grants for research and writing. The History Department of Carnegie Mellon University offered supplementary support and generous travel allowances for research in Russia. The exchange between Carnegie Mellon University and the Russian State University for the Humanities (RGGU) proved invaluable in aiding my work in libraries and archives in Moscow. I am indebted to Irina Karapetiants, Iuri Afanas'ev, John Lehoczky, and Joe Trotter for their continuing financial and administrative support for the exchange. I am also grateful to my Russian colleagues at RGGU. Aleksei Kilichenkov and Igor Kurukin, in particular, have aided me in numerous ways, large and small. Elena Nikulina provided able and efficient research assistance.

The staff at the State Archive of the Russian Federation (GARF) have been unfailingly helpful. Their professionalism and dedication in the face of numerous obstacles and hardships inspire great respect. I am especially grateful to Nina Abdulaeva, the head of the reading room, and to archivist Boris Sadovnikov, who acquainted me with the holdings of the All Union Central Council of Unions (VTsSPS) and unions. Without his guidance, I would never have found many of the materials included here. I am also grateful to Lydia Naumova, the head of the reading room in the Central Archive of Social Movements of Moscow (TsAODM), now the Central Archive of Social-Political History of Moscow (TsAOPIM), for her help in ordering documents and negotiating restrictions. Barry Schles, the head of interlibrary loan at Carnegie Mellon University's Hunt Library, has been highly resourceful in locating even the most difficult materials. The

Russian State Archive of Film and Photographic Documents (RGAKFD) allowed me to reprint selections from their archive of historical photographs, and the Tretiakov Gallery went to some effort to locate and reproduce Solomon Nikritin's powerful painting, *People's Court*, for the cover of this book. A portion of this book first appeared as an article, "Stalinist Terror and Democracy: The 1937 Union Campaign," in *American Historical Review*, December 2005.

William Chase, Donna Harsch, Carmine Storella, and Lynne Viola all offered excellent suggestions and comments on the manuscript. Naum Kats has been a wonderful colleague, and has aided my research over the years in many ways. I have learned much from my discussions with Moscow colleagues Andrei Sokolov and Sergei Zhuravlev. Colleagues from the Working Class History Seminar in Pittsburgh, the University of Toronto, the American Association for the Advancement of Slavic Studies, and the Russian Labor History conference under the auspices of the International Institute for Social History all offered stimulating comments on portions of the manuscript. I worked in TsAODM over several summers with Simon Pirani, a friend, comrade, and colleague, and I am grateful for our spirited discussions about Russian politics, past and present. J. Arch Getty was unfailingly generous with sources and references, kindly answering every query. I fondly remember one bright summer afternoon in his Moscow apartment when we painstakingly reconstructed and reviewed the key arrests and political events of the late 1930s month by month. Donald Filtzer read the entire manuscript with great care and generously shared his extensive knowledge of Russian workers and factories with me. His comments were invaluable in revising the manuscript. His own meticulous research and passionate engagement with the big political issues of Soviet socialism serve as a model of what scholarship can and should be.

Finally, I would like to thank my husband, Marcus Rediker, who has accompanied me and walked many a mile in a field far from his own. Our political discussions over the years have deepened my understanding of the Soviet experiment. He still asks the hardest, the smartest, and the most useful questions.

Introduction

Toward a Social History of the Terror

The "Great Terror" is one of the most important events in Soviet and, indeed, in twentieth-century history. The Russian revolution in 1917, based on the simple principle that working people should control the wealth they create, inspired movements throughout the world. The terror's lawlessness, violence, and killing, however, thoroughly discredited and destroyed the world's first socialist experiment. It raised critical and difficult questions: when did "terror" begin? What were the causes? Who was responsible? Who benefited, and who lost? In a prison camp in the 1930s, a young communist woman captured the urgency of these questions in an anguished poem:

> We must give an answer: who needed
> The monstrous destruction of the generation
> That the country, severe and tender,
> Raised for twenty years in work and battle?[1]

Historians generally agree that the terror began with the assassination of Sergei M. Kirov, the head of the Leningrad party committee, in December 1934 and ended with the removal of Nikolai I. Ezhov, head of the People's Commissariat of Internal Affairs (NKVD), in November 1938. The most intense phase of repression is known in Russia as the Ezhovshchina or the "time of Ezhov," synonymous with his leadership of the NKVD from November 1936 to November 1938. In these two years, millions of people were arrested, interrogated, shot, and sent to labor camps. The NKVD arrested more than 1,575,000 people in 1937–8, the vast majority

---

[1] Yelena Vladimirova, a Leningrad communist who was sent to the camps in the late 1930s, wrote the poem. It is reprinted in full in Roy Medvedev, *Let History Judge: The Origins and Consequences of Stalinism* (Columbia University Press, New York, 1989), p. 634.

(87 percent) on political grounds. Of the total arrested, approximately 1,345,000 were convicted, and 681,692 executed for counterrevolutionary crimes. An additional 1,473,424 died of disease, cold, hunger, accidents, and other causes in the camps, in exile, or in prison.[2] From 1934 to 1940, 3,750,000 people, sentenced for criminal and political offenses, passed through the vast labor-camp system. In 1937 and 1938, there were so many arrests that the camps were thrown into crisis, unable to feed, clothe, or house the sheer numbers of new prisoners.[3] Although political arrests and party purges occurred before and after the Ezhovshchina, the terror reached its height in 1937 and 1938, marking the Soviet experiment in ways that could never be eradicated or forgotten.[4]

If historians largely agree about the timing of the "Great Terror," they disagree on almost every other aspect: the intent of the state, the targets of repression, the role of external and internal pressures, the degree of centralized control, the number of victims, and the reaction of Soviet citizens. One long-prevailing view holds that the Soviet regime was from its inception a "terror" state. Its authorities, motivated by the desire to gain total political control, sent a steady stream of people to their deaths in camps and prisons. The stream may have widened or narrowed over time, but it never stopped flowing. In this view, the terror grew from the Bolsheviks' commitment to a profoundly antidemocratic ideology. From the very moment they took power, they sought to crush civil society. Terror allowed them to consolidate power and to victimize all strata of a prostrate population. Scholars who advocated this interpretation were interested primarily in political history. Most, although not all, considered the Soviet Union a "totalitarian" state in which a small group of party leaders wielded total control over all aspects of social, economic, and

---

[2] J. Arch Getty, Gabor Rittersporn, and Viktor Zemskov, "Victims of the Soviet Penal System in the Pre-War Years: A First Approach on the Basis of Archival Evidence," *American Historical Review*, 98, 4 (October, 1993), pp. 1022–4.

[3] Oleg Khlevniuk, *The History of the Gulag: From Collectivization to the Great Terror* (Yale University Press, New Haven, 2004), pp. 306, 309, 177–81.

[4] "Ezhovshchina" and "the Terror" are terms that encompass purge, repression, and the general climate of fear. The term "purge" or *chistka* refers to a process within the Communist Party in which members were reviewed at periodic intervals and sometimes expelled for corruption, passivity, moral laxity, political opposition, or other reasons. In the late 1930s, these purges turned deadly, and expulsion was often, although not always, the prelude to arrest, imprisonment, or execution. Purge is also sometimes used to describe expulsions from an institution. The term "repression" refers to the wider phenomena of arrest, imprisonment, and execution affecting people within and outside the Party.

political life. As a result, in charting the political course of the state, they attached great importance to the actions of a few leaders, and little to the activities of workers, peasants, women, or other social groups.[5]

In the 1980s, a new interest in social history prompted a "revisionist" challenge to this view. Historians began to take a closer look at the fissures and tensions within the Soviet state. They charted sharp vacillations in policy, relationships between central and local authorities, conflicts between campaign-style justice and the rule of law, and the effect of foreign and internal social threats. They explored a dynamic dialectic between state policies and social responses in which social tensions influenced state actions, producing in turn unforeseen consequences, which led to increasingly draconian solutions. They identified specific targets and episodes of repression.[6] A few historians investigated institutions and groups, uncovering complex interactions between state initiatives and social or community interests. They began to explore "popular elements" in the terror, discovering that workers and peasants used its rituals and rhetoric to denounce managers and officials for abuse. The focus on the

[5] Robert Conquest, *The Great Terror: A Reassessment* (Oxford University Press, New York, 1990); Stéphane Courtois, Nicolas Werth, Jean-Louis Panné, Andrzei Paczkowski, Karel Bartosek, and Jean-Louis Margolin, *The Black Book of Communism: Crimes, Terror, Repression* (Harvard University Press, Cambridge, MA, 1999); Alexander Solzhenitsyn, *The GULAG Archipelago: An Experiment in Literary Investigation, 1918–1956* (Harper and Row, New York, 1974); Marc Jansen and Nikita Petrov, *Stalin's Loyal Executioner: People's Commissar Nikolai Ezhov* (Hoover Institution Press, Stanford, 2002); Oleg Khlevniuk, in *In Stalin's Shadow: The Career of "Sergo" Ordzhonikidze* (M. E. Sharpe, New York, 1995) and *1937-i: Stalin, NKVD i sovetskoe obshchestvo* (Izdatel'stvo Respublika, Moscow, 1992), presents a similar view of the state, but focuses mainly on the Ezhovshchina.

[6] J. Arch Getty, *Origins of the Great Purges: The Soviet Communist Party Reconsidered, 1933–1938* (Cambridge University Press, New York, 1985); Getty, "State and Society Under Stalin: Constitutions and Elections in the 1930s," *Slavic Review*, 50, 1 (1991), pp. 18–35; Getty, "Pragmatists and Puritans: The Rise and Fall of the Party Control Commission," *Carl Beck Papers in Russian and East European Studies*, 1208 (1997); Getty and Oleg Naumov, *The Road to Terror: Stalin and the Self-Destruction of the Bolsheviks* (Yale University Press, New Haven, 1999); James Harris, *The Great Urals: Regional Interests and the Evolution of the Soviet System, 1934–1939* (Cornell University Press, Ithaca, 1999); Roberta Manning, "Government in the Soviet Countryside in the Stalinist Thirties: The Case of Belyi Raion in 1937," *Carl Beck Papers in Russian and East European Studies*, 301 (1984); E. A. Rees, ed., *Centre-Local Relations in the Stalinist State, 1928–1941* (Palgrave Macmillan, Basingstoke and New York, 2002); Gabor Rittersporn, *Stalinist Simplifications and Soviet Complications: Social Tensions and Political Conflicts in the USSR, 1933–1953* (Harwood Academic Publishers, Chur, 1991); Peter Solomon, *Soviet Criminal Justice Under Stalin* (Cambridge University Press, New York and Cambridge, 1996).

reactions of various social groups raised new and fascinating questions about the relationship between interests "from below" and orders "from above" in sparking and spreading repression but, with a few exceptions, historians did not develop these initial findings.[7] Historians also began to focus on personal subjectivities, charting the inner psychology as well as the outward public reaction to repression in an attempt to understand how individuals responded to the terror.[8]

In the 1990s, newly released archival materials provided important information on Stalin's role and the targets of repression. The documents provided incontestable proof of Stalin's close personal involvement

---

[7] On workers and industry, see Sheila Fitzpatrick, "Workers Against Bosses: The Impact of the Great Purges on Labor-Management Relations," in Lewis H. Siegelbaum and Ronald Grigor Suny, eds., *Making Workers Soviet: Power, Class and Identity* (Cornell University Press, Ithaca, 1994), pp. 311–40; J. Arch Getty and Roberta Manning, eds., *Stalinist Terror: New Perspectives* (Cambridge University Press, New York, 1993), included pioneering articles on repression in the factories, countryside, military, and other places, such as Roberta Manning, "The Soviet Economic Crisis of 1936–1940 and the Great Purges" (pp. 116–41), Robert Thurston, "The Stakhanovite Movement: The Background to the Great Terror in the Factories, 1935–1938" (pp. 142–60), and David Hoffman, "The Great Terror on the Local Level: Purges in Moscow Factories, 1936–1938" (pp. 163–7); Wendy Goldman, "Stalinist Terror and Democracy: The 1937 Union Campaign," *American Historical Review*, 110, 5 (December, 2005), pp. 1427–53; Lewis Siegelbaum, *Stakhanovism and the Politics of Productivity in the USSR, 1935–1941* (Cambridge University Press, Cambridge, 1988); Robert Thurston, "Reassessing the History of Soviet Workers: Opportunities to Criticize and Participate in Decision-Making," in Stephen White, ed., *New Directions in Soviet History* (Cambridge University Press, Cambridge, 1992), pp. 160–90. Only Thurston developed these initial ideas into a monograph: *Life and Terror in Stalin's Russia, 1934–1941* (Yale University Press, New Haven, 1996). See also Sergei Zhuravlev, "Terror Against Foreign Workers in the Moscow Elektrozavod Plant, 1937–1938," in Barry McLoughlin and Kevin McDermott, eds., *Stalin's Terror: High Politics and Mass Repression in the Soviet Union* (Palgrave, Basingstoke, 2003), pp. 225–40. See also William Chase, *Enemies Within the Gates? The Comintern and the Stalinist Repression, 1934–1939* (Yale University Press, New Haven, 2001); and Asif Siddiqi, "The Rockets' Red Glare: Technology, Conflict, and Terror in the Soviet Union," *Technology and Culture*, 44, 3 (July, 2003), pp. 470–500, on the dynamics of repression in institutions. On peasant responses, see Sheila Fitzpatrick, *Stalin's Peasants: Resistance and Survival in the Russian Village After Collectivization* (Oxford University Press, New York, 1994), pp. 286–312.

[8] Sheila Fitzpatrick, *Everyday Stalinism. Ordinary Life in Extraordinary Times: Soviet Russia in the 1930s* (Oxford University Press, New York, 1999); Veronique Garros, Natalia Korenevskaya, and Thomas Lahusen, *Intimacy and Terror: Soviet Diaries of the 1930s* (New Press, New York, 1995); Igal Halfin, *Terror in My Soul: Communist Autobiographies on Trial* (Harvard University Press, Cambridge, MA, 2003); Jochen Hellbeck, "Fashioning the Stalinist Soul: The Diary of Stepan Podlubnyi, 1931–1939," in Fitzpatrick, ed., *Stalinism: New Directions* (Routledge, New York and London, 2000), pp. 77–116. This list does not include memoirists and novelists, who explore the reactions and psychology of the individual in great detail.

in repression. Peppered with Stalin's signature and marginal notes, they revealed his hand to be quite literally everywhere. The archives also yielded new information about victims. Earlier estimates of arrests and executions in 1937–8 proved to be highly inflated. Historians originally estimated the number of people arrested to be between 7 million and 20 million. New figures, based on archival materials, show that approximately 2.5 million people were arrested, for both political and nonpolitical crimes. Similarly, historians had estimated the number of executions at roughly 7 million, but the actual number, 681,692, turned out to be one-tenth of that estimate.[9] Although the number of victims was discovered to be smaller than previously thought, the range of groups within the population targeted for repression turned out to be far wider. New findings substantially expanded the categories of victims beyond the economic managers, party and military leaders, former oppositionists, and foreign communists previously identified by historians. "Order 00447" for "mass operations" in July 1937 set target numbers for the imprisonment or execution of criminals, village clergy, religious activists, former kulaks, *lishentsy* (nobles, industrialists, and others deprived of voting rights), and other "hostile elements." It was followed by "Order 00486," which mandated the arrest of wives of men convicted of counterrevolutionary crimes, and a series of "national operations" aimed at Germans, Poles, Romanians, Finns, Latvians, and other groups.[10] The mass operations alone resulted in the arrest of 766,000 people, of which 385,000 were executed. These findings led to a new subset of research, which one historian termed "victim studies."[11]

---

[9] The 2.5 million figure covers political and nonpolitical charges and includes the 1.575 million arrested by the security police. See Getty et al., "Victims of the Soviet Penal System in the Pre-War Years," pp. 1022–3.

[10] J. Arch Getty, "'Excesses Are Not Permitted': Mass Terror and Stalinist Governance in the Late 1930s," *Russian Review*, 61 (January, 2002), pp. 113–38; Paul Hagenloh, "Socially Harmful Elements and the Great Terror," in Fitzpatrick, *Stalinism: New Directions*, pp. 286–308; Oleg Khlevniuk, "The Objectives of the Great Terror, 1937–1938," in J. Cooper, M. Perrie, and E. A. Rees, eds., *Soviet History, 1917–1953: Essays in Honor of R. W. Davies* (St. Martin's Press, New York, 1995), pp. 83–104; Barry McLoughlin, "Mass Operations of the NKVD, 1937–1938: A Survey" (pp. 118–52), Nikita Petrov and Arsenii Roginskii, "The 'Polish Operation' of the NKVD, 1937–1938" (pp. 153–70), and David Shearer, "Social Disorder, Mass Repression and the NKVD During the 1930s" (pp. 85–117), all in McLoughlin and McDermott, *Stalin's Terror*; Melanie Ilic, ed., *Stalin's Terror Revisited* (Palgrave, Basingstoke, 2006), pp. 5–6.

[11] Shearer, "Social Disorder and the NKVD in the 1930s," p. 103; McLoughlin and McDermott, "Rethinking Stalinist Terror," in McLoughlin and McDermott, *Stalin's Terror*, p. 3. See also Ilic, *Stalin's Terror Revisited*.

New findings from the archives had a mixed influence on debates over the terror. They reinforced the longstanding contention of proponents of the totalitarian thesis that Stalin played a large personal role in the repressions. His role in mandating the mass operations encouraged some historians to conceptualize the terror more narrowly as "a series of centrally directed punitive actions." In the words of Oleg Khlevniuk, "Mass repressions started and ended on orders from above, whenever Stalin considered an action appropriate." Even local "excesses" were "determined by the central directives themselves."[12] Discovery of the mass operations, however, also sparked interest in the social tensions that pushed central party leaders into authorizing such sweeping arrests. Some historians argued that Stalin initiated the mass operations in order to eliminate disgruntled social groups that might serve as a "fifth column" in the event of war. Barry McLoughlin noted that the impetus for Order 00447 to a certain extent "came from below" and "definitely went beyond the Stalin-Ezhov axis." Regional party leaders, concerned about how disaffected social groups would vote in the upcoming democratic elections to the Supreme Soviet, welcomed and widened the mass operations.[13] Historians investigating NKVD initiative on the local level also challenged the notion of total central control.[14]

Moreover, new research blurred the sharp distinction between proponents of the totalitarian thesis and revisionists. Leading revisionists were in fact the first to reveal Stalin's great personal role in the repressions, a key tenet of the totalitarian thesis.[15] At the same time, new documents challenged the idea that Stalin's obsessive drive for power was the main force behind the terror. Vacillation, switchbacks, and backtracking marked the Party's winding "road to terror." Stalin and party leaders even hesitated over how to interpret the Kirov murder, an event that in retrospect served as the main catalyst for the terror.[16] And if "revisionists," so attuned to

---

[12] Oleg Khlevniuk, *The History of the Gulag*, pp. 140, 331. See Khlevniuk's review of Jansen and Petrov, *Stalin's Loyal Executioner*, and J. Arch Getty's response in "To the Editors," in *Kritika: Explorations in Russian and Eurasian History*, 4, 3 (2003), pp. 760–7, and 5, 1 (2004), pp. 233–5.

[13] Hiroaki Kuromiya, *Freedom and Terror in the Donbas: A Ukrainian-Russian Borderland, 1870s–1990s* (Cambridge University Press, Cambridge, 1998); Jansen and Petrov, pp. 79–111; McLoughlin, "Mass Operations of the NKVD, 1937–1938," pp. 123–4.

[14] Getty, "'Excesses Are Not Permitted'"; McLoughlin, "Mass Operations of the NKVD, 1937–1938"; A. Vatlin and N. Musienko, "Stalinist Terror in the Moscow District of Kuntsevo," in McLoughlin and McDermott, *Stalin's Terror*, p. 127.

[15] Lynne Viola, William Chase, and J. Arch Getty, all labeled "revisionists" at one time, made important contributions to our understanding of political repression.

[16] See Getty and Naumov, *The Road to Terror*.

social history, made significant contributions to the new political history, some political historians, dissatisfied by the narrow focus on Stalin and a few central party leaders, raised important questions about the connections between terror and "the recurring tremors of the industrialization and collectivization upheavals."[17] Finally, new political findings enriched, rather than invalidated, earlier attempts to explore the element of terror "from below" by clarifying the dynamic between central orders and social responses.[18] Most of the new archival discoveries, however, still centered on central party authorities. Apart from a few pioneering articles and books, historians have yet to engage either the influence of social pressures on central party policies or the responses of various social groups to repression, two critical elements in developing a social history of the terror.

This book shifts attention from the machinations of top party leaders to the mechanisms by which repression engulfed Soviet society. It explores how terror spread downward and outward through the hierarchical layers of the unions, a network that encompassed 22 million members and reached from the All Union Central Council of Unions (VTsSPS) to factory and shop committees. It argues that repression was a mass phenomenon, not only in the number of victims it claimed, but also in the number of perpetrators it spawned. Party leaders presented the murderous abrogation of civil rights that we presently term "the Terror" as patriotic "*anti*-terror" measures. They stressed that vigilance and denunciation were duties of all loyal citizens. Moreover, they couched these "anti-terror" measures in the language of antibureaucratization, socialist renewal, and mass control from below, appeals with strong popular resonance. While recognizing the importance of state signals and actions, the book argues that *repression was also institutionally disseminated.* People participated as perpetrators and victims, and sometimes both, through their membership in factories, unions, schools, military units, and other institutions. The complex issues and rivalries unique to these organizations helped fuel the political culture of repression.

In the factories and the unions, the social tensions of industrialization were critical to the spread of terror. Workers, shop foremen, local party members, and union leaders adopted the slogans of repression and used them, often against each other, to redress longstanding grievances,

[17] McLoughlin, "Mass Operations of the NKVD, 1937–1938," p. 142.
[18] Fitzpatrick, "How the Mice Buried the Cat" and *Stalin's Peasants*; Manning, "Government in the Soviet Countryside in the Stalinist Thirties"; Michael Ellman, "The Soviet 1937 Provincial Show Trials: Carnival or Terror?," *Europe-Asia Studies*, 53, 8 (December, 2001), pp. 1221–33.

shift blame for intractable problems in production, and advance personal agendas. Party and union leaders strongly encouraged workers and union members to attack and remove corrupt and abusive officials. Highly publicized campaigns for secret-ballot, multicandidate elections in the unions, the soviets, and the Party accompanied the terror. The slogans of repression were intimately intertwined with those of democracy. Superficially, these two phenomena appear in sharp contradiction. What could denunciations, spy mania, fear, mass arrests, extralegal trials, and executions possibly have in common with secret ballots, new elections, official accountability, and the revitalization of democracy from below? *Terror and Democracy in the Age of Stalin* examines this paradox and the troubling questions it raises about mass participation and support for repression.

The terror was not simply a targeted surgical strike "from above" aimed at the excision of oppositionists and perceived enemies, but a mass, political panic that profoundly reshaped relationships in every institution and workplace. It provided new concepts and language – "unmasking enemies," "suppressing criticism from below," "wreckers," "family circles," "lickspittles," and "toadies" – that gave workers and officials new avenues to pursue their interests. The unions, the VTsSPS, and the party committees in the factories all participated in a process of "self-devouring" in which their own members enthusiastically accused and denounced each other in ritualized exposures and expulsions. The perpetrators of purge often became victims of the very processes they had initially promulgated. Members of unions and local party organizations frequently became the agents of their own demise.

This internal dynamic, with its complicated organizational and psychological mechanisms of self-destruction, differed sharply from the mobile killing squads and genocidal death camps of Nazism. If the rhetoric of Nazism was aimed at the "enemy" without, the rhetoric of the Soviet terror centered on "unmasking" the "enemy" within. In this sense, the analogy between Hitler and Stalin, so commonly invoked, does little to illuminate the dynamics of the Soviet terror.[19] The Nazis' genocidal policies

---

[19] On comparative approaches to terror, see Omer Bartov, "Review Forum. Rewriting the Twentieth Century: Extreme Opinions," *Kritika*, 3, 2 (2002), pp. 281–302; Alan Bullock, *Hitler and Stalin: Parallel Lives* (Knopf, New York, 1992); Sheila Fitzpatrick and Robert Gellately, eds., *Accusatory Practices: Denunciation in Modern European History, 1789–1989* (University of Chicago Press, Chicago, 1997); Gellately and Ben Kiernan, *The Specter of Genocide: Mass Murder in Historical Perspective* (Cambridge University Press, New York, 2005); Ian Kershaw and Moshe Lewin, eds., *Stalinism and Nazism: Dictatorships in Comparison* (Cambridge University Press, Cambridge, 1997);

were perhaps closest to the mass operations, which also targeted specific social and national groups for arrest, deportation, or execution, but the Soviet terror was far broader than the mass operations. It transformed every workplace and institution with its ritualized "unmasking" of trusted workmates, internal reviews, accusations, and denunciations. A worker, party member, engineer, or official could as easily become a victim as a perpetrator. No one fully understood why certain victims were selected. Party members struggled in shocked incomprehension to explain the arrest of relatives and spouses at party meetings. Unlike the German genocidal war against the Jews, the line between victims and perpetrators in the Soviet case was blurred. Yesterday's denouncer often became tomorrow's victim.[20]

Mark Mazower, *Dark Continent: Europe's Twentieth Century* (Knopf, New York, 1999); Eric Weitz, *A Century of Genocide: Utopias of Race and Nation* (Princeton University Press, Princeton, 2003). On parallels between debates in German and Soviet historiography on Nazism and Stalinism, see Tim Mason, "Intention and Explanation: A Current Controversy About the Interpretation of National Socialism," in Mason, *Nazism, Fascism and the Working Class* (Cambridge University Press, Cambridge, 1995), p. 212; Martin Malia, "To the Editors," *Kritika*, 2, 4 (2001), pp. 707–11. See also Ian Kershaw, *The Nazi Dictatorship: Problems and Perspectives of Interpretation* (Oxford University Press, New York, 2000); "From the Editors. Really-Existing Revisionism?," *Kritika*, 3, 3 (2002), pp. 569–71; Christopher Browning, "Beyond 'Intentionalism' and 'Functionalism': A Reassessment of Nazi Jewish Policy from 1939 to 1941," in Thomas Childers and Jane Caplan, eds., *Reevaluating the Third Reich* (Holmes and Meier, New York, 1993), pp. 211–33. On the Soviet debate, see *Russian Review*, 45, 4 (1986), pp. 357–413, and 46, 4 (1987), pp. 379–431, and more recently Martin Malia, "Judging Nazism and Communism," *National Interest*, 69 (Fall, 2002), pp. 63–78, and Michael David-Fox, "On the Primacy of Ideology: Soviet Revisionists and Holocaust Deniers (In Response to Martin Malia)," *Kritika*, 5, 1 (Winter 2004), pp. 81–105.

[20] On popular responses to Nazi terror, see Christopher Browning, *Ordinary Men: Reserve Police Battalion 101 and the Final Solution in Poland* (Harper, New York, 1998); Norman Finkelstein and Ruth Birn, *A Nation on Trial: The Goldhagen Thesis and Historical Truth* (Metropolitan Books, New York, 1998); Robert Gellately, *Backing Hitler: Consent and Coercion in Nazi Germany* (Oxford University Press, Oxford, 2001); Michael Geyer and John Boyer, eds., *Resistance Against the Third Reich* (University of Chicago Press, Chicago, 1994); Daniel Goldhagen, *Hitler's Willing Executioners: Ordinary Germans and the Holocaust* (Vintage Books, New York, 1997); Raul Hilberg, *Perpetrators, Victims, Bystanders: The Jewish Catastrophe, 1933–1945* (Aaron Asher Books, New York, 1992); Eric Johnson, *Nazi Terror: The Gestapo, Jews, and Ordinary Germans* (Basic Books, New York, 1999); Ian Kershaw, *Popular Opinion and Political Dissent in the Third Reich: Bavaria 1933–1945* (Oxford University Press, Oxford, 1983); Claudia Koonz, *Mothers in the Fatherland: Women, Family Life, and Nazi Politics* (St. Martin's Press, New York, 1987); Detlev Peukert, *Inside Nazi Germany: Conformity, Opposition and Racism in Everyday Life* (Yale University Press, New Haven, 1987); Marlis G. Steinert, *Hitler's War and the Germans: Public Mood and Attitude During the Second World War* (Ohio University Press, Athens, 1977).

Terror and Democracy in the Age of Stalin traces the evolution of terror in the factories and the unions. Beginning with a broad overview of Soviet industrialization, it examines the initial apathy of workers and party members toward the hunt for "enemies," the concerted efforts of central party leaders to whip up hysteria over "wrecking" in industry, and the rapid descent into madness in the factories and the unions. In exploring the responses of workers, local party members, union officials, managers, and shop heads, it seeks to understand how fundamentally decent, normal people move, in clear, comprehensible stages, toward self-destruction.

The Social Crisis of Industrialization

"The engineers wear fox furs, receive meat, sugar, and other things. And the workers are starving. We have been starving here for three months. The unions and the economic organs are bureaucrats. We should demand that we all be equal. If there is hunger, everyone should be hungry, not just the workers alone."

— A worker addressing a meeting of 500 construction workers in the Kolomenskii machine building works, Moscow province[1]

At the height of the terror in 1937, the Union of Nonferrous Metal Miners held a long-overdue national meeting. The union's leaders extolled the "new democratic order." The unions were unmasking enemies in their ranks and busting up old leadership circles based on patronage. The country was at last experiencing "a political turnabout." Emboldened by the new rhetoric, a miner named Shadabudinov shyly stepped up to the rostrum. "Comrades," he began nervously, "I cannot speak as well as the comrades who have spoken, but I would ask you to hear me out." Shadabudinov explained that he wanted to say "several words about my pit which today gives the country so much copper." He "fell into this plenum by accident," and had never met the head of his union until this day. Union officials rarely visited his settlement and, when they did, they never went down into the pits. The local union tried to help the workers, but "things do not always go right, especially when wreckers interfere." And, in 1936, "we had a lot of wrecking." Sixteen miners had died, four in the past four months alone. Many more had been wounded, blinded, and crippled in accidents. "So frankly, this is a horror," Shadabudinov said quietly. Even worse, officials seemed not to care. Under the guise of political education,

[1] Gosudarstvennyi arkhiv Rossiiskoi federatsii (GARF), fond 5515, opis' 33, delo 50, "Sektor informatsii Otdela orgraboty i proverki ispolneniia VTsSPS. Svodka no. 5," list 1140b.

the party organizer did nothing but read the newspaper aloud. "He tells us fairytales," Shadabudinov said in disgust; "And for this he gets 400 rubles a month." The mine director was unresponsive, and the secretary of the party committee (*partkom*) was in the director's back pocket. The director had recently given him 4,000 rubles and a fine fur coat, which he sported around the frozen pits. Shadabudinov had written repeatedly to various officials about the situation, but none had responded. Finally he had gathered copies of all his letters, glued together a makeshift envelope from old newspaper, and sent the package off to Nikolai I. Ezhov, the head of the Commissariat of Internal Affairs (NKVD). "I did not receive an answer, but all the same, I feel something was done," Shadabudinov noted with satisfaction. "Five days ago, the Party Control Commission demanded to see the director and the secretary of the party committee."[2] Shadabudinov's denunciation opened an investigation of the director and the party committee secretary. Denounced for "wrecking," in all likelihood they suffered fates resembling those of countless other victims of the terror. Yet in Shadabudinov's view, who, if not these "wreckers" in fur coats, should answer for the dead and maimed miners?

The conflict that Shadabudinov described between miners and officials was just one of many. Industry in the 1930s was crisscrossed with high tension wires, humming with stress. Unremitting pressure from Moscow to meet unrealistic production targets, shop loyalties and rivalries, labor turnover, high accident rates, low wages, and painful living conditions all created serious tensions. The Party's rank and file were increasingly alienated from its policies, the unions were unable to represent workers' interests, and workers lacked any collective, officially recognized outlets to express their grievances. In and of themselves, these tensions would not have given rise to the terror of the 1930s.[3] Yet coupled with strong efforts by party leaders to involve workers and union officials in the elimination of "wreckers," they fueled the hunt for enemies. The terror provided a variety of groups with a new language to express their conflicting interests and grievances. As the hunt for enemies gained momentum, it overtook

---

[2] GARF, f. 7679, o. 3, d. 86, "TsK Soiuza rabochikh dobychi tsvetnykh metallov IV plenuma. Steno. Otchet," ll. 3–8, 66–67.

[3] Roberta Manning, "The Soviet Economic Crisis of 1936–1940 and the Great Purges," in J. Arch Getty and Manning, eds., *Stalinist Terror: New Perspectives* (Cambridge University Press, New York, 1993), pp. 116–41, argues that the economic crisis of 1936 was a cause of the purges. However, R. W. Davies, "The Soviet Economy and the Launching of the Great Terror," in Melanie Ilic, ed., *Stalin's Terror Revisited* (Palgrave, Basingstoke, 2006), pp. 12, 29, maintains that industry was "a resounding success" in 1936.

and subsumed the more focused attack on former oppositionists and transformed the culture of the workplace. Millions of people were drawn into the process as victims and as perpetrators, and sometimes both. In factories, mines, and mills, on vast new construction sites, in dormitories and crowded communal apartments, the terror was shaped and driven by the pressures particular to Soviet industrialization. This chapter sets the background for the 1937 conflagration, a fire that was lit and assiduously fanned by party leaders, but that found substantial fuel in the wider grievances, tensions, and resentments of the industrial workplace.

The Politics of Accumulation

In 1928, party leaders launched the first five-year plan, setting high targets for industrial production and construction. Thousands of workers migrated to vast new construction sites in Siberia, the Urals, and the Don basin to build great *kombinaty* of iron, steel, and chemicals. They dug new mines, erected great hydroelectrical dams, and expanded older factories. New methods of production wiped out traditional skills, undermining the power of older "masters" in the shops and foundries. Millions of new workers, including unprecedented numbers of women, entered the waged labor force for the first time. From 1929 to 1933, the number of people working for wages almost doubled from 11,873,000 to 22,649,200.[4] New migrants crowded the cities and workers' settlements, sleeping in earthen dugouts (*zemlianki*), hastily erected barracks, apartment corners, hallways, and even the "hot shops" and canteens of the factories. Peasants, fleeing newly collectivized villages, women, driven by the fall in real wages, and youth, eager for work, joined older workers with complex political histories in factories, in mines, and on construction sites. All these groups, marked in different ways by the country's tumultuous history, pitched headlong into the upheaval and chaos of industrialization.

In tandem with the industrialization drive, the Party launched a fierce struggle with the peasants to collectivize agriculture. Food prices rose precipitously as the stocks of vegetables, meat, butter, milk, eggs, and grain plummeted. The government introduced bread rationing in February 1929 in an attempt to guarantee food to workers and their families, halt speculation, and offset the declining purchasing power of the wage. Although rationing ensured a basic minimum for workers, it did not address the problem of shortage. Workers were still forced to buy much of

---

[4] *Trud v SSSR: statisticheskii spravochnik* (Moscow: TsUNKhU Gosplana, 1936), p. 25.

their food in private markets where high prices cut the purchasing power of the wage by half.[5] In an attempt to control prices, the government assumed control of food distribution, establishing closed workers' cooperatives attached to workplaces. Yet the new distribution system worked poorly, often failing to deliver food to towns and workers' settlements. Even bread, the mainstay of workers' diets, was often unavailable. Workers suffered painful shortages of all consumer items, including clothing, needles, thread, blankets, plates, cutlery, and shoes. Shortages of coal, fuel, timber, nails, glass, coal, machine parts, and tools plagued every workplace.

In launching the first five-year plan, the Party was faced with a vicious circle. In order to increase real wages and achieve greater prosperity, the price of commodities had to fall. Yet a decrease in prices was dependent on greater productivity. Wage increases alone would only lead to a larger number of people chasing a small number of goods, a classic prescription for a rise in prices – if not in state stores, then in informal resale markets. Party leaders maintained that workers' productivity would have to rise faster than their remuneration for a brief period. Eventually, goods would be produced more cheaply, and price decreases would ensure a rise in real wages and growth in overall prosperity. Above all, this plan required sacrifice and high output from workers.[6] Party leaders applied enormous pressure to managers to meet ambitious targets set in Moscow for every industry and workplace. Economic planners tinkered endlessly with the relationships among state prices, wages, norms of production, and capital investment in an attempt to reconcile the needs of hungry workers with the demands of industrialization.

Yet the perfect balance between accumulation and consumption, combining a high rate of investment, low prices, and decent wages, remained elusive. A stubborn three-way tug of war ensued among workers, party and union officials, and managers over the wage fund. Workers took every opportunity to raise their wages. Party and union officials tried to

---

[5] On the history and politics of rationing, see Elena Osokina, *Ierarkhiia potrebleniia: o zhizni liudei v usloviiakh stalinskogo snabzheniia, 1928–1935 gg.* (Izdatel'stvo MGOU, Moscow, 1993). On retail trade, see R. W. Davies, *Crisis and Progress in the Soviet Economy, 1931–1933* (Macmillan, Basingstoke and London, 1996), pp. 58–64; on the fall in real wages, see Wendy Goldman, *Women at the Gates: Gender and Industry in Stalin's Russia* (Cambridge University Press, New York, 2002), pp. 76–82.

[6] The conflict between "productivism" and "workerism" went back to the Civil War. "Productivism," however, reached its apogee with the industrialization drive in the 1930s. See Diane Koenker, *Republic of Labor: Russian Printers and Soviet Socialism, 1918–1930* (Cornell University Press, Ithaca, 2005), pp. 45–76, 260.

keep wages down while raising labor productivity. And managers were caught in the middle. By 1930, the high unemployment of the 1920s was replaced everywhere by labor shortages. Enterprises were desperate for workers.[7] Managers, anxious to retain workers to meet production targets, tried to maintain higher wages and lower production norms at state expense. In tandem with workers, they siphoned as much money as possible from the national wage fund, leaving union and party officials to uphold Moscow's directives. All three groups proved highly ingenious in advancing their interests. No sooner did workers wrest a rise in nominal wages than union and party officials raised production norms.[8] When the growth in wages outstripped labor productivity in 1931, the Party and unions countered with a new wage scale, a "great movement toward norming" in thousands of jobs, piecework, elimination of pay for down time (machine stoppage), and an increase in retail prices. In December 1931, the Politburo made a secret decision to raise prices. By spring 1932, retail prices had increased by 30 percent in state stores. V. V. Kuibyshev, head of the State Planning Commission, admitted the state was forced to adopt this "extremely undesirable measure" to provide funds for capital construction.[9]

Workers varied widely in their responses. Some willingly accepted the prevailing party line: "Fulfill the plan and prices will come down." One said, "We don't need to decrease the tempo of construction. What the capitalists did in many decades, we did in four years. It is better to live through some hardship than to be dependent on capitalist imports." Others, however, questioned party policy. If the socialist state set prices on behalf of the workers, why did the Party adopt policies so inimical to workers' interests? Workers in one Moscow factory, for example, readily agreed to price increases, but added, "We demand a corresponding increase in wages." One worker articulated the general confusion when he asked, "In capitalist society, prices are regulated by the market, but we have a planned economy, and prices still rise. Why is this so?" Others,

---

[7] Donald Filtzer, *Soviet Workers and Stalinist Industrialization: The Formation of Modern Soviet Production Relations, 1928–1941* (M. E. Sharpe, Armonk, NY, 1986), pp. 51–3. Filtzer notes that labor shortages led to skyrocketing labor turnover.

[8] Norms, based on time-and-motion studies, set output quotas for jobs. In 1924, norm setting was extended throughout industry and became a key means for raising productivity. See ibid., p. 22.

[9] GARF, f. 5451, o. 43, d. 31, "Material dlia TsK partii. Materialy k dokladu 'Zarabotnaia plata za 3 goda, 1930–1933,'" ll. 19–21; Davies, *Crisis and Progress in the Soviet Economy*, pp. 22–4, 54, 131–2, 194–5, 207–9.

with less faith in state policies, cynically explained that prices rose because "the state had ruined agriculture and there was no food."[10] Many workers felt betrayed by the Party's promises, and couched their dissatisfaction in the Party's own rhetoric. A mechanic in a mineral water factory declared: "They are not fulfilling the instructions of Comrade Stalin to improve the conditions of the workers. Wage rates were revised downward, but prices have increased." A party member and worker in a cotton-printing factory noted angrily, "This is the opposite of what Comrade Stalin said to do." An older woman worker in the Frunze factory, however, made no distinction between Stalin and the Party. She told her shopmates, "We must hang these thieves." When asked whom she meant, she replied, "The communists."[11]

Workers found their own ways to counter speed-up and falling wages: they left their jobs in search of better terms. In 1930, labor turnover, measured by the percentage of the workforce discharged each year, reached 115 percent. Although turnover fell steadily thereafter, in 1936, more than 87 percent of industrial workers left their jobs.[12] Factory managers, pressured to retain workers and meet their production targets, spent freely on overtime for "storming" at the end of every month. As a result, the Party was not successful in holding wages down: in 1932, the national wage bill ran 1,211,000,000 rubles over budget.[13] The Central Committee and Central Control Commission responded with a secret commission in December 1932 to draft a new plan for 1933. In an effort to halt the upward wage/price spiral, the commission directed managers to increase output norms, decrease the amount paid for piecework, and cut overtime sharply. Managers were expressly forbidden to increase wages beyond levels set by the collective contracts without government approval.[14] Yet the new plan, too, was not entirely successful, and the state instituted another round of price increases in 1933 to finance the construction of housing and the infrastructure needed to support the growing towns. Party and union

[10] GARF, f. 5451, o. 43, d. 13, "Svodka no. 2 'O povyshenii tsen,'" ll. 89, 890b. See Filtzer, *Soviet Workers and Stalinist Industrialization*, pp. 76–81, on workers' reactions to speed-up and shock work.

[11] GARF, f. 5451, o. 43, d. 13, "Informatsionnaia spravka no. 10 o nastroeniiakh rabochikh v sviazi s povysheniem tsen," ll. 9, 10.

[12] Filtzer, *Soviet Workers and Stalinist Industrialization*, pp. 51–3.

[13] GARF, f. 5515, o. 33, d. 50, "Postanovlenie ekspertnoi komissii po voprosu o pereraskhode fondov zarplate v 1932 g.," "Narkomu truda t. Tsikhonu," ll. 2, 150–1500b.

[14] GARF, f. 5515, o. 33, d. 50, "Politbiuro TsK VKP (b)," ll. 96–97. The commission planned for labor productivity to rise by 14 percent and wages by 9 percent, and prices to decrease by 3.9 percent.

officials grimly shouldered the task of explaining price increases to the workers.[15] Workers in the machine shop of Dinamo responded angrily, "You say that everything is fine and sufficient, that we are growing, but the fact is that you have nothing. They sing your praises in the newspapers, but you don't know what to do except fire people, decrease provisions for workers' families, and take away their ration cards."[16] Many workers felt that the state was squeezing them too hard.

The 9th Trade Union Congress was held in April 1932 under the slogan "From wages to production." The Party instructed union officials to mount "an energetic campaign" to increase norms in 1933 in the hope of raising an additional 82 million rubles to finance industrialization. Union officials were directed to organize brigades of young shock workers (*udarniki*) to bust old norms. Drawing on youthful enthusiasm for building socialism, they encouraged young workers to set new records and compete for awards.[17] The 1933 campaign built on a long string of similar efforts to raise productivity through competition between shops, factories, and individual workers, as well as through piecework or "payment by results." Planners developed complex "progressive piecework" calculations whereby the rate of remuneration rose with each successive unit of output. By the mid-1930s, schemes for wage payment had become so complicated that often workers, union leaders, and even managers could not explain how wages were calculated.[18] The All Union Central Council of Unions (VTsSPS) frankly admitted that most competitions, particularly in coal mining, were poorly organized and unsuccessful.[19]

The campaigns to bust norms split the working class. While young workers often responded enthusiastically, older workers resented the

---

[15] GARF, f. 5451, o. 43, d. 27, "Predsedateliam TsK soiuzov, respublikanskikh, kraevykh, oblastnykh sovprofov," ll. 1–2.

[16] GARF, f. 5451, o. 43, d. 27, "Sektor informatsii Otdela orgraboty i proverki ispolneniia VTsSPS," l. 9.

[17] On shock work and Stakhanovism, see R. W. Davies and Oleg Khlevnyuk, "Stakhanovism and the Soviet Economy," *Europe-Asia Studies*, 54, 6 (2002), pp. 867–903; Filtzer, *Soviet Workers and Stalinist Industrialization*; Hiroaki Kuromiya, *Stalin's Industrial Revolution: Politics and Workers, 1928–1932* (Cambridge University Press, New York, 1988); Lewis Siegelbaum, *Stakhanovism and the Politics of Productivity in the USSR, 1935–1941* (Cambridge University Press, New York, 1988); Kenneth Straus, *Factory and Community in Stalin's Russia* (University of Pittsburgh Press, Pittsburgh, 1997); Robert Thurston, "The Stakhanovite Movement: The Background to the Great Terror in the Factories, 1935–1938," in Getty and Manning, *Stalinist Terror*, pp. 142–60.

[18] Goldman, *Women at the Gates*, pp. 244–51. On attitudes toward piecework, see Davies, *Crisis and Progress in the Soviet Economy*, pp. 55–8.

[19] "Material dlia TsK partii," ll. 21–24.

faster pace. In a dye-trimming factory in Egorevsk, workers circulated a letter explaining that they refused to compete because they were on the edge of starvation. "We scarcely have the energy to drag our legs as a result of the sour cabbage soup they feed us in the canteen all the time. The old workers will not do this. There will be no more competition until we are fed properly."[20] The VTsSPS received complaints from workers in numerous industries about increased norms. Miners were upset because the horses were too famished to meet the haulage norms.[21] Workers on old, faulty machines blamed managers for failing to create conditions that would allow them to compete. Shock work (*udarnichestvo*) and its successor, Stakhanovism, introduced new tensions and grievances in the workplace, pitting old workers against young, workers in undercapitalized industries against their managers, and managers and engineers against party and union activists. Managers in undercapitalized industries, such as textiles, and industries with new technologies, such as steel, doubted the potential of shock work and Stakhanovism to increase productivity. The Party's euphoria with Stakhanovism was short-lived. By July 1936, about a year after Aleksei Stakhanov set his coal-mining record, party leaders recognized that record breaking and storming created more problems than they solved.[22]

Union officials and managers struggled over wages and norms, but their positions were the reverse of those held under capitalism. The VTsSPS noted that managers, not unions, "were guilty of driving up wages." Soviet managers, unlike their capitalist counterparts, initially worried little about wages, which were drawn from state funds. Outwardly acquiescent to Moscow's high output targets and norm-busting competitions, they dispensed generous wage bonuses to encourage production, colluded with workers to lower output norms, and tried to maintain pay scales, especially for less-skilled workers.[23] In 1933, union officials and managers clashed in several industries when managers tried to raise wages and the unions attempted to hold them down. Factory managers in Leningrad ignored the plan and insisted on raising the wage scale. Union officials

---

[20] "Svodka no. 2 'O povyshenii tsen,'" l. 84; see Filtzer, *Soviet Workers and Stalinist Industrialization*, pp. 77–8.

[21] GARF, f. 5451, o. 43, d. 27, "Svodka pisem rabochikh, signalistov VTsSPS," ll. 180b, 18.

[22] Davies and Khlevnyuk, "Stakhanovism and the Soviet Economy," pp. 887–96; Siegelbaum, *Stakhanovism and the Politics of Productivity in the USSR, 1935–1941*, pp. 247–93.

[23] See Filtzer, *Soviet Workers and Stalinist Industrialization*, pp. 222–9, on managerial concessions to workers.

dragged the director of the Leningrad stamp trust to court to prevent him from raising wages.[24] Workers and managers also colluded on "fictitious piecework." The Supreme Council of the National Economy (VSNKh) and the VTsSPS retreated from progressive remuneration in 1933 in response to "overspending" of the wage fund. They sternly cautioned managers that progressive remuneration was not to be applied without a corresponding increase in output.[25] The costs had come to outweigh the benefits. Despite orders from Moscow, many managers simply refused to reevaluate output norms, an enormous task that required assessment of hundreds of jobs. And if norms were raised, managers and foremen tried "to soften the impact."[26] When norms were raised in the Stalino, Voroshilovgrad, and Shakhty mines, directors tried to ensure that wages did not fall.[27]

Party leaders were not solely responsible for the pressures on workers, but were themselves subject to demands from the commissariats to increase investment. In 1934, despite hopes for a more moderate tempo of construction, they realized that the second five-year plan (1933–7) could not be fulfilled without greater investment. After much debate, they adopted a more ambitious plan for 1936, in the hope of building up defense as well as railways, light industry, schools, and the consumer sector. Forty percent of industrial growth was expected to come from increases in labor productivity. Workers and party leaders, riding their respective horses, "Wages" and "Productivity," continued the race for capital appropriation. In 1933, the Party introduced higher norms. In 1934, the increase in wages once again outstripped the gains in labor productivity. The Party responded with a norm revision in April 1935, but wages continued to rise. Norms were increased again in 1936, spurring productivity to surpass wages. Yet workers did not abandon the field: despite the greater increase in productivity in 1936, the wage fund was still overspent by 2,019,000,000 rubles.[28] Party leaders spoke constantly

---

[24] "Material dlia TsK partii," ll. 11–12, 17; GARF, f. 5451, o. 43, d. 30, "V TsK VKP (b). Dokladnaia zapiska ob itogakh provedeniia koldogovornoi kampanii i peresmotra norm vyrabotki," l. 159 (this delo, as well as some others, numbered backwards).

[25] GARF, f. 5451, o. 43, d. 30, "V TsK VKP (b) tov. Stalinu, v SNK SSSR tov. Molotovu, v VTsSPS tov. Shverniku," l. 210; GARF, f. 5451, o. 43, d. 31, "Material dlia TsK partii," ll. 28–32.

[26] "V TsK VKP (b). Dokladnaia zapiska ob itogakh provedeniia koldogovornoi kampanii i peresmotra norm vyrabotki," ll. 159–157.

[27] GARF, f. 5451, o. 43, d. 83, "TsK VKP (b) tov. Andreevu A. A.," ll. 140–139.

[28] Davies and Khlevnyuk, "Stakhanovism and the Soviet Economy," pp. 872–5, 897, 896, 876.

about building a new society of prosperity for workers, who, in turn, publicly endorsed their goals. Yet in daily practice, workers and the state engaged in an unremitting struggle over capital appropriation. Industrialization required a high degree of sacrifice; socialism promised a better life. The seesaw between productivity and wages revealed that neither side was fully willing to accept the position of the other.

Disruption in Consumption

Real wages fell by about 50 percent among industrial workers during the first five-year plan (1929–1932), and continued to fall until 1934. They made a slow recovery from 1935 to 1938, yet even in 1937 they stood at only 66 percent of their 1928 level. According to one historian, living standards could not have dropped further after 1931 without causing "a complete disintegration of economic life." By the end of 1932, free-market prices were sixteen times greater than 1928, and state store prices had doubled.[29] Food shortages and high prices were compounded by problems in the food delivery system. Hardships were greatest in undercapitalized industries such as textiles, in new and distant workers' settlements, and in families with many dependants and few earners. Yet chronic shortages of meat, dairy products, vegetables, fish, and even bread were everywhere. A woman worker in the Krasnaia Talka textile factory in Ivanovo, for example, wept as she explained to a fellow worker, "I stood in line for three days for bread and got nothing. I live in a dormitory. When my children run out into the corridor, they snatch the bread from people's hands. I am ashamed, but I can do nothing. They are starving."[30] By 1932, the food situation was grim. Although grain collections in 1931 surpassed the record level set in 1930, the grain harvest had been poor. The large state collections left the peasants with little seed grain for planting and contributed to the famine of 1932–3. Meat, dairy, and fish collections also decreased. Workers in Moscow and Leningrad, comparatively well provisioned in comparison with other towns, went hungry. Stores did not even have enough food to honor ration cards. Factories, short of funds,

---

[29] Solomon Schwarz, *Labor in the Soviet Union* (Praeger, New York, 1951), pp. 139–64; Janet Chapman, *Real Wages in Soviet Russia Since 1928* (Harvard University Press, Cambridge, MA, 1963); R. W. Davies, *The Soviet Economy in Turmoil, 1929–1930* (Harvard University Press, Cambridge, MA, 1989), pp. 304–9; Eugene Zaleski, *Planning for Economic Growth in the Soviet Union, 1918–1932* (Chapel Hill, University of North Carolina Press, 1971), p. 392; Goldman, *Women at the Gates*, pp. 76–82; Davies, *Crisis and Progress in the Soviet Economy*, p. 459.

[30] GARF, f. 5451, o. 43, d. 12, "Spets. spravka," l. 355.

failed to pay wages. And prices in the free peasant markets skyrocketed. Productivity declined as turnover increased. The economy was in crisis.[31]

In Ivanovo, a textile region, the situation was particularly dire. In late spring, workers' brigades, empowered to check prices and provisions, discovered that the cooperative stores had received only 13 percent of the consumer goods allotted by the plan. The cooperatives contracted with collective farms for 94,215 liters of milk in May, but received only 1,359. There were similar shortages of meat and produce. Many workers were completely dependent on the cooperative stores. In Sverdlovka, workers could not even buy a cup of tea in the factories. Workers in Teikovo fled the textile factories because there was nothing to eat. Fights over food broke out in the canteens and the militia was called in to restore order. Hungry peat-bog cutters tried to beat up union officials and the head of the Teikovo party committee.[32] In Ivanovo, the distribution system was in chaos. Food stores and factory canteens kept almost no records, leading to mass pilfering and corruption. When the head of Canteen No. 1 ran out of food, he sent a short note over to a friend in the store, "Niura, send over four kilograms of bread." Managers lost, mislaid, or spent money for food on other needs. Retail clerks raised prices illegally and pocketed the difference. They took bread off the shelves of the cooperative stores and resold it at high profits in the market. Widespread pilfering further reduced the small number of products available for sale. Prices rose dramatically in the free markets.[33]

On the anniversary of the October revolution in 1932, the lack of food underscored how many hopes of the revolution were still unfulfilled. Bread deliveries to the stores were late, and workers in Ivanovo went hungry. Workers from the Krasnaia Talka textile factory spent the anniversary standing in bread lines. In Metal Factory No. 4, a line of 200 people formed at a produce counter at 6:00 A.M., and stood patiently for the entire day. In the Zinoviev factory, 150 people stood in line for six hours,

---

[31] Hiroaki Kuromiya, *Freedom and Terror in the Donbas: A Ukrainian-Russian Borderland, 1870s–1990s* (Cambridge University Press, Cambridge, 1998), pp. 151–200; Davies, *Crisis and Progress in the Soviet Economy*, pp. 176–82, 234–43.

[32] GARF, f. 5451, o. 43, d. 12, "Oblastnoi sovet professional'nykh soiuzov Ivanovskoi promyshlennoi oblasti," ll. 185, 182, 181. See also Jeffrey Rossman, *Worker Resistance Under Stalin: Class and Revolution on the Shop Floor* (Harvard University Press, Cambridge, MA, 2005).

[33] GARF, f. 5451, o. 43, d. 12, "Signal'naia svodka no. 1. Voprosy rabochego snabzheniia," ll. 127, 126. On the food crisis, see also Davies, *Crisis and Progress in the Soviet Economy*, pp. 195–6.

waiting for bread and flour. There were similar problems in other factories throughout the province.[34]

Food distribution on the vast new construction sites was also prone to disruption. Often there were no food deliveries for three to four days at a stretch. In Zlatoustroi, a large construction site in the Urals, the workers' cooperatives received no bread for days at a time, and no shipments of flour, fish, or meat for up to three months. Groats, sugar, butter, and oil were unavailable. The cooperative stores in Kuznetsstroi received only 50 percent of their allotted flour, 20 percent of the groats, 20 percent of the meat, and a mere 4 percent of the fish in spring 1932. In the Donbas region, many cooperative stores did not receive any groats, fat, or sugar. In April, the stores received no food at all, and workers ate the remnants of the March shipments. And in the Tul'skii metal factory, no bread cards were distributed for two weeks in May, and workers received no bread. In June, no food cards were issued.[35]

In response to the food crisis, the state cut food rations in 1932 and 1933, and again in 1934. Various groups were shifted to lower categories of provisioning or denied rations altogether. The state shifted responsibility for ration size and allocation to the regions, heralding the breakdown of the centralized rationing system. Workers fled their factories in search of jobs providing higher rations. In the Bronitskii glass factory, for example, workers, reassigned to lower norms, left in droves. Managers all around the country reported "mass departures" and "mass refusal to work."[36] A VTsSPS representative wrote, "People are running from the factory as a result of poor provisioning and very low wages."[37] Workers in an agricultural machine-building factory in Berdiansk, for example, were moved to a lower ration category, dropping from 700 to 600 grams of bread, and white-collar personnel were removed from the ration list entirely. The cuts produced a flood of desperate complaints from workers in Grozny, Leningrad, Omsk, Buriat-Mongolia, Kontora, Konstantinovka, Ural'sk, Ostashkov, and Zinov'evsk.[38] The head of the Union of

[34] GARF, f. 5451, o. 43, d. 12, "Spets. spravka o provedenii godovshchiny oktiabria na predpriiatiiakh IPO," l. 355.

[35] GARF, f. 5451, o. 43, d. 13, "Signal'naia svodka no. 28," l. 35.

[36] GARF, f. 5515, o. 33, d. 33, "Narkomtrud SSSR," l. 79; Davies, *Crisis and Progress in the Soviet Economy*, pp. 185, 177–82.

[37] GARF, f. 5515, o. 33, d. 33, "O neblagopoluchenom polozhenii na zavode im. Stalina," "Informsektor VTsSPS. Signal'naia svodka no. 19," ll. 217, 218–218ob.

[38] GARF, f. 5451, o. 43, d. 67, "Sekretariu VTsSPS tov. Shverniku. TsK Soiuza s/kh mashinostroeniia tov. Volkovu," "Sekretariu VTsSPS tov. Shverniku. Dokladnaia zapiska," ll. 216, 212–209.

Leather Workers wrote to the VTsSPS about "an extraordinarily difficult situation for workers" in Ukraine, the Urals, and the Middle Volga. Dependents had been removed from the bread-ration lists, yet there was no commercial sale of bread in state stores, and prices in the private market were prohibitive. Starving workers were eating the raw materials in the factories: the fleshy sides of the hides, raw leather, and glue. The head of the Union of Wool, Silk, and Tricot Workers sent a similar report.[39] Many workers penned angry letters to *Trud*, the national union newspaper, complaining about cuts in bread norms, the lack of bread and fats, and the elimination of bread cards for dependents, invalids, and pensioners. One worker wrote, "We have been sitting here for two months without bread."[40]

In families with many dependents – children, the elderly, or invalids – the old peasant calculus of worker to eater was critical in determining consumption. Ivan Voronin, a garment worker, was representative of the most impoverished sector of the working class. Employed in a low-priority industry, his wages were low and he was the sole earner for a wife and six young children. When union officials discovered the family, they were living in a cold, dank cellar, swollen with malnutrition. For several days, the family had eaten nothing except a dog, and they had just finished the last of its hide. The union quickly found employment for Voronin's wife and placed the children in preschool, where they would be fed.[41] The family's situation was extreme, but not uncommon.

Workers in light industry, a low investment priority, were most strongly affected by the food crisis, but workers in all sectors suffered. The crisis in consumption was at its worst from 1929 to 1933. Peasant resistance to collectivization, famine in 1932–3, elimination of private traders, and poor organization of the food distribution network all created serious problems. Millions died of starvation. Surviving peasants fled famine-stricken villages for towns and industrial settlements. The food situation began to improve in 1934, yet the VTsSPS continued to receive reports from local union and party officials about malnourished workers. In 1937, for example, the VTsSPS authorized extra shipments of food to workers in Rostov, Cheliabinsk, Perm, Stalingrad, Saratov, and other towns in

[39] GARF, f. 5451, o. 43, d. 67, "Sekretariiam VTsSPS, t.t. Shverniku i Veinbergu. Biuro Sotsstrakha, t. Kotovu," "TsK VKP (b), VTsSPS – tov. Shverniku, NKLP – tov. Liubimovu," ll. 134, 28.
[40] GARF, f. 5451, o. 43, d. 67, "Sekretariat VTsSPS. Tov. Rykovu," l. 254.
[41] GARF, f. 5451, o. 43, d. 30, "V sekretnuiu chast' VTsSPS. Vystupleniia otdel'nykh rabochikh vo vremia koldogovornoi," l. 131ob.

response to reports that workers were suffering from hunger and scurvy due to lack of fruits, vegetables, and potatoes.[42]

Working and Living Conditions

The decrease in consumption was accompanied by a severe housing shortage in towns and new workers' settlements. Peasant migrants found jobs easily, but they could not get housing. Workers moved constantly in search of housing, higher rations, and better wages, creating major disruptions in production. Plant directors, municipal authorities, and party leaders could not provide enough housing for new arrivals. People lived in rickety barracks and earthen dugouts (*zemlianki*), without kitchens, toilets, heat, running water, furniture, and bedding. Workers in the Eastern Chemical, Lacquer/Paint, and Dye Trusts, for example, were poorly housed in barracks and dugouts located ten miles from the plants. Local transportation was still in the planning stage. There was no running water or sewage disposal.[43] Apartments in older towns were subdivided repeatedly to make room for newcomers. Municipal services, such as plumbing, electricity, sewer lines, and garbage collection were overstrained or absent. Workers, having nowhere else to eat, overwhelmed the factory canteens. Crowded and filthy, the canteens lacked cutlery, dishes, seating, and decent food. The canteen in the Red October agricultural machine-building factory in Odessa province in 1934, for example, served only cabbage. The food in Iaroslavl's canteens was equally dismal.[44] Canteens improved over time, but many suffered from insufficient, low-quality food, shortages of utensils, and long lines through the 1930s. As late as 1940, the canteen attached to the Artem mine had only eight spoons, twenty-five forks, and seventeen plates for the seventy-five workers who relied on the facility for their meals.[45]

Squalid housing, inadequate sewage facilities, food shortages, overcrowding, and high labor turnover characterized thousands of construction sites and factories with large numbers of new workers.[46] In the Red

[42] GARF, f. 5451, o. 43, d. 72, "Postanovlenie sekretariata VTsSPS," "Postanovlenie sekretariata VTsSPS," ll. 47, 48; Davies, *Crisis and Progress in the Soviet Economy*, pp. 368–9, 380–1.

[43] GARF, f. 5451, o. 43, d. 67, "Predsedateliu Sovnarkoma i STO tov. Molotovu," l. 4.

[44] GARF, f. 5451, o. 43, d. 67, "Odesskii oblastnoi gorsovet," ll. 7, 6.

[45] GARF, f. 5451, o. 43, d. 83, "TsK VKP (b) tov. Andreevu A. A.," l. 131.

[46] On conditions in Magnitogorsk, see Stephen Kotkin, *Magnetic Mountain: Stalinism as a Civilization* (University of California Press, Berkeley, 1995), pp. 106–97.

October machine-building plant in Stalingrad, the nonferrous mill met only one-third of the plan for May 1932, and only 13 percent of what was produced was quality metal. In the blast furnace, where temperatures routinely rose to more than 100 degrees, the workers had no access to water.[47] A. K. Abolin, a VTsSPS secretary, visited the Petrovskii iron and steel works in Dnepropetrovsk in 1933 at the height of the famine in Ukraine. His horrifying report prompted the Central Committee to recall the heads of the provincial party and factory committees to Moscow. The Petrovskii works employed 28,500 workers, 40 percent of whom had worked there for less than a year. The plant overspent its wage fund, did not meet production targets, and experienced constant disruptions in production, displaying, in Abolin's words, "all the illnesses of the iron and steel industry." In one nearby settlement of 30,000 people, the outdoor toilets were broken and boarded up. People relieved themselves outside on the ground, creating vast "Egyptian pyramids" of waste. The dormitories had no kitchens, no water during the day, and only occasional water at night. The canteens were vastly overburdened. One canteen, equipped to serve 150 people, routinely served 4,000. Meals were three to six hours late, and lines of 200–300 people stretched out the door. Workers often left without eating in order to return to work. Most of the canteens had no cutlery. The one canteen that supplied spoons compelled workers to hand over their hats, mess kits, and even party and union membership cards as collateral. Bread, the mainstay of workers' diets, rarely accompanied the watery cabbage soup, and the food supply was sporadic. Abolin wrote in despair, "We must ask how can people lead such lives? Where are the union and party organizations?" Union officials, overwhelmed by the filth and chaos, stayed resolutely away from the dormitories and their "pyramids." The shop committees did little social work or political education, and their methods were crude. In the spike shop, for example, union officials labeled anyone who failed to attend meetings "an enemy of the USSR," and deprived the absentees of food, an action that could hardly have endeared them to their hungry members.[48]

Abolin discovered that thirty-one people had died in the hospital from starvation and exposure, and 123 more were suffering from malnutrition, including the head of a party cell, party members, production workers with long seniority, and new migrants. Some had lost their ration cards; others were sending money home to the village. One woman was

[47] GARF, f. 5451, o. 43, d. 13, "Signal'naia svodka no. 3," l. 210b.
[48] GARF, f. 5451, o. 43, d. 30, "VTsSPS N. M. Shverniku. Pis'mo no. 2," ll. 118–113, 114.

scrimping on food in an attempt to buy a warm coat. The unheated dormitories had no blankets and workers slept in all their clothing. Abolin moved quickly to rectify the worst conditions, creating a brigade to visit malnourished workers. Chaotic records and labor turnover, however, soon stymied his best efforts. Abolin sharply questioned Chernov, the head of the Commission of Mutual Help, an organization dedicated to workers' social welfare. Chernov, overwhelmed by the seemingly insurmountable problems of the plant, explained helplessly, "We couldn't find addresses for fifteen of these people. In the factory, workers told us that they had once worked in the shops, they knew them, but that they didn't work there anymore. Where they work now – no one knows." Abolin replied, "Maybe they are lying in the hospital." Chernov shrugged. "Maybe." Finally, Chernov asked, "Comrade Abolin, what can we do with starving workers who have been in the factory for only five or six months?" Abolin snapped, "Even if they've worked five days! If a person is swollen from hunger, he needs help."[49]

Abolin also met with the doctor of the plant's hospital, who described the effects of the Ukrainian famine. The Petrovskii plant had been inundated with starving peasants, desperate for food. The doctor, who did not understand the full extent of the famine, claimed that, although his malnourished patients called themselves "collective farmers," they must have been "dekulakized peasants" and homeless teenagers because they lacked documents or passports. By day, they waited patiently near the factory for unskilled day labor, hoping to be hired within the factory itself. At night, "masses of people" broke into the hot shops and canteens to sleep on the floors and tables. Homeless and poorly clothed, constantly dodging the militia, they gradually "became exhausted and fell into the hospital." The doctor had already buried a number of them.[50]

The attempt to build industry, housing, municipal services, schools, hospitals, and transportation simultaneously forced officials to scramble for scarce resources. Managers often used the wage fund, one source of ready cash, to pay for materials. In one district in Ivanovo, white-collar employees had not been paid for six months. As a result, the medical personnel fled and the hospitals closed. School personnel received no wages for more than two months, and children's institutions received nothing but spoiled millet. Crowds of angry parents gathered every day in the

---

[49] GARF, f. 5451, o. 43, d. 30, "Strakh. punkt zavoda im. Petrovskogo," ll. 112–108.

[50] GARF, f. 5451, o. 43, d. 30, "Bol'nitsa zavoda im. Petrovskogo, Dnepropetrovsk," "Soobshcheniia tovarishchei, obsledovavshikh kvartiry rabochikh, znachashchikhsia v spiskakh opukhshikh ot goloda," ll. 107–103, 101–99.

district party office and the cooperative headquarters to protest.[51] In a porcelain factory in Rybinsk, wage arrears, coupled with increased prices and decreases in the bread ration, led to a short strike and a riot. The workers yelled, "Stop work! You want to starve us. It's you devil communists who have brought us to this. Let there be war." The director had spent the wage fund on other pressing needs of the factory.[52]

Accidents

The pressure to reach high production targets, new and unfamiliar technology, and an inexperienced workforce all combined to produce a high accident rate throughout the 1930s. The most hazardous occupations were in the coal and iron ore mines, oil extraction, construction of railroad lines, and the iron and steel industry. In 1934, the injury rates (number of production injuries per 100 workers) in these industries ranged from 20 to 33 percent, which meant that up to one-third of the workforce suffered an injury in the course of the year. Yet even in the safest industries, such as the porcelain, printing, textile, and garment sectors, injury rates were about 5 percent. In the majority of industries in 1934, between 10 and 20 percent of the workforce was injured on the job. Moreover, almost 75 percent of industries showed an increase in injury rates from 1934 to 1936. Only in 1937, with the new, concerted attention to labor safety and "wrecking," did injury rates drop: more than 90 percent of the unions reported significant decreases compared to 1936.[53] There were also high numbers of fatal work accidents, especially in coal and nonferrous metal mining, railroad car construction, and the iron and steel industry. Of 660,800 coal miners in 1936, 1,076 died in fatal work accidents. From 1935 to 1936 fatalities increased by 27 percent in coal, and 8.7 percent overall.[54] Among 12,000 workers within the Moscow construction trust, there were more than 1,000 accidents, 65 resulting in serious injuries leading to 6 deaths.[55]

[51] GARF, f. 5451, o. 43, d. 12, "Signal'naia svodka no. 1. Voprosy rabochego snabzheniia," l. 122.

[52] GARF, f. 5515, o. 33, d. 50, "Sektor informatsii Otdela orgraboty i proverki ispolneniia VTsSPS. Svodka no. 4," ll. 116–116ob.

[53] The figures, reported by seventy-nine unions for 1934–7, covered work injuries that resulted in lost time. Injuries rose in fifty out of sixty-nine unions that reported statistics for 1934 and 1936. Of the forty-eight unions that reported injury rates for 1937, forty-four noted a decrease. See GARF, f. 5451, o. 43, d. 74, "Tablitsa: proizvodstvennyi i bytovoi travmatizm v 1934–1937," ll. 1–3.

[54] GARF, f. 5451, o. 43, d. 74, "Chislo smertel'nykh nechastnykh sluchaev za 9 mes. 1936," l. 8.

[55] GARF, f. 5451, o. 43, d. 73, "Prezidiumu VTsSPS. Dokladnaia zapiska," l. 166.

Until 1937, union officials and managers largely ignored labor safety. Managers often failed to spend safety funds allocated by the state or diverted them to other purposes. The funds were often useless in the face of chronic shortages. Coal tunnels and faces, for example, were poorly reinforced because timber was unavailable at any price. Union officials and managers disregarded safety rules and the fines imposed for violations.[56] Not surprisingly, the high rate of accidents and fatalities created enormous resentment among workers toward managers, foremen, and local party and union officials. In fall 1936, party leaders mobilized this anger in a national campaign against "wrecking," sparked by an explosion in the Kemerovo mines. Workers were encouraged to equate all accidents with deliberate wrecking by union officials and managers. Union leaders of the State Farm Grain Workers and the Railroad/Metro Construction Workers were among the many accused in 1937 of overlooking fatalities, lacking sympathy for the families of the dead and injured, and failing to enforce labor safety.[57]

Workers' Moods

Although Soviet achievements generated enthusiasm and pride, food shortages, accidents, and strained services eroded support for party policies. Many workers questioned why the revolution had done so little to improve their immediate situation. Judging policy by what it produced in the short run rather than what it promised for the future, they blamed the state for the precipitous drop in their living standards. The Bolsheviks demeaned these views as the "politics of the stomach," a narrow, politically unsophisticated insistence on instant gratification.[58] In Krasnyi Putilovets, a Leningrad machine-building factory with a hallowed revolutionary history, party organizers installed a large board where workers could post questions. The board was peppered with complaints. One posting read:

Why did they stop providing the milk ration for children in 1932? Lenin said, "We need a young healthy generation." A child cannot be healthy on black bread alone. Not everyone is in a position to be able to buy milk for two rubles or to

---

[56] GARF, f. 5451, o. 43, d. 70, "Voprosy okhrany truda, zarplaty i massovoi raboty profsoiuzov na proizvodstve," ll. 2–13.

[57] See, for example, GARF, f. 5451, o. 43, d. 73, "Sekretariu VTsSPS. Tov. Shverniku. Dokladnaia zapiska," "Prezidiumu VTsSPS. Dokladnaia zapiska," ll. 156–158 and 164–167.

[58] Koenker, *Republic of Labor*, pp. 45–76, 260.

stand in line for three hours and get a liter for one ruble. In our turbine shop, we have a poster hanging on the wall, which says the situation with milk products will improve in 1932, but the fact is we have nothing. We are now living through all these difficulties, we are building socialism, but how long can our children wait?[59]

Workers questioned how much they should be expected to sacrifice to finance industrialization. When the price of a cup of tea tripled in the Shcherbakova textile factory in Moscow, the workers felt they had reached their limit: they did not have enough energy to work on what they were fed. One exclaimed, "They are building socialism backwards: they steal from us, but we cannot work without eating."[60] Some claimed that conditions were worse than in the pre-revolutionary period. One worker noted angrily, "Look, everyone knows that earlier we were exploited by the capitalists, but living then was better. Now we talk about the economy, but this economy is strangling us." A mechanic told the director, "We have to lower prices so we can eat because I cannot even fulfill my norm."[61] When an older worker in Moscow's Kauchuk rubber factory was transferred to a new job in 1934, his wages dropped to 120 rubles a month. He marched into the factory committee office, removed his hat, and told the union organizer, "I want to thank you as a representative of Soviet power. After thirty-five years of work, I am guaranteed starvation."[62] Many workers doubted whether party policy, with its high investment in heavy industry, would ever improve consumption. Apprentices in the Izhorskii machine-building works in Kolpino in Leningrad province wrote a letter to the VTsSPS in 1933 complaining about conditions. The factory administration had neglected to provide 150 apprentices with passes to the canteen for four days. The dormitories had no toilets, and "the guys go wherever they can." There was no firewood or coal for heat, and many of the young men had no shoes. The apprentices joked bitterly, "At the end of the second five-year plan, we will eat tractors."[63]

Workers not only distrusted party policy on investment and wages, but agriculture as well. Many new migrants and workers with relatives in the countryside, a significant proportion of the labor force, did not believe the Party's accounts of collectivization and rural prosperity. A

[59] GARF, f. 5451, o. 43, d. 13, "Signal'naia svodka no. 28," l. 35.
[60] "Svodka no. 2 'O povyshenii tsen,'" l. 4.
[61] "Sektor informatsii Otdela orgraboty i proverki ispolneniia VTsSPS," l. 9.
[62] GARF, f. 5451, o. 43, d. 67, "Sekretariu VTsSPS tov. Shverniku," l. 252.
[63] "Sektor informatsii Otdela orgraboty i proverki ispolneniia VTsSPS. Svodka no. 5," l. 115ob.

note in a Moscow garment factory was passed up to the rostrum after a pep talk by a union official. It read, "How long will you continue to deceive us? You say that the state and collective farms are sowing more land and increasing the herds of cattle, but provisioning for us is worse and worse. We have stopped believing you. In the first five-year plan, they fed us meat bones; in the second, they will feed us dog meat."[64] Nor did many workers accept the Party's explanation that kulaks were responsible for food shortages. A worker in the Dzerzhinskii iron and steel works in Dnepropetrovsk countered flatly, "There never were any kulaks in the countryside. They took every last thing from poor people in bast shoes [*lapti*]." A worker in a machine shop offered an even darker view: "There is widespread famine in the Soviet Union. The collective farms are serfdom. People in railroad stations are eating potato peelings. The papers say there is famine abroad, but on the contrary, there is famine in our country."[65] Streams of rural migrants brought fresh news from the villages to the factories. In the barracks of Factory No. 45, about forty workers became involved in a heated discussion about collectivization. One worker declared, "You speech-makers try and persuade us of achievements. The fact is, the communists have brought the country to the point where they are trading human meat. Buying sausage, I discovered human fingers, with nails!" Another worker added bitterly, "We read in the daily paper in an article by Stalin himself that 35 percent of the population [kulaks] must be destroyed." When other workers objected, a man lying on his bed sarcastically asked a young, recent migrant, "Tell me, Vania, did you have to leave the countryside because of famine or because of your rich life?" "Of course, because of famine," Vania replied. "And tell me please," the worker continued, "where is the grain of the *muzhik*?" "Taken away by the state," Vania said. "And where are the cattle, the cows, and the horses?" "They took the cows," Vania answered simply. "The horses died of hunger because there was nothing to feed them." Finally, a cleaning woman intervened, declaring that Soviet power had freed her and her mother from poverty. The worker sneered, "Only to you they gave a life."[66]

Mistrust over state policy sometimes hardened into outright hostility against the Party. In Proletarskii Trud, a machine-building factory, one

[64] "Sektor informatsii Otdela orgraboty i proverki ispolneniia VTsSPS," l. 90b.
[65] "Sektor informatsii Otdela orgraboty i proverki ispolneniia VTsSPS. Svodka no. 5," ll. 113–114.
[66] Ibid., l. 115.

old worker declared, "The Bolsheviks have led us to the point where soon everyone will croak from hunger. Once again, we see lines everywhere. They increase the work load, but they give us nothing."[67] A woman worker asked, "What kind of devil makes a revolution, and afterwards people die from hunger? The factory committee does not even know that several workers have died of hunger. If Lenin was alive it would be better."[68] For many, the optimism of union and party officials rang increasingly false. Tired of listening to long speeches, one worker in Elektrosila, a Leningrad electrical engineering plant, asked sarcastically, "How long will the communists torture people with their 'correct' policies?" And a painter in a railroad car factory exclaimed, "A good state would be one without communists because they only promise to better the position of the workers. When will we finally see this improvement? The first five-year plan is already ended and where are their promises?"[69] Another arrived at the simple conclusion, "The communists are all thieves and bandits."[70]

In 1931, Stalin spoke before a conference of managers, urging an end to wage "leveling" and the introduction of sharp pay differentials between skilled and unskilled work.[71] To provide incentive, the Party developed elaborate hierarchies of consumption and privilege, creating differentials among workers in heavy and light industries, in various regions, and at different skill levels. Families, too, were subject to the differentials among breadwinners. Dependents of workers in heavy industry, for example, received a larger ration than those in light industry. The policies aimed to encourage workers to raise their skills, but they also fomented resentment against those with greater privileges. Workers in light industry could find neither justice nor logic in the differentials for family members. A worker and party member in Saratov asked in angry astonishment, "Why do we distribute bread in this way? The wife of a worker in the Kombin factory gets 400 grams of bread, but the wife of a garment worker receives 100 grams." An older garment worker called the 100-gram ration his wife received "slow death." "When we made the October revolution,"

---

[67] GARF, f. 5451, o. 43, d. 13, "Signal'naia svodka no. 3," l. 21.

[68] "V sekretnuiu chast' VTsSPS," l. 131.

[69] GARF, f. 5451, o. 43, d. 27, "Svodka o polozhenii otdel'nykh predpriiatniiakh i uchastkakh raboty," l. 11.

[70] "V sekretnuiu chast' VTsSPS," l. 131.

[71] Joseph V. Stalin, *The New Russian Policy* (New York, Stratford Press, 1931); Filtzer, *Soviet Workers and Stalinist Industrialization*, pp. 102–7; Davies, *Crisis and Progress in the Soviet Economy*, pp. 65–76.

he declared, "we said there would be equality and brotherhood, but we don't have this. Our workers are dying from hunger. The garment workers in Moscow do good work, but we are not considered equal to others."[72] Workers on the outskirts of Moscow were angry that the capital was better provisioned than other regions. One worker in the outlying Liuberetskii agricultural machine-building factory wrote, "The working class, thanks to the policy of the Party, is leading an existence of semi-starvation. Moscow, this parasite on the workers of the whole country, receives goods in abundance, which it uses not only for personal consumption, but to sell to those coming in from the surrounding towns. At the same time, we have nothing. Supposedly, it is impossible to give us in Liubertsy even kerosene. The workers go to work in the morning and they cannot even make themselves a cup of tea."[73] Other workers were convinced that Jews or other ethnic groups were taking advantage of Russians. A worker in the Frunze factory simply shook his head in amazement after an official's speech about economic achievement, "They talk so well, they must be Jews or Armenians. Our Russians don't talk like that."[74]

Workers scrutinized the differentials between their wages and those of party and union officials. Depending on skill and industry, workers' base pay was between 150 and 500 rubles a month (without overtime or piecework). In 1936, the secretaries of the VTsSPS earned 1,100 rubles per month, the heads of the unions, between 700 and 900 rubles, and the chairs of the republic, province, and district union committees between 600 and 800 rubles. Union officials, like workers, were also subject to differentials depending on whether they worked inside or outside Moscow and Leningrad or in a union in heavy or light industry. Their salaries were roughly comparable to those of party and state officials at similar levels.[75] Officials were entitled to numerous privileges, including regular food packages and access to stores with a better array of goods. The wage differentials and privileges separating workers and officials were not great, yet even the smallest differentials provoked resentment among those in want. One construction worker asked, "Why do we workers not have the right to buy things in the stores for engineering and technical

[72] "V sekretnuiu chast' VTsSPS," l. 131.
[73] GARF, f. 5451, o. 43, d. 13, "Svodka o povyshenii tsen," l. 16.
[74] "Sektor informatsii Otdela orgraboty i proverki ispolneniia VTsSPS," l. 90b.
[75] GARF, f. 5451, o. 43, d. 71, "Postanovlenie 1068," "Postanovlenie prezidiuma VTsSPS," ll. 471, 472. For 1940 figures, see GARF, f. 5451, o. 43, d. 84, "Predsedateliu ekonomicheskogo soveta pri SNK Soiuza SSR tov. Mikoianu," l. 54.

personnel? We also need food."[76] Many workers spoke in favor of wage leveling. Others were more critical, maintaining that a new elite was being created at the expense of their labor. A woman spinner in Krasnaia Talka wondered in 1932, "How long can we endure such a life? This is very bad: someone is getting fat, but for the workers there is only a crust of bread and we work for it! They are leading us to the grave!"[77] According to one machine-tool operator, the state was growing fat as the workers grew lean. Protesting the decrease in the bread ration in the spring of 1932, he noted, "They feed the workers on bony fish, but they send the ham to the Kremlin."[78]

Promise of Plenty

The Party's economic program was based on short-term sacrifice in exchange for long-term prosperity.[79] Workers who failed to grasp this concept were considered politically "backward," unable to grasp any policy beyond the rumbling of their own bellies. Nowhere was this promise of deferred plenty so evident as in the loans floated by the state to finance industrialization. The loans contributed significantly to the state budget, providing 10 percent of the planned revenue increase in the budget in 1931.[80] Party and union officials encouraged workers to subscribe to loans, based on deductions from their wages. Although the loans were voluntary, in practice workers had little choice but to subscribe. Party and union officials, under great pressure to demonstrate unanimous support, cajoled, hounded, and threatened workers until they assented.

Workers' responses to the loan campaigns revealed the limits of their support for state policies. In some cases, resentment was so great that workers collectively refused to subscribe. Workers in lumber factories in Minsk, Borisov, Gomel, and other Belorussian towns, for example, simply refused to sign up. In the forge and foundry of the Kommunar machine-building factory in Minsk, workers refused to endorse the new loan in 1932. One worker spoke for all when he proclaimed, "We are not going to subscribe to anything more." A brigade leader insisted, "Not one kopek will you get for a new loan." And another worker yelled out in

---

[76] "Sektor informatsii Otdela orgraboty i proverki ispolneniia VTsSPS. Svodka no. 5," l. 114.

[77] "Spets. spravka," ll. 355, 354.   [78] "Signal'naia svodka no. 3," l. 21.

[79] Sheila Fitzpatrick, *Everyday Stalinism. Ordinary Life in Extraordinary Times: Soviet Russia in the 1930s* (Oxford University Press, New York, 1999), pp. 89–114.

[80] Davies, *Crisis and Progress in the Soviet Economy*, pp. 3, 112.

support, "Not one kopek! Let the shock workers sign up." Even a communist and factory committee member said angrily, "About the loan, they don't forget, but about special work clothes, they have already forgotten." When organizers pushed workers to sign up, one declared, "Comrades, we have still not subscribed to this, and they still hold this noose around our necks. How can the workers answer this? I am already left barefoot, and my family at home is starving, and we still have this loan. I definitively declare that I will not sign for this loan. Let them do what they want with me. I have no more strength to give. We must stop work." After the organizers threatened and hectored, a majority finally voted in favor. One worker abstained, noting bitterly, "On the soup you feed us, I am too weak to raise my hand." In the Voroshilov machine-building factory in Minsk, boiler shop workers responded to the loan announcement with angry jeers: "Let the state take out its own loans, no one has the right to force us to sign up." "Let them give us back the money they spent on the previous loan, then we'll vote for a new one." Only 14 of 200 workers voted for the loan. One worker explained, "The workers are truly not able to sign up because everything is so expensive. Prices rise, wages don't rise. Milk was twenty-seven kopeks and now it is forty-five." When another worker asked him how the workers could help the state, he replied cynically, "Help whom? Those who go to a health resort twenty times?" In the forge and repair shop, workers tore posters promoting the loan from the walls, and scrawled false signatures on the sign-up sheets.[81] Frustrated workers, pushed to the limit of endurance, disrupted meetings everywhere. In Ivanovo, workers in the Nogin factory interrupted the meeting with angry outbursts: "Again a loan!" "Again, they are robbing the people!" "Start feeding us and then we'll sign up!" "Give us ten kilograms of flour!" The meeting ended in pandemonium.[82]

Most of the workers' objections were based on low wages and the high cost of food. One worker in a candy factory explained, "I receive seventy-five rubles a month. I cannot subscribe to the loan because to live on this money is impossible." Many argued that they could not subscribe because their wages were "not enough to sustain life." Women workers in Minsk's Krupskaia factory explained, "We cannot subscribe every year.

[81] GARF, f. 5451, o. 43, d. 12, "Gor. Moskva," ll. 108–104. Workers in a glass factory in the Western province also refused to sign and tore the slogans from the walls: GARF, f. 5451, o. 43, d. 12, "Ob otritsatel'nykh nastroenniiakh vyiavlennakh v kampanii po zaimu," l. 114.

[82] GARF, f. 5451, o. 43, d. 12, "Spets. spravka no. 2," l. 157.

They provision us too poorly." Workers at the lower end of the wage scale were particularly resentful of the demands of the Party. A washerwoman in a paper factory noted indignantly, "Put us on the first priority list for provisioning and then we'll subscribe to the loan. We have low wages, they don't provide work clothes, we get 250 grams of bread. We are hungry and they present us with loans!"[83] These workers did not oppose the loans in principle, but because of poverty.

Many workers, however, were critical not only of the loans but also of party policy. They complained that they got no benefit from the forced subscriptions. A worker in a tram depot noted, "The state doesn't give us much bread, they cut rations further, and then they ask us for money. They force us to subscribe to a monthly deduction. Only a fool would sign up for this. They have squeezed enough juice from the workers." Others were disgusted by the Party's practice of presenting every campaign as if the workers themselves had initiated it. A former Trotskyist in the Voroshilov machine-building factory in Druzhkova in Ukraine told a group, "Now they lead us with beautiful phrases. They say the workers demand a new loan...They have unanimous votes in the factories, and they carry out the campaigns in our name." Outraged by the lack of democracy in the factories, he deemed the loan nothing more than "a compulsory tax." A group of former Trotskyist workers in a Moscow shoe factory also refused to sign up, but capitulated after they were threatened with dismissal.[84]

Party and union activists, confounded by the widespread resistance, turned to threats. In a woodworking factory in Ivanovo, workers explained that officials had "tormented them to death" about the loan. In an interminable meeting, they "exhausted the patience" of the workers, who signed out of sheer weariness. One foreman in a textile factory brusquely announced, "I will fire anyone who doesn't sign up."[85] Party and VTsSPS leaders were critical of such methods, yet local organizers often felt they had little choice. Activists responsible for collecting signatures confessed that they did not know how to convince their fellow workers. A brigade leader in a textile factory in Klin asked party officials, "What am I supposed to do with the workers when they don't want to sign? I told them that they must sign to support the other workers, but they have refused, and so we still have not resolved this business." Several of the more honest activists simply told the workers to make the best of

---

[83] "Gor. Moskva," ll. 108–105.
[84] Ibid., l. 105.
[85] "Spets. spravka no. 2," l. 157.

a bad situation: "It doesn't matter, there's no way out. You must sign up and it's better to do it now. At least they won't pester you every two weeks because you will have already paid."[86] In another factory, a worker help-lessly threw up his hands: "They entrusted me with collecting signatures, and look," he explained, "I went to the workers. But this is all shameful to me because I know the present condition of our workers. One worker said to me, 'Isn't it embarrassing for you to talk to me about a loan when my children are hungry?'"[87]

The Role of the Unions

In the 1920s, unions had an active, albeit limited, role in defending work-ers' interests. They negotiated wage and production contracts and suc-cessfully defended workers in thousands of industrial disputes over wages, compensation, hiring, dismissal, and safety. Strike activity fluctuated in the 1920s, decreasing after 1922 and rising in the second half of the decade, yet most strikes were brief and limited to one factory or shop. In lieu of striking, unions encouraged workers to pursue grievances through official arbitration channels. Unions wielded considerable influence as part of a managing "triangle" in the enterprises, which also included representa-tives from management and the Party. And they maintained a limited but distinct independence from the state. They defended workers' interests, for example, in 1926–7 in heated debates with the Supreme Council of the National Economy over wages and productivity.[88]

Yet, even in the 1920s, the unions did not act as fully independent rep-resentatives of the workers. Their role in the triangle gave them greater influence, but also compromised their relationship with management. M. P. Tomskii, the head of the VTsSPS, recognized that melding the inter-ests of managers and union representatives worked to the disadvantage of workers. With the adoption of the first five-year plan, central planners set wage and production targets, usurping the role of the unions in negotiating

---

[86] "Gor. Moskva," l. 108.

[87] "Ob otritsatel'nykh nastroenniiakh vyiavlennakh v kampanii po zaimu," l. 114.

[88] Filtzer, *Soviet Workers and Stalinist Industrialization*, pp. 22–4; E. H. Carr and R. W. Davies, *Foundations of a Planned Economy, 1926–1929*, vol. I, part 2 (Macmillan, New York, 1969), pp. 563–4, 549; Kevin Murphy, "Strikes During the First Third of the Twen-tieth Century: From Working-Class Militancy to Working-Class Passivity," in D. Filtzer, W. Goldman, G. Kessler, and S. Pirani, *A Dream Deferred: Studies in Russian Labor His-tory* (Peter Lang, forthcoming); and Murphy, *Revolution and Counterrevolution: Class Struggle in a Moscow Metal Factory* (Berghahn Books, Oxford and New York, 2005). On the Union of Printers, see Koenker, *Republic of Labor*, pp. 109–73.

collective contracts. The unions, stripped of their previous functions, were reoriented toward improving labor discipline and productivity. During the 8th Trade Union Congress in December 1928, Stalin and his supporters attacked union leaders for championing the "so-called 'purely workers' point of view" at the expense of industrialization. L. M. Kaganovich, a staunch ally of Stalin, was placed on the presidium of the VTsSPS as a counterweight to Tomskii, who resigned as head of the VTsSPS. The struggle sharpened in the spring when the Central Committee criticized Tomskii, N. I. Bukharin, and A. I. Rykov for "setting the unions against the Party" and concealing "trade unionist" tendencies. In June 1929, Tomskii was removed entirely from the VTsSPS. His removal, coupled with the adoption of the first five-year plan, marked an end to the limited independence the unions had exercised in the 1920s. Stalin and Kaganovich subsequently supervised a thorough purge of the VTsSPS and the unions. In Tomskii's words, "the entire leadership" was removed, including more than two-thirds of the unions' central committee and factory committee members. The purge of the unions continued through 1931 as older union officials and activists were replaced by young shock workers.[89] Stalin and his supporters labeled the former leaders undemocratic, bureaucratic, and corrupt, and their members did not protest.[90]

The vast expansion of the economy in the 1930s further weakened the unions, which were repeatedly divided according to territory and specialty. In 1931, the VTsSPS split the Union of Miners into four separate unions, and the once-powerful Union of Metal Workers into six, including separate unions for iron and steel, and machine building. In 1934, the Union of Iron and Steel Workers split again into three regional unions, and the Union of Machine Building Workers split into six new unions based on machine type. Between 1934 and 1935, the total number expanded from 47 to 159 unions with 19,041,000 members, covering 81 percent of wage earners in industry, construction, transport, public dining, education, state farms, and other areas. There were seventy-seven industrial unions alone, encompassing the largest group (42 percent) of wage earners.[91] Each union had central, regional, and workplace committees (*fab-, zav-, or mestkomy*, abbreviations for factory, plant, or workplace committees).

---

[89] Carr and Davies, *Foundations of a Planned Economy, 1926–1929*, vol. I, part 2, pp. 547–8, 549, 552, 560, 563; Kuromiya, *Stalin's Industrial Revolution*, pp. 40–9, 196–7.
[90] Koenker, *Republic of Labor*, pp. 247, 252–9.
[91] *Trud v SSSR*, pp. 56–62; *XVII S"ezd Vsesoiuznoi kommunisticheskoi partii (b): Stenograficheskii otchet* (Gosudarstvennoe Izdatel'stvo Politicheskoi Literatury, Moscow, 1939), p. 157.

As the unions proliferated, they spawned a growing bureaucracy. The central committees each employed about twenty paid personnel, as well as cultural, physical, and political instructors for workers on the local level. In 1936, the unions employed 71,500 paid staff members. Fully 79 percent of members' dues were devoted to administrative costs, which totaled 402,000,000 rubles. In 1937, the staff was cut in half to 35,000, and administrative expenses by 42 percent to 221,000,000 rubles. Yet the staff quickly ballooned again, rising to 213,568 people in 1939. In 1940, it was cut back to 79,341 people (twice the number in 1937) and allotted 1,363,000,000 rubles. It appeared almost impossible to hold staff numbers and costs down.[92]

The VTsSPS served as an umbrella organization of the unions, setting policy, responding to complaints, disbursing funds, and monitoring labor conditions. In June 1933, the People's Commissariat of Labor was abolished and its staff and social service functions, including management of workers' compensation funds, were transferred to the VTsSPS. By 1936, the VTsSPS employed more than 340 people. Headed by N. M. Shvernik, it was governed by an elected secretariat (Shvernik, Abolin, G. D. Veinberg, V. I. Polonskii, N. N. Evreinov), and a presidium, which included the five secretaries and ten additional members. It contained labor and cultural-club inspectorates; departments for labor statistics, foreign workers, planning and wage regulation, finance, and the journal *Voprosy Profdvizhenie*; a scientific library, the Bureaus of Social Insurance (Sotsstrakha) and Physical Culture, the research institutes, and a secret section, dealing with internal politics and classified information on strikes, disturbances, accidents, and conditions.[93]

After the purge of Tomskii and the rightists, the Party defined the role of unions ever more narrowly to serve industrialization. In January 1933, a joint plenum of the Central Committee and the Central Control Commission summarized their tasks: to strengthen labor discipline, prevent overspending of the wage fund, maintain high production norms, and encourage workers to increase their skills and master new technology. Their function did not differ appreciably from that of a capitalist manager.

[92] "Sokrashchenie profsoiuznogo apparata," *Voprosy profdvizheniia*, 3 Fevral' and 5–6 Mart, 1937, pp. 56, 58; GARF, f. 5451, o. 43, d. 76, "V TsK VKP (b). Tov. Andreevu A. A.," l. 314.

[93] GARF, f. 5451, o. 43, d. 69, "Sekretariu VTsSPS. Tov. Shverniku," "Spisok sotrudnikov VTsSPS na poluchenie posobii," "Spisok sotrudnikov VTsSPS na poluchenie putevok," ll. 2–9, 16–19, 21–25.

The factory committees, which had seized and run the factories in 1917, were instructed to review workers' wages to ensure they were not inflated through illegal overtime or piecework.[94] In essence, the unions became cheerleaders for production and watchdogs over the wage fund.

The unions and the VTsSPS officially adhered to their prescribed roles, but factory committee activists found it difficult to promote policies counter to their members' short-term interests. When the state increased food prices in 1932, for example, many union activists asked: "Are the real wages of workers going to be maintained?"; "Will an increase in wages reflect the increase in prices?"; and "Why are we violating the decree of the 16th Party Congress (1930) which stated that we would struggle for an increase in real wages?"[95] Rather than fighting for wage increases, however, union activists were dispatched to teach retail sales clerks how to respond to workers' angry queries about prices. They were to propound the Party's line: price increases would permit further economic development.[96] The activists did a poor job of propagandizing the clerks. When angry customers asked why prices had risen, clerks responded that too much capital was invested in heavy industry. Others noted flatly, "Food collection is going poorly." A union activist in Leningrad asked a store manager, "Did you educate your staff about the price increase?" The manager shrugged, "Let Stalin educate them." When a worker in the canteen of the Pravda printing factory asked the salesgirl why the price of tea had risen from 2 to 5 kopeks, she answered tartly, "Say your thanks that we have water, because soon we won't have that either."[97]

In addition to explaining price increases, union activists were mobilized in a national campaign to transform the new collective contract "into a lever for increasing labor productivity." Not surprisingly, workers greeted the campaign with anger. Confounded and depressed by their new assignments, union activists did little. Veinberg, a VTsSPS leader, reported to the Central Committee that many factory committees ignored the campaign, held no discussions with their members, and simply signed the contract on their behalf. The collective contracts, once negotiated in good faith by factory committees representing workers' interests, were viewed as a

---

[94] GARF, f. 5515, o. 33, d. 50, "Rezoliutsiia Biuro fraktsii VTsSPS po dokladu tov. Shvernika 'O vypolnenii profsoiuzami reshenii ianvar'skogo ob"edinennogo plenuma TsK i TsKK VKP (b),'" l. 200.

[95] GARF, f. 5451, o. 43, d. 13, "Informatsionnaia spravka no. 10 o nastroeniiakh rabochikh v sviazi s povysheniem tsen," l. 5.

[96] "Svodka o povyshenii tsen," l. 14.   [97] Ibid., ll. 12, 13, 15.

sham by union members and activists alike. One worker noted contemptuously, "The collective contract is a useless scrap of paper."[98] Union activists were also reluctant to curtail "overspending" of the wage fund. They turned a blind eye when managers created "fictive shock workers" in order to maintain wages, and were unenthusiastic about shock work and other forms of "socialist competition." Veinberg accused them of "failing to agitate for high labor productivity and labor discipline."[99] Union activists were uncomfortable promulgating policies that cut the already meager wages of their members. Challenged by the workers, they did not know how to respond. In a shop meeting in the Marti factory, a worker passed an anonymous note to the podium. "Why does the union struggle so hard for technical norming and oppose overspending of the wage fund? Why doesn't it struggle when they increase prices for food and goods?"[100] Workers did not understand the purpose of unions that supported the state's efforts to extract maximum surplus for industrialization and opposed management's efforts to maintain the wage scale. They resented mandatory meetings to ratify contracts that undermined their interests. One brigade leader explained that there was no reason to attend a meeting to discuss a contract that provided nothing.[101]

By 1935, the unions had ceased to play any role in negotiations over the collective contract, output norms, and wage scales, which became the exclusive purview of the economic organs.[102] Stripped of any role in negotiating terms of employment and unable to defend their members, they tried to alleviate the most egregious conditions by speeding emergency deliveries of food and work clothes, improving food distribution and housing, and responding to complaints.[103] They enrolled new members, supervised cultural, political, sport, and educational activities, dispensed compensation for accidents and sickness, and provided passes

---

[98] GARF, f. 5515, o. 33, d. 50, "V MK VKP (b). Kratkii otchet o sobranii aktiva partiinykh, professional'nykh i khoziaistvennykh organizatsii," ll. 308–309.

[99] "V TsK VKP (b). Dokladnaia zapiska ob itogakh provedeniia koldogovornoi kampanii i peresmotra norm vyrabotki," ll. 162–160. There was widespread collusion among workers, managers, and union activists. See Filtzer, *Soviet Workers and Stalinist Industrialization*, pp. 208–32.

[100] "Sektor informatsii Otdela orgraboty i proverki ispolneniia VTsSPS. Svodka no. 4," l. 117ob.

[101] GARF, f. 5515, o. 33, d. 58, "Iz vystuplenii na sobranniiakh rabochikh po obsuzhdeniiu koldogovora Stalgres," l. 146.

[102] "Voprosy okhrany truda, zarplaty i massovoi raboty profsoiuzov na proizvodstve," ll. 13–18.

[103] See, for example, "Sekretariiam VTsSPS, t.t. Shverniku i Veinbergu. Biuro Sotsstrakha, t. Kotovu," "TsK VKP (b), VTsSPS – tov. Shverniku, NKLP – tov. Liubimovu," ll. 134, 28.

to vacation and rest homes. As boosters of economic development, the unions were occupied with alleviating conditions created by policies that they could neither challenge nor address.

Workers' Protests

The transformation of the unions made it difficult for workers to pursue their grievances collectively. As a result, they tended to bypass the unions, expressing their dissatisfaction with wages, shortages, and conditions through a variety of individual and collective strategies, including complaints, quitting, passive resistance, and short collective protests. In some cases, individual strategies became collective: quitting, a personal decision, was so common as to create "labor turnover," a collective phenomenon that damaged production. Collective protests included disruption of meetings, slow-downs, walkouts, strikes, and riots. Protests tended to be spontaneous, brief, small, and easily defused, rarely spreading beyond a single shop or factory. The VTsSPS was successful in quelling discontent with promises to redress grievances, arbitration, and emergency food deliveries. It is perhaps a measure of how strongly workers supported socialism that the deep social strains of industrialization did not produce more sustained protest. Yet the absence of large-scale protest was hardly a sign of satisfaction. Hardship, doubt, mistrust, and malaise were slowly eroding the close connection party leaders once had with their working-class base. The Party was losing touch with the class that had brought it to power and in whose name it ruled.

Discontent was sharpest among workers in light industry, and the largest, most coordinated, and sustained protests occurred among textile workers. The state raised wages in heavy industry and at the upper end of the wage scale in an effort to attract workers and motivate them to improve skills. Both these differentials worked to the disadvantage of workers, particularly women, who were concentrated in light industries and less-skilled jobs. Light industry in general was undercapitalized, its aging machinery prone to frequent breakdowns, which cut into workers' earnings. Some of the sharpest protests came from women textile workers. A wave of strikes in the Ivanovo region in April 1932 involved more than 16,000 textile workers.[104] When the state lowered ration norms for

---

[104] Jeffrey Rossman, "The Teikovo Cotton Workers' Strike of April 1932: Class, Gender, and Identity Politics in Stalin's Russia," *Russian Review*, 56 (January, 1997), pp. 44–69. Only sporadic reports of strikes are contained in the VTsSPS, previously classified *opis'*

children at the end of 1932, the textile factories again erupted in protests. When party and union officials tried to discuss the new policy in the Lezhnevskii factory, women workers insisted on large factory- or shopwide meetings in place of smaller groups, where they could be easily silenced. When union officials refused, the women yelled, "Then we're leaving." In the weaving department, angry women peppered the head of the party committee with questions: "Can we countermand this decision to lower the norms of provisioning?" "Why are you lowering the norms for children?" Finally, they shouted him down. "In no case can we decrease the ration packets for children." "You are torturing us," they yelled. "How long are you going to do this?" In several meetings, communist workers took the side of their workmates, and spoke out against official policy. One party member declared to strong applause, "The Party is split now, and it is not listening to the voice of the people. They only feed the officials. We have endured enough. We must demand that they do not decrease the ration packets. Workers will not support the Party. It is becoming impossible to live." Similar protests roiled other factories.[105]

Despite better wages for heavy industry and skilled positions, protests were not confined to the textile industry or women workers. Increased norms, revisions of the wage scale, food shortages, and wage arrears provoked workers in heavy industry as well. There were short strikes in the Nikopol iron and steel works, in Moscow's Krasnyi Fakel machine-building works, in Leningrad's Krasnyi Putilovets machine-building works, in the Donbas mines, among dock workers in Leningrad, Arkhangel'sk, and Odessa, and the Sormovo shipyard.[106] In the Malenkov machine-building factory, a prize-winning young shock worker called for a strike when the norms were raised. He succinctly summarized the situation, "They reconsidered the norms, lowered the wage scale, and decreased the provisions in the cooperatives. Therefore, we must walk out of the factory." Young workers were frequently the most militant, and shock workers and party activists often played leading roles. When new rules about not paying for defective production (*brak*) went into effect in 1932, many workers took sharp pay cuts. Two workers in Krasnyi

---

(f. 5451, o. 43). It is possible that the severe labor disturbances that Rossman documented in Ivanovo occurred in other places as well: Davies, *Crisis and Progress in the Soviet Economy*, pp. 188–92.

[105] GARF, f. 5451, o. 43, d. 13, "Obkom VKP (b) predsed. TsK soiuza tov. Evreinovu," l. 17.

[106] Filtzer provided the first overview of labor disruptions: *Soviet Workers and Stalinist Industrialization*, pp. 81–90.

Putilovets walked out after the norms were raised and penned a declaration to the second and third shifts not to come to work. Workers on the third shift also threatened to walk out.[107]

Price increases in January 1932 prompted workers in Moscow, the country's best-provisioned city, to strike. Workers in a construction-materials factory agitated during their break for a factorywide strike. They said, "They pay us little, the norms are high, the payscale is low, and prices are increasing. What are we working for? No matter what we do, we are half-starved." A group of workers quit in protest, but party and union officials persuaded them to stay. A series of "explanatory conversations" followed, but the workers were not convinced. "It isn't right. You are just throwing dust in our eyes," they replied. In the Donbas, miners responded to the price increases with anti-Soviet proclamations.[108]

Workers also walked out when managers failed to pay wages or issue food cards. In 1932, workers in Vishkhimzavod, a chemical factory in the Urals, walked out when they did not receive their wages.[109] The factory lacked fuel and raw materials, and the director may have diverted the wage fund to maintain production. Workers in the railroad car–building factory in Mytishchi in Moscow province received no wages in November 1932. A painter went to the factory's party secretary in desperation, "You need to have your head cut off. You are always propagandizing that now we have these supposed difficulties on the finance front that we need to overcome. I want to tell you that to endure much more is not possible; we will have an uprising in three months. I myself cannot sacrifice my life and my children, and I cannot endure any more."[110] In 1933, seventy workers in the Izhorskii machine-building works in Leningrad province stopped work for three hours to protest the fact that they had not received ration cards or wages for three months.[111] Workers in the Provskii factory in Eastern Siberia declared an "Italian'ka" (slow-down) after the administration failed to distribute ration cards for flour, and workers in two shops walked out for three hours. When workers in a glass factory in Ivanovo were not paid for two months, they presented the administration with an ultimatum: "Give us the money within the next two hours, or we shut

[107] "Signal'naia svodka no. 3," ll. 21, 210b; see Filtzer, *Soviet Workers and Stalinist Industrialization*, p. 87, on the militancy of young workers.

[108] "Svodka no. 2 'O povyshenii tsen,'" ll. 3–4.

[109] GARF, f. 5451, o. 43, d. 14, "Informsektoru VTsSPS," "Protokol po zasedaniia signal'nogo posta VTsSPS na Vish. kombinate," ll. 71, 69.

[110] "Svodka o polozhenii otdel'nykh predpriiatiiakh i uchastkakh raboty," l. 11.

[111] GARF, f. 5451, o. 43, d. 27, "Sektor informatsii," l. 9.

the factory down."[112] After rations were cut for workers in Liudinovo's locomotive factory in the Western province in 1932, workers called for a strike. About half the workers were new migrants, still seething about collectivization. Mensheviks and Socialist Revolutionaries were also active in the factory, offering a political critique of Bolshevik policies. Workers in the repair shop gathered in a train car and sent a small delegation to other shops to organize support for a strike. On May Day, someone scrawled an appeal on the wall in one shop: "Workers, Restore Power to the Soviets!," a slogan based on the revolutionary "All Power to the Soviets," popular in 1917 but subsequently rendered subversive by the dictatorship of the Party. The workers sent an appeal to a neighboring glass factory to join the strike. The district party committee quickly commandeered and distributed two train cars of bread, forestalling the strike. Yet these were only temporary measures. A local VTsSPS representative noted that workers received no bread or sugar in June, and the food situation was still very precarious.[113]

The full history of Soviet labor relations still remains hidden in NKVD and party archives. Scattered data assembled here suggest that protests were not confined to the undercapitalized, low-wage textile industry, but were everywhere: in heavy as well as light industry, in Moscow and Leningrad as well as distant construction sites and mines. New migrants, older workers, women, skilled, and unskilled all participated. Their protests tended to be short, spontaneous, and effective in prompting immediate action from managers and officials. Wages, weeks or months in arrears, miraculously appeared; food deliveries were rushed to the stores. Emergency aid was effective in quelling protest, but it did not create lasting change. Although conditions improved in the middle of the decade, they worsened again as the country began to prepare for war in the late 1930s.

Doubt in the Party

The strains of industrialization not only undermined workers' confidence in the Party, but also promoted wavering within its own ranks. Former oppositionists in leading posts, appalled by the hunger and suffering in the cities and the countryside, discussed alternatives to Stalin's leadership and policies. Rank-and-file members, too, found it increasingly difficult

[112] GARF, f. 5451, o. 43, d. 27, "Svodka no. 4," ll. 12–12ob.
[113] GARF, f. 5451, o. 43, d. 12, "VTsSPS. Dokladnaia zapiska," ll. 67–66.

to support the Party's policies. Working-class communists faced the same hardships as other workers. Among the workers suffering from malnutrition in the Petrovskii iron and steel works, for example, were the secretary of a party cell and other party members.[114] Communist workers were often more sympathetic to the complaints of their workmates than to the prevailing party line. Many workers with rural relatives blamed collectivization for food shortages, and dismissed party propaganda about rural prosperity. At a meeting of the senior production workers in the Kompressor machine-building factory in Moscow, a party member with thirty years' seniority asked angrily, "Why did we have good food and clothes in 1924, and now there is nothing?" An older worker responded with a denunciation of collectivization, "Provisioning is very bad here, and I think the reason why is because we collectivized the peasantry. The collective farms don't meet the demands for production. If individual farmers could raise more cattle, then there would be more meat and other agricultural produce in the markets."[115] A candidate party member and worker in the 1905 factory also stated that the lack of food in the cities was tied to the failure of collectivization. "Supposedly, there is no war communism now," he said, referring to the Bolsheviks' policy of forced grain requisitioning during the Civil War, "but the peasants and collective farmers are robbed worse than under war communism."[116] Although party leaders expected such sentiments from "backward" rural migrants, they were widely shared by party and nonparty workers, who communicated regularly with rural relatives and brought news from the villages to the factories.

Many communist workers balked at enrolling others in the national loan campaigns. One report noted that their mood "was about the same as the mood of the workers." Some defied party discipline and spoke out against the loans. One communist lathe operator in a machine shop in Briansk announced at a meeting, "What is this loan for? Why do we need a second five-year plan when we haven't gotten anything from the first? It's impossible to live now. Let them improve the position of the workers and then we can subscribe to a new loan and build the second five-year plan." In the Marti factory, an old worker and party member stood up at a union meeting and announced, "The provisioning of the workers gets worse every day. They press on the workers' circles, they lower our

---

[114] "Strakh. punkt zavoda im. Petrovskogo," l. 112.
[115] "Signal'naia svodka no. 3," l. 21.
[116] "Sektor informatsii Otdela orgraboty i proverki ispolneniia VTsSPS," l. 9.

wages." He pulled out his party card, threw it down, and declared, "You won't shut me up."[117] A woman textile worker and party member in Ivanovo refused to attend a party meeting about the loan. "I am not going and don't you sign me up," she announced. "Everywhere, there are only rogues. Justice cannot be found. If you sign me up, I will leave the Party."[118] Many communist workers, deeply offended by the growing differentials between workers and officials, felt that the burden of the loans should be borne by the more privileged. One communist worker in a leather factory in Klin declared, "Let them sign up the officials who receive better salaries and have their own stores." Another candidate party member in the same factory responded angrily to an activist's attempt to add him to a subscription list. "Have you fed us, have you given us bread?" he demanded. "You agitate well for the loan, but you are fat and satisfied and we are hungry. Yes, everyone now is hungry. As long as you don't stand in line with us, and you don't get the same rations, and you don't improve the situation, not one worker will subscribe for a single kopek."[119]

Many party members felt they could not in good conscience persuade workers to sacrifice further for industrialization. When a new round of price increases went into effect in 1933, the Party called meetings to explain the policy. One party member remarked to another in embarrassment, "How can we explain this to the workers when some groups receive so very little?"[120] When norms were raised in the Kamenskii paper factory in Moscow province in 1932, the norming expert himself denounced the increases at a workers' meeting. "Not in a single capitalist country are the workers so exploited as in the Kamenskii factory," he thundered to loud cheers and applause. "Here they steal the workers' wages and improperly measure their output." Neither the Party, union, nor Komsomol members said a word in response. The outspoken norming official and the head of the factory committee were fired soon afterwards.[121]

Some communist workers denounced party policies and the unions outright. Egorov, a party member in the Paris Commune factory in Ivanovo, bitterly dismissed the unions as "worse than in the capitalist countries."

---

[117] "Sektor informatsii Otdela orgraboty i proverki ispolneniia VTsSPS. Svodka no. 4," ll. 117–117ob.

[118] "Spets. spravka," l. 153.

[119] "Ob otritsatel'nykh nastroenniiakh vyiavlennakh v kampanii po zaimu," l. 112.

[120] "Sektor informatsii Otdela orgraboty i proverki ispolneniia VTsSPS. Svodka no. 5," l. 113.

[121] GARF, f. 5451, o. 43, d. 14, "Signal'noe soobshchenie no. 1," l. 1.

And a party member in the Kozitskii factory in Leningrad told his fellow workers, "All their talk in meetings – this is just throwing dust in our eyes. And then in the papers they write about our active participation." In the Krasnoe Sormovo machine-building works in Nizhnii Novgorod province, a party member angrily rebuffed a union activist seeking support, "It's your law, your power – you do whatever you want."[122] Hunger, chaos, falling wages, and the suffering of fellow workers and peasants placed enormous pressure on rank-and-file communists. Many found it difficult to justify policies that created such hardship. The wavering and disillusionment in the ranks found its echo among party leaders. By 1932, they had transformed the inchoate discontent into an incisive critique of Stalin's industrial and agricultural policies.

The Remnants of Oppositionism

Throughout the 1920s, numerous groupings had formed within the Party expressing different approaches toward foreign affairs, economic policy, unions, culture, law, and family relations. Scarcely an issue emerged that did not engender passionate debate. Party members grouped and regrouped within shifting alliances accommodated within a flexible political culture.[123] At the same time, the Party was also rent by deeper, more divisive struggles over fundamental policies and power. In 1923, many members rallied to Trotsky's critique of the burgeoning state bureaucracy and erosion of party democracy.[124] Party leaders G. E. Zinoviev and L. B. Kamenev adopted a similar platform in 1925 in response to Stalin's growing power. In 1926, Trotsky joined Zinoviev and Kamenev in a "United Opposition," which found wide support in the factories, among students, and in Zinoviev's Leningrad stronghold. Yet by 1927 Stalin and his supporters had successfully outmaneuvered the opposition. Trotsky was expelled from the Party, and eventually exiled abroad, and

---

[122] "V TsK VKP (b) dokladnaia zapiska ob itogakh provedeniia koldogovornoi kampanii i peresmotra norm vyrabotki," ll. 154–153.

[123] See, for example, Wendy Goldman, *Women, the State and Revolution: Soviet Family Policy and Social Life, 1917–1936* (Cambridge University Press, New York, 1993); Lynn Mally, *Culture of the Future: The Proletkult Movement in Revolutionary Russia* (University of California Press, Berkeley, 1990); Richard Stites, *Revolutionary Dreams: Utopian Vision and Experimental Life in the Russian Revolution* (Oxford University Press, New York, 1991).

[124] Leon Trotsky, *The New Course: The Challenge of the Left Opposition (1923–1925)* (Pathfinder Press, New York, 1975); Isaac Deutscher, *The Prophet Unarmed: 1921–1929* (Random House, New York, 1977).

Zinoviev and Kamenev were removed from their posts. Their supporters were silenced; some quietly abandoned their protests, others were expelled or exiled.

In 1929, with the adoption of the first five-year plan, many of Trotsky's earlier supporters recanted and rejoined the Party. Eager to work in industry, they took up prominent positions. At the same time, party leaders Bukharin, Rykov, and Tomskii, opposing the Party's new policy of forced grain requisitioning and collectivization, were deemed "right deviationists," and also forced to recant. Tomskii was dismissed as head of the VTsSPS, and the unions thoroughly purged of his supporters. Many of these "rightists" found new jobs in the Commissariat of Labor, moving back to the unions and the VTsSPS when the commissariat was dissolved in 1933.

By 1932, small oppositional groups of both leftists and rightists had revived. Several former leftists, now occupying leading industrial posts, met with Trotsky and his son in Berlin. M. N. Riutin, a "rightist" expelled from the Party in 1930, organized a clandestine oppositional group to protest Stalin's policies and methods. Numerous copies of its 194-page manifesto, known as the "Riutin Platform," circulated among party members in various cities. The "Riutin group" was expelled from the Party and arrested. The Riutin Platform terrified the Stalinist leadership and would figure prominently in later accusations against party leaders. Other party members of the left and right, including Tomskii, Rykov, V. V. Shmidt, and I. N. Smirnov, were demoted, censured, expelled, or arrested. Yet all the oppositions retained former supporters in prominent posts in the unions, industry, economic organs, and other institutions. At the January 1933 Central Committee Plenum, one delegate noted that the party and state organizations were filled with discontented critics. "If you want repulsive anecdotes about the work of the Party," he said, "sit in the Sovnarkom [Council of People's Commissars] dining room."[125]

Of all these groups, only the Trotskyists developed a base of support among workers. Yet even the Trotskyists found themselves increasingly isolated from young, militant workers. Although they shared their grievances, they were appalled at the "anti-Soviet," even antisocialist,

---

[125] "Stalin i krizis proletarskoi diktatury. Platforma 'Soiuza marksistov-lenintsev' (Gruppa Riutina)," *Reabilitatsiia politicheskie protsessy 30–50-x godov* (Izdatel'stvo Politicheskoi Literatury, Moscow, 1991); J. Arch Getty and Oleg Naumov, *The Road to Terror: Stalin and the Self-Destruction of the Bolsheviks, 1932–1939* (Yale University Press, New Haven, 1999), pp. 52–4; Davies, *Crisis and Progress in the Soviet Economy*, pp. 245–6, 328.

views of the new peasant migrants. Frightened to make common cause with such people, they were increasingly isolated from any potential base.[126] By 1934, no active, organized opposition to Stalin's policies from either the left or the right remained. Former oppositionists continued privately to exchange information, maintain contact, and share doubts and opinions. Some assumed high posts, others remained in the factories, a scattering of politically sophisticated comrades with complex histories, long memories, and deep reservations about Stalin and his policies.

Conclusion

By 1934, the Party had weathered the most difficult social and economic crisis of its existence and created a strong base for further development. Its success was a testament to workers' deep commitment to the greater ideals of socialism. Informants reported much grumbling and bitterness, but nowhere in the archives do their reports suggest that workers hoped to restore the nobility and capitalists to power. But the Party's victory came at a steep cost. Its aims for the first five-year plan, to reduce prices and increase real wages, foundered on unrealistic production targets, unanticipated imbalances, and fierce resistance to collectivization. Although the economy began to stabilize by 1934, workers were increasingly alienated by the painful costs of industrialization. Working-class party members and union activists found it difficult to uphold the party line. Forced to choose between an embattled working class and party policies, many experienced a crisis of faith. How could they endorse collective contracts that provided no benefits and loans that reduced meager paychecks? Even strong proponents of socialism were increasingly dismayed by the Party's insistence on false shows of participation and consent. The unions' factory committees, once vital and militant representatives of workers' interests, now did little more than enroll members, and organize meetings with preset agendas and outcomes.

Party leaders were aware of the deepening malaise and discontent. Official investigators, informers (voluntary and paid), and union and party activists regularly surveyed the "mood of the workers" on an array of issues.[127] Some reports provided no personal information about the

---

[126] Aleksei Gusev, "The Bolshevik Leninist Opposition and the Working Class, 1928–29," in Filtzer et al., *A Dream Deferred*.

[127] The Party, the Commissariat of Labor, the unions, and the VTsSPS all gathered information from informers, worker activists, investigatory brigades, and local officials.

workers they profiled, serving mainly to apprise leaders of reactions to new policies. In other instances, however, informants carefully identified outspoken workers by name, job, shop, and factory. So-called anti-Soviet comments prompted investigations of workers' backgrounds and sometimes resulted in loss of job, union membership, and living quarters or even arrest.[128] Workers spoke fairly openly in the early 1930s, but they undoubtedly became more cautious as they saw the potential consequences. Those without passports or with dubious class backgrounds were at highest risk, and many undoubtedly kept silent out of fear.

At the local level, working-class party and union activists were torn by doubts about party policy and alienated from leaders who were more privileged, and better paid and provisioned. Former oppositionists in leading posts buzzed with discontent, but had no base of support among the workers. Former oppositionists still working in the factories were critical of party policy yet appalled by the anti-Soviet moods among new migrants and other workers. They offered workers no organized alternative to Stalinist policies. Party leaders, caught between the need to industrialize and the resentment their policies evoked, were aware of the slow erosion of support among workers, the doubts within party ranks, and the secret, steady hum of criticism. Although workers widely supported socialism, their support for party leaders was not fully assured. The Party had survived a tumultuous social and economic transformation, but just barely. It was riddled by doubters above and below, and its social base had eroded. Most importantly, many industrial tensions and difficulties remained unresolved. Workers had numerous grievances, but no official outlet for collective redress.

Mikhail Aleksandrovich Panin, a 29-year-old coal miner from Donetsk and a Red Army volunteer, best captured the situation in a letter he wrote to the Commissariat of Labor in 1933 in the midst of the famine. He explained that the miners had gone without wages for more than two months, a managerial practice that was creating "artificial starvation." Rations had been cut, and many families had received nothing but bread for the past month. Despite numerous suggestions from miners to officials to sift the flour, the bread was full of chaff. Miners had begun to swell from malnutrition; twelve miners from his pit alone were lying in the

---

[128] Workers who spoke out against the collective contract campaign in 1933, for example, were investigated: "V TsK VKP (b). Dokladnaia zapiska ob itogakh provedeniia koldogovornoi kampanii i peresmotra norm vyrabotki," ll. 154–153; "V sekretnuiu chast' VTsSPS," ll. 131–131ob.

hospital. The horses, too weak from hunger to pull the wagons, died in their traces. Mining in the deeper recesses of the pits had stopped, and production plummeted. Miners were so desperate that they were hacking up the dead horses and eating them. "Is it really possible," Panin asked, "that we workers have struggled for this: to eke out such an existence, to pilfer the fallen, discarded horses from the pit stables, who are deliberately treated as nothing more than uncollected forage?" "It has been intolerable to see all that has been done deliberately by local officials," Panin wrote. "You can judge the mood of the workers by what I have told you. Not only here, but everywhere."[129] By 1937, local officials were being called to account. The chaff in the bread, the dead horses, the failure to meet production targets had a new name. It was called "wrecking."

[129] GARF, f. 5515, o. 33, d. 58, "Biuro Zhalob pri Narkomtrud," ll. 155–156.

1. Serp i Molot (Hammer and Sickle) factory, 1935. Courtesy of RGAKFD

2. Serp i Molot, 1935. Courtesy of RGAKFD

3. Krasnyi Proletarii (Red Proletarian) factory, 1935. Courtesy of RGAKFD

2

From Murder to Mass Conspiracy

"Horrible and monstrous is the guilt of these criminals and murderers who raised their hands against the leaders of our Party, against Comrades Stalin, Voroshilov, Zhdanov, Kaganovich, Ordzhonikidze, Kosior, and Postyshev."

> – A. Ia. Vyshinskii, Procurator General, first Moscow
> show trial, August 1936[1]

"This event [the Kirov murder] was fatal for the country and for the Party."

> – G. S. Liushkov, NKVD official[2]

Late in the afternoon of December 1, 1934, a former employee of the Institute of Party History, Leonid V. Nikolaev, slipped into Leningrad party headquarters and shot and killed Sergei M. Kirov, the head of the Leningrad party committee. Kirov, a popular organizer and staunch supporter of Stalin, had been sent to Leningrad in 1926 to win over the Leningrad party organization, a stronghold of G. E. Zinoviev and the left opposition. Kirov replaced G. E. Evdokimov, a member of the left opposition, as secretary of the Leningrad party committee in February 1926. Evdokimov would later be tried, with fifteen other defendants, for Kirov's murder, found guilty, and shot. The assassination is still shrouded in mystery, the subject of numerous conspiracy theories. Some argue that Kirov was a popular political moderate who challenged Stalin's leadership, and that Stalin secretly engineered the murder. Others contend that there is no evidence to support either Kirov's "moderation" or Stalin's

---

[1] *The Case of the Trotskyite-Zinovievite Terrorist Center: Report of Court Proceedings* (People's Commissariat of Justice USSR, Moscow, 1936), p. 117 (hereafter cited as *Report of Court Proceedings*).

[2] "O tak nazyvaemom 'Antisovetskom Ob"edinennom trotskistsko-zinov'evskom tsentr,'" *Izvestiia TsK KPSS*, No. 8, 1989, p. 88.

involvement in the crime.[3] Both Khrushchev and Gorbachev established commissions to investigate the murder. Drawing on hundreds of documents and interviews, both commissions concluded that Nikolaev had acted alone.[4] All agree, however, that Kirov's murder touched off a reaction that would culminate in sweeping arrests within the Party, industry, the unions, academia, the government, and other institutions. The very day of the murder, the state passed an anti-terrorist law abrogating civil liberties and judicial rights. Investigations of "terrorism" were to be completed within ten days. The accused were to be informed of the charges twenty-four hours before trial, they were denied legal counsel for their defense, their sentences could not appealed, and a death sentence was to be carried out immediately. In September 1937, these provisions were extended to other crimes, including wrecking and subversion.[5] By 1937, the entire country was gripped by an insidious culture of denunciation and witch hunting.[6]

Although party leaders responded immediately, they were initially unsure what meaning to ascribe to the Kirov murder. Was it a tragic but isolated crime, or was it part of a larger terrorist conspiracy? In the immediate aftermath of the assassination, arrests were confined to Nikolaev and his circle. Over the next two years, however, the investigation widened in fits and starts to include former left oppositionists, foreign communists, "rightists," and others. The state's narrative of the murder and its political meaning also broadened to include ever more elaborate terror and murder plots. In the factories, however, at the base of the Party's organizational pyramid, the party committees (*partkomy*) continued to function much as they had before. Unsure how to implement the center's instructions urging vigilance and action, they continued to focus on production, campaigns, and problems in the shops. Workers showed

---

[3] Robert Conquest, *Stalin and the Kirov Murder* (Oxford University Press, New York, 1989); Amy Knight, *Who Killed Kirov? The Kremlin's Greatest Mystery* (Hill and Wang, New York, 1999); J. Arch Getty, "The Politics of Repression Revisited," in Getty and Roberta Manning, eds., *Stalinist Terror: New Perspectives* (Cambridge University Press, New York, 1993), pp. 40–62; Gabor Rittersporn, *Stalinist Simplifications and Soviet Complications: Social Tensions and Political Conflicts in the USSR, 1933–1953* (Harwood Academic Publishers, Chur, 1991), pp. 5–6.

[4] Knight, *Who Killed Kirov?*, p. 19.

[5] Peter Solomon, *Soviet Criminal Justice Under Stalin* (Cambridge University Press, Cambridge, 1996), p. 236.

[6] See Chapter 6 in this book on the factory party committees, and Sheila Fitzpatrick, *Everyday Stalinism: Ordinary Life in Extraordinary Times* (Oxford University Press, Oxford and New York, 1999), pp. 190–217.

great interest in the Kirov murder, but they, too, did not consider it their personal business. Apart from an occasional reference to a Trotskyist or wrecker, both the party rank and file and the workers were largely impervious to the political squall at the top. Terrorism, in their view, was the business of the NKVD. This chapter traces and contrasts responses to the Kirov murder "from above" (among party leaders) and "from below" (within the factories). As party leaders became increasingly obsessed with hidden terrorists and enemies, the workers and *partkomy* proved much slower to respond. Their general apathy, failure to "unmask" enemies, and tolerance infuriated party leaders, who in turn made every effort to involve them in the hunt for enemies. This dynamic between party leaders and their base was critical to the spread of the terror, the development of mass participation, and the change of political culture in the factories.

The Murder Plot Expands

The Politburo entrusted N. I. Ezhov, deputy chairman of the Party Control Commission, and Ia. S. Agranov, deputy commissar of the Commissariat of Internal Affairs (NKVD), with investigating the Kirov murder. Although Ezhov's aggressive investigation and conspiracy theories would eventually propel him to a position as the head of the NKVD, the investigators initially limited their search to a small group of suspects. Within the month, Nikolaev and thirteen others had been arrested, tried, and executed in accordance with the new law of December 1. In a second trial on January 15–16, 1935, Zinoviev, Evdokimov, L. B. Kamenev, I. P. Bakaev, and fifteen others were convicted of establishing a so-called Moscow center, which allegedly guided the activities of various counterrevolutionary groups, including the one convicted of murdering Kirov. Yet Zinoviev and Kamenev both denied that they had played any part in Kirov's murder. Convicted only of "abetting" the murder by encouraging opposition, they were sentenced to prison.[7]

The day after the trial ended, Stalin summarized the political situation in a letter to the Politburo. On January 18, the Central Committee sent this letter, in "closed" secret form, to all party organizations for discussion. Prepared under Stalin's personal supervision, the letter explained that a group of "Zinovievites" had been arrested for Kirov's murder, found

---

[7] J. Arch Getty and Oleg Naumov, *The Road to Terror: Stalin and the Self-Destruction of the Bolsheviks, 1932–1939* (Yale University Press, New Haven, 1999), pp. 144–7.

guilty, and sentenced.[8] In other words, the murderers had been found and punished, the case solved. The letter's jerky syntax and rambling exposition were unusual in an important communiqué from above. Marked by clumsily inserted clauses and repetitions, the letter read as if drafted by a shaky and hesitant hand. It closely followed the narrative presented by the prosecution at the trial of the "Moscow center": Kirov was killed by a "Leningrad center," headed by a center in Moscow, which encouraged terrorism but was unaware of the assassination plans. Both centers shared a "Trotskyist-Zinovievite platform," and aimed to place their members, many of whom were in the Party, into leading posts. Having lost all support within the Party and the working class for their program, they resorted to terrorism and allied with the Latvian consul in Leningrad, a supporter of German fascism. The letter emphasized repeatedly that these two centers did not offer a socialist alternative to Stalin's leadership, and were not to be viewed as another grouping in the Party's long, fractious history. They were terrorists, fascist collaborators, representatives of "the expiring bourgeois classes." The letter presented the defendants as genuine counterrevolutionaries, discredited them personally, and even smeared their relatives. It stressed that the former oppositionists of the 1920s were not "tame and harmless," as many party members believed. They were "double-dealers" who professed loyalty to the Party's policies and its leaders, while secretly preparing terrorist acts. Holding party cards and occupying important posts, they "masked" their true intentions. In fact, the lack of vigilance within the Leningrad party organization, and specifically the Leningrad NKVD, had enabled them to carry out Kirov's murder. Moreover, the letter warned that other "masked" oppositionists still remained in the Party and in high posts. It demanded the exclusion, arrest, and exile of all "remnants of antiparty groups within the Party," and encouraged members to study party history so they could recognize these "remnants" and destroy them.[9]

Some historians believe that the letter gave "a straightforward directive" not only to exclude oppositionists from the Party, but to arrest them.[10] Yet the text offered no specific course of action beyond heightened vigilance and study. The last open opposition within the Party had been

[8] "O tak nazyvaemom 'Antisovetskom Ob"edinennom trotskistsko-zinov'evskom tsentr,'" pp. 78–81.

[9] "Zakrytoe pis'mo TsK VKP (b). Uroki sobytii, sviazannykh s zlodeiskim ubiitstvom tov. Kirova," *Izvestiia TsK KPSS*, No. 8, 1989, pp. 95–100.

[10] "O tak nazyvaemom 'Antisovetskom Ob"edinennom trotskistsko-zinov'evskom tsentr,'" p. 81.

vanquished in 1927, and most party members in 1935 did not believe that their local organizations contained "remnants of antiparty groups." They readily acknowledged that some members may have voted for Trotskyist resolutions, or even been active in oppositional circles, but they believed that these people had long since abandoned their earlier views. Party members were respectfully attentive to the letter, but did not find it directly applicable to their own organizations.

Shortly after sending the letter, the Politburo, on Stalin's initiative, undertook wider reprisals against the former left opposition. It exiled 663 Zinovievites from Leningrad, and transferred 325 party members, former "leftists," to work outside the city. The Leningrad NKVD arrested an additional 843 former Zinovievites in January and February. During their interrogations, the version of the Kirov murder presented at the trial and in the letter began to expand to include more perpetrators, plots, and targets. Ezhov elaborated the new version in a manuscript, "From Fractionalism to Open Counterrevolution and Fascism," which he sent to Stalin in May 1935 with a cover letter requesting further instructions. According to the manuscript, former Trotskyists had also opted for terror and abetted the Zinovievites. That summer, Ezhov instructed the NKVD to find and liquidate a still-hidden "Trotskyist center." Former members of the left opposition, in exile, in prison, and in leading posts, were arrested or brought back to Moscow to be interrogated or reinterrogated.[11] The circle of alleged perpetrators was expanding rapidly.

Vigilance and Drift

The widening scope of the investigation now included former Trotskyists as well as Zinovievites, creating a larger pool of potential suspects. People who had long abandoned oppositional activity were transferred, exiled, and in some cases arrested and repeatedly interrogated. Yet, on the local level, the *partkomy* in the factories responded slowly to the letter and the ongoing investigation, thus insulating their members from arrests. Naturally, they were aware of Kirov's murder. They attended meetings and memorials, and read countless articles devoted to Kirov's achievements and "villainous murder." They paid lip service to "vigilance," but by and large they continued to regard earlier oppositional activity as a harmless survival of the Party's once-vibrant culture of debate. Officials from the Proletarskii district committee (*raikom*) organized discussions of the Kirov

[11] Ibid., pp. 81–2.

murder in the huge factories, Dinamo, AMO, and Serp i Molot (Hammer and Sickle). A secretary of the Moscow party committee, M. M. Kulikov, reported unhappily that many party members maintained a tolerant view of former oppositionists. Despite the steady drumbeat against Trotsky, Zinoviev, Kamenev, and others in the press and at the upper levels of the Party, the rank and file retained considerable respect for them. One party member from the rolling mill in Serp i Molot declared, "We should not forget the merits of Trotsky, Zinoviev, and Kamenev in the Civil War." Kulikov indignantly responded, "Is this the question? The question now is, who would work against the Party." Yet many party members and workers refused to demonize former oppositionists. Loyal to their memories of the revolution, their views of the Kirov murder did not always follow the "lessons" the Central Committee had carefully outlined in its January 1935 letter. In Bread Factory No. 3, a worker stood up and told the official speaker, "You are still too much of a greenhorn to be criticizing Zinoviev and Kamenev." Kulikov fumed, "And two communists were sitting right there and did nothing."[12]

In Trekhgornaia Manufaktura, a large textile factory in Moscow, the letter had little impact. The *partkom*'s plenum met regularly throughout 1935 to discuss administrative housekeeping tasks: enrollment of "sympathizers," the party school, pension problems, members who lost party cards, and production issues. Between sixteen and sixty people attended the meetings, which included shop heads, union officials, and managers. In response to the letter, the plenum invited some members to discuss their political views. Its overall approach through 1935 was tolerant and low-key: few members tried to grandstand or demonstrate their own vigilance at their comrades' expense. The cases illustrated the range of oppositional activity as well as the *partkom*'s response. Each case followed a similar procedure. The party member under investigation presented his or her history of opposition, and the plenum members asked questions, discussed the case, and rendered a decision concerning the member's future in the Party.

Kapluna, a former Zhenotdel (Women's Department) activist who joined the Party in 1920, confessed that she had been active in the opposition until 1925. Despite Stalin's slogan, "Socialism in One Country," she had doubted whether socialism could be built without strong allies. Kapluna's politically muddled confession suggested that she had never

---

[12] Tsentral'nyi arkhiv obshchestvennykh dvizhenii Moskvy (TsAODM), f. 80, o. 1, d. 528, korobka 32, "Stenogrammy soveshchanie sekretarei partkomov RK VKP (b)," ll. 1–8.

fully understood the debates of the 1920s. "I didn't believe in the strength of the proletariat," she explained. "The opposition was frightened of the peasant kulak and did not know how to oppose him. Kamenev said to give a horse to every poor peasant. This was lacking in perspective." She also admitted that she had agreed with the opposition's critique that the Party was reducing socialism to state control of capital. Kapluna explained that she joined the left opposition in a factory in the early 1920s after meeting an organizer, who distributed oppositional literature. She participated in a faction that voted as a bloc at party meetings and even paid dues. Eventually, she came to believe that the opposition was unprincipled and quit. But she insisted that she had never been a "double-dealer." In fact, the Party, fully aware of her record, had already excluded and reinstated her with a strict reprimand. She had never mentioned her past to the Trekhgornaia *partkom* because she had long since renounced her earlier ideas. Her husband, a manager in an economic trust, had also broken with the opposition. Kapluna finished, "I messed up in becoming a follower of Zinoviev ... The Party believed in me. I think I have worked honestly, and that I can make up for my mistakes and continue to work in the Party."[13]

The plenum's discussion of Kapluna's case focused less on her previous activities than on whether her change of heart was genuine. One member argued, "She is politically literate and it is impossible to say that she entered unconsciously into opposition." Others were concerned that she had distributed opposition literature. But no one contended that her past activities were grounds for expulsion. Moreover, Kapluna had already been expelled and restored by a higher party organization. It made no sense to revoke her reinstatement if the Party had already forgiven her. The plenum resolved to retain her in less responsible work, and to watch her carefully. In its view, prior opposition, even of the most active sort, was not grounds for expulsion.[14]

The case of Fokin was also favorably resolved. Fokin confessed that, although he "always stood for the line of the Party," he had doubts about its agrarian policies. Working in a shop with many peasant seasonal workers, he explained that he "thought the peasantry was very pressed." His fellow workers "were often dissatisfied with the policies of Soviet power." A plenum member replied, "Fokin is not speaking completely openly. He had vacillations and he should admit it openly. He has confused a lot of

[13] TsAODM, f. 369, o. 1, d. 154, "Protokol no. 3 plenuma partkoma Trekhgornoi manuf.," ll. 10–100b.
[14] Ibid.

things." He was concerned that Fokin, a party member, "did not strike a blow for vigilance" and correct the misapprehensions of the seasonal workers. The plenum members, however, concluded that Fokin was confused. They warned him to formulate his ideas more carefully in the future, and vowed to check that he "struggled for the general line."[15]

Khvostov, the deputy director of the factory's party school, fared somewhat worse in the plenum's deliberations. Khvostov confessed that he had voted for the Trotskyist opposition as a young student in Sverdlovsk University in 1923. He claimed that he was initially swayed by Trotsky's speeches but, within three months, "when the line of the Party became clearer, I understood the wrongness of my view." Once again, party members debated whether Khvostov had truly accepted the Party's policies. Khvostov's downfall, however, resulted not from his past mistakes, but from recent missteps. Several people reported that he had questioned the "difference between capitalist and socialist forms of labor competition." Most dangerously, he made light of Kirov's murder, joking that, "Nikolaev wanted to straighten Kirov out." The combination of past opposition coupled with present criticism proved Khvostov's undoing: the plenum voted to expel him from the Party.[16]

The plenum's discussions suggested that its members, aware of the prevalence of oppositional activities and ideas in the 1920s, were reluctant to expel or even censure others for past "mistakes." Of the three party members, Trekhgornaia's plenum voted to expel only one, Khvostov, for voicing negative comments about Kirov and labor competition. Honest doubts and prior opposition, however, remained within the limits of sanctioned behavior. Kapluna, like hundreds of others, had already been censured and forgiven by the Party. Fokin's doubts about collectivization and rural life were common. Many communists on the shop floor had trouble maintaining the party line in the face of complaints from their fellow workers. In these two cases, neither past activity nor vacillation was sufficient to justify expulsion. The factory's *partkom* still took a reasonably tolerant approach to both.

Throughout the spring of 1935, the NKVD continued to arrest and interrogate former oppositionists, but Trekhgornaia's plenum largely ignored the hunt for enemies. They excluded one party member for concealing that his father was a kulak, and another, Al'tshuller, for "careerism." Small ripples from these expulsions touched others. The secretary of the

---

[15] Ibid., l. 11.   [16] Ibid., ll. 3–10.

partkom wrote to the Party Control Commission requesting an investigation of those who had recommended and hired Al'tshuller. The plenum also made further inquiries about Kapluna. It discovered that she had organized opposition groups in two tobacco factories, had been active for longer than she claimed, and had been expelled from the Party not once but twice for "vacillation from the general line." Her failure to be honest damaged her more than her past. The plenum agreed that she still held oppositional beliefs and "had succeeded in masking herself, pretending to be an honest worker." This time she was excluded.[17]

With these few exceptions, meetings continued more or less routinely. Occupied with the concerns of the factory's largely female workforce, the plenum focused on children's diets, schools, housing, awards for good parenting, and its own personnel issues. It officially reprimanded a weaver who "consciously ran waste" on her looms, a clerk who put real communism into practice by *lowering* prices in a food store and selling fish to workers at a small fraction of the state-mandated price, and other members for public drunkenness, anti-Semitism, and financial impropriety.[18] *Partkom* members tempered their usual concern with work and personal behavior with a slightly sharper approach to former oppositionists. Yet despite a few expulsions and higher "vigilance," the Kirov murder and the Central Committee's January letter did not greatly disturb local political life. Members were disciplined for drinking, playing Robin Hood, messing up their jobs, and occasionally acting like bigots. In other words, throughout the spring of 1935, the political climate on the local level darkened but slightly. By and large, party life in the factories went on much as before.[19]

Sharpening Vigilance

Tension increased substantially in the Central Committee in the early summer, when members of the Kremlin service administration were accused of participating in a terrorist group aimed at the assassination of Stalin and other party leaders. At the June 1935 Central Committee Plenum, Ezhov

---

[17] TsAODM, f. 369, o. 1, d. 154, "Protokol no. 6 plenuma partkoma Trekhgornoi manufaktury," "V Komissiiu partiinogo kontrolia pri MK VKP (b)," "Protokol no. 10," "Protokol no. 11," ll. 18–34.

[18] Ibid. A "reprimand" or "strict reprimand" was an official form of censure entered in a party member's record. It could also be removed.

[19] In Krasnyi Bogatyr, a Moscow rubber factory, a similar pattern prevailed. See, for example, TsAODM, f. 462, o. 1, d. 18, k. 2.

presented his latest version of the Kirov case, accusing Zinoviev, Kamenev, and Trotsky of *direct* involvement in Kirov's murder as well as in the recently discovered Kremlin plot. Zinoviev and Kamenev had confessed to abetting terrorism by encouraging opposition, but the new accusations were considerably more serious. Ezhov also accused Avel Enukidze, the secretary of the Central Executive Committee (CEC) responsible for Kremlin administration and security, of aiding the terrorists. According to Ezhov, "alien and hostile" elements "wove their counterrevolutionary nest" in the CEC administration. Evidence suggested that Enukidze was mainly guilty of ignoring the rumors, gossip, and jokes about Stalin and other party leaders that circulated among the CEC staff. When a Kremlin commandant wanted to denounce a cleaning woman to the NKVD for anti-Soviet remarks, Enukidze waved him off. "Look into it once again," he told the commandant. Ezhov also accused Enukidze of supporting a motley assortment of aging revolutionaries with state funds. For his part, Enukidze could not understand what was wrong with helping penurious Mensheviks, former oppositionists, and their dependents. He responded to Ezhov's charge with genuine surprise.[20]

Despite Ezhov's harsh charges, the Central Committee plenum was not sure how to treat Enukidze. Both Stalin and Voroshilov chided him gently: "What are you – some kind of a child? If your heart bled for someone, you could have asked any of us." And Stalin added, "Why ask? Let Enukidze hand money out from his own pocket, if that's what he wants to do, from his own pocket and not from state funds." Enukidze apologized, but at the same time refused to admit that he was entirely wrong. "I was in no condition to refuse such requests," he said simply. "Call it what you will." One historian noted, "Politically, he was still reading from a different page." After a split vote and much hesitation, the Central Committee removed Enukidze from the Central Committee and expelled him from the Party.[21]

The new accusations against Zinoviev and Kamenev, the discovery of plots in the Kremlin itself, and the expulsion of Enukidze marked a critical shift in the political climate. Antistate jokes, criticisms, and gossip now appeared in a different light. The Central Committee Plenum chastised Enukidze for tolerating an "atmosphere" that encouraged enemies, yet the leadership was still uncertain how strictly to enforce its new definition of

---

[20] Getty and Naumov, *The Road to Terror*, pp. 170–1.
[21] Ibid., pp. 172, 176–9.

"loyalty." The Central Committee failed to follow up on Ezhov's charges against Zinoviev and Kamenev, never published Ezhov's manuscript on factionalism and counterrevolution, and readmitted Enukidze to the Party a year later. Six months after the Kirov murder, the leadership was still unsure how to interpret it.[22]

As Central Committee members were getting their first lessons in "vigilance," the *partkomy* were jolted into activity by an organizational verification (*proverka*) followed by an exchange of party documents (*obmen*). Launched in the Party in June 1935, the verification began as a "housekeeping affair." According to the screening instructions, its purpose was to eliminate members who no longer belonged in the Party, organize membership records, and ensure that members' documents were correct; no mention was made of the Kirov murder. Regional and district party leaders, responsible for carrying out the *proverka* and *obmen*, were confused about its procedures and aims. Did past oppositional activity constitute an offense? Were they required to send information to the NKVD about members who had been expelled? Did they need permission from the procurator to involve the NKVD in an investigation? Ezhov addressed the regional secretaries in September 1935 in an effort to clarify the roles of the Party, the procuracy, and the NKVD. Minimizing the role of the procurator and the courts, he encouraged party secretaries to develop a closer relationship with the NKVD. Investigation was the job of the NKVD, not the Party, but the NKVD should expand their investigations to include those party members who recommended anyone who was expelled. By December, the NKVD had assumed a more aggressive role in the Party's purge, forwarding compromising materials on party members to regional party leaders.[23] Local leaders, however, continued to regard the *proverka* and *obmen* much like the routine purges that preceded it: members could expect a careful review of their documents, biographical data, personal behavior, and activities.

Local party organizations kept notoriously poor records. Members frequently lost or misplaced their party cards, and failed to record their dues

[22] Ibid., pp. 176–8. Getty notes that, according to the first version of the stenographic report of the Central Committee plenum, the vote on Enukidze was split. Subsequent versions showed the vote to be unanimous. Getty makes a convincing argument for vacillation at the top.

[23] Ibid., pp. 197–8. See also Getty, *The Origins of the Great Purges: The Soviet Communist Party Reconsidered, 1933–1938* (Cambridge University Press, New York, 1985), pp. 58–91, and Rittersporn, *Stalinist Simplifications and Soviet Complications*, pp. 73–4.

payments. In the *partkom* of the Serp i Molot iron and steel plant, for example, twenty people were expelled from June to October 1935 for a variety of transgressions, including poor attendance at meetings, discrepancies in their documents, false biographical claims, and antistate and -party comments. One Il'in, an older foundry worker with twenty years' seniority and a decade of party membership, was expelled for complaining about the state loans. Party members admitted that the loan campaign in Serp i Molot had created "a very tense situation" among the workers, who could barely meet basic expenses. Il'in was overheard complaining, "Here they are stealing from us again, they take it all from us, yes from us."[24] Although the *partkom* sharply scrutinized its members, there was little discussion of "masked enemies," "wreckers," or oppositionists. The purge, at least in its initial phase, differed little from those the Party had conducted in the past.

In Krasnyi Bogatyr, a large Moscow rubber factory, the *partkom* responded to the heightening political tension in the Kremlin with the standard vow to increase "political literacy." Yet it carefully distanced itself from responsibility. Playing to the January letter's recommendation to study, it claimed that managers, foremen, and other leading party members in the factory were "not able to be vigilant because they are politically illiterate." And while they humbly promised to remedy everybody's deficiencies, they focused mainly on production. Few were versed in the finer points of past political debates, and fewer still cared to revisit these issues. Ignorance provided the ideal excuse for not getting involved in what was clearly proving a messy and unpleasant business. "We informed the higher organizations about alien people and no steps were taken," one party member announced with a shrug. Everyone admitted that there was "wrecking" in the factory: "A blockhead did the ordering and buying." "There were great piles of rags obstructing production." But no one seemed especially alarmed. "Everyone needs to increase their political level," they assented. When the *partkom* held a meeting to commemorate the one-year anniversary of the Kirov murder, the speeches were formulaic: "Kirov is not with us, but his courage remains." "The murder of Kirov tells us the class struggle continues." Once again, everyone agreed that there were wreckers in the factory. When the *partkom* hung portraits of the country's leaders in the machine shop, someone poked out the eyes and mutilated the faces. But no one could identify the wreckers

[24] TsAODM, f. 429, o. 1, d. 126, "Stenogramma prenii zakrytogo partiinogo sobraniia zavoda 'Serp i molot,'" l. 6.

and, more importantly, no one was especially alarmed.[25] At the time, a rhetorical endorsement of vigilance seemed sufficient to satisfy the rumblings in Moscow.

Statistics partially explain the complacency in the factories. In 1935, party members at the local level were still fairly insulated from attacks on former oppositionists. From July 1935, when the verification campaign began, to December, the Party expelled 9.1 percent (177,000) of its 1,945,055 members; the vast majority for routine causes, including moral corruption, embezzlement, hiding class origins, and discrepancies in documents. Only a small fraction (2.8 percent or 4,956 people) was expelled for Trotskyist-Zinovievite opposition. Of the total number expelled, about 8.6 percent were arrested (15,218 people), less than 1 percent of the Party's total membership. It is not possible to know the fates of those expelled, but even if everyone expelled for opposition had been subsequently arrested, this group still accounted for only one-third of the total arrests, suggesting that the remaining two-thirds of party members who were arrested were charged with non-political crimes such as embezzlement.[26] The lack of concern within the *partkomy* about "Trotskyist-Zinovievite terrorist groups" resulted in a low level of expulsions, which in turn provided some protection against subsequent arrests for political reasons. The low number of arrests, in its turn, ensured that the "unmasking" of trusted workmates did not disturb the committees' daily routines. All in all, throughout 1935, the apathy of the *partkomy* served as an excellent buffer against intensifying machinations at the top.

The Case Widens

In January 1936, there was a major shift in the Kirov case. Ezhov's expanded version of the murder plot, presented first to Stalin in May 1935,

---

[25] TsAODM, f. 462, o. 1, d. 18, k. 2, "Protokol zakrytogo partsobraniia," "Protokol partiinogo zakrytogo sobraniia sm. B," "Protokol obshchego sobraniia chlenov partii VKP (b)," "Protokol zakrytogo partsobraniia iacheiki VKP (b)," "Protokol obshchego zakrytogo partsobraniia Mekhstroi transportnogo otdela," ll. 1–12.

[26] Getty and Naumov, *The Road to Terror*, p. 198. Getty and Naumov provide additional figures for the 1935 *proverka*, noting that by February 1937, 263,885 or 13.6 percent of the membership had been expelled, of which 2.8 percent or 7,504 were expelled for Trotskyism or Zinovievism. In the general population (party and nonparty members), 30,174 "counterrevolutionaries" were sentenced in 1935. See J. Arch Getty, Gabor Rittersporn, and Viktor Zemskov, "Victims of the Soviet Penal System in the Pre-War Years: A First Approach on the Basis of Archival Evidence," *American Historical Review*, 98, 4 (October, 1993), p. 1035.

was revived by a confession extracted from V. P. Ol'berg, a former member of the German Communist Party who had fled fascism, acquired Soviet citizenship, and settled in Gorky.[27] It is not clear whether interrogators forced Ol'berg to confess to their specific fabrications or if he unwittingly supplied information that reinforced Ezhov's expanded version of the plot. Within a month of his arrest, however, Ol'berg confessed that Trotsky instructed him to assassinate Stalin and create a counterrevolutionary terrorist organization. More than 100 alleged Trotskyists were arrested in other cities, and charged with terrorism.[28] The investigations spawned new terrorist subplots linked directly to Trotsky. According to the rapidly evolving narrative, supporters of Trotsky and Zinoviev had formed a "united center" in 1932 aimed at assassination and terror. Ezhov had accused Zinoviev and Kamenev in June of direct involvement in Kirov's murder, but the latest variant went even further by positing a whole new list of suspects and targets in a growing conspiracy of terror.

Over the spring of 1936, NKVD investigators used a wide variety of illegal methods, including torture, sleep deprivation, psychological abuse, and isolation to extract and shape confessions from former oppositionists. In February, G. E. Prokof'ev, the deputy commissar of the NKVD, sent a directive to local NKVD organs to eliminate the entire Trotskyist-Zinovievite underground, resulting in widespread arrests. In March, G. G. Iagoda, the head of the NKVD, suggested that the underground's members be handed over to the Court of the Military Kollegiia, sentenced under the law of December 1, 1934, and shot. A. Ia. Vyshinskii, Procurator General of the USSR, agreed and added that Trotskyists "carrying out active work" in exile or expelled from the Party in the *proverka* be sent to distant labor camps. Stalin accepted the suggestions and entrusted Iagoda and Vyshinskii to draw up a list of people to be brought before the court. Soon after, the NKVD directed its local organs to undertake the "full destruction of all Trotskyist forces." The tempo of arrests quickened. In April, 508 more "Trotskyists" were arrested and interrogated, providing in turn more names and widening the scope of the investigation. During the arrest of I. I. Trusov, a nonparty assistant at the Communist Academy, NKVD investigators found a "personal archive" of Trotsky's papers from 1927.

---

[27] William Chase, *Enemies Within the Gates? The Comintern and the Stalinist Repression, 1934–1939* (Yale University Press, New Haven and London, 2001), pp. 134–5.
[28] "O tak nazyvaemom 'Antisovetskom Ob"edinennom trotskistsko-zinov'evskom tsentr,'" p. 82.

The discovery prompted Stalin to suggest that Ezhov assume responsibility for interrogations, a suggestion the Politburo accepted unanimously.[29]

Up to this point, arrests were still limited mainly to former oppositionists and foreign communists.[30] The circles widened as these people were interrogated and forced to name others. Yet even through the spring of 1936, the factory *partkomy* were still relatively undisturbed. In Krasnyi Bogatyr, between 300 and 450 party members met regularly. In May, they expelled a woman for her low level of political awareness and lack of initiative in production, but also decided to send her to a rest home and then to school. They dealt with problems in the shops, and management's failure to reward Stakhanovite workers after a 24-hour storming session produced a record number of galoshes. In June, they discussed the Central Committee Plenum in a very short meeting and, once again, unanimously affirmed the need to struggle against the Zinovievite opposition. Later that same month, they vowed to increase the number of subscriptions to another state loan. In July, they complained that workers were unhappy about the subscriptions. And they heard a steady stream of declarations from party members who had failed to pay dues, attend meetings, verify their documents, and keep track of their party cards. They issued reprimands and heard appeals. Only one case was connected with the widening terror: a woman was reprimanded for failing to tell the *partkom* that her husband had been exiled for counterrevolutionary activity.[31]

While the Krasnyi Bogatyr *partkom* plodded along, disciplining its members, prodding its workers, and trying to improve daily life in the factory, the Kirov case, fueled by new arrests and confessions, was assuming greater momentum. Neither the Politburo, the Central Committee, nor the procurator's office resisted the quickening juggernaut launched by Ezhov. Spinning at greater speed and in widening circles, it generated ever more astounding plots of attempted mayhem and murder. The only resistance came from a surprising source. Both Iagoda, the head of the NKVD, and G. A. Molchanov, head of its Secret Political Department, tried to slow the broadening investigation. Examining the written records of the confessions used to build the case, Iagoda scrawled "Untrue," "Nonsense,"

[29] Ibid., pp. 83–4.
[30] Chase, *Enemies Within the Gates?*, pp. 102–45.
[31] TsAODM, f. 462, o. 1, d. 19, "Protokoly obshchikh zavodskikh partsobranii," "Protokol partiinogo sobraniia," "Protokol obshchezavodskogo partiinogo sobraniia, sovmestno s Komsomolom i sochuvstvuiushchimi," "Protokol obshchezavodskoi teoriticheskoi partiinoi konferentsii po ustavu VKP (b)," "Obshchezavodskogo partiinogo sobraniia," "Protokol zakrytogo partsobraniia," ll. 1–51.

and "Lie" across one defendant's claim that Trotsky had directed him to murder Soviet leaders.[32] Stalin and Ezhov interfered, however, and several key oppositionists were reinterrogated to strengthen the new version. Their "evidence" soon became the basis for the first of the Moscow show trials. In June, Vyshinskii and Iagoda, responding to Stalin's earlier request, delivered a preliminary list of eighty-two people for trial. Stalin instructed the NKVD through Ezhov to prepare for a trial of Trotskyists and Zinovievites together. From June 1936 on, state efforts were directed at building the case of a "united center."[33]

At the end of July, Ezhov sent Stalin a draft of a letter, outlining the case against Zinoviev, Kamenev, and other defendants. Stalin made numerous corrections. On July 29, 1936, the Central Committee sent this "closed" secret letter to the party organizations. The case, as sketched in the letter, had grown considerably in the eighteen months since Kirov's murder. Zinoviev and Kamenev, previously charged with "arousing terrorist moods," were now charged with Kirov's murder, as well as the attempted murders of Stalin and other party leaders. The letter made a tight organizational link between Zinovievites and Trotskyists, claiming that the two groups united in 1932 and subsequently formed terrorist groups in major cities. Trotsky sent this "United Trotskyist-Zinovievite Center" instructions from abroad to murder Kirov, Stalin, and other party leaders. The new targets – Stalin, K. E. Voroshilov, L. M. Kaganovich, A. A. Zhdanov, S. V. Kosior, P. P. Postyshev, and G. K. Ordzhonikidze – each had a terror cell devoted to his assassination, involving a slew of new plotters, including former Zinovievites I. P. Bakaev, G. E. Evdokimov, M. N. Iakovlev, M. N. Motorin, I. I. Reingold, and R. V. Pikel, and Trotskyists I. S. Esterman, I. N. Smirnov, S. V. Mrachkovskii, E. A. Dreitser, and V. A. Ter-Vaganian. According to the letter, after Kirov's murder Trotsky had instructed his supporters to move quickly against Stalin, organize terror cells in the army, and seize power in event of war. I. K. Fedotov, the director of the Gorky Pedagogical Institute, was charged with heading

---

[32] Agranov, the deputy head of the Moscow *oblast* NKVD, announced at the February–March 1937 Central Committee Plenum that Iagoda and Molchanov tried to limit the investigation, and did not believe the extracted confessions. Agranov noted, "Such was the mood" in the NKVD, indicating that they were supported by other NKVD officials: "O tak nazyvaemom 'Antisovetskom Ob"edinennom trotskistsko-zinov'evskom tsentr,'" p. 85. See Agranov's testimony at the February–March 1937 Plenum in Getty and Naumov, *The Road to Terror*, p. 249.

[33] "O tak nazyvaemom 'Antisovetskom Ob"edinennom trotskistsko-zinov'evskom tsentr,'" pp. 82–4.

a Trotskyist terror cell, which aimed to kill Stalin in Red Square during the May Day demonstration. Fritz David, a Comintern official, and K. B. Berman-Iurin were accused of plotting to kill Stalin at a Comintern Congress, a charge that set off a chain of arrests in the Comintern.[34] D. A. Shmidt, an army commander, was charged with plotting to kill Voroshilov, a Politburo member and Red Army general. Workers in the Kaganovich leather factory were charged with plotting to kill Kaganovich. A number of German communists who had escaped Hitler and settled in the Soviet Union, including Berman-Iurin, M. I. Lur'e, N. L. Lur'e, E. Konstant, P. Livshits, V. P. Ol'berg, F. David, Kh. Gurevich, and M. Bykhovskii, were accused of terrorism and spying on behalf of Russian fascist émigré organizations and the Gestapo. The letter also claimed that "terrorists" had infiltrated the Gorky party organization, the staff of *Leningradskaia Pravda*, the Academy of Science, and a weapons factory in Tula. G. M. Arkus, the deputy chairman of Gosbank, the main state bank, was accused of funding them, and at least one "terror cell" was accused of planning robberies or "expropriations." One short but stunning line introduced the possibility that "rightists," too, had participated in the plots against Stalin. According to the letter, Kamenev confessed that the plotters "would accept the participation of the rightists, Bukharin, Tomskii, and Rykov, in the organization of a new government."[35]

Most importantly for rank-and-file party members, the letter linked the *proverka* to the Kirov murder. These two events, only vaguely connected in the screenings of the past year, were now firmly associated. The letter criticized the *partkomy* for failing to uncover "terrorists" in their organizations, noting that the NKVD had subsequently arrested party members who passed successfully through the *proverka*. This terrible breach in security was the result of the Party's loss of "revolutionary vigilance." The letter stressed, "The indelible mark of every Bolshevik under the present conditions should be the ability to recognize an enemy of the Party, no matter how well he may be masked."[36]

---

[34] Chase, *Enemies Within the Gates?*, pp. 146–77.

[35] "Zakrytoe pis'mo TsK VKP (b). O terroristicheskoi deiatel'nosti Trotskistsko-zinov'evskogo kontrrevoliutsionnogo bloka," *Izvestiia TsK KPSS*, No. 8, 1989, pp. 100–15. Chase, *Enemies Within the Gates?*, pp. 162–3, notes that the Party's Department of Cadres notified Georgii Dimitrov, the general secretary of the Comintern, that it sent material to the NKVD on 3,000 foreign communists and émigrés living in the USSR suspected as spies, provocateurs, and wreckers.

[36] "Zakrytoe pis'mo TsK VKP (b). O terroristicheskoi deiatel'nosti Trotskistsko-zinov'evskogo kontrrevoliutsionnogo bloka," pp. 100–15.

In early August, Vyshinskii composed the first draft of the indictment against twelve defendants based on the text of the July letter. Stalin corrected the draft by strengthening the link between the Trotskyists and the Zinovievites (a critical point, in his view), and added two more people to the list of defendants. The indictment was sent back to Stalin again in mid-August and he redrafted it once more, adding two more defendants. By August 14, Vyshinskii had prepared the final indictment, which was read aloud when the trial opened on August 19.[37]

The case, which began in December 1934 with a domestic murder and a lone gunman, now involved sixteen defendants, multiple murder plots, foreign spies, fascist contacts, and terrorist conspiracies. The initial objective, to find and punish Kirov's assassin, had expanded into a nationwide attack on the former left opposition. Kamenev's confession hinted at rightist participation, opening the possibility of further investigation. The letter, with its obsessive concern with "masked" oppositionists, pushed local party leaders to transform the *proverka* into a new, mass exercise in "unmasking enemies." Stalin and his supporters knew well that the opposition had never been limited to a few famous revolutionaries. Tens of thousands of party members in factories, universities, and other institutions had participated in the fierce debates and raucous meetings of the mid-1920s. In fact, all party members at that time had been exposed to the ideas and activities of the opposition, voting in meetings, caucusing in smoky hallways, and passionately debating the left's critiques. With war looming in the West, Stalin was terrified by the thought that the Party was honeycombed with secret, hidden opponents.

Production versus Politics

The Central Committee's July 29 letter aimed to shake the *partkomy* out of their lethargy and dispel their complacency that their organizations were free of enemies. It did not, however, have the desired effect. Party members assented to the letter in the abstract, but most refused to view their comrades as potential "masked enemies" or production problems as "wrecking." In Serp i Molot, eighty party members met in a closed session in mid-August, two weeks after receiving the Central Committee's

[37] "O tak nazyvaemom 'Antisovetskom Ob"edinennom trotskistsko-zinov'evskom tsentr,'" pp. 78–81. Stalin added E. S. Holtsman, Fritz David (I. I. Kruglianskii), K. B. Berman-Iurin, and N. L. Lur'e to the list of defendants: *Report of Court Proceedings*, pp. 9–39.

letter, to discuss the plant's latest failure to meet its production targets. The meeting included party members at all levels: workers, shop organizers, foremen, *partkom* leaders, managers, and the director. Although party members were quick to defend themselves and blame others for problems, the "blame game" involved few allegations of sabotage or wrecking. Several party members advanced the notion that "hidden enemies" might be responsible for the plant's problems, but P. F. Stepanov, the director, bluntly quashed all "political" explanations. Similar meetings were held in factories throughout Moscow, for the city had failed to meet its plan as well. The Moscow party committee (*gorkom*) had met earlier that day with representatives from the factories to discuss the city's "pitiful" industrial performance. The main problem, everyone acknowledged, was rapid turnover of the workforce. Peasants arriving from the countryside easily found work but not housing. In fact, Aleksandr I. Somov, the secretary of Serp i Molot's *partkom*, arrived at the meeting late because he was detained at the citywide gathering.[38]

In Somov's absence, the deputy secretary opened the meeting with a short speech on obstacles to fulfilling the plan. "We will discuss not only the reasons known to all of us, but also the question of wrecking. A counterrevolutionary Trotskyist-Zinovievite group has shown its face, and gathered people around it." Stepanov, however, immediately rejected this idea. In his keynote speech, he concentrated on specific technical difficulties. The open hearth, for example, where the molten steel was poured out, was a site of endless bungling. Tons of steel had been ruined because a crane and ladle were not available to pour it out. When the foreman responded that the shop needed more workers, Stepanov sharply retorted that the operator of the crane and ladle (a party member no less!) had disappeared from the shop at a critical moment. Stepanov noted, "I look for a worker with a crane in order to get a ladle. I ask the worker where he was. He answers, 'I was looking for class enemies.' And I told him, 'And you didn't find any except yourself.'" Class enemies, as Stepanov made clear, were people who did their jobs poorly.[39]

Izotov, a party organizer in the cutting foundry, also tried to blame problems in the open hearth on wreckers. He explained that, when the cranes broke down, the foreman and mechanic took off on vacation. One

---

[38] TsAODM, f. 429, o. 1, d. 145, "Stenogramma zakrytogo partiinogo soveshaniia zavoda 'Serp i molot' po voprosu o nevypolnenii zavodom proizvodstvennoi programmy," ll. 30–31.

[39] Ibid., ll. 1–2, 40b.

Mints then tried to fix them. The repairs, which should have taken less than an hour, took twenty. As a result, only one crane with a 25-ton ladle was available to pour out forty tons of molten metal. Izotov maintained that Mints intentionally disabled the cranes in order to kill workers. He noted indignantly, "This would have produced a huge accident. All the workers would have been incinerated." Everyone at the meeting knew that repairs often took longer than necessary because it was difficult to procure needed parts. Yet Mints, the one person who had taken responsibility and tried to fix the broken equipment, had recently been arrested as a Trotskyist.[40] He was a readymade scapegoat.

Stepanov, however, refused to lay the blame on Mints. He noted sharply that the mechanic never bothered to report that the cranes were broken, and that when the foreman went off on vacation the mechanic promptly followed him. Stepanov blamed most production problems on the shop foremen. They were all in "a vacation mood," thinking "about health resorts." Coordination of labor and materials was poor. Sometimes workers sat around with nothing to do; at other times, there were too few to handle the job. Stepanov noted, "I went to one shop at night. The workers surrounded me, 'Comrade Stepanov, we have no work to do, we will get no wages.' At the same time, the shift boss, a communist, declares he has no workers." In his judgment, a good foreman was able to retain his workers and meet the plan. "Take the steel extrusion shop," he said, "There are three shifts. One has a full staff of workers. Now here is a shift boss! The workers don't try to get out of the shop. There is no turnover. The boss doesn't drink. He meets the plan 100 percent." The foremen on the two other shifts, however, had constant problems. "Three shift bosses – and three different results." In Stepanov's view, production was the ultimate test of politics. A person who did a poor job in the factory could not be considered a good communist. On the other hand, poor work was not a crime. Stepanov noted, "In the cable department, they fulfill 130–140 percent of the plan, but the open hearth doesn't work. Yet communists work in the open hearth as well. Is this stupidity or a crime?" The failures in the open hearth, he contended, were the result of "stupidity." Irresponsible party members, not criminal terrorists, were the source of the factory's problems.[41]

Most *partkom* members supported Stepanov. They paid lip service to the possibility of "wreckers," but were easily deflected by local concerns. When Bogdanovich, the deputy director of the factory, opined that poor

---

[40] Ibid., ll. 18–18ob.   [41] Ibid., ll. 3–6ob.

work resulted from a lack of "Bolshevik confidence in the decisive struggle with counterrevolutionaries," he was quickly sidetracked by a far more compelling topic: animals in the dormitories. Orlov, the party secretary of the rolling mill, complained that the workers were upset because they were forbidden to keep even a kitten in the barracks. Bogdanovich, forgetting completely about counterrevolutionaries, replied indignantly to Orlov, "We put a comrade from your shop into the dormitory, and he immediately brought a chicken into his room." He added sarcastically, "Perhaps it is possible to bring in chickens, cows, and pigs. But then it will be a barn, and not only in the room because the chickens also block up the corridor. It's not necessary to have chickens walking around in the corridor." "Anyway," he concluded in exasperation, "the issue is not about cats, but the fact that we are now working poorly."[42]

In general, party members did not treat accusations of wrecking seriously. When two workers in the cold rolling mill got into a fight, one called the other a bastard. The other replied, "I won't give you the materials you need." The materials, according to Somov, stayed in the shop for ten days. "The shop boss thinks they're just fighting," Somov declared, "but I consider this wrecking." D. Sagaidak, the head of the cold rolling mill, however, entirely ignored Somov's accusation of wrecking. He burst out in defense of his shop, "The materials did not lie around for ten days!"[43]

The meeting was characterized by an easygoing tolerance, even toward groups that party leaders officially demonized. Party members joked easily about the "kulak" backgrounds of new workers in the plant. Bogoliubskii, the head of the steel extrusion shop, explained that his shop was short of labor: "They sent a recruiter to the countryside around Riazan to bring collective farm workers to the factory..." Stepanov interrupted him, "First he excludes eight people from the Party as kulaks, and then they bring him a whole new batch!" The meeting burst into laughter.[44] Party members could still joke about the fierce political rhetoric emanating from Moscow. They felt no need to demonstrate their loyalty to Soviet socialism; it was based on their dedication to the plant, not on their ability to "unmask" their comrades.

Serp i Molot was not free of problems, and party members did not hesitate to blame each other. Yet accusations did not have a political cast. If Stepanov blamed foremen for the plant's problems, they in turn blamed the raw materials, the machinery, and the workers. A party organizer in

---

[42] Ibid., ll. 26–27.
[43] Ibid., ll. 30–31.
[44] Ibid., l. 17.

the rolling mill argued that the mill failed to meet its production quota because it was running on low-quality coal. "Our shop could meet the plan if we got help from above," he told Stepanov. "Get us good coal." He also noted that the workers would be more productive if the ventilators worked properly, a constant complaint in shops with high temperatures. Orlov, the party secretary of the rolling mill, blamed the mill's rollers, which constantly malfunctioned.[45] The rollers were but one example of breakdowns and stoppages that frustrated workers and managers throughout the country. New equipment, costing millions of gold rubles, had been purchased for the industrialization drive, yet few people were adept at installing, running, or repairing it.

Some party members blamed bad "moods" among the workers, especially recent migrants. Although the newspapers were largely silent about problems on the new collective farms, workers regularly visited friends and relatives in the countryside and exchanged tales of crop failure, hunger, and poor living conditions. "The moods of backward collective farmers affect workers who spend time there on vacation," noted the deputy secretary of the *partkom*. "These moods are carried here." The peasants in Riazan province, for example, were so disaffected that party organizers coined the phrase, "Riazanskii mood" to describe the bitter attitudes of workers who returned from the province. Some foremen complained about the workers' lack of labor discipline. Bogoliubskii, the head of the steel extrusion shop, noted, "In our shop, the master doesn't come in, people are late, and the workers give us an ultimatum, 'You don't provide, we don't produce.'"[46] Sokol, an organizer in the calibration shop, complained that the factory's doctor excused workers from heavy labor at the slightest complaint, placed them in easier jobs, and prescribed vacations. He was especially annoyed with labor legislation that compelled managers to place pregnant women in lighter work. "This corrupts the workers," he declared. "A woman comes to me, it's true, she is pregnant, and she says that she can't work the night shift. The doctor told her that she should work only in the morning. She works on the motors. Now how is she supposed to work on the motors seven hours a day only in the morning?"[47] Somov, the *partkom* secretary, responded angrily to Sokol, noting that foremen frequently disregarded doctors' orders. "The doctor

---

[45] Ibid., ll. 7, 13–130b.

[46] Ibid., ll. 1, 2, 17. Other agricultural provinces that experienced problems included Kursk and Voronezh.

[47] Ibid., l. 20.

recommends light work, and the shop boss throws the recommendation in the garbage. Work is physically hard." He blamed the foremen for inexcusably rude behavior. "We see a barbarous relationship to workers everywhere," he charged. And he noted that turnover was a serious problem in all Moscow's factories. "Not a single boss asks why workers leave," he said. "We send them off to the *partkom*, the factory committee, the director, as if the *partkom* or the director had housing somewhere. But we don't solve the problem."[48]

Serp i Molot's difficulties were typical of factories, mines, and construction sites throughout the country. Shops failed to meet their production targets. Workers and managers struggled with new machinery, unpredictable deliveries, and high norms. Housing could not keep pace with the influx of new workers. Obstacles and problems abounded, the unavoidable consequences of rapid industrialization. Under pressure to meet Moscow's targets, everyone blamed someone else: officials in the Commissariat of Heavy Industry blamed Stepanov, who blamed his foremen, who in turn blamed poor-grade coal, malfunctioning machinery, lazy workers, and even pregnant women. Party members were touchy, anxious to defend their own shops at the expense of others. Yet despite the growing hysteria among party leaders over hidden Trotskyist-Zinovievite terrorists, party members were not frightened of each other, nor did they accuse each other personally. Their discussions of "wrecking" or "enemies" were vague, not directed at any particular individual. Most party members shared Stepanov's credo that hard work, organization, and motivation would eventually overcome even the greatest obstacles.

The Trial of the "United Center"

The sixteen defendants of the "United Trotskyist-Zinovievite Center" were finally tried in open court in Moscow on August 19–24, 1936.[49] The accused all declined the assistance of counsel; their confessions and mutual denunciations constituted the main evidence. During the trial, Vyshinskii guided the defendants through the confessions they had already provided to investigators. The trial transcript followed the July 29 letter closely as the defendants recounted various plots to kill Stalin and other party

---

[48] Ibid., ll. 30–31.

[49] The defendants were G. E. Zinoviev, L. B. Kamenev, G. E. Evdokimov, I. N. Smirnov, I. P. Bakaev, V. A. Ter-Vaganian, S. V. Mrachkovskii, E. A. Dreitser, E. S. Holtsman, I. I. Reingold, R. V. Pickel, V. P. Ol'berg, K. B. Berman-Iurin, Fritz David (I. I. Kruglianskii), M. Lur'e, N. Lur'e.

leaders. The Party officially admitted in 1991 that the confessions, extracted under torture and duress, were false.[50] The trial transcript was thus useless as a record of the defendants' actual activities or beliefs. Yet viewed as an imaginative script, conceived and written by the Stalinist leadership, it offered an uncannily accurate reflection of the leadership's deepest anxieties and fears. The confessions, stripped of their falsified activities, contained hard truths on which both the procurators and the defendants agreed: the Party had barely survived the economic crisis of the early 1930s, peasants and workers were embittered by collectivization and the drop in living standards, and many former oppositionists retained strong misgivings about Stalin. Repelled by his policies, they remained within the Party, outwardly professing loyalty while inwardly maintaining their reservations. These two fears – the alienation of workers and peasants and the presence of hidden doubters within the Party – were the subtext of the state's accusations.

Both Vyshinskii and the defendants referred repeatedly to the social discontent created by the upheavals of the first five-year plan. Kamenev testified, for example, that in 1932 he was confident that the country's "insuperable difficulties, the state of crisis of its economy, the collapse of the economic policy of the party leadership" would expose the mistakes of Stalin's policies. Kamenev's alleged hopes were identical to Stalin's fears. Stalin, too, understood that the country was seething with discontent. As Vyshinskii reminded the court, Stalin predicted that "remnants of the dying classes" would try to mobilize "the backward strata of the population" against Soviet power. In 1936, the "backward strata" were everywhere: among hungry *kolkhozniki*, disaffected workers, former kulaks. The Party's obsession with "masked" enemies was a direct expression of these fears. Kamenev testified that, in the event of war, Trotsky told him, "Our task will be to unite and take the lead of the discontented masses."[51] Was this a fabrication? If so, it was not unrealistic given the country's wrenching social and economic transformations, the Party's own faction-ridden history, and the rise of fascism.[52]

The defendants were forced not only to confess to deeds they had never planned or committed, but also to praise Stalin's strength and the leadership's unity. The trial took flattery of the leader to new heights. Vyshinskii

[50] "O tak nazyvaemom 'Antisovetskom Ob"edinennom trotskistsko-zinov'evskom tsentr,'" p. 78.
[51] *Report of Court Proceedings*, p. 119.
[52] Anna Larina, *This I Cannot Forget: The Memoirs of Nikolai Bukharin's Widow* (W. W. Norton, New York and London, 1993), p. 332.

set the tone, invoking the great victory of "the Leninist-Stalinist general line," "the great Stalin," "Comrade Stalin, the great executor and keeper of Lenin's will and testament." Zinoviev spoke of Stalin as "a mighty oak" surrounded by "young saplings" such as Kirov. Zinoviev allegedly told Reingold, "It is not enough to fell the oak; all the young oaks growing around it must be felled too." Reingold in turn testified, "The leadership that had grown up was made of too hard a granite to expect it would split of itself." Whether the defendants thought up these hackneyed compliments on their own, or were forced to memorize them by poorly educated NKVD investigators is unknown, but all testified that Stalin was central to the leadership, and that he, above all others, "had to be physically destroyed."[53] The defendants not only paid tribute to Stalin's policies, but also denied that they offered an alternative. The trial's audience at home and abroad would find no "new course" here.[54] The defendants were not socialists, Vyshinskii stressed, but criminals and murderers, motivated solely by a common hatred of Stalin and his victories. Evdokimov admitted in his final plea that he and the other defendants differed little from fascists.[55]

The vague imputations against the rightists in the Central Committee's July 29 letter assumed greater substance during the trial when the defendants connected prominent "rightists" with a variety of plots. Reingold claimed that the Trotskyist-Zinovievite center began meeting with Rykov, Bukharin, and Tomskii in 1932. Kamenev, too, testified, "We counted on the Rightist group of Rykov, Bukharin, and Tomsky." Kamenev's testimony did not directly link Bukharin, Rykov, and Tomskii to a specific crime, but strongly undermined their professed loyalty to the Party. Zinoviev's testimony, too, cast a long shadow of guilt over the former rightists as well as every opposition in the Party's faction-ridden history, including the Workers' Opposition, groups of leftists, and smaller groups clustered around I. T. Smilga and G. Ia. Sokolnikov, members of the Central Committee in 1917. Zinoviev provided the NKVD with enough leads to keep its investigators busy for years. On August 21, in the middle of the trial, the State Procurator's Office opened an investigation of Bukharin,

---

[53] *Report of Court Proceedings*, pp. 14, 131, 113, 16, 118, 121, 123, 32, 128. On Smirnov's and Trotsky's opinions of Stalin, see Roy Medvedev, *Let History Judge: The Origins and Consequences of Stalinism* (Columbia University Press, New York, 1989), p. 88.

[54] "The New Course" was the title of Trotsky's oppositional platform presented in 1923. See Leon Trotsky, *The New Course: The Challenge of the Left Opposition, 1923–1925* (Pathfinder Press, New York, 1975).

[55] *Report of Court Proceedings*, pp. 41, 167, 166, 123–5.

Rykov, Radek, Tomskii, and others implicated by the defendants. Tomskii promptly committed suicide. The defendants were found guilty of organizing a terrorist center, murdering Kirov, and attempting to murder Stalin and other Soviet leaders. All sixteen were sentenced to the "supreme penalty" and shot the day after the trial.[56] The Kirov murder, however, was still not "solved."

Workers Respond to the Trial

The Party made a great effort to mobilize workers and local party organizations around the trial. There were meetings in factories and huge open-air demonstrations. Hundreds of thousands of workers met after every shift, in small groups and in mass meetings. Workers demanded the death penalty, testified tearfully to the achievements of Soviet power, and shouted for the blood of the defendants. Although many asked thoughtful questions about the trial, the emotional atmosphere made public disagreement difficult. When workers spoke privately in small groups or pairs, however, they voiced a far wider array of opinions.[57] Yet even the most rabid workers and party members regarded the trial as a distant spectacle unfolding on a national stage far from their own factories.

The first set of meetings in the factories took place on August 15, four days before the trial opened. Organizers read aloud the lead editorial in *Pravda*, "Enemies of the People Caught Red-Handed," a carefully edited version of the secret Central Committee letter of July 29.[58] Workers were intensely interested. One participant later noted, "the meetings took place in an atmosphere of absolute electrification ... In the meeting hall there was dead silence as the indictment was read, and a forest of hands demanding that the article be read down to the last word. No one walked out, even though the meeting lasted until very late."[59] In Factory No. 46, 1,300 workers showed up during the dinner break to hear the news read aloud.[60] Party organizers skillfully used the threat of terrorism to elicit an outpouring of support for the state and its leaders. A sixty-year-old woman textile

---

[56] Ibid., pp. 55–6, 65, 68, 71–2, 178–80, 117; "O tak nazyvaemom 'Antisovetskom Ob"edinennom trotskistsko-zinov'evskom tsentr,'" pp. 78–81.

[57] Many comments were recorded by informers and forwarded to local party organizations and the Moscow party committee with the name, shop, and factory of the speaker.

[58] "Vragi naroda poimany s polichnym," *Pravda*, August 15, 1936, p. 1.

[59] TsAODM, f. 3, o. 49, d. 129, "V ORPO MK VKP (b)," l. 64.

[60] TsAODM, f. 3, o. 49, d. 129, "MK VKP (b) ORPO informatsionnnoe soobshchenie," l. 8.

worker (nonparty) said, "In the years when we lived through hardship, Comrade Stalin led us out of these difficulties and we began to live better. These scoundrels wanted to mess up our business, to kill our best leaders and Comrade Stalin. We must deeply investigate the case and not leave a single enemy."[61] An old worker, a recent candidate for party membership, vowed with tears in his eyes, "I am seventy-four years old. All my life, before the revolution there was poverty, hunger, and humiliation by the brutal landowners. Only under Soviet power did I see what life might be. There is no father who cares so much for a son, who teaches him so much, as Stalin... For Soviet power, for Comrade Stalin, I would go to any front and die."[62] By depicting the defendants as counterrevolutionary fascists who sought to resurrect tsarist oppression, party organizers provoked emotion-choked testimonials to Soviet achievements.

Both party and nonparty members angrily demanded the death penalty. A party member in a typographical factory stated, "An open trial gives us the chance to show the whole world the vile activities Trotsky, Zinoviev, and Kamenev directed against Soviet power and its leaders. I think that if fascists use terror against the working class, then we should also use terror against those reptiles who are in the direct service of the fascists."[63] "I never imagined that in our country there were such people who might prepare an attempt on our leaders," said an older, nonparty woman worker; "We should shoot them even for thinking about such a crime. Zinoviev and Kamenev, direct participants in the murder, should be shot quickly."[64]

Not only did the workers demand that the defendants be executed; many declared the trial a waste of time and effort. One nonparty worker from the Bolshevik factory explained, "Let's finish with the Trotskyists and Zinovievites; it's not necessary to try them, to waste time. Just shoot them." Another declared, "Court? What for? Shoot them all without the court, and don't waste time on this. And if it's necessary to investigate the case further, then leave a few of them."[65] The workers showed little respect for the "legal niceties." "Hang them," "Shoot them," they yelled. "Why let them live when they murdered Comrade Kirov?"[66] Several declared that Zinoviev and Kamenev should have been shot two years

---

[61] TsAODM, f. 3, o. 49, d. 129, "Informatsionnoe soobshchenie ob otklikakh rabochikh g. Moskvy na soobshchenie TASS o predanii sudu Tsentra trotskistsko-zinov'evskogo bloka," l. 2.

[62] TsAODM, f. 3, o. 49, d. 129, "V MK VKP (b) informatsiia," l. 85.

[63] "Informatsionnoe soobshchenie ob otklikakh rabochikh g. Moskvy," l. 1.

[64] Ibid., l. 2.　　　　　　　　　　　　[65] Ibid.

[66] "MK VKP (b) ORPO informatsionnoe soobshchenie," l. 12.

earlier, immediately after Kirov's murder. "Those bastards should have been annihilated a long time ago," stated an old nonparty worker in the Dzerzhinskii factory. "They have repeatedly betrayed the party. Zinoviev and Kamenev even revealed the plan for the armed uprising in October 1917. They should have been shot for that." A turner and party member from the Kalibr instrument factory demanded, "Why wasn't the entire counterrevolutionary group shot after the Kirov murder? We have coddled them too long. It's time to put an end to this business."[67] In Factory No. 95 in Kuntsevo district in Moscow, workers declared, "Enough standing on ceremony!" and "Further patience is impossible." "Shoot this group so that it cannot exist in our land as traitors to our country."[68]

The highly emotional tenor of the meetings made it difficult to ask questions about the trial or the evidence. Yet many workers did speak up. Some were honestly puzzled about the development of the case. They asked, "Why did the investigation of this case take so long?" and "Why were the Trotskyist and Zinovievite groups not decisively eliminated after the murder of Kirov?"[69] Other questions were more provocative, noting that at least one group had already been tried for Kirov's murder. "Why are they trying people for Kirov's murder a second time?" asked one worker. Others asked about the death penalty: "Can a proletarian court sentence people to be shot?" Some worried about the effect of the trial on international opinion, wondering if the Soviet Union had the right to judge people who were not Soviet citizens. They asked, "How does the capitalist world look at the information of the procurator?" "Will the bourgeoisie protest the trial of terrorists from abroad?"[70]

In private, workers expressed more varied opinions and ideas, reflecting the experiences of the groups among them. Many older workers had vivid personal memories of the revolution. They had participated in the overthrow of tsarism and fought with the Red Army in the Civil War. A number recalled Trotsky with great respect, rejecting Stalin's attempt to rewrite the history of the revolution. A packer in the Garden Trust told a party organizer, "Trotsky was a brilliant, prominent person who made great contributions, which the Party is now hiding and not discussing."

[67] "Informatsionnoe soobshchenie ob otklikakh rabochikh g. Moskvy," l. 2.
[68] "MK VKP (b) ORPO informatsionnoe soobshchenie," ll. 7–8.
[69] TsAODM, f. 3, o. 49, d. 129, "Rabochie sobraniia i besedy po egor'evskomu raionu o ter-roristicheskoi deiatel'nosti Trotskogo, Zinov'eva, Kameneva, i dr.," "V informatsionnyi sektor ORPO MK VKP (b). Ot shelkovskogo RK VKP (b)," ll. 5, 39.
[70] TsAODM, f. 3, o. 49, d. 129, "Otkliki na soobshchenie Prokuratory SSSR o predanii sudu Trotskistsko-zinov'evskuiu kontr-revoliutsionnuiu terroristicheskuiu gruppu," ll. 18, 19.

He added that older histories of the Party discussed Trotsky, but made no mention of Stalin.[71] A distributor in a calibration shop said, "Trotsky is a representative of the intelligentsia. He led from above, but we must give him credit, he is a good orator and he always led the masses."[72] Several workers remembered the trial of Ramzin, an engineer accused of wrecking in 1928. One said, "Our Party should not shoot such smart people, but reeducate them like Ramzin. They should send back those who came from abroad. There is a communist party there. Let them unmask and reeducate them."[73] Many workers privately expressed doubts about the death penalty if not the guilt of the defendants. Referring to Zinoviev and Kamenev, one said, "We should consider their previous contributions." Another explained, "Considering their previous revolutionary activities, I would hardly shoot them." A nonparty mechanic from a chemical factory said, "It would be better to send them abroad than to shoot them."[74] Some workers considered the trial a frame-up. In the Malenkov factory, Frolov, a party member, and Gusarev, a nonparty member, working side by side, spoke about the trial. Frolov said, "There is a good article today in *Pravda*." Gusarev replied, "Yes, the article is good but, all the same, Trotsky had great force and great success in the Red Army." When Frolov tried to argue, Gusarev ended the conversation. "This is all nonsense," he said flatly.[75] And even young workers with no personal memories of Trotsky had the sense that he had made a great contribution to the revolution. A young Komsomolets in a garment factory announced to a party member in the workers' dormitory, "Trotsky made a revolution in Russia in 1917, and the reason everything went bad was because they expelled him. But he was a great person, he commanded the Red Army, and without Trotsky we never would have had a revolution."[76]

A few workers, unaware that their comments would be reported to higher authorities, came out in support of the defendants. Some referred to the betrayal of the revolution's ideals. A timekeeper in a factory in Dedovsk in Moscow province told his fellow workers a joke: "Lenin, lying in the mausoleum, told Stalin, 'Turn me face down so that I won't have to see everything that you are doing.'"[77] One welder said, "It's understood

---

[71] TsAODM, f. 3, o. 49, d. 129, "V ORPO MK VKP (b). Informatsionnaia svodka," l. 79.
[72] "Informatsionnoe soobshchenie ob otklikakh rabochikh g. Moskvy," l. 4.
[73] "V ORPO MK VKP (b). Informatsionnaia svodka," ll. 79–80.
[74] "Informatsionnoe soobshchenie ob otklikakh rabochikh g. Moskvy," l. 3.
[75] Ibid., l. 4.
[76] "V ORPO MK VKP (b). Informatsionnaia svodka," ll. 79–80.
[77] TsAODM, f. 3, o. 49, d. 129, "Informatsionnaia svodka," l. 16.

that Trotsky and Zinoviev want power. But they have their convictions. Perhaps they wanted to make a second revolution. Lenin said that everyone will be free, but in reality there is no freedom. Here, for example, if I don't want to go to a meeting, they force me to go, and if I don't want to work, they force me."[78] A greaser in a spinning factory who had been excluded from the party openly called for a new revolution at a workers' meeting: "Terror was, is, and will be!" he cried; "Yes, and at the same time, it's necessary to overturn everything! Gather the working class . . . They [the authorities] have completely ruined everything!"[79] At a gathering of forty workers in a dormitory in Factory No. 46, an unemployed worker and former party member challenged the organizer assigned to read *Pravda* aloud. "Trotsky was a friend of Lenin's," he explained, "but after Lenin's death they began to push Trotsky aside." The NKVD, informed that he was living in the dormitory without a passport, arrested him that evening.[80]

Some workers, concerned about "rightists" and other party leaders linked to various plots, urged further investigation. One Komsomol worker demanded, "I believe there is still much to be revealed and uncovered . . . We must sweep these low agents of fascism and evil enemies of the people off the face of the earth."[81] Other workers demanded that Bukharin, Rykov, Tomskii, Uglanov, Sokolnikov, Piatakov, and others be investigated. One nonparty shop foreman stated, "All the leftists and rightists pledge their loyalty and, at the same time, they betray the party in critical ways. Rykov, Bukharin, and Tomskii admitted their mistakes. They work in important jobs. How can we trust them? How can we believe them in the future? We should hold them accountable in court."[82] And a weaver in the Nogin factory stated, "The Supreme Court should investigate the counterrevolutionary activities of the leaders of the right deviation and other former Trotskyists. Our sentence frightened that scoundrel Tomskii. He was obviously not innocent because he ended his life by suicide."[83] Yet not all workers agreed. A large crowd, abuzz with rumors,

---

[78] "Informatsionnoe soobshchenie ob otklikakh rabochikh g. Moskvy," l. 4.

[79] "Rabochie sobraniia i besedy po egor'evskomu raionu o terroristicheskoi deiatel'nosti Trotskogo, Zinov'eva, Kameneva, i dr.," l. 6. The worker's appeal played on a slogan in a popular Soviet poster: "Lenin was, is, and will be!"

[80] "MK VKP (b) ORPO informatsionnoe soobshchenie," l. 13.

[81] "Informatsionnoe soobshchenie ob otklikakh rabochikh g. Moskvy," l. 1.

[82] "V informatsionnyi sektor ORPO MK VKP (b). Ot shelkovskogo RK VKP (b)," ll. 76–77.

[83] TsAODM, f. 3, o. 49, d. 129, "V Otdel rukovodiashchikhakh partorganov MK VKP (b)," l. 87.

gathered spontaneously on the street in front of Tomskii's apartment after his suicide. Several people were overheard to say that Tomskii had left a note for Stalin, stating that he had always been loyal to the Party. He committed suicide because he could not stand the slander.[84]

The Party used the trial to push several agendas. Party organizers spoke about the need "to strengthen discipline and increase the productivity of labor." Workers were asked to pledge their support for Stakhanovism and higher productivity as a way of rebuffing "enemies." In one factory, for example, workers vowed, "We, the workers, in response to the sally of the class enemy, will demonstrate even greater Bolshevik vigilance and still more broadly develop Stakhanovite methods of work, rallying closely around the Central Committee and our beloved leader of the people, Comrade Stalin."[85] These formulaic endorsements convinced some workers that the trial was just another gimmick to increase productivity.

A large segment of the working class had recently migrated from the countryside. Many of these former peasants were bitter about collectivization but ignorant of the debates that had animated the Party in the 1920s. Less sophisticated politically, they viewed all Soviet leaders as scoundrels bent on extorting the last drop of blood from workers and peasants. "Left" or "right," it made no difference. They doubted whether party leaders, who always protected each other's privileges, would execute their own comrades. A nonparty worker in a watch factory explained to a party member, "They cooked up all this foolishness in order to lead some kind of campaign. Zinoviev is in the Kremlin, and he has five good apartments in Moscow."[86] An apprentice weaver also doubted whether the trial was genuine: "Who cares what you say about Zinoviev and Kamenev," he said to a party organizer; "Nothing will happen to them because they are Stalin's friends."[87]

Workers' opinions of the trial thus ran the gamut from harsh denunciation of the defendants, to stubborn insistence on the "truth" of the revolution, to blanket condemnation of the Bolsheviks as new exploiters. Yet whatever their opinions, workers were deeply engaged. Many asked if they could take off from work to attend. "Can we go to court and look at these vermin?" asked one. Others asked permission to attend the trial, send

[84] "V ORPO MK VKP (b). Informatsionnaia svodka," l. 85.

[85] "Rabochie sobraniia i besedy po egor'evskomu raionu o terroristicheskoi deiatel'nosti Trotskogo, Zinov'eva, Kameneva, i dr.," ll. 6, 5.

[86] "Informatsionnoe soobshchenie ob otklikakh rabochikh g. Moskvy," l. 3.

[87] TsAODM, f. 3, o. 49, d. 129, "V moskovskii komitet VKP (b). Otdel rukovodiashchikh partorganov (ORPO). Informatsiia," l. 60.

representatives from their factories, and listen to the court proceedings over the radio.[88] The defendants' shocking confessions animated the factories for weeks, providing a welcome distraction from heavy labor. Yet the trial did not substantially change relations among workers or the daily routines of the *partkomy*. Even workers who staunchly supported the execution of the defendants showed little interest in broadening the hunt for enemies to the factories. The trial was a deeply engrossing spectacle, but it was a diversion from daily life, not a part of it.

Hunting Enemies Everywhere

By September 1936, central party authorities had become increasingly impatient with the failure of the regional committees to purge their ranks. The regional organizations in turn pushed the city and district committees to uncover and expel "persons of questionable or wavering loyalty" who were connected "in the present or past with Trotskyism or Zinovievism."[89] The city and district committees responded by pressuring the *partkomy* in the factories. The *partkomy* had responded tepidly to the Central Committee's letter of July 29 as well as to a stronger subsequent letter from the Moscow party committee.[90] Local leaders did not dispute the leadership's contention that there were enemies in high places, but they showed little inclination to look for Trotskyists under their own beds.

In the middle of September, the Moscow party committee sent one of its secretaries, S. Z. Korytnyi, to investigate the results of the *proverka*. Korytnyi was highly displeased at what he uncovered in his visits to seven districts. By dint of aggressive questioning, he discovered that district officials had proceeded haphazardly with the review and exchange of party documents. They did not know the local party leaders in their jurisdictions, misunderstood the purpose of the purge, and kept poor records. Many smaller factories, workshops, and institutions did not have a single party member, and some had never received a visit from a party organizer. In the Taganka district, for example, only 152 out of 500 workplaces had party organizations. The majority of party organizers were scattered

---

[88] "Informatsionnoe soobshchenie ob otklikakh rabochikh g. Moskvy," l. 4; "MK VKP (b) ORPO informatsionnoe soobshchenie," l. 9; "V informatsionnyi sektor ORPO MK VKP (b). Ot shelkovskogo RK VKP (b)," l. 39.

[89] Getty and Naumov, *The Road to Terror*, pp. 269, 263–8.

[90] TsAODM did not allow me to see the letter from the Moscow party committee, although it is mentioned and quoted in other documents.

through the city in small groups. They knew and trusted one another, and did not take a strict approach to the *proverka*. The larger organizations, overwhelmed by the work involved in checking every member, also had a lax approach.[91] The Party was astoundingly disorganized at every level. In the Frunze district, members waited for hours in long lines to have their documents reviewed. Many were approved although they lacked the requisite documents or photographs. Faced with the task of compiling a list of local party secretaries, the Frunze district committee tried to recall acquaintances in various places: "Here is Ivanov in such and such an enterprise with such and such a number of members." Officials in the Taganka district committee were somewhat better organized, but knew only about two-thirds of their 152 party secretaries. In the Kuibyshev district, the party members who conducted the *proverka* and *obmen* were barely literate. The district was large, with 318 primary party organizations. Yet due to a lack of qualified personnel willing to devote time to the *proverka*, party cards were filled out so carelessly that the bearer's gender was often incorrect. The district's records were a mess: registered party members had disappeared, and active members had no cards. The Moscow committee found more than 600 errors in the records *after* the *proverka* was completed. Local officials, barely able to manage the demanding paperwork, had little time left over for identifying "enemies."[92]

Many party members in important jobs viewed the *proverka* as a dull, bureaucratic exercise that stole time from more pressing tasks. Officials in the Sverdlov district, which encompassed state institutions such as Gosplan, the Soviet Control Commission, and the Commissariat of Forestry, initially refused to abandon their work to help organize the *proverka*. District officials, fearful of offending leading party members with impertinent questions about their biographies, concentrated their attention on workers in the district's main factory. Korytnyi, dissatisfied with their double standard, urged them to review *everyone's* record by combing through biographical data, past speeches, and minutes of meetings.[93]

Not only were district officials tentative in their approach to party members in leading posts, but they also lacked authority over their fractious rank and file. The case of Otdel'nikov, a party member and head of a garment workshop, was typical of the apolitical, petty tempests that roiled

[91] TsAODM, f. 3, o. 49, d. 119, "Stenogrammy soveshchanii sekretarei RK VKP (b) po itogam proverki partdokumentov po partorganizatsiiam g. Moskvy," ll. 4, 11, 24, 92. Only seven enterprises in the Taganka district had more than 100 party members.
[92] Ibid., ll. 100, 7, 94, 44–5, 50.   [93] Ibid., ll. 126–127.

the district committees. Otdel'nikov refused to rehire a worker who had been expelled from the Party and his job for counterfeiting, even though a party investigation had restored his candidacy. The district *partkom* pressured Otdel'nikov, who angrily retorted that he would let the workers in his shop decide. The workers met, voted to support Otdel'nikov, and vented their anger against the district committee, yelling, "The district committee is full of swindlers. Otdel'nikov is our savior. He gave us a crust of bread." The mismanaged affair was typical of "politics" on the local level. In the end, the tussle for power ended badly for Otdel'nikov. District officials combed through their records, found some compromising material, and excluded him from the Party. One party member summarized the tale with disgust: "They wanted to remove one fool and put another one in his place."[94] Clearly, this was not what central authorities envisioned in purging the Party of "enemies."

What *Is* a "Trotskyist-Zinovievite"?

As late as fall 1936, district committee officials were still confused about what constituted a political enemy. The letters from the Central Committee and the Moscow committee strongly directed them to scrutinize their records for former oppositionists. Yet after carefully reviewing the letters, district officials were still unsure how to identify a "Trotskyist-Zinovievite." Was it someone who voted for a Trotskyist resolution in 1923 or someone involved in oppositional activities in the present? It seemed unfair to punish hardworking, loyal comrades for a "mistake" made more than a decade ago. On the other hand, there did not seem to be any party members currently engaged in Trotskyist activities. And if these people were "masked," how were they to be uncovered? When the director of a factory in the Taganka district was arrested as a Trotskyist, his fellow party members were astounded. "He was a political illiterate," said one. Another exclaimed, "How can a person with such narrow horizons suddenly be a Trotskyist?" No matter what Stalin and the newspapers said, these party members thought of "Trotskyists" as educated Marxists with a good grasp of politics. How could the director, a "political illiterate," possibly be a Trotskyist?[95]

Given the general confusion, the policy toward party members who had participated in the oppositions of the 1920s differed widely from one district to another. The Moscow party committee's letter warned against "a

94 Ibid., ll. 5–7.   95 Ibid., ll. 58–9, 13.

mechanical approach to unmasking," but officials were unsure what this meant. Korytnyi concluded that the purge lacked a political edge, a finding consonant with national and citywide statistics. The *proverka* of 1935 and *obmen* in 1936 did not result in many expulsions for political reasons. Nationwide, about 8.8 percent of those excluded from the Party (3,324 people) were expelled for Trotskyism or Zinovievism.[96] Data from the seven districts in Moscow that Korytnyi reviewed revealed similar results. The largest group was excluded for petty offenses, such as poor attendance at meetings, missing dues payments, or failure to study. In the Pervomai district, about 30 percent of exclusions were for "passivity." Korytnyi angrily upbraided the district officials, "These were not the people you needed to strike off." The party secretaries generally fared worse than the general membership. In the Kiev district, about one-quarter (40 of 170) of the party secretaries were removed from their posts, and in the Taganka district it was about one-fifth (30 of 152). Yet most were replaced for poor organizing or failing to meet the production plan, not political opposition. As of September 1936, 4,050 party members and 4,000 candidates had passed through the *proverka* and *obmen* in the Taganka district. Of these, 105 were excluded from the Party, 24 as Trotskyist-Zinovievites (about 6 percent of the district's members). Moreover, the overwhelming majority of these (17 out of 24) were expelled only after the letters from the Central Committee and the Moscow party committee. Korytnyi was furious about the sluggishness of the Taganka district officials. He noted that that they had not bothered to investigate a single one of the forty denunciations they received. "What are you waiting for?" Korytnyi demanded of them. "If one of these people is an enemy, then your dawdling is a crime." Yet the district committee showed little interest in investigating these "leads." Korytnyi scolded them, "Stop making excuses, such as 'the person has gone to Bashkiria.'"[97]

A few districts took a harsher approach. In the Sverdlov district, officials initially excluded everyone who had participated in the left opposition. The Kuibyshev district officials took an even harder line, expelling anyone who had participated in either the left or right oppositions. A district official said, "After they made such big mistakes, why should we

---

[96] Getty and Naumov, *The Road to Terror*, p. 275.

[97] "Stenogrammy soveshchanii sekretarei RK VKP (b) po itogam proverki partdokumentov po partorganizatsiiam g. Moskvy," ll. 168, 170–1, 12, 36, 37, 102, 76–7, 87, 63, 1. In Frunze district, only fifty-seven people were excluded. In Molotov district, officials reviewed 2,225 members, expelled 38 "enemies," and investigated 85 people who had ties with the left opposition.

leave these people in the Party?" He explained that they had expelled 105 former members of the left opposition, and several former rightists. He admitted, "The figures frightened us a little." Yet even in the Kuibyshev district, some party secretaries in the factories were reluctant to expel people for previous deviations, and tried to protect them. And despite the district's hard line on expulsion, officials never checked those who sponsored former oppositionists for party membership. By refusing to expand their investigations to include sponsors, workmates, relatives, and friends, they created a firewall against the spread of repression. Korytnyi lectured the district officials to take a stricter approach. "You whitewashed this business," he told them angrily. "Undoubtedly there are several people you need to look at again." He urged them to look over their members "extraordinarily closely."[98]

District officials were also confused about how to treat people who had already been expelled and reinstated by the Party. In the Pervomai district, officials were indignant when Korytnyi rebuked them for not expelling a woman who had been expelled and reinstated twice in the 1920s for participation in the left opposition. One district official retorted, "She was rehabilitated twice by the Moscow committee!" They did not understand how a lower party organization could punish a member for an infraction that the higher levels had already forgiven. And what about party members who concealed relationships with Trotskyists? In the Molotov district, a member was excluded because she failed to inform the *partkom* that her husband held "Trotskyist views," and another for not mentioning that her husband was exiled for counterrevolutionary activities. Yet officials questioned whether these exclusions were correct.[99]

The Moscow party committee was especially disturbed that district officials had allowed members to pass through the *proverka* who were later arrested. Why had the district failed to identify these enemies who were subsequently unmasked by the NKVD? In one peculiar case, the Taganka district committee requested new party documents for a member who was expelled and then restored by the Party Control Commission. Yet by the time the Moscow party committee received the request, the member had been arrested. District officials were forced to explain why they were requesting documents for an enemy. "What were we supposed to do?" asked one of the district officials helplessly. The district was caught between the NKVD and the Party Control Commission, powerful bureaucracies working at cross-purposes. Korytnyi also rebuked Taganka

[98] Ibid., ll. 112, 45–8, 54.   [99] Ibid., ll. 172–3, 87.

officials for overlooking factories that were once centers of left oppositional activity. A nucleus of former oppositionists from Moscow's Garment Factory No. 4 had moved to Garment Factory No. 2. These older
party organizers still met faithfully with workers in study circles. Korytnyi
pressed Taganka district officials for more information, but they seemed
clueless. Korytnyi also upbraided the Stalin district committee for failing to exclude a single party member from its Factory No. 24, although
many had contact with V. V. Lominadze, a prominent left oppositionist,
who had once worked there. Some of these party members had passed
through the *proverka*, only to be arrested by the NKVD. Only after this
political embarrassment did the Stalin district committee begin pressuring its *partkomy* to "unmask a series of enemies." One district official
explained, "In the beginning they were slow, but after they were reprimanded they began to study people closely, to unmask them, and they did
not allow the party organizations to shirk this task."[100] Korytnyi, through
a combination of bullying and cajolery, tried to dispel the district committees' general apathy and prod them into action. Yet as late as September
1936, a full month after the trial, his investigation showed that the district
and party committees were still reluctant to hunt for "enemies" in their
own ranks.

Conclusion

By the end of 1936, Stalin and his supporters had transformed the Kirov
case from a single murder by an embittered former party member into
an international terror plot aimed at the Soviet government. Within a
month, former oppositionists in Leningrad and Moscow were tried alongside Nikolaev. Throughout the spring of 1935, the investigation moved
forward fitfully with the discovery of a terrorist group in the Kremlin and
Enukidze's expulsion from the Party. Tension subsided slightly between
June and December 1935, although Ezhov had already crafted a new,
expanded version of the murder plot and arrests of former oppositionists continued. In January 1936, Ol'berg's confession opened new lines
of investigation, which led in turn to more arrests. Stalin played a strong
role in shaping the case throughout the spring of 1936, implicating former
Trotskyists and adding an international dimension to the growing conspiracy. The August trial of the "United Trotskyist-Zinovievite Center,"
a potent mixture of party fears and fantasy, revolved around hidden

[100] Ibid., ll. 63, 17–18, 129, 161–2.

oppositionists and the social tensions of industrialization. It placed the deepest anxieties of the leadership on public display.

The district and factory party committees lagged well behind central authorities in hewing to the evolving script of the Kirov murder. Local officials did not connect the unmasking of "terrorists" at the top with their own *proverka* and *obmen*. Initially, they ignored the Central Committee's July 19 letter about vigilance and "masked enemies." Unsure who the "masked" enemies were, and not particularly motivated to find them, they voted unanimously for the death penalty and returned to their own business. "Unmasking," in their view, was the job of the NKVD. The Moscow party committee later rebuked them strongly for acting as if the *proverka* had nothing to do with the trial.[101] Workers, too, remained distant from the trial. Publicly, they endorsed the verdict but, privately, they did not embrace it wholeheartedly.

If party leaders had focused only on eliminating former oppositionists, if the hunt for enemies had not spread to the *partkomy* and other institutions, the Stalinist terror would have been strictly limited. Yet party leaders feared that it was impossible to remove all oppositionists "from above." They needed the participation of the district and primary party organizations. By fall 1936, district and factory party committees were under increasing pressure from above to sharpen the *proverka*'s political edge. The Central Committee pressured the regional and city committees, which in turn leaned on the district and party committees to take action. Repression, limited thus far to former oppositionists, would soon overtake the local party organizations, the unions, and the factories. The rank and file, under pressure from above, would find its own reasons to join the hunt for enemies. The firewall, solidly built by the party committees of apathy, disorganization, and a good measure of common decency, would soon be engulfed in flames.

[101] Ibid., l. 161.

4. Funeral of Sergei M. Kirov with Stalin by the coffin. Courtesy of www.newizv.ru

5. Nikolai I. Ezhov, head of the People's Commissariat of Internal Affairs. Courtesy of www.hrono.ru

6. Nikolai I. Ezhov. Courtesy of www.hrono.ru

3

Mobilizing Mass Support for Repression

"I think our Bolshevik leaders resemble Antaeus and should be like Antaeus. Their strength exists because they do not want to break or weaken the tie with their mother who bore and fed them, with the masses, the people, the working class, the peasantry, with the little people."

> – I. V. Stalin in his keynote speech to the Central Committee Plenum, February–March 1937[1]

"Do you really believe the people are still behind you? It bears you, dumb and resigned, as it bears others in other countries, but there is no response in its depths... A long time ago we stirred up the depths, but that is over. In other words, in those days we made history; now you make politics."

> – Rubashev, a fictional oppositionist in response to his interrogator[2]

By September 1936, party leaders had become increasingly impatient with the complacent attitudes of district and party committees toward former oppositionists. Until the end of August, party leaders had concentrated on the Kirov murder and political plots against Stalin and his supporters. The August 1936 trial of the "United Trotskyist-Zinovievite Center" had emphasized high politics: both the defendants and their alleged victims were prominent party figures. In the fall, however, party leaders shifted the public focus of repression from political assassins to industrial wreckers. Workers were cast as the new victims of "masked" enemies. The shift began with an explosion in the Kemerovo coal mines that killed ten workers and injured fourteen others. The impact of the explosion was initially quite muffled: the national press failed to report it. Yet, within a month, a

---

[1] "Materialy fevral'sko-martovskogo plenuma TsK VKP (b) 1937 goda," *Voprosy istorii*, Nos. 11–12, 1995, p. 20 (hereafter cited as "Materialy fevral'sko-martovskogo plenuma").

[2] Arthur Koestler, *Darkness at Noon* (Bantam Books, New York, 1966), p. 68.

group of former oppositionists and mine managers were brought to trial for the accident. Widely covered by the press, the trial indelibly imprinted the accident on the Soviet national consciousness. And the reverberations of the explosion continued long after the miners were buried and the defendants sentenced. Party leaders urged workers, union activists, and party members to consider problems in industry, especially those related to safety, as wrecking. The hunt for enemies was not the sole responsibility of the NKVD, but the duty of every party member and citizen. The emphasis on wrecking helped mobilize the rank and file in the Party and the unions, dispelling the apathy that had so effectively insulated them against the spread of repression.

The Kemerovo disaster became a major leitmotif in the second great Moscow show trial of the "Anti-Soviet Parallel Trotskyist Center" in January 1937. The two trials reshaped the message of the terror for a wide, popular audience. By emphasizing industrial wrecking and workers as victims, they successfully spread the hunt for enemies into every factory and union organization. The February–March 1937 Central Committee Plenum took this message one step further. Party leaders, insisting on democracy and multicandidate, secret-ballot elections, attempted to bust up the controlling "family circles" within the unions and party organizations. They urged the rank and file to exercise their democratic rights, expose hidden oppositionists, and oust entrenched leaders from power. Taken together, these three national events shifted attention from political assassination to industrial wrecking, featured workers as targets of "enemy" oppositionists, managers, and engineers, and mobilized the rank and file to criticize and remove union and party officials. The new message, a blend of democracy, industrial wrecking, and local grievances, proved an extraordinarily potent catalyst in the spread of repression.

The Kemerovo Trial

The NKVD shifted its investigations to industry in the summer of 1936, targeting former left oppositionists who had returned to the Party in 1929 and assumed leading posts. G. I. Malenkov, the Central Committee's head of membership registration, began checking the party records of several hundred officials in economic posts that summer. A review of 2,150 officials revealed "compromising material" on 526, and 50 were removed from their posts.[3] A review of the 743 party members in the

---

[3] J. Arch Getty and Oleg Naumov, *The Road to Terror: Stalin and the Self-Destruction of the Bolsheviks, 1932–1939* (Yale University Press, New Haven and London, 1999), p. 281.

Commissariat of Heavy Industry (NKTP) in December 1936 revealed that
160 had recently been expelled (22 percent), 12 were former Trotskyists
(2 percent), and 80 had belonged to other groups before joining the Party
(11 percent).[4] By 1937, almost 1,000 economic managers were in prison.[5]
Subject to grueling interrogation, they confessed to elaborate schemes
of industrial wrecking, which in turn led to further arrests. The terror
widened its scope to include those who had returned to the Party as well
as their intimates, mentors, and fellow managers. A. Ia. Vyshinskii, the
zealous procurator of the August trial, opened an investigation of G. L.
Piatakov, the deputy commissar of heavy industry, after several defendants
implicated him in their testimonies. Piatakov, a former member of the left
opposition and close associate of Trotsky, was expelled from the Party
on September 11 for maintaining close ties with Zinoviev and Kamenev,
and arrested the following day. Getty notes, "His arrest for sabotage
and 'terrorism' sent shock waves through the industrial establishment."[6]
After lengthy interrogation, Piatakov confessed to economic wrecking
and sabotage. Brought from prison to a Politburo meeting in January, he
looked, as Bukharin later noted, like "a skeleton with his teeth knocked
out."[7]

Eleven days after Piatakov's arrest, on September 23, 1936, a terrible
explosion rocked the Kemerovo coal mines, located in the Kuznetsk basin
(Kuzbas) in Western Siberia. Gas in an underground chamber ignited,
killing ten miners and badly injuring fourteen others. The problems in
the Kemerovo mines were common throughout the industry: numerous
accidents, poorly planned tunnels, and insufficient internal scaffolding.
Mining in the Kuzbas dated back to the nineteenth century, but the government only began to develop the region's rich potential in the 1930s,
constructing a huge mining, metallurgical, and chemical complex. Railroad cars took coke from the Kuzbas to the new iron and steel base in
Magnitogorsk and returned with iron ore for the new metallurgical plant
in Stalinsk (Novokuznetsk). The population of Kemerovo, a small mining
town, had grown sixfold since 1926 to more than 100,000 people.[8] The

---

[4] Oleg Khlevniuk, *1937-i: Stalin, NKVD i sovetskoe obshchestvo* (Izdatel'stvo Respublika, Moscow, 1992), pp. 116–17.

[5] Getty and Naumov, *The Road to Terror*, p. 282; Oleg Khlevniuk, "Economic Officials in the Great Terror, 1936–1938," in Melanie Ilic, ed., *Stalin's Terror Revisited* (Palgrave, Basingstoke, 2006), pp. 38–67.

[6] Getty and Naumov, *The Road to Terror*, pp. 286, 283.

[7] Anna Larina, *This I Cannot Forget: The Memoirs of Nikolai Bukharin's Widow* (W. W. Norton, New York, 1993), p. 312.

[8] S. S. Balzak, V. F. Vasyutin, and Ya. G. Feigin, *Economic Geography of the USSR* (Macmillan Co., New York, 1949), pp. 193, 192, 250.

September explosion was hardly the first. An earlier explosion in December 1935 had killed two workers and injured several others. The national and labor press, not in the habit of reporting work accidents, never mentioned either the December or September explosions. Two days after the explosion, on September 25, Stalin, on vacation in Sochi, sent a telegram to the Politburo requesting that G. G. Iagoda be removed as head of the NKVD and replaced by N. I. Ezhov. L. M. Kaganovich, a member of the Politburo, explained, "Yagoda had turned out to be too weak for such a role."[9] On September 29, the Commissariat of Justice sent a circular to regional and local procurators: "Reconsider all cases of technical safety, and every explosion, accident and fire, which have occurred in industry in the past three years."[10] As procurators began combing their case files for Trotskyist links, the NKVD began its investigation of the Kemerovo explosion, arresting leading managers and engineers. In prison, the managers joined a number of former Trotskyists from the West Siberian district arrested earlier in the spring. Within weeks, the NKVD had linked the mine managers and the former Trotskyists in an elaborate plot to wreck the Kemerovo mines and murder workers.

The Kemerovo explosion was not the first industrial accident to result in state prosecution. The Criminal Code contained a section on "service crimes," which covered "misuse of authority" to "criminal negligence." Misuse of office for the purpose of harming the state was classified as "wrecking." In 1928, the Supreme Court made it easier to obtain a wrecking conviction by ruling that procurators did not need to prove "counter-revolutionary intent," only intent to commit the act. In 1929, the Party launched a big campaign against "bourgeois specialists" (former tsarist officials and technical experts), adding a class dimension to the prosecution of service crimes. Judicial organs began prosecuting managers, engineers, and economists for accidents and failures in industry, trade, and transport. The campaign reached its apogee in 1931 in the trial of a group of former Mensheviks working as economists and planners. The Party retreated from the attack in the spring of 1931, taking measures to protect specialists. In 1933, in the wake of the famine, officials of the Commissariats of Agriculture and State Farms were tried for wrecking. The trial, however, was secret and party leaders made no attempt to whip up

---

[9] Getty and Naumov, *The Road to Terror*, p. 280.
[10] GARF, f. 8131, o. 37, d. 84, "Stenogramma doklada tov. Vyshinskogo ob itogakh plenuma TsK VKP (b) na sobranii partaktiva Prokurator soiuza RSFSR gor. Moskvy i Pravovoi akademii," l. 108.

popular support. British engineers were also accused in 1933 of spying and wrecking electric power stations, but this trial, too, was not accompanied by a wider popular campaign against specialists. In fact, after 1931, party leaders favored specialists with material privileges unavailable to workers, and were reluctant to attribute industrial accidents to wrecking.[11]

The lull lasted roughly until fall 1935, when Aleksei Stakhanov set a coal-mining record, which launched the Stakhanovite movement. Party leaders, euphoric over the possibility of raising labor productivity, set more ambitious production targets and encouraged workers in all industries to adopt Stakhanovite work methods. Factory managers were skeptical of the benefits of norm busting, but nonetheless urged foremen and engineers to comply with the campaign. Some workers, eager to raise their wages, pressured managers to supply them with the necessary equipment and materials to break records. Others resisted, seeing the campaign as one more ploy by the Party to extract maximum effort from an underfed working class. The Party initially met resistance with repression. The NKVD equated any activity harmful to a Stakhanovite worker, including failure to supply needed materials and tools, with sabotage. Workers and managers were arrested for deriding the campaign. When a mine roof collapsed and killed a group of Stakhanovite miners in Cheliabinsk, six engineers were found guilty of wrecking. Yet, by summer 1936, party leaders were beginning to doubt Stakhanovism's productive potential. The Central Committee, increasingly reluctant to blame common safety hazards and industrial problems on sabotage, called a halt to the persecution of industrial managers.[12]

The hiatus in persecution, however, was short-lived. The NKVD arrested the Kemerovo mine officials soon after the explosion in September. The trial began on November 20 in Novosibirsk, and the miners' deaths were announced the same day. A group of nine former Trotskyists and managers were charged with deliberately engineering the explosions. The Kemerovo trial built on earlier trials, but the combination of charges for spying, political opposition, and deliberate murder was new. The defendants included I. A. Peshekhonov, the head engineer of the Kemerovo

---

[11] Peter Solomon, *Soviet Criminal Justice Under Stalin* (Cambridge University Press, Cambridge and New York, 1996), pp. 139–40; R. W. Davies, *Crisis and Progress in the Soviet Economy, 1931–1933* (Macmillan, London, 1996), pp. 38–40, 46, 82–3, 336–9, 351, 452.
[12] R. W. Davies and Oleg Khlevnyuk, "Stakhanovism and the Soviet Economy," *Europe-Asia Studies*, 54, 6 (2002), pp. 882–7; Donald Filtzer, *Soviet Workers and Stalinist Industrialization: The Formation of Modern Soviet Production Relations, 1928–1941* (M. E. Sharpe, Armonk, NY, 1986), pp. 199–200.

mine complex, and E. P. Shtikling, a German national and head engineer of the complex's Severnaia mine. The other defendants, who worked in the Tsentral'naia mine where the explosion occurred, were I. I. Noskov, the mine's director, V. M. Andreev and I. E. Kovalenko, its head engineers, N. S. Leonenko, its manager, I. T. Liashchenko, its director of ventilation, F. I. Shubin, a foreman, and M. A. Kurov, a former Trotskyist and worker. Peshekhonov had received three years' exile in the Shakhty trial in 1928. After serving most of his sentence in Western Siberia, he was eventually appointed as head engineer of the Kemerovo mine complex. Six additional men were also implicated, but tried later in what became the second Moscow show trial of the "Parallel Trotskyist Center." They were Ia. N. Drobnis, deputy chief of construction in Kemerovo, N. I. Muralov, an old revolutionary and former Trotskyist exiled to Novosibirsk in 1928, A. A. Shestov, director of a Kuzbas zinc mine, M. S. Stroilov, chief engineer of the Kuzbas Coal Trust, M. S. Boguslavskii, the head of Siberian Machine Construction, and V. V. Arnol'd, a chauffeur. With the exception of Arnol'd, a picaresque adventurer with a sheaf of false passports and aliases, the group scheduled for trial as the "Parallel Trotskyist Center" were all former oppositionists. The Military Kollegiia of the Supreme Court, chaired by V. V. Ul'rikh and composed of two additional members, tried the case. These infamous military *troiki*, or groups of three, had been established after the Kirov murder to hear cases of "terrorism" and "treason."

The Kemerovo defendants were charged with committing multiple crimes in 1935–6 to disrupt the mining industry. The procurator built an elaborate tale of industrial wrecking, murder, espionage, and opposition, which began when Drobnis, a former Trotskyist, was reassigned to Kemerovo in 1934 from a post in Central Asia. Drobnis would be tried later in the January 1937 trial, but he played a pivotal role in the plot. According to the procurator, before leaving for Kemerovo, Drobnis visited Piatakov in his apartment in Moscow. Piatakov instructed him to contact Muralev and Boguslavskii, two former oppositionists exiled to Novosibirsk. These three became the nucleus of a Trotskyist terror cell in Western Siberia. In the spring of 1935, Piatakov met again with Drobnis to tell him about his meeting abroad with L. Sedov, Trotsky's son and representative. Sedov allegedly urged Piatakov to activate the Trotskyist network to assassinate party leaders and sabotage industry, especially metal, coal, and chemicals. Piatakov then instructed Drobnis to begin wrecking the mines. Drobnis, deputy chief of construction in Kemerovo, soon recruited Noskov, the director of the Tsentral'naia mine. After two meetings in

August and November 1935, Noskov recruited Kurov, a worker, and Shubin, a foreman, both former left oppositionists.[13] Over the next year, Drobnis, Noskov, Shubin, and Kurov recruited engineers and managers in the Tsentral'naia mine, including Liashchenko, Leonenko, Andreev, and Kovalenko, and several foreigners to their group.[14] Peshekhonov, the head engineer of the Kemerovo complex, embittered by his earlier conviction in the Shakhty trial, was eager to sabotage the mines. Stroilov had allegedly contacted Peshekhonov in 1933 and encouraged him to create "blind alleys" in the mines that could be filled with gas. He introduced Peshekhonov to Shtikling, a German engineer and alleged Gestapo agent, and the two formed a "counterrevolutionary fascist group." In October 1935, Shestov, the director of a nearby zinc mine, urged Drobnis to unite his Trotskyists with Peshekhonov's fascists, and the two groups merged soon thereafter.[15] The procurator recounted, "The wrecker Shakhtyite Peshekhonov and the Trotskyist counterrevolutionary Noskov found a common language and basis for activity with the fascist Shtikling."[16] They intentionally allowed the mines to fill with gas, hoping that an explosion would disrupt production and "embitter the workers."[17]

The trial was a web of interlocking testimonies in which the defendants incriminated themselves and each other. There was no evidence apart from their own confessions. Noskov, for example, testified, "Drobnis told me to organize acts of physical annihilation of workers by poisoning and explosions in the mines." And Kurov, in turn, testified, "Noskov told us that explosions in the mines would be very effective even if some of

---

[13] Shubin was a former Trotskyist who had participated in underground meetings held by Trotsky in 1927 before his exile from the USSR. The newspapers mentioned Kurov's occupation only once, noting that he worked "in production." See "Protsess kontrrevoliutsionnoi Trotskistskoi vreditel'skoi gruppy na kemerovskom rudnike," part 1, *Trud*, November 20, 1936, p. 3.

[14] The trial also featured a minor subplot, which carried strong echoes of the 1936 August trial. Arnol'd, Boguslavskii, and Muralov, who were tried in January 1937, were charged with plotting to kill R. I. Eikhe, the district's party secretary, and V. M. Molotov, the head of the Council of People's Commissars, in fall 1934 in a car accident: "Protsess kontrrevoliutsionnoi Trotskistskoi vreditel'skoi gruppy na kemerovskom rudnike," part 3, *Trud*, November 22, 1936, p. 3.

[15] Ibid.

[16] "Protsess kontrrevoliutsionnoi Trotskistskoi vreditel'skoi gruppy na kemerovskom rudnike," part 2, *Trud*, November 21, 1936, p. 3; "Soderzhanie prigovora," *Trud*, November 23, 1936, p. 2; "Protsess kontrrevoliutsionnoi Trotskistskoi vreditel'skoi gruppy na kemerovskom rudnike," part 3.

[17] "Protsess kontrrevoliutsionnoi Trotskistskoi vreditel'skoi gruppy na kemerovskom rudnike," part 1.

the workers suffered."[18] Shubin, informed of the plan, allegedly crowed with delight, "Soon our dear brother workers will croak in the mines like rats." Mocking Stalin's famous phrase that life was becoming better and happier, he said, "We'll show the workers a happy life." These comments, highlighted and repeated in numerous newspaper articles, became the signature phrases of the trial.[19] As one article explained, "They will not stop at the murder of any number of workers. On the contrary, the more victims, the better for the Trotskyist bloodsuckers because such are the commands of their masters – the fascists."[20]

The Message to Workers

Workers, mere spectators of the August 1936 trial, assumed prominent roles as victims and witnesses in the Kemerovo trial. The head of the Stakhanovite brigade in the Tsentral'naia mine testified that the indicted managers sabotaged the Stakhanovite movement to create dissatisfaction among the best workers. Another miner testified that workers had repeatedly reported gas accumulations and requested ventilators, but Liashchenko, the head of ventilation, told them, "We will install ventilators when Soviet power becomes wealthier." The procurator asked Liashchenko, "Was your declaration made with the aim of increasing workers' dissatisfaction? Was this the method of your counterrevolutionary activity?" Liashchenko replied, "Yes." When workers refused to enter gas-filled tunnels, Liashchenko accused them of disrupting production, and told them to dispel the gas by waving their jackets. A labor inspector testified that the tunnels were often filled with gas, and that he had ordered Liashchenko to install ventilators. Leonenko, manager of the Tsentral'naia mine, testified that he deliberately left standing water in the tunnels to create hardship for the miners, and Noskov, the mine's director, confessed that he planned multiple "blind alleys."[21] The procurator urged the defendants to admit that they *deliberately* aimed to murder workers. He asked Shubin, "Do you recognize that your actions in essence were tantamount to the murder of workers?" Shubin replied,

---

[18] Ibid.; "Protsess kontrrevoliutsionnoi Trotskistskoi vreditel'skoi gruppy na kemerovskom rudnike," part 2 and part 3.

[19] "Do kontsa iskorenit' Trotskistskikh merzavtsev!," *Trud*, November 20, 1936, p. 1.

[20] "Prigovor ozverelym vragam naroda," *Trud*, November 23, 1936, p. 1.

[21] "Protsess kontrrevoliutsionnoi Trotskistskoi vreditel'skoi gruppy na kemerovskom rudnike," part 2.

"It would not be hard to recognize that this was so." He asked Kovalenko, the mine's head engineer, "Would it be correct to conclude that you, as a member of this organization, consciously aimed to murder workers?" And he asked Leonenko whether he had "consciously poisoned tens of workers." Each of the defendants was required in turn to admit that the fatalities were not the result of negligence, but of conscious and deliberate action.[22]

The trial, like its August predecessor, blended the plausible with the fantastic. In fact, the mines were often filled with gas, the tunnels were poorly planned, and ventilators were absent. The procurator claimed that Kemerovo's managers *deliberately* refused to spend the state funds allocated to the mine for safety. More than three-quarters of the fund was "frozen" or unused. Unspent safety funds, however, were hardly unique to Kemerovo. Many managers did not spend monies allocated for safety, housing, or cultural services because shortages of building materials rendered them useless. Yet the procurator cast the unspent monies as proof of deliberate wrecking. He asked Andreev, the head engineer, what he had done to eliminate the "abominable conditions" in the mine. "Nothing," Andreev replied.[23] The problems in the Kemerovo mines, high accident rates, shoddy planning, and managerial negligence existed in every industry. They were the inevitable result of rapid industrialization and pressure to meet high production targets. The trial deflected blame, however, from the state to "enemies, who aimed to destroy the faith of workers in Soviet power."[24] The nine defendants, convicted solely on their interlocking testimonies, were shot.[25]

The message of the trial quickly found a receptive audience. Zakharov, a nonparty corer in the Stankolit factory, told his shopmates, "We have so much gas in the shop while we are working...The ventilators don't work despite the demands of the workers. We need to look around. Perhaps this is the work of the same bastards who poisoned the workers by gas in the Kuzbas."[26] Zakharov immediately interpreted the case to suit the workers' interests: perhaps someone would fix the ventilators if the

[22] Ibid.   [23] Ibid.

[24] "Soderzhanie prigovora."

[25] "Rech' gosudarstvennogo obvinitelia – zam. Prokuratora Soiuza SSR tov. Roginskogo," *Trud*, November 23, 1936, p. 2.

[26] TsAODM, f. 3, o. 49, d. 129, "Sekretariu MK i MGK VKP (b) tov. Khrushchevu N. S., sekretariu MGK tov. Kulikovu M. M., sekretariu MGK tov. Korytnomu S. Z.," ll. 119–120.

workers found a "wrecker" to blame. And he was not the only worker to grasp the utility of the case. Workers rapidly equated poor safety conditions, accidents, shoddy housing, and other problems of daily life with "wrecking." Did they believe that enemies deliberately sought to murder them? It is impossible to know. They did, however, realize that even a whisper of wrecking gained immediate attention from their supervisors.

After the Kemerovo trial, the factory newspapers were full of allegations. One newspaper openly asked, "If there are systematic disruptions in construction, violations of government instructions, freezing of millions of rubles, isn't this the work of enemy hands?" G. K. Ordzhonikidze, the commissar of heavy industry, received numerous letters from industrial directors complaining that they had become scapegoats for every difficulty. S. P. Birman, the director of the Petrovskii iron and steel works in Dnepropetrovsk, begged for "direction and advice." He explained that party directives encouraging "criticism and self-criticism" had been misused: "The foreign word *kritika* is often confused here with the Russian word 'to prattle' [*trepat'sia*]...Many here understand it to mean pouring rudeness all over each other, and primarily on leading officials, namely the managers and directors of large factories, who, according to the wave of a secret magic wand, are made the central target of their criticism." Birman charged that regional party officials were now occupied solely with agitating against managers. The Central Committee also received numerous letters of complaint. Stalin himself intervened after a director of an aircraft-engine factory complained that he and his fellow managers, all former Trotskyists, were being attacked solely for their past political mistakes. Stalin fired off a telegram to the Perm party secretary requesting that he "protect the director and his officials from defamation, and create around them an atmosphere of full confidence."[27] And, alongside complaints of persecution, Ordzhonikidze also received numerous denunciations, which he forwarded to Ezhov for further investigation.[28] Once the campaign against wrecking caught on, it proved irresistible to a variety of groups searching for scapegoats or solutions. Stalin's efforts to halt the campaign in this or that instance proved meaningless in the larger scheme of events.

---

[27] Cited by Molotov in his report on wrecking: "Materialy fevral'sko-martovskogo plenuma," *Voprosy istorii*, 8, 1993, pp. 20, 18–19.

[28] By the end of 1936, 43 of 823 leading managers in the NKTP had been expelled from the Party and arrested: Oleg Khlevniuk, *In Stalin's Shadow: The Career of "Sergo" Ordzhonikidze* (M. E. Sharpe, Armonk, NY, 1995), pp. 112–14, 116.

The Trial of the "Anti-Soviet Parallel Trotskyist Center"

The Kemerovo trial served as a dress rehearsal for the second Moscow show trial, which opened on January 23, 1937. Almost half of the defendants – Piatakov, Muralov, Drobnis, Boguslavskii, Shestov, Stroilov, and Arnol'd – had been implicated in the Kemerovo trial, and several had testified. Two members of the court were also veterans of the Kemerovo trial: Ul'rikh served again as chair of the Military Kollegiia of the Supreme Court, and N. M. Rychkov as a member of the *troika* that judged the case. Moreover, wrecking in Kemerovo was one of three conspiracies that constituted the January trial. Seventeen defendants were tried for treason, espionage, and wrecking, including Piatakov, the deputy commissar of heavy industry, K. B. Radek, *Izvestiia* editor and member of the Constitutional Commission, and Sokolnikov, the deputy commissar of foreign affairs. Most of the defendants were former Trotskyists, and several, including Piatakov, Radek, Muralov, and Serebriakov, had been personally close to Trotsky. Some were arrested well before the Kemerovo explosion, others soon after.[29]

The January trial featured numerous plots, and a complex chronology of oppositional activities dating back to the late 1920s. Vyshinskii, reprising his role as procurator, charged that the defendants had formed a "Parallel Trotskyist Center" to serve as a reserve in the event that the "Trotskyist-Zinovievite Center" was exposed. Motivated by a profound hatred for Stalin, they aimed to cripple and sell off Soviet industry, restore capitalism, disband the collective farms, and weaken the country's defense. Promising territorial concessions to the Germans and Japanese, they planned to take power once the USSR was defeated in war.[30] As in the August 1936 and Kemerovo trials, the state's case hinged entirely upon the defendants' confessions. The case was built around three loosely connected wrecking conspiracies, linking mining, railroads, and the chemical industry. Coal mined in the Kuzbas was shipped by rail to iron and steel

---

[29] *Report of Court Proceedings in the Case of the Anti-Soviet Trotskyite Centre* (People's Commissariat of Justice, Moscow, 1937) (hereafter cited as *Case of the Anti-Soviet Trotskyite Centre*). The defendants were Iu. L. Piatakov, K. B. Radek, G. Ia. Sokolnikov, L. P. Serebriakov, N. I. Muralov, Ia. A. Livshits, Ia. N. Drobnis, M. S. Boguslavskii, I. A. Kniazev, S. A. Rataichak, B. O. Norkin, A. A. Shestov, M. S. Stroilov, I. D. Turok, I. I. Grashe, G. E. Pushin, and V. V. Arnol'd. Muralov, for example, a former member of the left opposition exiled to Novosibirsk in the late 1920s, had been arrested in spring 1936. He refused to admit any wrongdoing, however, and held out against his interrogators until December.

[30] *Case of the Anti-Soviet Trotskyite Centre*, pp. 6–18, 372, 574–5.

plants, where it was used in the coking process to produce nitrogenous fertilizers and other chemical byproducts. The defendants were grouped by industry and region: Muralov, Drobnis, Boguslavskii, Norkin, Shestov, Stroilov, and Arnol'd in Western Siberia; Rataichak and Pushin in the chemical sector in Ukraine; and Serebriakov, Livshits, Kniazev, and Turok on the southern railroads. As in the Kemerovo trial, the prosecution linked former Trotskyists with industrial managers, and presented innocent workers and soldiers as the main victims. Vyshinskii also described several subplots of attempted murder of Soviet leaders, but these were mere embellishments to the primary motifs of opposition, wrecking, and fascist espionage.

The threads of the conspiracy all led back to Piatakov, the central figure in the trial. An active member of the left opposition in 1926–7, Piatakov was briefly expelled from the Party. He recanted and rejoined in 1928, allegedly encouraging other Trotskyists to follow. The Party, short of dedicated organizers, put many former oppositionists to work in leading industrial posts. Radek testified that, despite outward expressions of loyalty, they continued to harbor strong doubts about policy. They also maintained close ties, hired each other for jobs, and shared information about problems in industry and agriculture.[31] His description of the mindset and activities of the former oppositionists seemed utterly plausible. Radek and the defendants also confessed that they stayed in contact with Trotsky. Their testimonies repeated confessions already heard in the Kemerovo trial. Once again, several testified that Piatakov and Shestov, a member of the Eastern and Siberian Coal Trust, met with Sedov, Trotsky's son, on a buying trip in Berlin in May 1931. Sedov allegedly told them to resume the struggle against the Stalinist leadership using terrorism and wrecking. When Shestov returned to the Kuzbas, he contacted engineers from the Shakhty case, instructed Arnol'd, a chauffeur, to prepare an auto accident involving Molotov, and began wrecking in the mines. Piatakov set up a phony buying scheme with a German firm to funnel state funds to Trotsky.[32] According to the plot, Shestov returned to the Soviet Union in November 1931 with letters from Trotsky for Piatakov and Muralov hidden in a pair of shoes. Piatakov testified that Trotsky's letter instructed him to use "every means" to remove Stalin, unite the opposition, and wreck industry. Piatakov began reviving his old Trotskyist

---

[31] Ibid.; see testimony of V. F. Loginov, the manager of a coke trust in Kharkov, and Radek's last plea, pp. 176–9, 541–51.

[32] Ibid., pp. 160–2, 21–45.

contacts, including Livshits, the head of railways in Ukraine. In the summer of 1932, Piatakov went abroad, and once again met Sedov in Berlin. When he returned to Moscow in the fall, he met with Kamenev, who told him that he had established a "Trotskyist-Zinovievite center" and urged him to create "a parallel center." In the fall of 1932, Piatakov established the "parallel center," which began active wrecking in the mining and chemical sectors. Radek joined in November.[33]

According to the charges, Piatakov, as deputy commissar of heavy industry, was superbly positioned to place Trotskyists in key industrial posts. He appointed Drobnis deputy chief of construction in Kemerovo and put him in contact with other Trotskyists, including Shestov. Vyshinskii charged that this West Siberian group wrecked in the mines, delayed the construction of coke plants, ensured that "vast structures were in a perpetual state of construction," wasted money, and drafted poor designs. Coal from Kemerovo was so poor in quality that it produced explosions at the district power plant. The Kemerovo coke-oven industry deliberately shipped poor-quality coke to Urals iron and steel plants. At the same time, wreckers in the Urals built housing downwind from the fumes of the Central Urals Copper Works to poison the workers. Other wreckers on the railroads created accidents, disrupted freight traffic, refused to increase the running norms for boxcars and engines, and underused engine capacity by running empty boxcars. Vyshinskii badgered the defendants to admit that they wanted and intended workers to die.[34] The wrecking charges comprised a full and accurate summary of existing problems in industry and transport: construction delays, train accidents and mine explosions, disrupted rail shipping, poorly planned workers' settlements, and wasted chemical byproducts. These problems, however, stemmed largely from new and unfamiliar technology, labor shortage and turnover, and inexperienced planners and engineers, all unavoidable consequences of rapid industrialization.

The defendants firmly implicated the "rightists" in the plot to overthrow the government, a connection only hinted at in the August 1936 trial. Piatakov testified that Kamenev told him in fall 1932 that his "center" had made contact with Bukharin, Rykov, and Tomskii. Radek testified that Bukharin admitted in 1934 that he and N. A. Uglanov had taken the terrorist path. Uglanov, "a tough-minded and reliable anti-Trotskyist," had been appointed secretary of the Moscow party committee in 1924 to

[33] Ibid., pp. 32, 85–7, 216–33.
[34] Ibid., pp. 46, 205–15, 168–75, 211–14, 51.

oversee the purge of leftists. He had served as head of the Commissariat of Labor until 1930, and in the Commissariat of Heavy Machine Construction until 1933. Piatakov reported that he met with Bukharin, Tomskii, and Sokolnikov in the summer of 1935, and by December the rightists had joined the "parallel center."[35] The charges once again blended fact and fantasy. Sokolnikov, the deputy commissar for foreign affairs and the only "rightist" among the defendants, did arrange a meeting between Zinoviev and Bukharin in 1928 in an attempt to create common cause. In the January 1937 trial, he was forced to replay his earlier role as link between right and left by implicating Bukharin and other "rightists."[36]

The defendants had been carefully coached, yet some of their testimonies appeared strangely unscripted and intensely moving. Piatakov displayed the pitiful remnants of a shredded revolutionary honor. He testified calmly to fantastic murder plots and wrecking, but balked at Vyshinskii's suggestion that he had spoken negatively about Soviet workers. Several defendants spoke eloquently about their disagreements with Stalin's policies. In the August trial, Vyshinskii repeatedly insisted that the defendants had no alternate political program. In January, the defendants carefully described the Riutin Platform of 1932 and the painful social costs of industrialization and collectivization. In foreign policy, too, they hinted at hidden disagreements among party leaders. Radek testified, for example, that some state and military circles supported "the Rapallo line" or rapprochement with Germany. While it seemed unbelievable in 1937 that dedicated communists would ally with fascists, Stalin's nonaggression pact with Hitler in 1939 suggested that Radek may have truthfully rendered one current of opinion. And Radek, in his final plea, reminded the court that the prosecution's entire case rested entirely on Piatakov's confession and two letters from Trotsky that had been "burned." "All the testimony of the other accused," he cautioned, "rests on our testimony." Finally, the political doubts that Vyshinskii elicited from the defendants were not implausible. It would have been far odder if these strong, independent-minded former oppositionists had become ardent and uncritical Stalinists upon their return to the Party. Yet the purpose of the trial was not to extract the truth but to make criminal accusations plausible by imbedding them in partial truth. The verdict was set before the trial

---

[35] Ibid., pp. 23, 34, 99, 66; Catherine Merridale, "The Reluctant Opposition: The Right 'Deviation' in Moscow, 1928," *Soviet Studies*, 41, 3 (1989), pp. 385–6.

[36] Samuel Oppenheim, "Between Left and Right: G. Ia. Sokolnikov and the Development of the Soviet State, 1921–1929," *Slavic Review*, 48, 4 (1989), p. 613.

began. With the exception of Sokolnikov, Radek, and Arnol'd, who each received ten years, and Stroilov, who received eight, the defendants were all shot.[37] Sokolnikov and Radek were both later murdered in prison.

On the last day of the trial, the Moscow party committee and the unions called a mass meeting to announce the verdict. Thousands of workers crowded into Red Square to hear N. S. Khrushchev, secretary of the Moscow committee, and other speakers from the factories. Khrushchev appealed directly to the workers: "Trotskyists wanted to destroy the seven-hour working day, to destroy our great laws on labor, rest, education, to resurrect the horrors of unemployment which the workers of our country escaped through the victory of socialism." To deafening applause, he summarized the charges: "They organized explosions in the enterprises, they spied for fascist intelligence, they murdered and poisoned workers and Red Army soldiers, adults and children. They permitted the derailment of trains [carrying] our glorious soldiers, wrecked transport, and received money from Japanese counterintelligence... Raising a hand against Comrade Stalin, they raised it against all the best that humanity has because Stalin is the best hope, aspiration, and beacon of progressive humanity. Stalin is our banner, Stalin is our will, Stalin is our victory." As the workers cheered, the orchestra struck up the Internationale. Another speaker asked the workers to approve the sentence, and thousands of hands shot up in the air. He read, "The sentence of the Trotskyist band brought by the proletarian court; this is the sentence of all the Soviet people."[38] Like the huge factory meetings held in August, the rally sought to ensure that the workers understood the trial's message and collectively endorsed its verdict.

The February–March 1937 Plenum

Less than a month after the trial ended, the Central Committee Plenum met from February 22–March 7, 1937. Many historians recognize the plenum as a turning point in the development of the terror, although for years its proceedings were known only through rumor and hearsay.[39]

---

[37] *Case of the Anti-Soviet Trotskyite Centre*, pp. 444–5, 51, 543.

[38] TsAODM, f. 3, o. 50, d. 5, "Stenogramma obshchemoskovskogo mitinga trudiashchikhsia," ll. 1–13.

[39] Gabor Rittersporn, *Stalinist Simplifications and Soviet Complications: Social Tensions and Political Conflicts in the USSR, 1933–1953* (Harwood Academic Publishers, Chur, 1991), pp. 114–39; J. Arch Getty, "The Politics of Repression Revisited," in Getty and Roberta Manning, eds., *Stalinist Terror: New Perspectives* (Cambridge University Press,

The editors of *Voprosy Istorii* noted, "the signal for a new wave of mass repression was given at the February–March plenum."[40] J. Arch Getty and Oleg Naumov argued that it redirected the purge from lower party cadres to regional leaders.[41] Yet few historians have analyzed the plenum's proceedings, and interest has centered mainly on the fates of Bukharin and Rykov. The plenum, however, was a rich and complicated affair. The "new wave of mass repression" was prompted not only by the arrest of Bukharin and Rykov, but, more importantly, also by a new and unprecedented emphasis on "democracy." Several keynote speakers, including Stalin and A. A. Zhdanov, secretary of the Central Committee and the Leningrad regional and city committees, stressed the need for multicandidate, secret-ballot elections for posts within the Party, the soviets, and the unions. They sharply criticized a political culture that had grown increasingly ossified and bureaucratic, stressing the need to reinvigorate governing institutions from below. The plenum, which would provide the future marching orders for the Party, thus opened the door to a whirlwind of mass mobilization.

The agenda of the plenum included the fate of Bukharin and Rykov, industrial wrecking, the upcoming elections to the soviets, the need for greater party and union democracy, and Trotskyism. The discussion of Bukharin and Rykov, marked by rude accusations and piteous defenses, ended with the Central Committee's vote to expel them from the Party, and to march them directly from the plenum to prison. They were both executed a year later in the last of the Moscow show trials.[42] The plenum's two major themes, repression and democracy, appearing as polar opposites at first glance, proved to be closely intertwined. Speakers used the word democracy (*demokratiia*) to include secret ballots, direct elections, single candidates in place of lists, open debate of candidates' merits,

New York, 1993), pp. 55–59; Khlevniuk, *1937-i: Stalin, NKVD i sovetskoe obshch-estvo*, pp. 72–153. Roy Medvedev, *Let History Judge: The Origins and Consequences of Stalinism* (Columbia University Press, New York 1989), pp. 364–8, contains an accurate description of the Bukharin and Rykov cases. William Chase, *Enemies Within the Gates?: The Comintern and the Stalinist Repression, 1924–1939* (Yale University Press, New Haven and London, 2001), pp. 221–8, describes the effect of the plenum on the Comintern. The full stenographic report was published in *Voprosy Istorii* in installments from 1992 to 1995. Getty and Naumov provide a long excerpt in English dealing mainly with the cases of Bukharin and Rykov: *The Road to Terror*, pp. 364–419.

[40] "Materialy fevral'sko-martovskogo plenuma," *Voprosy istorii*, 2–3, 1992, p. 3.

[41] Getty and Naumov, *The Road to Terror*, pp. 358–9.

[42] Ibid., pp. 364–419. On the third Moscow show trial, see Wladislaw Hedeler, "Ezhov's Scenario for the Great Terror and the Falsified Record of the Third Moscow Show Trial," in Barry McLoughlin and Kevin McDermott, *Stalin's Terror: High Politics and Mass Repression in the Soviet Union* (Palgrave, Basingstoke and New York, 2003), pp. 34–55.

criticism from below, popular empowerment, and mass control. Stalin, for example, insisted not only on secret-ballot elections, but on the accountability of leaders to the people they represented.[43] Party leaders, angry at the inability of lower organizations to purge themselves of oppositionists, moved to mobilize the rank and file. Democracy was thus a way to increase support, invigorate the rank and file, and, at the same time, ensure a more thorough purge of regional elites.

Although party leaders invoked the ideals of democracy, the plenum itself was far from democratic. Politburo leaders scripted and carefully vetted the key speeches and final resolutions in advance.[44] In the unscripted discussions that followed the keynote speeches, plenum delegates did not debate each other or present conflicting opinions. Stalin received a large measure of sycophantic deference. V. M. Molotov, chairman of the Council of People's Commissars, and once described by Bukharin as a "lead butt who was still struggling to understand Marxism,"[45] groped repeatedly for some serviceable quote from Stalin to provide the ballast he needed to navigate the choppy political waters. Contention surfaced mainly in the form of personal attack. V. I. Polonskii, a secretary of the All Union Central Council of Unions (VTsSPS), launched a sharp attack on N. M. Shvernik, its first secretary. Ia. A. Iakovlev, the head of the Party Control Commission, undermined the creditability of N. S. Khrushchev, the head of the Moscow city and regional party committee, and A. A. Andreev, Central Committee secretary, denounced S. Kh. Vardanian, the head of the Taganrog party committee. In other words, the plenum presented the odd spectacle of leading party members defending democracy by denouncing each other's bureaucratic practices. The theme of democracy proved even more explosive at the lower ranks. It unleashed "serious insurrections" within the Party as local cadres turned on their leaders.[46] And it spilled beyond the Party, provoking one of the few unscripted decisions of

---

[43] "Materialy fevral'sko-martovskogo plenuma," *Voprosy istorii*, 11–12, 1995, pp. 20, 14–15.

[44] Khlevniuk, *In Stalin's Shadow*, pp. 143–6. An expanded group of Politburo and Central Committee members met before the plenum to draft and affirm resolutions based on the main speeches. The group included Stalin, Andreev, Voroshilov, Kaganovich, Kalinin, Mikoian, Molotov, Ordzhonikidze, and Chubar; candidate members Zhdanov and Petrovskii; and Central Committee members Antipov, Bauman, Bubnov, Vareikis, Gamarnik, Krupskaia, Litvinov, Mezhlauk, Piatnitskii, Khrushchev, and Shvernik, members of the Party Control Commission and the Soviet Control Commission; and others.

[45] Larina, *This I Cannot Forget*, p. 113.

[46] Getty and Naumov, *The Road to Terror*, pp. 358–9.

the plenum: to organize secret-ballot elections within the unions. Within less than a month, the principles of democracy articulated by the plenum would turn the unions upside down and create a frantic scramble for power and survival.

The Hunt for Wreckers

The plenum opened in the shadows of the Kemerovo and January trials. G. K. (Sergo) Ordzhonikidze, the commissar of heavy industry, scheduled to give the keynote speech on wrecking, killed himself on February 18. His suicide delayed the opening of the plenum by several days.[47] Throughout the fall of 1936, Ordzhonikidze had been reluctant to accept the new politicization of production. He recognized that baseless allegations of wrecking could only weaken industry by providing political excuses for organizational and technical problems. Yet, after the trials, he was clinging to a tightrope of rationality in a rising gale of hysteria. On February 5, Ordzhonikidze sent a technical expert, Professor N. Gel'perin, to Kemerovo to investigate how to improve production in the wake of the arrests. His carefully worded instructions suggested that he was interested in technical issues rather than politics. He told Gel'perin, "You yourself have most likely been influenced by the most recent trial. So remember that cowardly, insufficiently conscientious people may wish to blame everything on wrecking because, so to say, they bury all their own mistakes in the wrecking trial." He cautioned him, "It would be essentially wrong to allow this. We would not be able to get a precise picture of the consequences and we would not know how to correct them. You must approach this business as a technician. You must attempt to distinguish conscious wrecking from involuntary mistakes." In not so many words, Ordzhonikidze asked Gel'perin to ignore allegations of wrecking and concentrate on technical issues. Gel'perin returned to Moscow on February 17 and delivered his report to Ordzhonikidze later that evening. Ordzhonikidze asked him many technical questions about Kemerovo's nitrogen plant and the mood of the engineering and managerial personnel. He seemed particularly worried that morale had collapsed and that baseless allegations had become a substitute for work. He asked Gel'perin to deliver his written report within two days, but Gel'perin never had the opportunity. Ordzhonikidze arrived home after midnight to find

---

[47] Khlevniuk, *In Stalin's Shadow*, p. 144; Solomon, *Soviet Criminal Justice Under Stalin*, p. 240.

that the NKVD had searched his apartment. After a stormy conversation with Stalin, he remained sequestered at home the following day. Toward dusk, he shot himself. Gel'perin, serving as an honor guard, next saw Ordzhonikidze in his open casket.[48]

The suicide, known only to a handful of party leaders, was presented to the plenum delegates and the general public as a heart attack. Coming in the wake of the trials and arrests of managers, Ordzhonikidze's speech was to have summarized the current situation in industry. In his absence, Molotov delivered the speech.[49] Apologizing to the delegates for his unfamiliarity with the subject, he began by reviewing the confessions of the defendants in the January trial. Once again, the delegates heard the grisly recital of mining, railroad, and chemical accidents. "Bourgeois specialists" had been involved in wrecking since 1917, Molotov explained, but the current wreckers were "protected by party cards." Led by Piatakov, they had deliberately placed unskilled workers on complicated machinery, produced constant stoppages, and created "complete chaos" in copper smelting, nonferrous metallurgy, construction, and other sectors. They were responsible for wage arrears, poor housing, accidents, fires, and poisoning. "I speak mainly about heavy industry," Molotov explained. "This doesn't mean there is no wrecking in other branches." Opening the door to a new wave of arrests, he noted that there was wrecking in light industry as well, "although we still have not discovered it."[50]

Amplifying the message of the Kemerovo and January trials, Molotov stressed that workers were the primary victims of these plots. Wreckers, eager to turn workers against Soviet power, deliberately created harsh working and living conditions. In an industrial town near Moscow, wreckers designed the sewer and factory waste pipes to empty into the river upstream of the workers' settlement. Workers, who used the river water for drinking, cooking, and washing, suffered repeated epidemics of dysentery and typhoid fever. Not understanding that wreckers were trying to poison them, they blamed the Party and the government for polluting the river. Molotov clearly stated that difficulties on the job, in housing, and with the food supply were likely the result of wrecking. His

[48] N. Gel'perin, "Direktivy narkoma," *Za industrializatsiiu*, February 21, 1937, p. 8. On the hours leading up to Ordzhonikidze's suicide, see Khlevniuk, *In Stalin's Shadow*, pp. 143–9.

[49] Khlevniuk argues that Ordzhonikidze's speech would have been more moderate than Molotov's: *In Stalin's Shadow*, pp. 164–5. Yet Molotov, too, vacillated on how broadly to define wrecking.

[50] "Materialy fevral'sko-martovskogo plenuma," *Voprosy istorii*, 8, 1993, pp. 7–8, 10, 11.

speech, reprinted in part in newspapers, provided workers with a new rhetoric for their longstanding grievances, and a quick remedy for painful conditions.

Yet Molotov's speech was not without its caveats. Enemies were not responsible for *every* industrial problem. How was a party member or worker to determine the difference between enemy wrecking and honest mistakes? Molotov had no clear answers. Instead, he offered the delegates several contradictory examples. On the one hand, he sharply criticized a mine manager for protecting one of his engineers. The manager had called the engineer "a fool, not a wrecker," but in the wake of an explosion, cave-in, flood, and avalanche, the engineer confessed to the NKVD that he had deliberately wrecked the mine. The manager, Molotov noted, was sheltering an enemy, a serious crime in itself. On the other hand, he urged party leaders and managers not "to dump guilt on each other" or make false and dangerous assumptions. He explained, "We cannot take the position that, just because this or that official was once a Trotskyist, or spoke against the Party, we should refuse to use them." Many former Trotskyists, in his estimation, were doing excellent work. Molotov thus sent the delegates a confusing and frightening message: he counseled moderation in approach and dire consequences for failure. His only real piece of advice was that the delegates should "know the people below them closely."[51] This seemingly benign counsel set off a witch hunt in the factory party committees. Armed with Molotov's words, and terrified by the arrests, members began checking each other's biographies, requesting data from distant party committees, and uncovering new suspects with each fresh investigation.

Andreev and Stalin both supported Molotov, criticizing party leaders for disregarding "politics" in their single-minded focus on industrialization. Andreev, Central Committee secretary, noted that in the Azov-Black Sea region, all the party secretaries in the large towns as well as scores of leaders in the soviets, industry, trade, training schools, and the Komsomol had been arrested as "Trotskyists." They had set up little fiefdoms, where they flaunted their power before the workers. Vardanian, for example, was transferred from the Central Committee of the Armenian party to head the Taganrog city committee. "Actually," Andreev sneered, "he became the prince of Taganrog." He surrounded himself by loyal toadies. The workers were so disgusted that they renamed the street where he lived, "Lickspittle Street." Vardanian was ultimately unmasked as a

---

[51] Ibid., pp. 21, 20, 18, 19.

"Trotskyist" and arrested. Andreev argued that the Azov-Black Sea party organization was blind to the enemies in its midst because it had placed politics below economics. Deeply concerned with improving agriculture, its members were "all busy becoming first-rate agronomists."[52] Stalin, too, stressed the need to bring back "politics." The Party had failed to expose its enemies because its leaders were "fixated on plans, on fulfillment and overfulfillment." The economic successes of the first and second five-year plans had "created a mood of bragging, of parade-ism, parading our successes." Everything else, including the precarious international situation, had come to seem "petty and unimportant." Stalin mimicked the Party's economic leaders, "Strange people are sitting there in Moscow, in the Central Committee: they invent some kind of issue, push the idea of some kind of wrecking, they themselves don't sleep, and they don't let anyone else sleep." Stalin counseled party members to keep capitalist encirclement and the threat of spies and counterintelligence agents in mind at all times.[53] He decried the widely held "putrid theories" that successful managers could not be wreckers, that Trotskyists no longer posed a threat, or that wrecking was a Moscow fantasy. Successful performance was not synonymous with loyalty. In fact, success was often an enemy's most effective mask. In his concluding speech, Stalin urged party leaders to return to "politics," to stop selecting old personal acquaintances for posts, to promote local cadres, and to support secret ballots and direct elections.[54] "Democracy," in Stalin's view, was a powerful weapon against Trotskyists and wreckers.

Elections to the Soviets

The new emphasis on democracy in the Party was prompted not only by the hunt for enemies, but also by the upcoming elections to the soviets. A new constitution had recently been adopted, introducing an electoral system that extended voting rights to all citizens, including former nobles, White Guards, priests, dispossessed kulaks, and others groups formerly excluded from the political process (*lishentsy*). Urban votes would no longer be weighted more heavily than rural votes; all would be counted equally. Voting to the mid- and higher-level soviets would occur directly, by separate candidates rather than lists, and by secret rather than open

---

[52] "Materialy fevral'sko-martovskogo plenuma," *Voprosy istorii*, 8, 1995, pp. 3–10.
[53] "Materialy fevral'sko-martovskogo plenuma," *Voprosy istorii*, 3, 1995, pp. 11–14.
[54] "Materialy fevral'sko-martovskogo plenuma," *Voprosy istorii*, 11–12, 1995, pp. 12–15.

ballot. The Stalin Constitution, as it was widely known, marked "a turning point in the political life of the country."[55]

Although the plenum delegates uniformly praised the new constitution, they were deeply concerned about the outcome of the upcoming elections. Many feared that the Party lacked sufficient support to maintain its predominant political position. Zhdanov noted gravely that the introduction of democratic elections was "a very serious exam for our Party."[56] A gallows humor, based on anxiety that the Party might not weather a genuine referendum on its leadership, characterized many of the delegates' comments. When I. D. Kabakov, head of the Sverdlovsk regional committee, dully intoned, "Never have the masses of people been such active creators of socialist development and socialist society as after the acceptance of the constitution," A. I. Mikoian quipped to nervous laughter, "Yeah, there is going to be a big bang."[57] Zhdanov warned that the Party, lacking experience with secret-ballot elections and individual candidates, would face "enemy agitation and enemy candidates." Religious groups were already reviving and petitioning to reopen the churches.[58]

Various speakers voiced concern that the Party had little contact with people in isolated rural areas, impoverished urban neighborhoods, new workers' settlements, and enclaves of exiled kulaks. R. I. Eikhe, head of the Siberian and West Siberian regional committees and the Novosibirsk city committee, referred to the "unkempt desolate villages and similar areas in the towns" inhabited by embittered peasants, impoverished "former people," criminals, prostitutes, *bezprizorniki* (homeless children), and other poor and desperate castoffs of industrialization. In Western Siberia, large groups of exiled kulaks nursed deep grudges against the government and "would slander and provoke during the elections." If party candidates were to win, they would have to become "answerable to the people" and "closer to people in a real way."[59] Other delegates were anxious about voters in industrializing regions with rapid population growth. Kabakov admitted that harsh conditions sometimes created hostility to Soviet power. Labor shortages had "opened huge cracks for a stream of foreign elements." In the Sverdlovsk region alone, more than 1.2 million people had migrated from the countryside to the towns and

---

[55] "Materialy fevral'sko-martovskogo plenuma," *Voprosy istorii*, 7, 1993, p. 21.

[56] "Materialy fevral'sko-martovskogo plenuma," *Voprosy istorii*, 5, 1993, pp. 3–4.

[57] "Materialy fevral'sko-martovskogo plenuma," *Voprosy istorii*, 6, 1993, p. 27.

[58] "Materialy fevral'sko-martovskogo plenuma," *Voprosy istorii*, 5, 1993, pp. 4–5.

[59] "Materialy fevral'sko-martovskogo plenuma," *Voprosy istorii*, 6, 1993, pp. 5–6.

construction sites.[60] A. S. Kalygina, head of the Voronezh city committee, noted that the city had expanded tenfold since the beginning of the first five-year plan. She, too, had her doubts about how new workers would vote. There were only 2,000 communists for 50,000 workers, and only 550 actually worked "at the bench" or in production. No more than 1 percent of the workers in most of Voronezh's factories were party members. Moreover, the city, used as a place of exile, harbored many people hostile to the Soviet state.[61] S. V. Kosior, secretary of the Ukrainian Central Committee, was concerned about the craftsmen, workers in small factories, housewives, white-collar workers, technical intelligentsia, and "backward people" who comprised 50 to 60 percent of his electorate. He added anxiously, "We have done absolutely no work with these layers of the population." The Party had concentrated most of its organizing and educational efforts among industrial workers, believing it "beneath our dignity to work among white-collar employees," who were "considered second-class citizens." Even in the factories, as much as 80 percent of agitation work was "toothless." Several newly formed Ukrainian religious groups had recently sent greetings to Stalin and the Central Committee, praising the new constitution for its affirmation of religious freedom. Kosior added, "The comrades are totally bewildered. Should we forbid this? Well, the people have the right to send greetings to their leader. Should we allow this? The devil knows what will come of it." Democracy was reviving all sorts of tendencies the Bolsheviks had tried to discourage. And now all these people would be voting![62]

The pervasive anxiety of the plenum delegates was an indication of precisely how democratic the constitution intended elections to the soviets to be. If the leaders had not taken the rights prescribed by the constitution at face value, they would not have been fearful of the outcome. They would not have worried how exiled kulaks, rural migrants, new workers, small craftsmen, housewives, "former people" (*byvshie liudi*), and peasants might vote. In July 1937, these fears would provoke mass roundups of "hostile" elements in the "wild and desolate corners" in both town and country, but in February party leaders intended to face the election squarely.[63] They would have to rely heavily on rank-and-file members in

[60] Ibid., p. 27.
[61] "Materialy fevral'sko-martovskogo plenuma," *Voprosy istorii*, 7, 1993, pp. 3–5.
[62] "Materialy fevral'sko-martovskogo plenuma," *Voprosy istorii*, 6, 1993, pp. 6–9.
[63] J. Arch Getty, "State and Society Under Stalin: Constitutions and Elections in the 1930s," *Slavic Review*, 50, 1 (1991), pp. 18–35; Paul Hagenloh, "Socially Harmful Elements and the Great Terror," in Sheila Fitzpatrick, ed., *Stalinism: New Directions* (Routledge,

the factories, schools, and collective farms to create support for their program and their candidates. Yet in much the same way that the Party was disconnected from the people, party leaders were distanced from their own rank and file. A successful electoral outcome would require an invigorated party, a close connection between leaders and the rank and file, and active mobilization of the voting public.

Party Democracy

In his keynote speech on the erosion of democracy within the Party, Zhdanov advanced the idea that the Party needed to empower the rank and file. He highlighted the widespread practice of *kooptatsiia* or "appointments," which had replaced elections in staffing posts. *Kooptatsiia* promoted the formation of tight cliques, loyal only to the leader who appointed them. The practice had become so common that some local organizations did not have a single elected official. City, district, and primary party committees were supposed to be elected each year; regional and union republic central committees, every eighteen months. Yet the majority of party organizations had not held elections since 1934.[64] Moreover, when elections were held, the results were predetermined. Several days before a party conference, Zhdanov explained, the secretary of the primary party organization would "go into a corner somewhere" and draw up a list of candidates. The list would be formalized in advance in a small closed meeting, and the election "transformed into a simple formality" lasting no more than twenty minutes. Zhdanov complained that this "back-door" decision-making was "a violation of the legal rights of party members and of party democracy." In many factories, selected delegates rather than members at large elected the party committee, effectively "depriving two-thirds of our membership of the right to vote." General party meetings were disappearing altogether, in favor of smaller shop committee gatherings. When the rank and file met, they were unfamiliar with the agenda and the items were unrelated to their real concerns.

London, 1999), pp. 286–308; Barry McLoughlin, "Mass Operations of the NKVD, 1937–1939: A Survey" (pp. 118–52), and David Shearer, "Social Disorder, Mass Repression and the NKVD During the 1930s" (pp. 85–117), both in McLoughlin and McDermott, *Stalin's Terror.*

[64] More than 10 percent of members of the regional and national central committee plenums were appointed rather than elected. In the district and town committees, the numbers were even higher, reaching 60 percent: "Materialy fevral'sko-martovskogo plenuma," *Voprosy istorii*, 5, 1993, pp. 6–8, 9–10.

Resolutions were prepared in advance and there was no debate. Meetings had been reduced to mere formalities.[65]

The plenum's decision to promote democracy was not only related to the revitalization of the rank and file. Stalin and other leaders were concerned that a thorough purge of oppositionists was impossible as long as tight cliques or circles continued to control the regional and local party committees. These "circles of protection" appointed, shielded, and aided their members, often in contravention of orders from Moscow. Many had their origin in longstanding friendships dating back to the revolution, Civil War, and oppositions of the 1920s. Zhdanov invoked democracy not only as means to revitalize the Party but to eliminate enemies. Party members, appointed to important posts, brought entire entourages to fill the posts below them. They created an atmosphere of *semeistvennost'* or "family-ness" based on circles of mutual protection.[66] Several party leaders offered examples from their own regional organizations. Eikhe noted that party committee secretaries in Western Siberia were rarely elected. Secret-ballot elections would undermine the reigning code of mutual protection in "family circles."[67] Kosior pointed out that in some regions in Ukraine the *entire* leadership had been appointed. *Kooptatsiia* encouraged party leaders to cultivate personal connections "to build up their own positions."[68] Not beholden to an electorate, wielding vast power to hire and fire, they built up personal fiefdoms. A. I. Ugarov, former secretary of the Leningrad party committee, claimed that it was "blocked up" with counterrevolutionaries, supporters of Zinoviev, and rightists. The party organization had become ossified and complacent. "Parades, clamor, boasting, glorification of leaders, and toadyism" had replaced honest, direct relations. At a recent meeting, Ugarov noted, after a party committee secretary spoke to thousands of workers, the local newspaper rhapsodized, "The working class listened with great love to the secretary's speech." Ugarov noted with disgust, "This is obviously false and distorts our relationship with workers."[69] Eikhe, Kosior, and Ugarov all spoke in favor of reinvigorating the lower ranks by breaking up the family circles, which had become an obstacle to the identification and removal of former oppositionists or "enemies." Yet as secretaries of regional or city party committees, they too were participants in the system

---

[65] Ibid., pp. 9–11.   [66] Ibid., pp. 6–8.
[67] "Materialy fevral'sko-martovskogo plenuma," *Voprosy istorii*, 6, 1993, p. 3.
[68] Ibid., p. 10.
[69] "Materialy fevral'sko-martovskogo plenuma," *Voprosy istorii*, 10, 1995, pp. 22–4.

they criticized. As patrons with their own circles of power, their endorsements of democracy had an odd ring. Were they mobilizing their own rank and file against themselves? Within the next two years, all three men would fall victim to their own rhetoric, arrested and shot by the NKVD.

The resolutions adopted by the plenum, based on Zhdanov's speech, established the future policy of the Party. They aimed to eliminate *kooptatsiia* and restore the rules of election, to replace open voting by list with secret ballots and individual candidates, and to promote the "unlimited right to criticize." Elections were to be held at every level from the primary party organizations to the republic central committees by May 20. Time limits for elected offices were to be strictly observed. Direct elections were to be held in general party meetings, not smaller shop groups.[70] Taken together, the resolutions aimed to reinvigorate the Party and to reconnect its leaders with its base. The speakers did not see any contradiction between eliminating enemies and empowering the rank and file. In fact, both these policies were seen as part of the same aim: a revitalized and united Party.

"Trotskyists" and "Little People"

Plenum delegates also took up the review (*proverka*) and exchange (*obmen*) of party cards launched in May 1935 as part of their new emphasis on democracy. The results of the *proverka* had been an ongoing source of contention. Central party leaders argued that the party committees had expelled rank-and-file workers for trivialities, while allowing the real enemies to slip through. Ezhov and Stalin voiced strong dissatisfaction with regional leaders at the Central Committee plenums in June and December 1936. Representatives from the Moscow city committee personally upbraided the district organizers in September for their chaotic record keeping, disorganization, and lackadaisical approach. The city leaders' irritation with the district organizers was a direct response to Moscow's displeasure with them.

Eikhe and Ia. A. Iakovlev, the head of the Party Control Commission, raised the issue again at the February–March Plenum. Eikhe contended that a large percentage of those expelled from the Party in Siberia "were not enemies, but loyal to the Party and Soviet power." Most troubling,

---

[70] "Materialy fevral'sko-martovskogo plenuma," *Voprosy istorii*, 5, 1993, pp. 12–14; 7, 1993, p. 23.

the number expelled from the Party in his region was more than twice the number currently enrolled: 93,000 people had been expelled since 1926, and 43,000 remained. Ia. B. Gamarnik, head of the Political Directorate of the Red Army and deputy commissar for military and naval affairs, asked in astonishment, "How many?" Eikhe replied, "93,000." "So many!" Gamarnik exclaimed. Eikhe feared with good reason that many people, bitter about exclusion, would vote against the Party's candidates in the upcoming elections to the soviets.[71]

Iakovlev was also perturbed by how regional and city leaders had handled the purge. As head of the Party Control Commission, he received thousands of complaints and appeals for reinstatement from members who had been expelled. He singled out Khrushchev, head of the Moscow city and regional committees, for especially egregious behavior. The expulsion figures in Moscow's largest defense factories were shocking: in Kalibr, 110 of the 198 party members and candidates had been expelled, and in Spetsavtomashina 53 of 56! The Party Control Commission reviewed 155 cases from three factories: in the overwhelming majority, party organizations had expelled workers with long seniority and excellent production records. A turner from Kalibr, for example, who was a prized Stakhanovite, a party organizer in the Red Army, and a local union representative, was excluded for "political illiteracy." Iakovlev was livid. "What was the real problem?" he demanded. "He had missed a few study circles." A woman worker with long seniority in Kalibr who headed a women's brigade, and volunteered in the childcare center, reading circle, and union, was expelled "as ballast." She appealed, received no response, and then asked to do volunteer work for the Party. She was refused on the grounds that it would be "dangerous" to give responsible assignments to a nonparty person. Listening carefully to Iakovlev's story, Stalin blurted out, "This is disgusting!" Workers were excluded for passivity, political illiteracy, and failure to pay dues. Iakovlev charged, "We've created a shooting gallery under the heading of passivity." He strongly attacked Khrushchev and the Moscow party organization for ignoring Trotskyists, the real enemy, and expelling workers. Moreover, in Moscow's factory party committees, elections had not been held since 1933. The self-serving formulation, "According to the initiative of Nikita Sergeevich [Khrushchev]" preceded every declaration and resolution. Iakovlev charged that while

[71] "Materialy fevral'sko-martovskogo plenuma," *Voprosy istorii*, 6, 1993, pp. 5–6.

the Moscow party committee was busy with "self-eulogy," Trotskyists in leading posts were disrupting production.[72]

Stalin also derided party officials for bungling the purge. He noted that 10,000 party members had been excluded for "passivity," a policy that would "only help wreckers, Trotskyists, and enemies in general" by creating an embittered "army." Most importantly, Stalin provided a concrete numerical representation of the enemy threat that remained. He estimated that there were about 30,000 former oppositionists, of which 18,000 Trotskyists and Zinovievites had already been arrested, leaving 12,000 at large.[73] Not all of these were enemies; many had renounced their former views and a small number had already left the Party. "Yet," Stalin cautioned, "you don't need very many to mess things up." Stalin's calculation of 12,000 potential oppositionists had been revised upward considerably since June 1936, when he calculated that the Party should have expelled 600 former Trotskyists and Zinovievites. Stalin had clearly given careful consideration to the numbers, and his new estimate revealed that, between June 1936 and February 1937, the size of the threat had greatly increased in his mind. The number of party members expelled had also increased considerably in this time: Stalin now set the total at 300,000 – 100,000 more than Ezhov's estimate at the June 1936 plenum. "We have been inhuman, bureaucratic, and soulless in our attitudes toward the fates of individual party members," Stalin said. "All this is water turning the mills of our enemies."[74] The *proverka* had been mishandled: rather than targeting a limited number of "Trotskyists," it had attacked a much wider group of "little people." Both Stalin and Iakovlev emphasized that workers who were "politically illiterate," remiss in their dues, or absent from study circles were never the intended target of the purge. A member had to accept the Party's program, pay dues, and participate in its activities. Not every party member was required to be a Marxist or a master of

---

[72] "Materialy fevral'sko-martovskogo plenuma," *Voprosy istorii*, 5–6, 1995, pp. 16–20.

[73] Stalin arrived at this figure in the following manner: in 1927, there was an open discussion, a "real referendum," on the issues raised by the united opposition. Of 854,000 party members, 730,000 voted. Of this group, Stalin estimated that 4,000 had voted for the Trotskyists, and 2,600 had abstained, providing a total of 6,600 people who had favored the Trotskyist program. Adding 11,000 more from the group that did not participate in the election, he calculated a maximum number of 18,000 Trotskyists. Stalin then added 10,000 more who supported Zinoviev, and another 2,000 "whisperers" (purveyors of doubt) and rightists, for a total of 30,000 "antiparty cadres."

[74] "Materialy fevral'sko-martovskogo plenuma," *Voprosy istorii*, 11–12, 1995, pp. 21–2. For Ezhov and Stalin's figures at the June 1936 plenum, see Getty and Naumov, *The Road to Terror*, p. 236.

complex political theory. Eliciting uncomfortable laughter, Stalin joked, "I don't know if many members of the Central Committee have mastered Marxism."[75]

Stalin also summarized the new understanding of Trotskyism that had emerged from the Kemerovo and Moscow trials. Trotskyism was not an alternative path to socialism or "a political current in the working class," as it had been "seven or eight years ago." Trotskyists were "an unprincipled band of wreckers, diversionists, spies, and murderers, acting on the assignment of intelligence organs of foreign states" to restore capitalism. They hid behind "the party cards in their pockets."[76] Beneath the inflammatory rhetoric, Stalin's subtext was simple: the Soviet Union, threatened by fascism, could not afford an internal struggle for power.[77] Anyone who contemplated an alternative to Stalin's leadership, who listened privately to antigovernment opinions without informing the proper authorities, was in effect aiding an external enemy. A party member's greatest loyalty, Stalin explained, was to the Party. It took primacy over family and friends, and required members to report doubts and keep no secrets.[78] Stalin's notion of "total honesty," of vigilance above all other human loyalties, helped promote a quasi-religious, cult atmosphere within the Party. Soon a doubt not relayed to the proper authorities would itself become evidence of terrorism.

Yet Stalin's speech to the plenum, like Molotov's, offered a mixed message. He urged vigilance on the one hand, and counseled moderation on the other. Not every party member with a record of oppositionism was an enemy. "We have excellent people among former Trotskyists, you know this," he cautioned. "[There are] excellent officials who by accident fell into Trotskyism, then broke with it, and now work as real Bolsheviks." In the end, Stalin offered a surprisingly weak solution to the problems he identified: more political education courses and the addition of two deputies to aid every party secretary from the lowest party organizations

---

[75] "Materialy fevral'sko-martovskogo plenuma," *Voprosy istorii*, 11–12, 1995, p. 22.

[76] "Materialy fevral'sko-martovskogo plenuma," *Voprosy istorii*, 3, 1995, pp. 6–10.

[77] Ibid., pp. 3–6.

[78] See Stalin's cautionary tale about Ordzhonikidze's relationship with Lominadze, head of the Magnitogorsk city party committee. Although Ordzhonikidze listened to Lominadze's doubts about party policy, he refused to report him to the Central Committee. Later, Ordzhonikidze swung to the opposite extreme and wanted to shoot him. Stalin argued that he should not be shot, arrested, or even excluded from the Party, just removed from the Central Committee. Lominadze committed suicide in 1935. See "Materialy fevral'sko-martovskogo plenuma," *Voprosy istorii*, 11–12, 1995, pp. 16–17, and Getty and Naumov, *The Road to Terror*, p. 218.

to the highest.[79] His speech suggested a limited purge, targeting fewer than 12,000 party members with oppositional backgrounds. He warned against the thinking that would soon grip every party organization: "Let us now beat anyone to the right or to the left, who at some time walked along some street with some Trotskyist or ate in a dining hall at some time next to a Trotskyist."[80] Within a year, however, Stalin's parody would become a reality. Party committees would be gripped by elaborate investigations of the most trivial personal contacts. Regardless of what Stalin intended, his emphasis on absolute loyalty, mobilization of the rank and file, and the politicization of production quickly broadened the hunt for enemies beyond the relatively small circle of former oppositionists, to encompass anyone who had once "walked along some street with some Trotskyist."

Purging and Reviving the Unions

The decision to arrest Bukharin and Rykov marked the end of months of vacillation toward the former rightists. Ezhov summarized the accusations for the plenum delegates: rightists had formed underground terrorist cells, sanctioned the Kirov murder, spied, and plotted to kill party leaders. Their founding document was the Riutin Platform, a lengthy critique of Stalin's policies, which Ezhov now claimed was drafted by Bukharin, not Riutin, in 1932.[81] A. A. Andreev, the former commissar for railway transport and secretary of the Central Committee, presented the "evidence" of the tie between left and right oppositionists. First, M. P. Tomskii, the head of the VTsSPS until 1929 and known rightist, had committed suicide shortly after the August trial. Andreev noted, "People don't shoot themselves for nothing." Second, V. V. Shmidt, former deputy chairman of the Council of People's Commissars (SNK) and deputy commissar for agriculture, had recently been arrested and confessed that he met with N. A. Uglanov, Bukharin, and Rykov in 1932 to discuss and approve the Riutin Platform. Uglanov, former head of the Moscow party committee and the Commissariat of Labor, had also been arrested. Third, "rightists" were implicated in a variety of "crimes," including a plot to dismantle the state

---

[79] "Materialy fevral'sko-martovskogo plenuma," *Voprosy istorii*, 3, 1995, pp. 7–14.
[80] Ibid., p. 12.
[81] Getty and Naumov, *The Road to Terror*, pp. 357–9, 364–419; "Stalin i krizis proletarskoi diktatury. Platforma 'Soiuza marksistov-leninintsev' (Gruppa Riutina)," in *Reabilitatsiia politicheskie protsessy 30–50-x godov* (Izdatel'stvo Politicheskoi Literatury, Moscow, 1991), pp. 334–459.

and collective farms. "Double-dealers," they had repeatedly taken advantage of the Party's willingness to reinstate them in leading posts, "abusing the faith of the Party." The "rightists" may have recanted in 1930, but they had never abandoned their critique of Stalinist industrialization.[82]

Andreev's speech opened the door to a broad assault on the VTsSPS and its member unions. When "rightists" had been expelled from the unions in 1929, many had moved to the Commissariat of Labor under the welcoming wing of Uglanov. The Commissariat of Labor had been eliminated in 1933, and the VTsSPS had absorbed its staff and its departments. The "rightists" then migrated back to the VTsSPS. Andreev, aware of the transfer of cadres over the years, now claimed that the unions were riddled with enemies. "The unions work poorly and union leaders are covered with moss. We cannot leave this branch of the party political leadership in its current position."[83]

N. M. Shvernik, a Stalin supporter who had replaced Tomskii as head of the VTsSPS in 1929, delivered the main report on the unions. Shvernik announced that "wrecker diversionists from Trotskyist bands and rightist restorationists of capitalism" had succeeded in seizing key posts in the unions. Stalin seemed surprised by Shvernik's statement. "Who succeeded in seizing these posts?" he called out. Shvernik had a ready list: Gil'burg, the head of the Union of Coke-Oven Workers, had been arrested as a Trotskyist, and V. A. Kotov, a former deputy secretary to Uglanov in the Moscow party committee, had also been arrested.[84] Kotov had headed the Bureau of Social Insurance (Sotsstrakh), first under the Commissariat of Labor and then the VTsSPS. After his arrest, Kotov confessed that he had wasted millions of rubles in dispensing funds to disabled workers. Shvernik blamed the Commissariat of Labor for placing the Bureau of Social Insurance "in a horrible chaotic state." "Under VTsSPS it didn't get much better," Ezhov interrupted. "I assure you," replied Shvernik smoothly, "that it did get better under VTsSPS. If we got the bandit Kotov, then it does not mean that things got worse under us. It is correct that we blamed Kotov."[85] The brief thrust and parry between Shvernik and Ezhov was a hint of the chaotic free-for-all that would soon characterize party meetings. Ezhov did not hesitate to impugn Shvernik, even though he was a strong supporter of Stalin, and Shvernik deftly defended himself.

---

[82] "Materialy fevral'sko-martovskogo plenuma," *Voprosy istorii*, 8–9, 1992, pp. 3–8.

[83] "Materialy fevral'sko-martovskogo plenuma," *Voprosy istorii*, 8, 1995, p. 12; Junbae Jo, "Soviet Trade Unions and the Great Terror," in Ilic, *Stalin's Terror Revisited*, pp. 69–70.

[84] Merridale, "The Reluctant Opposition," p. 387.

[85] "Materialy fevral'sko-martovskogo plenuma," *Voprosy istorii*, 10, 1995, pp. 18–21.

The exchange, between two men supposedly on the same side of the fence, was typical of the allegations and attacks that would soon dominate the Party's political culture.

Shvernik argued that the unions, like the Party, lacked internal democracy. "I should say here, directly and with all frankness," he explained, "that the unions are in even worse shape." With the development of new industries during the first five-year plan, the country's 47 unions had split into 165, creating thousands of new jobs. Positions at every level were filled by appointment, rather than election. Echoing Stalin, Shvernik contended that the lack of democracy allowed "counterrevolutionary elements to build their nests." The paid union staff had become "large and cumbersome," creating a "wall between the broad masses and the possibility of self-criticism." In an effort to prune the bureaucracy, the VTsSPS had recently fired more than half of its paid staff, and planned to replace them with volunteers. Shvernik concluded his speech with the suggestion that elections were needed not only in the Party, but in the unions as well. Kaganovich responded in startled surprise, "By secret voting?" Shvernik replied dubiously, "I don't know about secret voting." A voice yelled out amid general laughter, "It's frightening." Shvernik responded slowly, "I think this would not be too bad. Perhaps the elections can be by secret ballot." Everyone laughed again. "I think this would clean our ranks of bureaucratic elements, closely connect us with the broad masses, and give the unions the chance to get closer to the masses."[86]

It is not clear what motivated Shvernik to suggest a replication of the campaign for democracy within the unions. He may have planned to use the elections to deflect attacks against him from within the VTsSPS, to curry favor with Stalin and other Politburo leaders, or to renew the connection between the unions and their members. No matter what his motive, however, within less than a month, this brief, seemingly unscripted exchange would spark a mass campaign for democracy, elections involving millions of workers, and waves of arrests within the unions.

Conclusion

Between September 1936 and March 1937, party leaders changed course in an attempt to involve the rank and file in the Party, the unions, and the factories in the hunt for enemies. The shift, sparked by investigations of former oppositionists in leading industrial posts, featured workers as

[86] Ibid.

victims, equated industrial problems with wrecking, and introduced multicandidate, secret-ballot elections to break up reigning "family circles." As Molotov pointed out, allegations of wrecking were not new. Yet for the first time, the so-called wreckers were carrying party cards. The trials provided workers with new opportunities for pressing their grievances against managers. In a speech to party activists in the Procuracy, Vyshinskii blasted the common belief that a successful manager could not be a wrecker. "Work is not proof of loyalty," Vyshinskii cautioned. "Wreckers who only do harm do not exist." He urged jurists to search for wreckers wherever safety was neglected and work rules ignored. The February–March 1937 Plenum directed the unions to review safety rules with engineers, technicians, and workers. The courts now had to take a more aggressive role in investigating accidents and prosecuting violations. It was time, Vyshinskii explained, to reconsider all accidents in light of potential wrecking.[87] The unions and the Procuracy were primed to give a strong political cast to workers' complaints.

By linking the hunt for oppositionists to party and union democracy, Stalin and other leaders ensured the involvement of rank-and-file party members and union officials at every level. Stalin used the Greek myth of Antaeus, the son of Poseidon, god of the sea, and Gaia, goddess of the earth, to explain the Party's new emphasis on democracy. Antaeus was so strong that his opponents considered him invincible. Yet the secret of his strength was in a special gift: whenever Antaeus was knocked down, he regained his energy from contact with the earth, his mother, and sprang back more powerful than before. Hercules defeated Antaeus by separating him from his mother earth, lifting him up, and strangling him in the air. Stalin's message was clear: the source of Bolshevik power was its connection to the people. Without this deep, ever-renewable source of strength, the Party, like Antaeus, was doomed.[88]

Was Stalin's invocation of democracy simply a smoke screen designed to hide the destruction of those who once offered alternative views? Was it a cynical ploy by Stalin and his supporters to strengthen and centralize power by inciting the rank and file against their regional leaders? Or was it part of a genuine belief that the Party could be purged of oppositionists and revitalized at the same time? At first glance, it would seem

[87] "Stenogramma doklada tov. Vyshinskogo ob itogakh plenuma TsK VKP (b) na sobranii partaktiva Prokurator Soiuza," ll. 90, 91, 100, 104–105, 106, 111.
[88] "Materialy fevral'sko-martovskogo plenuma," *Voprosy istorii*, 11–12, 1995, pp. 20, 14–15.

that the repression of former oppositionists was the antithesis of democracy. What could the arrest, torture, and execution of leading party figures possibly have in common with a renewal of democracy? The very pairing of these events is repellent. Yet a careful reading of the plenum suggests that there was no contradiction between repression and democracy in the political psychology of Stalin and his supporters. Party leaders defined democracy as multicandidate, secret-ballot elections, the accountability of leaders, greater rank-and-file participation, and elimination of the "mini-cults" surrounding local and regional leaders. This definition did not differ appreciably from that of Western liberal theorists. Yet there were important differences. Party leaders wanted to eliminate the creeping apathy in the lower ranks, but at the same time mobilize these ranks to break up the "family circles," which they saw as harboring former "oppositionists." Democracy thus became the means to a more thorough repression.

Some historians suggest that Stalin and his supporters used the slogans of democracy to mobilize the lower ranks against regional leaders in order to bring regional leaders under Moscow's control and to eliminate their independent power bases. The plenum was thus an expression of an organizational struggle between Stalin and powerful regional leaders, between the forces of central and regional power.[89] The plenum reveals, however, that Stalin and his supporters did not promulgate this policy solely or directly through the rank and file. On the contrary, they used the very regional leaders they allegedly aimed to target. In fact, the strongest critics of mini-fiefdoms at the plenum were regional leaders with their own family circles. Andreev, Zhdanov, and Stalin introduced the issue of party democracy, yet powerful regional leaders such as Eikhe, Kosior, Kalygina, and Kabakov supported them. Shvernik, the head of VTsSPS, Polonskii, his rival, and Iakovlev, head of the Party Control Commission, were also proponents of democratization. In fact, it is difficult to separate the proponents from their alleged targets. Why would regional leaders become ardent advocates of a program designed to remove them?

---

[89] J. Arch Getty, *Origins of the Great Purges: The Soviet Communist Party Reconsidered, 1933–1938* (Cambridge University Press, New York, 1985); Getty and Naumov, *The Road to Terror*, pp. 493–9; Getty, "Pragmatists and Puritans: The Rise and Fall of the Party Control Commission," *Carl Beck Papers in Russian and East European Studies*, 1208 (1997); Rittersporn, *Stalinist Simplifications and Soviet Complications*; James Harris, *The Great Urals: Regional Interests and the Evolution of the Soviet System, 1934–1939* (Cornell University Press, Ithaca, 1999).

The plenum suggests an explanation. For Stalin and his supporters, party democracy was a strategy to eliminate *kooptatsiia* and *semeistven-nost'*, two practices seen as protecting former oppositionists. The purpose of the campaign for democracy was not to eliminate the middle level of leadership, which was essential to the party structure, but to extricate the former oppositionists from their midst. "Family circles" were an obstacle to the hunt for enemies. Democratic, secret-ballot elections were a swift and effective way to break them up. Initially, regional leaders consented to the purge of oppositionists. They spoke sympathetically against syco-phancy and seemed eager to reinvigorate the rank and file. The campaign, per se, did not appear to threaten their power base. Yet the language of democracy proved open to many uses. Once the rank and file were roused, many of these regional leaders would be destroyed by the very slogans that they were initially so eager to promulgate.

With the rise of fascism, party leaders entered a new embattled phase that brooked no disagreement or doubt. As Stalin pointed out, only total loyalty was acceptable. "War is inevitable," Vyshinskii told the party jurists; "the fascist world is preparing for war, and it will use every means it can."[90] After Kirov's murder, Stalin and his supporters were convinced that silent yet stubborn oppositionists still lurked in the party and union organizations. They never fully accepted Stalin's program and quietly encouraged young people in vaguely oppositional sentiments. They were biding their time, waiting for a moment of weakness. By 1937, Stalin was bent on rooting out this silent opposition, destroying anyone not thor-oughly committed to his own leadership and program. Did Stalin hope for a carefully targeted purge within a newly democratic, invigorated Party? He did set a numerical limit on the removal of remaining opposi-tionists and cautioned moderation in defining the enemy. Or did he intend a blood bath from the beginning? His *intentions* cannot be known. A close reading of the plenum, however, suggests that Stalin aimed for a ruthless, yet limited attack on former oppositionists coupled with a new effort to educate, integrate, and empower lower party cadres. But regardless of what he intended, repression and democracy became intertwined. The hunt for oppositionists, fueled by new elections and attacks on managers, spread to every party organization and union. The various campaigns for democracy quickly amplified the hunt for oppositionists beyond the

[90] "Stenogramma doklada tov. Vyshinskogo ob itogakh plenuma TsK VKP (b) na sobranii partaktiva Prokurator soiuza RSFSR," l. 88.

limited parameters set at the 1937 plenum. Democracy was not peripheral, not a smoke screen, not a collection of meaningless slogans designed to mask the "real" meaning of events. It was the very means by which repression spread to every union, factory committee, and primary party organization. If the hunt for oppositionists ignited a fire within the Party and the unions, the campaign for "democracy" served as the gasoline.

7. Meeting of workers in Serp i Molot's open hearth furnace, 1936. Courtesy of RGAKFD

8. Meeting of workers in Trekhgornaia Manufaktura. Courtesy of RGAKFD

4

The Campaign for Union Democracy

"Do you know the mood of our union member? How he lives? What we need to do to help him in life and at work?"

    – Denisov, head of the Union of Nonferrous Metal Miners, 1937

"Now activism will revive. I know this because of what is happening in our mine. We have a lot of accidents as a result of explosions. When we held a meeting on wrecking in the mine, it lasted nine days. In this meeting, the workers said pointblank to me, 'Enough talk about Piatakov and Purishch, the former head of construction. Talk about yourself. We think you are also a wrecker.' The workers are in a sense right because we have no club, no running water in the bath house, no canteen, restaurant, or childcare center."

    – Krenov, head of a mine committee within the Union of Nonferrous Metal Miners, 1937[1]

In less than three weeks, Nikolai Shvernik's seemingly spontaneous suggestion to the February–March 1937 Central Committee Plenum to replicate the campaign for internal party democracy within the unions became official policy. In line with the broad extension of voting rights promised by the new constitution, the state also extended union membership to workers who had previously been barred for social origins.[2] The campaign for "union democracy" (*profdemokratiia*) was taken up by the VTsSPS (All Union Central Council of Unions) and quickly disseminated through more than 150 unions and their 22 million members.[3] At the

---

[1] GARF, f. 7679, o. 3, d. 86, "TsK Soiuza rabochikh dobychi tsvetnykh metallov. IV plenuma. Steno. Otchet," ll. 16, 71–72.

[2] GARF, f. 5451, o. 43, d. 69, "VTsSPS prezidiuma. TsK VKP (b) tov. Andreevu, A. A.," l. 239.

[3] Slogans of mass participation also preceded the purge of the "rightists" in 1928, when the Party launched a similar campaign against corrupt, bureaucratic, undemocratic union

6th VTsSPS Plenum in March 1937, representatives from the unions were instructed to organize multicandidate, secret-ballot elections. By the end of 1937, almost every union had held elections, and workers had swept out many of the old leaders. In raucous mass meetings, workers skewered their union leaders for disregarding occupational health, accidents, and horrific living conditions. Under the watchwords of democracy, better working conditions, safety, and antibureaucratism, workers voted for reform.

The campaign captured the striking paradox of terror and democracy so evident at the February–March Central Committee Plenum. The elections were accompanied by continuing attacks on former oppositionists and arrests of both older and newly elected officials. The campaign served simultaneously as an exercise in genuine electoral reform and as a highly politicized attack on the unions. Yet where was the balance between these two seemingly opposite forces? Did workers oust the "bureaucrats" and gain real power? Did Stalin and his supporters terrorize union officials into obedience? Did union officials protect their posts? A close examination of the campaign suggests that terror and democracy combined to create a complex upheaval in the unions involving many different interests. Party leaders, workers, and union officials all used the slogans of the campaign to pursue different aims. The campaign for union democracy set off pitched battles within the unions, and quickly became entwined with accusations of wrecking, the hunt for former oppositionists, and fears of spies and diversionists. It successfully spread the hunt for enemies into every union.

The Campaign Begins

The resolutions of the February–March Central Committee plenum quickly became the new marching orders for the unions. The editors of *Voprosy Profdvizheniia*, the union movement's journal, wasted no time in promulgating the new campaign for democracy. In a searing editorial in the March issue, they excoriated union and VTsSPS officials: "The insufficiencies characterizing the party characterize the unions to an even greater degree." They repeated the same phrases used by Zhdanov in his speech to the Central Committee Plenum: violations of democracy,

leaders. At the time, workers generated little enthusiasm for either criticizing or defending their leaders. See Diane Koenker, *Republic of Labor: Russian Printers and Soviet Socialism, 1918–1930* (Cornell University Press, Ithaca, 2005), pp. 248–59.

kooptatsiia, "bureaucratic perversions," "weakening ties with the masses," "arrogance," "toadying," and "suppression of criticism from below." They claimed that the unions were filled with "hidden oppositionists," former staff and supporters of Tomskii, the previous leader of the VTsSPS, and V. V. Shmidt and N. A. Uglanov, former heads of the Commissariat of Labor (NKT). The Bureau of Social Insurance, which provided support to sick and disabled workers, "was riddled with embezzlers and enemies of the people," who stole millions of rubles and "systematically disrupted pensions." Occupational health and safety and union finances, areas that closely affected workers' interests, were key targets for "wrecking by enemies of the people." The editors skillfully blended anti-oppositionist rhetoric with appeals to workers' needs. "Enemies of the people" had organized accidents, diversions, and horrible violations of safety rules. They had deliberately worsened labor conditions, filled the mines and copper-smelting works with poisonous gas, and curtailed housing construction and social services. Moreover, union officials had remained silent. Production meetings in the factories had "turned into occasions for empty speechifying," where everything "except the suggestions of the workers, masters, and technicians" was discussed. The editors strongly urged workers to speak out against "wreckers" and corrupt officials. Leading officials in the chemical, agricultural machine-building, and nonferrous metallurgical industries had already been arrested for "wrecking." Workers had a vital role to play in helping the NKVD identify others. "Enemies" were "able to pursue their dark, traitorous affairs because the unions did not encourage criticism, and did not heed the complaints and declarations of the workers." In sum, the unions were in "a peculiar crisis." Their staffs were "littered" with bureaucratic and alien elements. *Kooptatsiia* and noisy parades had supplanted democratic elections and honest meetings. Citing Zhdanov's speech, the editors asked, "Indeed, doesn't this criticism of the violations of the principles of elections and democracy in party organs apply to the unions?"[4]

The solutions proposed by VTsSPS were also identical to the Central Committee's resolutions on reform of the Party: to revive democracy, accountability, and self-criticism at every organizational level. The VTsSPS called for "sharpest criticism of those union 'hats,' who have overlooked wreckers," and elections to bring "fresh blood" into the unions. Invoking a return to "the authentic, Bolshevik Leninist spirit," it

---

[4] "Itogi plenuma TsK VKP (b) i zadachi profsoiuzov," *Voprosy profdvizheniia,* 5–6, (March 1937), pp. 4–8.

encouraged workers to sweep out the bureaucrats, take power into their own hands, and bring safety, housing, and health to the fore.[5] The call was quickly translated into action. Less than a month later, the VTsSPS convened a plenum with delegates from all the unions to promulgate the new approach.

The 6th Plenum of the VTsSPS

The VTsSPS held its 6th Plenum in April 1937, its first since 1931. More than 300 union officials attended, including leaders of the VTsSPS, unions, and local mine, workplace, factory, and railroad line committees.[6] The long hiatus figured prominently in Shvernik's keynote address, which charged that the unions had fallen apart after the purge of Tomskii and the rightists in 1929. Shvernik, who had first floated the idea of union democracy, now vigorously promulgated the new campaign. He sharply criticized union leaders for violating democratic principles, omitting elections and entrenching themselves in posts without a popular mandate. Many unions, in fact, did not have legally elected central, regional, or factory committees.[7] Officials were dismissive of the people they were supposed to serve, "insensitive toward complaints," and cavalier about safety rules, labor laws, housing, and occupational health.[8] Shvernik's repeated invocations of workers' rights were interspersed with references to wrecking, "enemies of the people," and loss of "class vigilance." Union officials had allowed enemies, Trotskyists, wreckers, and diversionists to flourish at every level.[9] Kotov, head of the Bureau of Social Insurance, Zharikov, head of the VTsSPS Bureau of Information, Kolotilov, head of the Union of Teachers, Kaiurov, secretary of the Union of Oil Refinery Workers, Chislov, a leader of the Union of Oil Workers of the Caucasus, and Gil'burg, head of the Union of Coke-Oven Workers, had been arrested as "enemies of the people." Shvernik broadened the attack further to include those "impermissibly politically blind, sluggish, and careless"

---

[5] Ibid., pp. 8–9.

[6] Junbae Jo, "Trade Unions and the Great Terror," in Melanie Ilic, ed., *Stalin's Terror Revisited* (Palgrave, Basingstoke, 2006), pp. 71–5.

[7] Each union was headed by a central committee, with regional (*oblast*) committees at mid-level, factory and shop committees, and the *profgrup*, the smallest unit, at the base. Some unions also had district (*raion*) committees.

[8] GARF, f. 5451, o. 21, d. 1, "Ob otchetakh profsoiuznykh organov v sviazi s vyborami poslednikh," l. 68.

[9] GARF, f. 5451, o. 21, d. 1, "Rezoliutsiia VI Plenuma VTsSPS 'Ob otchetakh proforganov v sviazi s vyborami poslednikh' po dokladu tov. Shvernika," ll. 126–129.

union officials who failed to help the NKVD in its hunt for enemies.[10] He urged union officials to participate actively in identifying and denouncing the enemies in their midst.

The delegates, prominent union and VTsSPS leaders, listened carefully to Shvernik's speech. Attentive readers of the party and union press, they were not surprised by his message. In the words of one quick-minded official, the unions were at a "turning point," and those who thought that everything would continue along the same track "had fallen out of their handcarts."[11] Yet this was the first time they responded publicly, as a group, to the change in course. Their reactions, initially defensive, spanned the gamut from fear to enthusiasm as they took up the new slogans to advance their own hopes and interests. In fact, the delegates' responses foreshadowed the range of reactions that would be replayed with growing intensity as the campaign spread. Some took advantage of the new course to advance the interests of their workers and expose conditions in the factories, some scrambled to blame their bosses, others publicly distanced themselves from union colleagues who had recently been arrested. Delegates fired criticism in every possible direction, including at Shvernik himself. Not even the head of the VTsSPS was off-limits.[12]

Several speakers picked up the theme, first voiced by Stalin and Zhdanov, that leaders had become separated from the people. N. V. Voronina, an older woman from Elektrozavod, a large Moscow electrical factory, who had worked in factories since 1900, used the opportunity to press the claims of women workers. Voronina's strong commitment to workers' needs had brought her to the attention of union officials who had appointed her to the VTsSPS presidium in 1933. Yet she roundly criticized the very leadership she had joined, angrily denouncing VTsSPS leaders for ignoring the needs of the 23,000 workers in her factory. "I'll tell you how we're working there," she said. "The place is a scandalous mess!" Workers contended with constant stoppages, low wages, chaos in production, and horrible living conditions. Five different chairmen headed the factory committee in three years, and not a single one had been elected. The Stalin Constitution promised everyone "the right to work, to education, and to rest," she explained. "But what do we have in the lamp department?" In this overwhelmingly female shop, "women workers, with two or three kids and no husbands, earn 150 rubles a month because of machine stoppages.

[10] "Ob otchetakh profsoiuznykh organov v sviazi s vyborami poslednikh," ll. 58–59.
[11] GARF, f. 5451, o. 21, d. 1, "Stenogramma VI Plenuma VTsSPS," ll. 187–192.
[12] Ibid.

They swear at the Party and the government, but they are not guilty. The unions and the managers who don't struggle with these stoppages are guilty. And, as a result, women receive miserable pay!" Voronina was also furious about the lack of childcare. She noted that, as a result of the 1936 decree prohibiting abortion, "we have 500 women on maternity leave, 300 more ready to take maternity leave, and 200 women bringing their babies to the factory committee. Did we build crèches? No." The factory director had promised to build a crèche for 180 infants, but a single crib had yet to appear. "Women workers say, 'Now where is the decree that said that, when we give birth, they will create institutions where we can leave our children?'" Millions of peasants had taken jobs in cities and new settlements, but housing had not kept pace. Workers slept in the factory and in makeshift houses built on poles. "You bang the door, the whole house shakes." Workers were deprived of their rightful insurance awards in an attempt to "economize" on social insurance funds, which then were never spent. Voronina exclaimed, "We have workers with tuberculosis and nervous disorders who go from one commission to another for years, and they are not able to go anywhere to restore their health, while a million rubles lie like dead capital. This is a disgusting situation." Voronina's words rushed out in a crescendo of criticism. Older workers spent forty years and more in the factory, but feared retirement on pensions of seventy-five rubles a month. They did little work and managers treated them as "a fixed expense." But they deserved better. There were no ventilators in the shops, and temperatures reached more than 130 degrees. When Voronina exclaimed in frustration, "We have already talked about this for five years and we still have no ventilators," the entire plenum burst into spontaneous applause.[13]

The response to Voronina's speech showed that an auditorium of union officials could still be moved by a heartfelt appeal to workers' interests. Yet their applause was also strangely displaced, for who was responsible for the lack of ventilation if not union and VTsSPS leaders? Voronina, for example, was a member of the presidium, the highest body of the VTsSPS. Yet she complained that no one told her what to do. She tried to meet with Shvernik, N. N. Evreinov, and other VTsSPS leaders, but "was not able to have a proper conversation with a single secretary." She had seen Shvernik only once in her factory since 1931. "Every month they send us protocols, I read them and put them away," she said. "I have

[13] Ibid., ll. 195–202.

a whole stack of them. What am I supposed to do with them?"[14] The delegates' predisposition to shrug off responsibility, and to cast themselves (together with the workers) as victims of *other* officials, was a constant theme in their speeches. Many echoed Voronina's excuse that "no one told us what to do." The VTsSPS secretaries came in for a drubbing by the plenum delegates, many of whom held leading positions in the union central committees and the VTsSPS. At times, it appeared that every delegate was looking for someone a little higher in the organization to blame. A. V. Artiukhina, head of the Union of Cotton Textile Workers in Moscow and Leningrad, blamed Shvernik, the head of the VTsSPS, Evreinov, its secretary, and its entire thirteen-member presidium (which included Voronina!) for their failure to provide leadership for the union central committees.[15] "Everyone knows about the completely unhealthy situation which exists in the secretariat," she exclaimed. V. I. Polonskii, a former VTsSPS secretary, had recently been transferred, "I'm not referring to him," she said. "But what about those remaining comrades? Every time I come to see Evreinov about work, I receive the same answer, 'Solve it yourself.'" Furiously she asked the plenum, "Where are Abolin, Evreinov, and the other secretaries?" Artiukhina noted that she represented a union with 350,000 members and a paid staff of forty-two. Echoing Voronina's complaint, she said, "We want help, not papers." She, too, was furious about the abortion decree and the lack of childcare facilities. "Why doesn't the VTsSPS concern itself about this?"[16]

S. L. Bregman, a member of the presidium and head of the Union of Shoe Workers, also shifted blame away from the presidium and union central committees to the VTsSPS secretaries. He complained steadily about all his local problems: "We have no help, we have no check-up, we have no controls." He whined so much about the upper-level leaders that one exasperated voice in the audience finally burst out, "But you're a member of the presidium!" Yet Bregman still refused to acknowledge responsibility, retorting quickly, "The secretariat and presidium of the VTsSPS are in the position of an orchestra without a conductor." He followed the oft-used strategy of humbly acknowledging all failures while shifting the blame to his own bosses. Critiquing the leaders of the VTsSPS, he righteously declared, "It is much better to sit in an office, to give orders,

---

[14] See also comments of Diachenko, the chairman of the factory committee of Serp i Molot in Ukraine: ibid., l. 224.

[15] The presidium of the VTsSPS had thirteen members in March 1937. Polonskii was later arrested, and other arrests followed.

[16] Ibid., ll. 209–216.

to defend the paper barricades." Bregman especially targeted Evreinov, the VTsSPS secretary. "It's a great event when the secretary goes to a factory," Bregman sneered. "In two years, Evreinov has gone to the Urals once. What kind of leadership is this?"[17] While Bregman sought to cast himself as a bold and outspoken fighter against the "bureaucrats," his own position on the VTsSPS presidium and as head of the Union of Shoe Workers undermined his heroic pose.

Several delegates, confused and frightened by the double message of purging bureaucrats and hunting enemies, sought to distance themselves from colleagues who had been arrested. Radianskii, the head of the Union of State Farm Beet Workers, noted that the secretary of his union was arrested for being a Trotskyist. He had been excluded from the Party earlier for participation in the left opposition, but concealed his political history from the union. When the presidium of the Beet Workers discovered his past oppositional activities, it fired him, and asked the VTsSPS to affirm its decision. The secretary then "ran off to Moscow" to plead his case before the Party Control Commission, which reinstated him, and ordered the Beet Workers to rehire him. Radianskii pressed for further investigation, but Evreinov refused. Eventually, he was hired by Evreinov himself, and finally arrested "within the walls of the VTsSPS." This story of expulsion, appeal, reversal, reinstatement, and arrest was not atypical. Radianskii painted himself as the scorned crusader who tried repeatedly to bring this "enemy" to the attention of the VTsSPS. His speech was partly an attempt to protect himself for, as head of the union, he worked closely with its secretary. Yet Radianskii also revealed the dilemma union officials faced when last week's colleague became yesterday's enemy, today's exonerated victim, and tomorrow's enemy again. In the end, the NKVD was the final arbiter of the drama's wild reversals of fortune. Arrest, the incontestable proof of guilt, revealed whether the supporting actors had cast their lot with an enemy. Yet by the time a colleague was arrested, it was too late to demonstrate "vigilance" by denouncing them. Radianskii thus attempted to shift the blame to the VTsSPS. "I was vigilant, comrades," he implied. "The guilt now is yours."[18] Many delegates were beginning to understand the advantages of the preemptive denunciation. This form of self-protection would in turn create more targets for the NKVD.

In its final report, the plenum identified *kooptatsiia* as a key weakness of the unions, undermining democracy and providing a haven for "enemies." The report noted, "Far and wide, officials snuck into the unions not

---

[17] Ibid., ll. 203–206.   [18] Ibid., ll. 218–219.

because they were politically or organizationally qualified, but because of 'personal connections,' 'convenience,' 'work harmony,' or 'friendly relations.'" In Dinamo, a large machine-building factory in Moscow, four successive chairmen of the factory committee had been installed without elections. In the copper-smelting works in Krasnoural'sk, six successive chairmen were appointed. Many union central committees lacked presidiums; the chairman and the secretary alone decided important issues. The unions rarely convened meetings of their members. When they were held, they had a "formal-declaratory" character: leaders broadcast slogans to a bored and sullen membership. There was no check on whether resolutions were ever implemented. The report also criticized the VTsSPS presidium for working in a "bureaucratic manner," showing "no initiative," and providing poor leadership to the union central committees, which in turn failed to lead the factory committees. Rife with "bureaucratic perversions, violations of financial discipline, and incorrect spending of state and union funds," the factory committees were blind to the working and living conditions of their members. The organizational structure, from top to bottom, was in need of serious reform. Finally, the report urged union officials to begin "unmasking" former supporters of Tomskii, Shmidt, and Uglanov in the unions and now-defunct Commissariat of Labor. It called for new, revitalized unions, purged of enemies, to replace the paid, ossified staff. The secretariat and the presidium of the VTsSPS were both reconstituted at the plenum. Of the secretaries, only Shvernik and Nikolaeva remained; P. G. Moskatov, E. N. Egorova, and Bregman replaced Abolin, Veinberg, and Evreinov.[19]

A Charter for Union Democracy

The resolutions adopted by the 6th Plenum demanded that the unions be recast, from top to bottom. New elections based on secret ballots were to be held in every union organization from central to factory committees. Union members would have "the unlimited right to reject and criticize" individual candidates. Voting by lists was forbidden. The plenum mandated deadlines as well: elections for factory and shop committees were to be held between June 1 and July 15, followed by regional (*oblast*) conferences, union congresses, and elections for higher-level posts between July 15 and September 15. The VTsSPS would hold its own capstone

---

[19] "Ob otchetakh profsoiuznykh organov v sviazi s vyborami poslednikh," ll. 56–58, 62, 60; Jo, "Trade Unions and the Great Terror," p. 74.

congress composed of the newly elected union officials on October 1. Every union central and factory committee was to begin a process of "criticism and self-criticism," actively solicit suggestions, and report to their members before the elections. Copies of these reports were to be widely distributed for discussion. Workers' suggestions would serve as "commands for the newly elected leaders." *Trud*, the national labor newspaper, was instructed to investigate various unions to ensure compliance. Control of funds was to be democratized. The factory committees in the larger enterprises (300 workers or more) were to organize soviets of social insurance consisting of fifteen to thirty people to study occupational illness and accidents, oversee disbursement of insurance monies, and ensure that managers strictly observed laws on overtime, rest days, and holidays. The union factory and central committees were instructed to stop the common managerial practice of withholding workers' wages to meet more pressing expenses and to ensure that workers were paid on time. Finally, permanent committees of union volunteers were to be attached to the soviets at every level to raise issues of housing, consumption, and conditions.[20]

The VTsSPS also decided to move the unions headquartered in Moscow to regions where their members worked. It aimed to improve workers' access to their leaders and break up a Moscow bureaucracy that was increasingly detached from regional problems. The headquarters of the Union of Oil Refinery Workers, for example, was moved to Baku, that of the Union of Glass Workers to Smolensk. The order sparked much moaning and wailing among Moscow's union officials. Forced to leave comfortable apartments in the country's best-provisioned city for dubious housing in areas beset by shortages, poor services, and few cultural amenities, officials fired off telegrams and letters to the VTsSPS detailing why the union staff could not possibly leave Moscow. Most argued that they required ready access to high officials to serve their workers effectively. The VTsSPS, however, was not swayed by these transparent pleas. The moves were accompanied by drunken "goodbye parties" (*provody*) which suggested that the officials were bound for a hanging rather than the hinterlands. (In the eyes of a well-provisioned Muscovite, these may have been one and the same.) As a result of the general collapse of morale,

---

[20] "Rezoliutsiia VI Plenuma VTsSPS 'Ob otchetakh proforganov v sviazi s vyborami poslednikh' po dokladu tov. Shvernika," ll. 130–137; "Ob otchetakh profsoiuznykh organov v sviazi s vyborami poslednikh," ll. 62–64. See also GARF, f. 5451, o. 21, d. 114, "Resheniia VI Plenuma VTsSPS," ll. 69–82.

it often took months for union leaders to establish functioning headquarters in their new towns.[21]

Shaking Up the Unions

Over the next two years, the unions went through a major shakeup. Officials not only were cast out of Moscow, but were also forced to campaign for their posts in multicandidate, secret-ballot elections. *Trud* and the VTsSPS sent investigators to check up on specific factories and unions. Such check-ups (*proverky*) were not uncommon, but after the VTsSPS Plenum they focused on union democracy as well as conditions.[22] Investigators discovered that many factory committees were occupied solely with enrolling new members. The process was cumbersome and, although it varied from plant to plant, it accounted for most of the unions' time. A new worker would write an application (*zaiavlenie*) for membership and submit it to the union group (*profgrup*), the primary organization. After a cursory background check, the *profgrup* would make a recommendation and pass the application to the shop committee, which would in turn make its decision, and pass it to the factory committee for final approval. In most cases, these reviews were *pro forma*; almost every worker gained admittance to the union. Yet the large size of many factories coupled with high labor turnover and poor records meant that many shop and factory committees did little more than process applications. In the metalworking factory, Proletarskii Trud, for example, the factory committee plenum discussed thirty or more applications at every meeting. In some months, the number of workers quitting exceeded the number hired. In the metal-threading shop, thirty-two of the sixty-five people accepted into the union left the factory within three months. When the factory director was arrested in March 1937 for wrecking and Trotskyism, the chaos created by high labor turnover was compounded.[23]

---

[21] GARF, f. 5451, o. 22, d. 11, "Beseda tov. Moskatov s sekretariami prezidiumov TsK soiuzov ot delov VTsSPS," l. 1; GARF, f. 5451, o. 22, d. 64, "V sekretariat VTsSPS," "Dokladnaia zapiska o resultakh proverki raboty TsK soiuza rabochikh stekol'noi promyshlennosti," ll. 145–146, 192–193.

[22] These reports, like the labor inspectorate reports of the nineteenth century, provide excellent information on living and working conditions.

[23] GARF, f. 5451, o. 21, d. 103, "Zavod 'Proletarskii trud,'" ll. 48–51. Membership was sometimes delayed because a worker made insulting comments to women, got in fights, or had "a foggy past." The factory committee (approximately twenty-five members) had been elected in 1931 and again in 1936.

The factory committees in general were paper shells of the once vital, rowdy organizations that had taken over the factories in 1917. Unlike in the 1920s, they did little to resolve workers' grievances. Disorganized and lacking initiative, they met rarely with workers, and often did not meet at all. An investigation of the Krasnyi Tekstil'shchik factory in April 1937 revealed that six chairmen had led the seven-member factory committee, which had not held an election since 1932. The full committee had never met, and kept no financial records. It had never called a factorywide union meeting, although it occasionally convened the workers to pass a resolution marking the anniversary of the October revolution or May Day.[24] The factory committee in Elektrozavod, a large Moscow electrical engineering factory, also kept no financial records and never discussed union expenditures with workers. Thirteen different chairmen had headed the factory committee since 1933, and not a single one had been elected. The factory committee received its monthly plan of work from the factory's party committee, which scripted its every move in advance.[25] The situation was slightly better in Moscow's Linen Factory No. 6, which had 2,600 workers. The factory committee had been elected in 1933. Some chairmen had been elected, others appointed. The factory committee did hold general meetings, but they were poorly attended and never discussed occupational health or accidents.[26] A similar situation prevailed in a Moscow cotton chintz and padding factory. The factory committee had last been elected in 1932, and maintained no written records.[27] Two workers in a Moscow gas factory summed up the role of union officials: "They sit like some kind of clerks in the factory committee, they never go to the shops, and they don't work with the politically active workers."[28]

The investigations and elections contributed to an increasingly charged atmosphere. Throughout 1937, the NKVD arrested union officials, directors, and technical specialists, blaming problems with production, wages, ventilation, and accidents on wrecking. The central committee of the

[24] GARF, f. 5451, o. 21, d. 103, "Sekretariu VTsSPS tov. Evreinovu. Dokladnaia zapiska," ll. 43–44.

[25] GARF, f. 5451, o. 21, d. 103, "Sostoianie orgmassovoi raboty na Elektrozavode," l. 58. On the Elektrozavod factory, see Sergei Zhuravlev, *"Malen'kie liudi" i "bol'shaia istoria": inostrantsy moskovskogo Elektrozavoda v sovetskom obshchestve 1920–1930kh gg.* (ROSSPEN, Moscow, 2000).

[26] GARF, f. 5451, o. 21, d. 103, "V uchstatsektor VTsSPS," ll. 45–46.

[27] GARF, f. 5451, o. 21, d. 103, "Dokladnaia zapiska: po voprosu o sostoianii profchlenstva i o profdemokratii na Sittsenabivnoi fabrike," ll. 55–55ob.

[28] GARF, f. 5451, o. 22, d. 11, "O perestroike raboty profsoiuznykh organizatsii v sviazi s sokrashcheniem platnogo apparata," l. 12.

Union of Metallurgical Workers of the East became embroiled in frightening accusations of wrecking in a factory in Cheliabinsk. The NKVD halted construction of the ferrous-molybdenum shop, accusing managers and union officials of wrecking because they spent 400,000 rubles over budget on equipment and disregarded technical safety.[29] Some union leaders, fearful of arrest, tried to protect themselves by casting blame on others. In Briansk, the central committee of the Union of Cement Workers hurriedly dispatched a labor inspector to a cement factory in Amvrosievka in the Donbas region after the director and head engineer were accused of wrecking in a series of accidents. The inspector reported that there were "mass accidents," "a ruinous housing situation," and no clean drinking water in either the factory or the nearby workers' settlement. Temperatures in some of the shops reached more than 125 degrees, and fires broke out constantly throughout the factory and the nearby settlements. The factory committee had done nothing to rectify the situation. The Union of Cement Workers sent their inspector's report to the procurator, urging him to bring criminal charges against the director if he did not make good on his promise to eliminate the problems within one month.[30] The officials' hasty effort to involve the procurator was motivated less by concern for the workers than by fear that they too would be pulled into the whirling vortex of accusations.

Fears of accusation, investigation, and arrest jolted complacent officials into action. The Union of Metallurgical Workers of the South discussed and drafted new safety rules for the entire industry.[31] The Union of Machine Tool Workers took up the growing number of accidents and eye injuries in the Stankolit factory, ordering the director to provide safety goggles, work boots and clothes, and other items. Henceforth, every accident in the factory was to be investigated.[32] The Union of Electric Power Station Workers charged that accidents in the Leningrad Electric Power Station had increased due to the "criminal and scornful" attitude of the director and negligence of safety rules. It recommended that the labor inspector be removed.[33] Factory committees throughout the country began forwarding records of their meetings to VTsSPS headquarters. The Union of Grain Industry and Elevator Workers in the South and

[29] GARF, f. 5451, o. 21, d. 114, "TsK Soiuzov metallurgov vostochnykh raionov," l. 1.
[30] GARF, f. 5451, o. 21, d. 114, "TsK Rabochikh tsementnoi prom.," ll. 1–3.
[31] GARF, f. 5451, o. 21, d. 114, "TsK Metallurgov iuga," l. 3.
[32] GARF, f. 5451, o. 21, d. 114, "Prezidium TsK Soiuza stanko-instrumental'noi prom.," l. 9.
[33] GARF, f. 5451, o. 21, d. 114, "TsK Soiuza elektrostantsii," l. 10.

East undertook a wide survey of housing conditions at grain-collection points.[34] The days of lax attendance and fiddling with membership applications seemed to be over.

Multicandidate, Secret-Ballot Elections

The elections produced a considerable shakeup in the leadership, sweeping out the old leaders, and creating a flurry of excitement among workers. The Union of Woolen Workers, for example, held "accountability" meetings in every factory in which workers had registered complaints. For the first time in years, workers actively participated in large, noisy meetings to choose new candidates for the upcoming factory committee elections. Of the more than 1,300 people elected to 195 factory committees in the woolen industry, 65 percent were new and 43 percent had never before participated in union activities. Almost half of the factory committee chairmen were new. Woolen workers elected more than 1,000 people to shop committees, and another 1,000 as union shop organizers. In Krasnyi Tkach factory, about one-sixth of the total factory workforce of 4,400 was elected to the shop committees, an unprecedented level of voluntary participation. Paid officials were eliminated from the shops and replaced with volunteers; the number of paid staff of the factory committee was cut by 15 percent. The new factory committee elected a plenum, which met regularly to discuss living conditions.[35] In August, the Union of Woolen Workers held its first congress with 245 delegates. They sharply criticized the central committee for its poor leadership, "deep violations of union democracy," lack of contact with lower organizations, and phony performances. The delegates voted out the old members and replaced almost half with Stakhanovites from the shop floor. The new central committee quickly established labor-protection commissions to improve ventilation, keep accident records, provide work clothes, and monitor overtime work.[36]

During the fall and winter of 1937, 116 unions held congresses attended by more than 23,300 delegates. The blame game, first played by the

---

[34] GARF, f. 5451, o. 21, d. 114, "Svodka o praktike rabote profsoiuzov," l. 22.

[35] GARF, f. 5451, o. 22, d. 64, "Dokladnaia zapiska o perestroike prof. raboty na osnove resheniia VI Plenuma VTsSPS," ll. 211–224. Forty percent of the new factory committee members belonged to the Party, while 17 percent were engineering or technical personnel.

[36] Ibid. Of the new 41-member central committee, only four had previously served: GARF, f. 5451, o. 43, d. 72, "Postanovlenie sekretariata VTsSPS," ll. 59, 60. The electoral shakeup in the Union of Woolen Workers was replicated in other unions, including the Union of Iron Ore Workers of the South and the Union of Dairy Workers.

delegates to the VTsSPS Plenum, now spread throughout the unions. A report noted that delegates "unmasked an entire series of individuals in leadership positions." Once again, each layer of leadership criticized the one above it. Delegates from the Union of Railroad Construction Workers criticized their central committee. The central committee of the Union of Central Cooperative Employees (Tsentrosoiuz) criticized its presidium. Hundreds of workers from electrical power stations, peat bogs, schools, and dining halls denounced their unions for "bureaucracy, separation from the masses, and ignoring the needs of their members." Workers embraced the campaign for union democracy, but they did not control it. Regardless of the rhetoric spouted at the podium, workers composed only about one-quarter of the delegates to the union congresses; the remainder included union officials, white-collar employees, engineering/technical personnel, and more than 600 directors of trusts and enterprises and their deputies. About two-thirds of the delegates were party members. The congresses, aimed at revitalization from below, were still dominated by paid union officials and managers.[37] Alongside genuine efforts by workers to reform their unions, officials replicated the peculiar exercise first performed by the VTsSPS Plenum in which "bureaucrats" trumpeted against bureaucracy, and the complacent railed against complacency.

By the end of 1937, new central committees were elected in 146 of the country's 157 unions. Party and union leaders proclaimed the campaign a great success. About 1,230,000 people or 6 percent of the 22 million membership were elected to union posts, including 31,000 to regional (*oblast* and *krai*) and republic committees, 830,000 to factory committees, 160,000 to shop committees, and 163,000 to group organizations (*profgrupy*). The VTsSPS nullified hundreds of elections that violated "the principles of union democracy" by not offering secret ballots and more than one candidate. This "made a deep impression on the workers," according to one report. At the lower levels, workers voted to reconstitute hundreds of thousands of *profgrupy* and shop committees, almost 100,000 factory committees, and 1,645 regional committees. The final election returns showed a serious shakeup in the composition of the unions. More than 70 percent of factory committee members were replaced, 66 percent of the 94,000 factory committee chairmen, and 92 percent of the 30,723 members of the regional committee plenums.

---

[37] GARF, f. 5451, o. 22, d. 64, "Dokladnaia zapiska o khode vyborov tsentral'nykh komitetov profsoiuzov i vydvizhenii bespartiinykh na rukovodiashchuiu profsoiuznuiu rabotu," ll. 12–13.

Many of the newly elected representatives were workers or "people from production": 65 percent of those elected to the *profgrupy* were Stakhanovites or shock workers as were 62 percent elected to the shop committees, 45 percent to the factory committees, and 25 percent to the regional committees. The figures indicated strong representation of workers, but they showed another trend as well. The higher the level within the union organization, the lower the percentage of workers elected to it. From the *profgrup* to the regional committee, for example, the percentage of workers elected dropped by 40 percent.[38] People who did not work in the industry represented by the union still occupied most positions at the upper levels. The wave of renewal weakened as it rolled toward the upper reaches of the unions.[39]

In elections for the highest level of union leadership, the central committees, union members also returned strong votes of no confidence. Electoral returns from 116 union central committees showed that more than 96 percent of 5,054 plenum members, 87 percent of presidium members, 92 percent of secretaries, and 68 percent of chairmen were replaced. Here, too, officials at the apex of the hierarchy retained a greater share of posts than those immediately below them: 96 percent of central committee members were replaced, but only 68 percent of chairmen. Moreover, the new chairmen and secretaries often transferred from other important party, managerial, or union posts. In about one-third of the central committees, they were former heads of factory committees.[40] The new electoral shakeup provided the greatest benefits to this group, catapulting them from leadership of the factories into positions of national prominence.

Party and VTsSPS leaders pointed with pride to the fact that many newly elected officials were *not* party members, evidence that "new people," "the best Stakhanovites," were becoming active in union affairs. Far more nonparty people could be found at the lower than the upper reaches of union leadership: 93 percent of *profgrupy*, 84 percent of the shop committees, 80 percent of the factory committees, 66 percent of the factory committee chairmen, 47 percent of the regional committees, 34 percent of the regional committee presidiums, 33 percent of the union

[38] Ibid., ll. 10–14.

[39] There was a similar pattern in the May 1937 party elections: the regional (*oblast* and *krai*) first secretaries retained their positions, while the district (*raion*) and primary party officials were voted out: J. Arch Getty, "Pragmatists and Puritans: The Rise and Fall of the Party Control Commission," *Carl Beck Papers in Russian and East European Studies*, 1208 (1997), p. 28.

[40] "Dokladnaia zapiska o khode vyborov," ll. 10–14.

central committees, and 19 percent of central committee presidium members did not belong to the Party.[41] Moving up the organizational ranks, the percentage of party members increased just as the percentage of workers decreased. Party leaders' active endorsement of nonparty candidates stood in sharp contrast to their usual policy of promoting their own members. In September 1937, Bregman, newly promoted to VTsSPS secretary, sharply reprimanded the heads of the unions for sending so many party members to the All Union Congress of Unions. "This is wrong," he wrote. "At least 35–40 percent of the delegates should not be party members."[42]

What was the VTsSPS's motivation in promoting nonparty members? Its aims were the same as Stalin and Zhdanov's program for the Party itself: to renew democracy from below and to remove former oppositionists. In the campaign for union democracy, "nonparty" served as a signifier for workers, just as "party member," especially among officials in leading posts, signified a greater likelihood of oppositional activity. By reducing the Party's role in elections, party leaders gave workers a sense of greater power.[43] Party leaders viewed mid- and upper-level union officials as the analog to the regional "princes" they had denounced at the February–March Central Committee Plenum. These union officials were more likely than nonparty workers to have complex political biographies and careers. Moreover, the workers resented them for their failure to address problems in the factories. By mobilizing workers to remove these officials, top party leaders were able to gain working-class support and target former oppositionists in much the same way as they sought to use the rank-and-file party cadres against their regional leaders.[44] Party and VTsSPS leaders viewed the removal of union officials as fulfilling both these aims.

[41] Ibid.

[42] GARF, f. 5451, o. 43, d. 69, "Vsem predsedateliam TsK Soiuzov," l. 147.

[43] In 1925, the Union of Printers tried to dispel apathy by giving more power to the workers and reducing the role of the Party. The purge of the rightists in 1929 was also accompanied by a campaign encouraging criticism from below. See Koenker, *Republic of Labor*, pp. 169, 254.

[44] J. Arch Getty and Oleg Naumov, *The Road to Terror: Stalin and the Self-Destruction of the Bolsheviks, 1932–1939* (Yale University Press, New Haven, 1999), pp. 263–8, 331–3, 442–3. Getty argues that regional party leaders were targeted for removal by Stalin and his supporters through a mobilization of the lower party ranks against the middle. In Getty's view, these regional leaders represented a threat to centralizing power as well as a pool of likely oppositionists. The process of mobilizing the lower ranks against the middle did not occur smoothly, but in advances and retreats from the June 1936 Central Committee Plenum through the February–March 1937 Central Committee Plenum.

Workers voted out the overwhelming majority of old officials, but did they succeed in replacing them with workers? Salary data shed some light on this question. In 1938, there were 5,484 chairmen, secretaries, and presidium members elected to union central and regional committees. At this highest level of leadership, salary data show that almost 60 percent of the newly elected officials either took a cut in salary or stayed at the same level. In other words, they did not move up from lower positions, and certainly not from the shop floor. Of the 40 percent who increased their salaries, the overwhelming majority did not make a big jump: they gained less than 200 rubles per month.[45] The newly elected chairman of the Union of Oil Refinery Workers, for example, was previously the head of a shop. As head of the union, he earned 1,000 rubles a month, 100 rubles less than he had earned as shop boss. The new chairman of the Union of Coal Miners of the East was previously the head of the Cadre Department of the Eastern Coal Transport Trust. He, too, took a pay cut, from 1,200 to 800 rubles. The new chairman of the Union of Construction Workers in Heavy Industry in the Far East previously headed the energy sector in the eastern town of Komsomol'ka, earning 1,540 rubles beforehand, but only 800 afterwards. The new chairman of the Union of Medical Workers had been director of a shoe workshop, the chairman of the Fish Workers Union was the former deputy chairman of the Murmansk town soviet, and the head of the Union of Iron Ore Workers had previously been the head of the Liebknicht mine.[46] In other words, the newly elected chairmen of the union central committees were not workers; they were leading officials in powerful local and regional posts, who moved up or laterally from managerial positions within the unions, industry, or government.

Compared to workers, these elected officials earned large salaries. Workers at the bottom of the wage scale earned about 150 rubles per month. Workers in the textile factories, for example, were frantic when stoppages further reduced their meager paychecks, because they had barely been able to feed their children on their regular monthly earnings. Highly skilled workers in heavy industry might earn 500 rubles or more a month. Yet union officials earned more than workers even at the highest end of the pay scale. They also received access to special goods, monthly

---

[45] GARF, f. 5451, o. 22, d. 75, "O zarabotnoi plate shtatnykh vybornykh rabotnikov v tsentral'nykh komitetakh i oblastnykh komitetakh profsoiuzov," ll. 2–4. The study covered 1,349 paid, elected officials.

[46] Ibid., ll. 3–4.

food packets, and other privileges. Throughout 1937 and 1938, officials were under fire everywhere. Lateral leapfrog was one way regional and local cliques protected each other. Leading officials stubbornly defended their privileges even through the unpredictable vagaries of "revitalization." Managers moved into unions, and former union officials were most probably appointed to management posts. If these men were representative of the newly elected officials, the higher union organizations appeared to have been "renewed" by the bosses!

Analysis of the elections suggests that many interests were at play. Stalin, Shvernik, and other party leaders aimed to gain workers' support and root out former oppositionists. The workers hoped to remove corrupt and complacent "bureaucrats." And regional and local leaders sought to preserve their standing by moving members of their own "family circles" from one leading post to another. The elections were not an unalloyed victory for any of these groups. Party leaders' attempts to break up "family circles" and root out oppositionists were circumvented by lateral leapfrog. The workers did not succeed in removing "bureaucrats." And regional and local leaders continued to be arrested even after assuming new posts. At least ten members of the new union central committees were arrested as "enemies of the people" soon after the elections. In the Union of Railroad Workers alone, nineteen newly elected officials were "unmasked" and arrested.[47] Throughout 1937 and 1938, the NKVD continued to cull the union ranks. These arrests encouraged union officials to denounce each other, which in turn prompted ever-widening circles of arrests.

After the Elections

The new elections did not end the process of "revitalization." On the contrary, they opened a Pandora's box of grudges, charges, and grievances. Workers successfully used the elections to shake up the unions, but they were not as successful in transforming union practices. In some unions, the new leaders proved even more corrupt and incompetent than those they replaced. In others, elections produced fierce factional fighting which drew attention away from workers' grievances. Throughout 1938, the VTsSPS continued to launch investigations of the unions, which fueled repression by identifying new sources of corruption, negligence, and opposition.

In the Union of Glass Workers, for example, union officials were completely absorbed in fierce factional rivalries generated by the elections,

[47] "Dokladnaia zapiska o khode vyborov," l. 23.

while the workers still struggled with the same miserable conditions that existed before the campaign for democracy. An older faction within the union intensely disliked the newly elected chairman of the central committee, and met secretly to try to unseat him. The central committee, deeply mired in internal squabbles, ignored the lower union organizations, the high accident rate in the factories, and the needs of its members. The union continued to disregard housing, daycare, dining halls, labor safety, cultural services, and international issues. It failed to hold secret-ballot elections for many positions. The factory committee of the Khrustal factory in Diat'kovo in Briansk province, for example, had three successive chairs in 1937, its shop committees were not elected by secret ballot, and union representatives continued to be appointed rather than elected. Union finances and membership records remained in a "chaotic state." More importantly, little changed in the lives of the workers. The barracks that housed many of the factory's 3,865 workers were collapsing. The floors were broken, there were not enough dressers or chairs, and the buildings were crawling with roaches and bedbugs. The workers produced glass, but their own windows were broken. There were no newspapers or chess or checker sets. With nothing to occupy them, the workers "drank, fought, and engaged in various debaucheries." Despite a high accident rate, the union gave scant attention to safety or medical aid. The Krasnyi Fakel glass factory in Ivanovo province was located four miles from a hospital, had no means of transportation, and lacked even a small first aid station for its 800 workers. The factory's daycare center possessed a total of twelve plates and three glasses for thirty-six children. The 787,000 rubles allocated by the state to the Union of Glass Workers for cultural/life services in 1937 had never been spent. On the other hand, union officials had overspent the fund for their own salaries by 201,000 rubles. In this union, the campaign for union democracy had bogged down in bureaucratic infighting. Although new leaders were elected, they paid no more attention to workers' needs than those they replaced. In fact, the struggle for power seemed to have absorbed whatever small energy the central committee had once placed in the service of its members.[48]

Elections in the Union of Coal and Shale Workers of the Center also failed to produce responsive leaders. The union's leaders were closely tied to the district party committee in a "family circle," which offered an

---

[48] "Dokladnaia zapiska o rezultatakh proverki raboty TsK Soiuza rabochikh stekol'noi promyshlennosti," ll. 187–193.

excellent example of the lateral leapfrog the elections so often produced. Fedin, the newly elected chairman of the union's central committee, had previously served as secretary of the party committee in the mines from 1930 to 1937. Union elections offered him the opportunity to move up, from party committee to the head of the union. In 1938, his former boss, Plotkin, the secretary of the district party committee, was arrested as an "enemy of the people." Plotkin's connections extended deeply into the union.[49] His arrest prompted the union's party organization and the VTsSPS to examine Fedin and the union's central committee more closely. Fedin submitted a declaration to the party group of the VTsSPS protesting: "I have no deviations and have never worked in opposition." Desperate to sever his connection to Plotkin, he portrayed himself as someone who had successfully denounced and unmasked others, a strategy designed to emphasize his own loyalty and rectitude. "I was elected and reelected," he stressed. "I unmasked some rabble as saboteurs and traitors . . . I uncovered and criticized and also unmasked those who did not fulfill the general line of the party." Fedin had moved easily from party to union post, most likely with Plotkin's help. Yet with Plotkin's arrest, Fedin quickly abandoned him. "I had no relation to Plotkin except in regard to my work. I never drank with him. Plotkin never attempted to move me from the general line." He blamed the union's poor record on the officials above him who were often absent from their posts: "They never gave me clear assignments." The VTsSPS investigation of the union's other leaders exonerated them of oppositional politics, but revealed them in all their sloppy greed, cupidity, and corruption. Savin, a member of the presidium, was accused of "drunkenness and carelessness." He had already received several party reprimands for drunkenness and hooliganism, but he was still drinking. Boldin, the head of the union's mass production department, was dirty and disheveled. He had received a strict reprimand for polygamy, and was paying alimony to two former wives. He kept passes for rest homes for his ex-wives and family instead of distributing them to the workers. Prodok, a member of the union's central committee, moved himself from a small town to a coveted residence in Moscow, overspent 500,000 rubles on sick leave and other things, and failed to distribute vacation passes to the workers. Two other central committee members were recently expelled from the Party, one for "drunkenness and debauchery." The VTsSPS investigator concluded that there was no "compromising data" on Fedin, but criticized him for being "politically blind in his failure to unmask Plotkin."

[49] GARF, f. 5451, o. 22, d. 64, "V sekretariat VTsSPS. Dokladnaia zapiska," ll. 93–94.

He also recommended that Savin and Boldin both be dismissed.[50] The new central committee, elected by the members of the Union of Coal and Shale Workers in the campaign for union democracy, turned out to be little more that a rogues' gallery of self-serving careerists, drunkards, and petty thieves.

The new leadership of the Union of Oil Refinery Workers was not much more impressive. After elections in 1938, the new central committee members had wasted no time in lining their own pockets and getting drunk. The newly elected young chairman, Makurin, had first entered a Baku refinery as a guard in 1928, and then moved up to boiler stoker. He entered the ranks of officialdom when he became secretary of the factory committee, and then assistant to the head of a shop. Although a party member, he never advanced beyond a primary school education. The other new members of the central committee also had little education. The one female member, Ikonnikova, was barely literate and, although she attended meetings regularly, she never spoke. After the elections, the central committee split in bitter fighting. Tolmadzhev, the head of the union's cultural department, denounced Makurin and the new leadership for squandering union funds and ignoring critical problems. He claimed that the union was still "blocked up" by "family circles," guilty of favoritism and corruption. The only activities they organized were drunken parties. Makurin spent most of his day in an alcoholic stupor, engaged in petty corruption. The infighting revealed other sordid incidents, as well. When union headquarters moved from Moscow to Baku in October 1938, members of the central committee got so drunk that they missed the train. For almost a month after the move, no one did any work. They spent 6,000 rubles more than the 11,500 rubles allocated in the budget "to help officials of the union central committee" and awarded themselves prizes and bonuses. They took the money allocated to print and post safety rules in the refineries, formed a "rules committee," and paid themselves 1,500 rubles for serving on it. The workers elected these people, but a VTsSPS investigator concluded, "This presidium is in no condition to do its job." He recommended removing most of the newly elected leadership, scheduling a new election, reviewing the union's central committee, and auditing its finances.[51] The

---

[50] GARF, f. 5451, o. 22, d. 64, "Sekretariu VTsSPS. Tov. Bregmanu. Dokladnaia zapiska," ll. 110–113.

[51] GARF, f. 5451, o. 22, d. 64, "V sekretariat VTsSPS. Tov. Shverniku, t. Nikolaevoi, t. Bregman. Dokladnaia zapiska. Sekretno," ll. 145–148. The report was written by the head of the Organization Department of the VTsSPS.

Union of Oil Refinery Workers had held democratic elections, but the people its members put into office were dishonest, disorganized drunks.

The Union of Cotton Textile Workers, too, was split by an ugly power struggle between the union's newly elected and older leaders in the wake of the elections. In 1938, the union had 300,000 members, with one-third located in the Moscow region. Light industry in general was undercapitalized, and aging machinery, frequent breakdowns, and low wages all contributed to poor morale. Workers consistently failed to meet the production plans set for their factories. In 1937, I. E. Liubimov, the head the Commissariat of Light Industry, was arrested along with many of his staff. Problems in the textile industry, however, persisted even after the arrests of the alleged "wreckers." In September, the Council of People's Commissars (SNK) issued a decree about "liquidating the consequences of wrecking" in the textile industry and the union held its congress to elect a new central committee. The problem of wage rates and production norms carried over from the old to the new central committee. In January 1938, the union turned the problem over to the SNK, but the government, too, failed to find a solution. In May 1938, a VTsSPS investigation of the textile industry discovered "wage distortions of a provocative manner that had consciously been planted by the old leadership of the Commissariat of Light Industry."[52]

Leaders of the VTsSPS met with the union's presidium in May to berate them about the wage issue. Moskatov, a VTsSPS secretary, charged that the system of wage payment had "in essence corrupted the workers." According to a complicated piece-rate formula, workers received higher wage rates when the machines stopped than when they ran. M. P. Stepanov, a member of the VTsSPS presidium, explained that textile workers fulfilled only about 60 to 75 percent of their production norms. VTsSPS officials knew that workers were entitled to 66 percent of the average piece rate during a stoppage. If the norms were set high, and workers consistently fulfilled less than 66 percent, they could conceivably receive higher wages for not working. Moskatov noted, "The status of norms is such that their nonfulfillment seems to benefit the textile workers!" Moskatov also claimed that management of the industry was riddled with "imposters, former White Guards, and every other kind of filth," and the central committee of the union was "also not without sin."[53] Artiukhina, the union's

[52] GARF, f, 5451, o. 22, d. 11, "Material k protokoly prezidiume VTsSPS ot 10/V/38. O polozhenii del v TsK Soiuza khlopchatobumazhnoi promyshlennosti," ll. 241–247.
[53] Ibid.

head, came under sharp attack. A daughter of weavers, Artiukhina had begun work in the textile factories at the age of twelve. She had joined the Union of Textile Workers in 1909, and was arrested and deported several times. In 1927, she had become head of the Zhenotdel (Women's Department) and had fought hard for women workers. Moskatov questioned Artiukhina aggressively about the wage rates. She admitted that she did not fully understand how they were calculated. Stepanov asked, "How can Artiukhina, an old textile worker experienced in leadership, not understand?" Stepanov argued that the wage problem was a direct result of union neglect: officials never visited the factories or improved the equipment. "Why doesn't the central committee undertake a program of repair?" he asked. Yet Stepanov, too, admitted that he did not understand the wage rates. In fact, no one seemed to understand the complex mix of progressive piecework bonuses, flat rates, and downtime rates for stoppages. Stepanov, pushed to clarify the wage formula, stumbled and fell back on the popular excuse: "The feeling is that enemies of the people aimed to confuse this business."[54]

VTsSPS officials instigated the newly elected union leaders to blame Artiukhina for the wage problems. Not all played the game. Riasin, the head of the Organization Department of the union's central committee, argued that it was unrealistic to expect union leaders to resolve complicated issues of wages, rates, and living conditions in every factory. Others, however, found Artiukhina a convenient scapegoat. Shiriaev, the newly elected union secretary, sensed that Artiukhina was on the brink of arrest and tried to protect himself. Professing "ignorance," he blamed her for not giving the new presidium members instructions and for disregarding their ideas. "I worked for two and a half months with Comrade Artiukhina," he complained, "and, during this entire time, there was not the smallest attempt to help raise us to the correct path, to organize our work correctly. On the contrary, in practical work, they attempted at every step to undermine the initiative of the new officials. In essence, we do not have a chair of the central committee, but are directed by firm, one-person rule." Yet Shiriaev also admitted that he bore a personal grudge against Artiukhina because she refused to release him to enroll in educational courses, a coveted privilege that offered greater upward mobility.[55]

Moskatov supported the new representatives unreservedly. Shiriaev was right, in his opinion. The "old guard" had entrenched itself in the union over the past six years, and it was difficult to get rid of them. He was hostile

---

[54] Ibid., ll. 241–248.   [55] Ibid., ll. 258–2660b.

to Artiukhina, but found it difficult to criticize her for, unlike many union leaders, Artiukhina constantly visited factories and spoke with workers. Moskatov derided her for too much contact. "Artiukhina visits a place, promises a full basket, but it's all for nothing," he said snidely. He accused Artiukhina of highhandedness, failing to identify enemies within the union, and "smoothing over sharp questions." He summed up her style of work with an old folk saying: "Don't take the garbage out of the hut, because we might lose something in the cleaning." He went on, "This putrid, non-Bolshevik position is the enemy of our party position." "Why do we have this stinking atmosphere?" he asked nastily. "First, I consider the leadership of the union central committee clearly bankrupt. It has politically discredited itself in the sense that many large, sharp political questions flew right by its nose." Moskatov suggested removing Artiukhina, convening a new union plenum to discuss the central committee's relationship with the factory committees, developing a plan to deal with the "consequences of wrecking," and instructing the VTsSPS department of wages to straighten out the wage-rate mess.[56]

Artiukhina, upset and unnerved by the criticism, maintained her composure. She calmly explained that the turnover of leadership in the union sparked by the 1937 elections had created new difficulties. A new cohort, with little experience, had to be trained. The production norms and wage rates were difficult to master. The SNK had considered the question, and Molotov himself had demanded revision of the norms. She noted humbly, "I am in agreement with everything that was said here about the mess. Perhaps I spoke poorly, I was more upset than I should have been, although I should be upset. I assure you, Comrade Moskatov . . ." Moskatov abruptly interrupted her, "What do you assure me of?" Unruffled, Artiukhina continued, "You heard me the first time, Comrade Moskatov. I wrote to the VTsSPS and asked for help in liquidating the consequences of wrecking. They did not call me, they did not respond." Just as Shiriaev and Moskatov had shifted blame from the newly elected leaders to Artiukhina, she, too, deftly shifted blame to her superiors in the VTsSPS. Artiukhina navigated the dangerous political waters with skilled resolve. She admitted that she had failed to resolve the wage issue, but she strongly denied that she was guilty of wrecking. "They say here that I covered up and continued the old wrecking practice. This is wrong," she said firmly. She asked the presidium for a chance to correct her work with their help.[57]

[56] Ibid., ll. 267–276.   [57] Ibid., ll. 276–277.

Arrests in the Commissariat of Light Industry, electoral rivalries, and fear encouraged union officials to blame each other. The real issue, however, could not be honestly named. The failure of textile workers to meet their production quotas was the result not of "wrecking" or of muddled wage rates, but of aging machinery and little new investment. Textiles were not a priority industry. Managers fiddled with wage rates in an attempt to decrease labor turnover by ensuring a minimum wage even when machinery broke. The union turned a blind eye. Workers and shop foremen also colluded in raising wages. Blaming Artiukhina, leaders of the Commissariat of Light Industry, or managers for wrecking would never solve the problems of an undercapitalized industry with aging machinery and a poorly paid labor force. More importantly, the VTsSPS insisted that the union enforce wage cuts. The workers had elected a new central committee, but not one of the newly elected leaders stated the truth: single mothers in the textile industry could barely support their children. Only Artiukhina admitted that a readjustment resulting in a wage decrease would have been unbearably painful. In response to Moskatov's assertion that the union had failed to cut wage rates, she said simply, "We were afraid to tell the workers the truth."[58]

The Limits of Union Democracy

Party and VTsSPS leaders openly admitted that the campaign for union democracy had two aims: "to liquidate stagnation in the unions" and "to root out the entrenched Trotskyist-Bukharinist agents of fascism and their supporters."[59] The leadership never regarded these aims as contradictory but, rather, envisioned a revitalized union movement eager to support Stalinist industrialization. The unions would not contest the state's policies of accumulation, investment, or wages but would still play an important role. They would ensure that state funds for housing, childcare, rest homes, social insurance, and safety were spent honestly and efficiently, oversee food distribution, and guard against corruption and shoddy construction. They would reduce accident rates and ensure observance of safety and overtime regulations. Union officials would be genuine representatives of the workers, elected regularly in secret-ballot, multicandidate elections. Party leaders realized that, in the absence of active members, union officials would become increasingly lazy and corrupt, geared solely toward

---

[58] Ibid., ll. 249–253.
[59] "Dokladnaia zapiska o khode vyborov," ll. 12–13.

bettering their own social and material interests. In essence, the Party crafted a new role for the unions as "social-welfare" managers. They could pressure industrial managers, and report safety violations to the courts. They could not, however, challenge state policy, offer an alternate economic program, or contest norms or wages.[60]

The most striking success of the campaign for union democracy was in the new attention to labor safety. Workers in every industry had suffered high accident rates in the early 1930s. In 1934, 25 to 33 percent of the workforce in the most hazardous industries suffered an accident on the job, and at least 10 percent in the majority of industries. The accident rate rose in more than 70 percent of industries between 1934 and 1936. In 1937, however, more than 90 percent of industries, with the exception of coal mining, coke ovens, chemical fertilizers, plywood, liquor and spirits, and road construction, showed a decline in the accident rate.[61] The new spotlight on wrecking undoubtedly encouraged managers and union officials to give more attention to labor safety. Yet it also may have encouraged shady bookkeeping. Officials in at least two unions were discovered to have shifted production accidents to the category of home accidents, which also required the unions to provide sick pay but did not entail political consequences. In a number of unions, work injuries appeared to decrease as home injuries increased.[62]

Stalin and his supporters in the VTsSPS and the Party did not consider the campaign for democracy to be at odds with the repression of oppositionists. They envisioned a workers' democracy within a limited sphere, emphasizing workers' oversight of consumer services, civic activism, and broad, popular participation. Workers were permitted, even encouraged, to criticize managers and officials, to speak out against abuses of power,

---

[60] On the limits of discussion, see Robert Thurston, *Life and Terror in Stalin's Russia, 1934–1941* (Yale University Press, New Haven, 1996), pp. 164–98.

[61] The most significant decreases occurred in tractor building (26 percent), agricultural machine building (23 percent), nonferrous metal working (22 percent), sawmill and wood working (22 percent), leather working (21 percent), railroad factories (20 percent), printing (19 percent), and municipal services and housing construction (18 percent). The figures were reported by seventy-nine unions for 1934–7, and included work and home injuries that resulted in lost time at work. Injuries rose in fifty of the sixty-nine unions that reported statistics for 1934 and 1936. Of the forty-eight unions that reported injury rates for 1937, forty-four noted a decrease. See GARF, f. 5451, o. 43, d. 74, "Tablitsa: proizvodstvennyi i bytovoi travmatizm v 1934–1937," ll. 1–3.

[62] GARF, f. 5451, o. 43, d. 74, "Kratkie poiasneniia k tablitse s proizvodstvennom i bytovom travmatizme za 1937," l. 5. Donald Filtzer notes that unions colluded with management in underplaying accidents in the postwar period: *Soviet Workers and Late Stalinism* (Cambridge University Press, Cambridge, 2002), pp. 203–13.

corruption, and poor working and living conditions. They were urged to write up abuses on wall newspapers in the factories, to write letters to the press, and government and party officials. But the democracy the campaign offered was limited, and discourse was not permitted to stray beyond clearly defined boundaries. In the Zhdanov factory, for example, during a discussion of the campaign for union democracy, four workers from the frame shop stepped outside these boundaries. One Chernostin, stubbornly rejecting the new campaign, asked resentfully, "Why do we need these worker meetings? They don't get the workers anything." Deev, his shopmate, declared that elections and factory committee meetings should be held without the participation of party members. And Kulikov and Malov, dismissing all the rhetoric about vigilance as a lot of nonsense, declared firmly, "There are no 'enemies of the people' among the working class and to look for them is just a waste of time and energy." If communists in leading circles wanted to cut each other's throats, the workers implied, let them. But they should leave the workers alone. These comments were deemed "enemy speeches." It was not acceptable to suggest that the new campaign was pointless, that workers would have better meetings without communists, or that the hunt for "enemies of the people" was a lot of nonsense. Informers duly noted these comments, and quoted them in a report to the VTsSPS with the name, shop, and factory of the speaker.[63]

Workers were clearly hopeful about the campaign and the elections. Yet even when they swept out officials that they regarded as corrupt or incompetent, they did not necessarily succeed in putting more honest or able leaders in their places. The officials elected by the Unions of Glass, Oil Refinery, and Coal and Shale Workers acted in much the same way as their appointed predecessors. Although they were less likely to be tied to the regional and district "family circles," they were equally prone to drunkenness, pilfering, and petty corruption. Many were barely educated. The general lack of competent administrators within the larger population was one of the main reasons, in fact, that *kooptatsiia* was so widespread. The double edge of the campaign, against negligence and petty corruption on the one hand, and political opposition on the other, placed the Party in a bind. While it aimed to remove the layer of officials entrenched since the late 1920s, the people who replaced them were often ill equipped to play the role the Party envisioned.

[63] "Resheniia VI Plenuma VTsSPS," l. 86.

The elections did not simply sweep out the old in favor of the new, but initiated a prolonged struggle within the unions. The old leaders fought hard to retain their posts, and were somewhat successful, especially at the upper levels. The unions were further destabilized by arrests in local and regional party organizations and their own industries. As more people disappeared into prison, union officials descended into vicious and fearful squabbling. The new leaders attacked the old, and everyone scrabbled frantically to find someone to blame for problems in the factories. In the end, the campaign was used to serve a variety of interests. It spread rapidly through the unions because it proved useful to so many ends. Although it brought some limited attention to working and living conditions, the new leaders were neither willing nor able to pursue genuine democratic reforms.

Finally, there was no substantive change in the role of the unions from 1929 to 1937. Workers were unable to use the campaign for democracy to transform the unions into genuine defenders of their interests. Elections, even with multiple candidates and secret ballots, meant little if the elected representatives had no power to win tangible benefits for their constituencies. Union representatives, no matter how honest and efficient, did not have the power to challenge wage rates, investment policy, or production norms. The only language available to workers, managers, and union officials for advancing their interests was the phrases promulgated by Zhdanov at the Central Committee Plenum and popularized by Shvernik through the VTsSPS: "wrecking," "weakening ties with the masses," "violation of democracy," "arrogance," "toadying," "lack of vigilance," and "suppression of criticism from below." This was the language of the terror and, as the only sanctioned outlet for expression, it was widely employed. Yet these phrases were of limited value in solving the real problem, which was rooted in rapid industrialization. Accidents, poor food distribution, shoddy housing, delayed construction, wage arrears, and low productivity were not the result of intentional "wrecking." In this sense, terror and democracy functioned as two sides of the same coin: democracy allowed workers to elect new officials, terror allowed them to remove the old, but neither permitted a challenge to the underlying structural problems.

9. Women workers in the Kauchuk Rubber Factory at an election meeting, June 1937. Reproduced from *Trud*, June 9, 1937, p. 2

10. Workers cast secret ballots in multicandidate elections for the factory committee in the Chicherin Machine Building factory, Moscow, June 1937. Reproduced from *Trud*, June 15, 1937, p. 3

5

Victims and Perpetrators

"People were literally thrown overboard here."
> – N. V. Voronina, head of the Bureau of Complaints, VTsSPS, discussing
> the purge of the Union of Railroad Workers, 1938[1]

"Irresponsibility and slinging charges have splintered authority among us. As a result, we have poor relations among us. Within the union, we have insulted each other with strong words, we just keep spitting on each other ... We are scattered and not sticking together according to a principle of respect and mutual understanding. This is a product of our own, personal relations, *which we ourselves are guilty of creating.*"
> – S. O. Kotliar, head of the Union of Employees of State Institutions, 1937[2]

The campaign for union democracy was from its very inception connected to the destruction of former oppositionists. Elections in the unions were accompanied by sweeping arrests of union and All Union Central Council of Unions (VTsSPS) leaders. The elections turned into bitter power struggles, which provoked a frenzy of backstabbing and denunciations. The VTsSPS, eager to prove its loyalty, initiated its own investigations, which caught the attention of the Party and the NKVD, and resulted in the arrest of numerous officials. Workers and union officials quickly discovered that "enemy of the people" and "wrecker" were magical phrases guaranteed to focus attention on long-neglected problems. In this atmosphere, workers' interests in improving conditions and eliminating corruption were rapidly submerged in a rising tide of chaos as people denounced each other in the same phrases for the same offenses. In successive waves of denunciation

---

[1] GARF, f. 5451, o. 43, d. 69, "Stenogramma soveshchaniia chlenov prezidiumov TsK soiuzov i otvetstvennykh rabotnikov VTsSPS," l. 275.
[2] GARF, f. 5451, o. 43, d. 73, "Vypiska iz stenogrammy piatogo plenuma oblastnogo komiteta Soiuza rabotnikov gosuchrezhdenii," l. 36 (italics mine).

and arrest, perpetrators sent victims to the camps, only to become the victims of new perpetrators, subject in turn to the same fate.

Historians have long tried to disentangle the skein of events in which so many people were caught and destroyed. Did the VTsSPS and the unions contribute independently to the repression, or did they simply carry out orders from above? What was the relationship among the Party, the NKVD, the VTsSPS, and the unions? What role did personal denunciations play? This chapter traces the progression of terror through the VTsSPS and the unions. From the first targeted purge of oppositionists to the free-for-all of mutual denunciation, it charts the organizational dynamics and personal behaviors that promoted and spread repression throughout the union movement.

The First Arrests

The first arrests within the unions were connected with attacks on former left oppositionists and the August 1936 trial of the "United Trotskyist-Zinovievite Center." Union leaders once active in the Trotskyist opposition were expelled from the Party and arrested. In Rostov, three leaders of the Union of Postal Employees – Kukuevskii, Ivanov, and Baburkin – were exposed as Trotskyists, expelled from the Party, and fired from their union posts. The investigation of Kukuevskii quickly broadened to include the officials who recommended him to the Party and appointed him to his union post. These arrests led to "a nest of Trotskyists," which included the director of Rostov's Central Telegraph Office, and members of the Azov–Black Sea regional party committee. The secretary of the Postal Employees replaced Kukuevskii with another union leader, Pivanov, who was also quickly "unmasked" as a Trotskyist.[3] The pattern of arrests would be replicated many times around the country in the coming months. Kukuevskii served as the hub of a wheel with multiple spokes, leading to a circle of contacts. A candidate for party membership had to be recommended by a party member, a practice that ensured that every party member was beholden to at least one mentor. Similarly, the widespread practice of *kooptatsiia* meant that many officials were appointed as part of "family circles" attached to a patron in a prominent post. Thus the "spokes of the wheel" were created by specific organizational practices. Any investigation led ineluctably to patrons and clients of the victim. The head of the Union of Canning Workers in Rostov, for example, got into

---

[3] "Trotskistskie posledyshi v rostovskom dvortse truda," *Trud*, August 22, 1936, p. 4.

trouble for promoting the party candidacy of a union official who was subsequently discovered to be a Trotskyist. The union's central committee was publicly warned in *Trud*, the national labor newspaper, that the recommendation or promotion of a person subsequently found to be a Trotskyist could be construed as a "criminal" act. This warning immediately implicated hundreds if not thousands of party members who had written recommendations or promoted people who were now discovered to be enemies.[4]

The first big wave of arrests hit the unions in the fall of 1936. The secretariat of the VTsSPS met regularly to consider requests from union leaders and to affirm personnel decisions made by the unions' central committees. Throughout the summer, their work was routine: a dull round of petitions from union leaders for sick leave, money, and rest-home vouchers for ailing wives. In October, routine business turned deadly. The secretariat began processing and affirming dismissals of union leaders who had been expelled from the Party and fired from their jobs by the unions. V. A. Dorokhov, the head of the Union of Timber Cutters and Floaters of the Central and Southern Districts, was expelled from the Party for participating in the Trotskyist opposition in 1923. The charge stated that he had hidden his oppositional activities for thirteen years, but had now been "unmasked." The central committee of his union fired him, and the VTsSPS secretariat affirmed the dismissal. In November and December, the secretariat affirmed the dismissals of several more union leaders who were also excluded from the Party for Trotskyism, including leaders of the Unions of Oil Refinery Workers of the Eastern Districts, Metal Workers, and Coal Miners of the East.[5] Gil'burg, the head of the Union of Coke-Oven Workers, and Zharikov, an aide to N. M. Shvernik, the head of the VTsSPS, who helped with the party *proverka* in the VTsSPS in 1935, were both arrested for Trotskyism.[6]

There were also arrests of former "rightists" in the VTsSPS. By December 1936, the NKVD implicated Bukharin and Rykov in the Kirov assassination and Trotskyist "plots" to kill other state leaders. These accusations signaled open season on their former sympathizers. Within the VTsSPS, the NKVD focused on the Bureau of Social Insurance, the Department of Labor Protection, and the labor safety institutes, all once part of the

[4] "Posobniki trotskistov zametaiut sledy," *Trud*, August 27, 1936, p. 2.

[5] GARF, f. 5451, o. 43, d. 71, "VTsSPS. Vypiska iz protokola zasedaniia sekretariata," "Postanovlenie sekretariata VTsSPS," "Vypiska iz protokola," ll. 355, 386, 401, 409.

[6] "Materialy fevral'sko-martovskogo plenuma TsK VKP (b) 1937 goda," *Voprosy istorii*, 10, 1995, pp. 18–21, 25–8.

Commissariat of Labor. The NKVD arrested Kotov, the head of the Bureau of Social Insurance, and charged him with wasting millions of rubles, along with Tsybal'skii, the head of the Department of Labor Protection, and many others in his organization.[7] Both former rightists and leftists were blamed for problems of great concern to workers: the high accident rate and the improper disbursement of workers' compensation funds. At this point, however, the axe was still falling very selectively.

The Fall of Polonskii

The February–March 1937 Central Committee Plenum marked the beginning of a wider attack on the unions and the VTsSPS. Several party leaders at the plenum had attacked each other for building small fiefdoms and "family circles." The meaning and purpose of this sniping was unclear. Ia. A. Iakovlev, the head of the Party Control Commission, for example, attacked N. S. Khrushchev, the head of the Moscow city and regional party committee. Were these personal vendettas or were they sanctioned at the highest levels? Or were they the only visible hints of intense, behind-the-scenes factional struggles? One of the most dramatic incidents involved V. I. Polonskii, a former VTsSPS secretary and supervisor of the Departments of Physical Culture and of Labor Protection. Polonskii launched a vicious attack on N. M. Shvernik, the head of the VTsSPS. Both men were staunch supporters of Stalin; both had been active in the purge of Tomskii and the rightists. The issues were murky because each used the same language to denounce the other. Yet the struggle between the two foreshadowed the infighting and wild accusations that would soon overwhelm the VTsSPS and the unions.

Polonskii had a long history of revolutionary labor activity. He joined the Bolshevik Party in 1912, and worked with the Union of Metal Workers. After the revolution, he helped to organize the Union of Miners and became head of the Southern Bureau of the VTsSPS. In 1920, he became head of the Nizhnii Novgorod regional committee of unions. He moved to Moscow in 1925 to become a member of the city party committee and, within two years, had become a candidate member of the Central Committee. In 1930, he served briefly as a VTsSPS secretary. In 1933, he became director of the Orgburo of the Central Committee, and deputy commissar of transport. In 1935, he again became a VTsSPS secretary. At

---

[7] Ibid.

the February–March Central Committee Plenum, Polonskii was already under a dark cloud, and had stopped working as a result of a bitter but obscure conflict with Shvernik over his organizational responsibilities.

Polonskii viciously attacked Shvernik and other VTsSPS leaders at the plenum. A witty speaker, he initially had the support of his fellow plenum members. Provoking laughter and quips from the audience, he began by insulting the VTsSPS, its leaders, and even the building in which they were housed. He charged the unions with "provincial, remote, political mustiness." The officials sat "in their mid-century building with its dark corridors, roaming like gloomy shadows. And even in the Palace of Labor, people find great satisfaction in doing nothing as the years roll by." Ia. V. Gamarnik, head of the Red Army's Political Directorate and deputy commissar for military and naval affairs, called out to the laughing delegates, "The building is very good." Polonskii noted that not one party leader had visited the VTsSPS headquarters in more than two years. Amid general laughter, he drawled, "In terms of the actual work, the basic order, the essential culture, well, we have a series of collective farms where things are not worse, and probably better."[8] Given the state of the collective farms, this was a serious insult, indeed.

Polonskii blamed Shvernik for permitting rightists to remain within the unions. M. P. Tomskii, purged in 1929, still managed "in the crumbling and bulky VTsSPS apparat and union central committees and local organizations to retain his avowed and hidden adherents." Retaining their "trade union habits," the unions continued to set workers against the state. Polonskii claimed that Tomskii had destroyed VTsSPS personnel records so that it was impossible to trace the officials still tied to him. In a broad hint to the NKVD, he recalled a list of ninety-three people who had voted against Stalin's decision to place L. M. Kaganovich, his supporter, on the VTsSPS presidium in 1929. If this list was investigated, he intimated, it would expose the hidden rightists in the VTsSPS. He noted that V. V. Shmidt, "Tomskii's brother-in-arms," and N. A. Uglanov had supervised the merger of the Commissariat of Labor and the VTsSPS. As a result, "the unions did not subordinate the Commissariat of Labor, but the Commissariat of Labor took them captive." Someone called out snidely from the floor, "And were you among this group?" Polonskii ignored the jibe, and continued his attack. A whole group of rightists had remained in the unions and moved into leading posts. The head of the VTsSPS's

[8] Ibid., pp. 25–6.

Department of Labor Protection, Tsybal'skii, had recently been arrested along with scores of others.[9]

These charges infuriated Shvernik, who fumed silently throughout Polonskii's speech. Finally, he burst out, "You're on the hunt, but you should talk about this in the context of self-criticism." "Don't you worry, Comrade Shvernik," Polonskii replied amid prolonged laughter; "You and I will never be accused of 'family ties' [*semeistvennost'*]." Polonskii continued his accusations. The leading officials of the VTsSPS and the unions were divorced from the workers, "swimming in a stream of bureaucratic papers." They had "lost their taste" for mass work, for elections, and for accountability before their members. Polonskii predicted that, if secret ballots were introduced, many of the union officials would be tossed out of office. Yet the more abusive Polonskii became, the colder his audience grew. Shvernik clearly had strong supporters among the delegates. Finally, Molotov interrupted the stream of charges, "You tell us how you personally tried to improve the situation." Ignoring Molotov, Polonskii continued. "Fear of the masses has become a chronic illness of union officials. It is not surprising that many of the leaders of the VTsSPS and the unions do not have the respect of the masses...Shvernik and Veinberg go everywhere like twins, either because they are inseparable or because they don't trust each other." The plenum delegates laughed again, but somewhat more uncomfortably now that Molotov had intervened. Shvernik, enraged, called out, "Why did you receive complaints for two years and do nothing?" Polonskii ignored him, returning to his list of VTsSPS transgressions: "There is no order in the questions they investigate. They are late in forming any resolutions to these questions, and they never provide any results in the general mess. They are politically senseless, and disorient the local unions. Look, in January, they considered 145 issues..." Kaganovich broke in, "And weren't you at these meetings?" "Excuse me," Polonskii said to Kaganovich, "but I have the floor now and I will speak." Someone else yelled out, "You knew earlier that they would ask you this question." And Veinberg interrupted again: "Why did you receive a salary for two years and do nothing?" Polonskii replied with a sneer to Veinberg, "You don't need to get upset, there is no possibility that you will be connected with me."[10]

Polonskii had begun his speech with brio, attacking the leadership of the VTsSPS in witty and offensive tones. At first, the plenum members were amused. But Shvernik, a longstanding supporter of Stalin, had his

---

[9] Ibid.   [10] Ibid., pp. 26–7.

own defenders on the Politburo. Molotov, Kaganovich, and Veinberg all objected strongly to Polonskii's accusations. Yet Polonskii pressed on, recalling the waste of money in the Bureau of Social Insurance. Shvernik yelled out in frustration, "But we, the VTsSPS, with the Central Committee uncovered this waste." Polonskii derided the VTsSPS solution. "Look here," he said, "Here is the decree of the VTsSPS. What does it say? If we read it, it is actually pretty funny." The decree established annual audits to be performed by newly formed committees of the unions. "Even this nonsensical, unserious decree is completely discredited. Why? The audit committee of the VTsSPS never met once in five years, never audited a single pay office, and never did anything." Veinberg interrupted again in a firm attempt to put an end to the accusations, "What did you do for two years in the VTsSPS?" Another voice yelled from the floor, "Talk about yourself, they say you sent a lot of telegrams." And Andreev, the chair of the meeting noted curtly, "Give the answers and finish up."[11]

Polonskii tried to begin again, "In a series of union organizations, beginning with the VTsSPS, a circle of mutual guarantees, nest-building, 'family' circles, the lowest specimens of swindlers..." Another voice called out, "Make a declaration! [*Zaiavlenie!*]" Polonskii readily named Bogoiavlenskii, the head of the party organization in the VTsSPS and an aide to Shvernik. Akulinushkin called out hastily, "He's a good official." "I think he was a useless official," Polonskii retorted sharply; "And you're the one who recommended him, Comrade Akulinushkin." Polonskii named Zharikov, another aide to Shvernik. "Shvernik saved this Zharikov, but he has now been unmasked as a Trotskyist and arrested. Another aide, Abolin, is also a Trotskyist who has been arrested. An entire series of Bundists and Mensheviks sat in the scientific research institute of VTsSPS. A former left SR heads the Scientific Institute of Labor. In many sections of the VTsSPS, we have counterrevolutionary elements who are using their positions for counterrevolutionary work." He blasted the paid staff, which was costing 3,336,000 rubles, only 40 percent of which was covered by members' dues. "And will this paid staff ensure democracy and attention for union members? Of course not." Finally, Polonskii turned to the subject of his own activities. He noted that he was sent to work in the VTsSPS against Shvernik's will and his own wishes. As he began to discuss his own work, however, Shvernik's supporters moved in to expose and embarrass him. They had waited long enough.[12]

---

[11] Ibid., p. 27.   [12] Ibid., pp. 27–8.

Voroshilov, the commissar of defense and a Politburo member, thrust a sheaf of papers into Polonskii's hands. "Here," he ordered. "You will read these several telegrams." Stalin said quietly, "A very interesting business." And a voice called out, "Read, read!" Polonskii slowly read the heading of the first telegram: "The Molotov Motor Vehicle Works ... " "Read, read further!" a voice insisted. "Signed Secretary of VTsSPS Polonskii." "Read the signature!" yelled the voice. "Signature – Polonskii," repeated Polonskii, unsure of what he held in his hands. "I sent many such telegrams," he noted quizzically. "Read further!" the voice yelled. Polonskii slowly read a short greeting. "What is bad here?" he asked in puzzlement. "I sent these telegrams to comrades with whom I was personally connected. I sent them to fellow workers, I demanded nothing from them." Stalin interceded, "And what was this personal business for?" Voroshilov quickly added, "How much money was spent on these telegrams?" Someone else shouted, "How many gifts were given out at VTsSPS expense?" Polonskii, stumbling now, tried to defend himself. He had sent the telegrams at his own expense, he presented workers who visited the VTsSPS office with books. Yet his initial verve was crumbling rapidly. Voroshilov summed up the problem in one short sentence: "These are 'family' telegrams," he said contemptuously. They showed that Polonskii used state funds to cultivate his own circle of loyalists, to build his own "nest."[13]

Molotov hammered the final question home. "Comrade Polonskii, is it true that you have already not gone to work for six months in the VTsSPS?" Shvernik turned on Molotov and said, nastily, "He doesn't go to work for six months. He doesn't obey [party] discipline, and you ask him, 'Why didn't you go to work?'" Polonskii broke down, his wit and swagger gone. "I cannot, comrades. I tried to get free of this work assignment, to make them let me go, because to work in this way is completely useless." L. P. Beria said sternly, "All the same, you have not been released from this job by a Central Committee decision." "I cannot be a mechanical human being," Polonskii cried; "I want to work in a real way, and there is no possibility for me to do that there. I'm done." Gamarnik and Beria added, "As long as you are not removed, you have to work." The last word, however, belonged to Stalin. Ever the public moderate, he added sympathetically, "We cannot consider him an undisciplined person. Obviously, it is hard for us to work."[14] Shortly thereafter, Polonskii was transferred to another post, deputy commissar for communications.

[13] Ibid., p. 28.   [14] Ibid.

Shvernik and Polonskii had no obvious political differences to justify their deep mutual animosity. Both were staunch Stalin supporters, both derided former oppositionists, and neither hesitated to denounce others and each other. Shvernik expected Polonskii's attack at the plenum, and had prepared his supporters. Using a handful of foolish telegrams costing no more than a few rubles apiece, he charged Polonskii with the cardinal sin of fostering "family circles." Polonskii tried to destroy Shvernik by casting political doubt on his leadership and tying him to rightists who had already been arrested. Both men's willingness, even eagerness, to hurl political charges was a harbinger of the hysteria that would soon engulf the unions.

Soon after the plenum, the VTsSPS launched an investigation of the Department of Labor Protection, previously under Polonskii's oversight, and its nine institutes for worker health and safety in Moscow, Leningrad, and other cities. The institutes had been created in the early 1920s under the Commissariat of Labor to reduce work-related accidents and illnesses. In July 1937, VTsSPS investigators reported that they were riddled with former oppositionists and spies. The NKVD had already arrested Shmerling, the director of the Leningrad Institute, Krasnovskii, the director of the Moscow Institute, his assistant, and a group in the machine shop. The VTsSPS investigators noted that at least ten employees of the Moscow Institute had relatives who had recently been arrested, and forty-three had received their higher education abroad, where they continued to maintain contacts. The investigators derided the institute's work as well as its personnel. Its four research departments – on protective gear, technical safety, acoustics, and hygiene – had developed numerous protective prototypes but the factories had not adopted any of them. Industry ignored the institute's standards for emissions and ventilation. The investigators urged the VTsSPS to purge the Moscow Institute of its "politically hopeless and foreign elements" and to begin promoting young people, trained under the Soviet system, in their places.[15]

As a result of the investigation, the VTsSPS removed the directors of the institutes in Kazan, Khar'kov, and Minsk in fall 1937, and ordered a purge of "foreign-class elements, enemies of the people, spies, and traitors" in all the institutes. In short order, officials discovered fifty-three sons of generals, nobles, officers, factory owners, and priests, seventeen employees with

---

[15] GARF, f. 5451, o. 43, d. 69, "V prezidium VTsSPS tov. Moskatovu," ll. 150–157. The official title of the Moscow Institute was the Moscow Scientific Research Institute for the Protection of Labor.

relatives who had been arrested, and fifty-seven more who corresponded
with relatives or colleagues abroad. All these people were promptly fired
and, in all likelihood, were subject to further investigation by the NKVD.[16]
Polonskii, as their former supervisor, also came under suspicion. He
was arrested that fall and shot at the age of forty-four on October 30,
1937.[17]

Polonskii's fall, like that of many highly placed people, pulled down
a number of others. M. G. Lagodinskii and E. E. Pavlova, chairs of the
Unions of Consumer Cooperative Workers in the Caucasus and the Central Districts respectively, both lost their jobs because they had allegedly
failed to report their meetings with Polonskii.[18] D. N. Meshcheriakov,
the head of the Union of Drivers in Moscow and Leningrad, also lost his
post. Meshcheriakov had worked under Polonskii in the Commissariat of
Transport and followed him into the VTsSPS, where Polonskii appointed
him head of the Union of Drivers. When Polonskii left the VTsSPS for the
Commissariat of Communications, he offered Mescheriakov a new post,
heading its Department of Cadres. The two men were still discussing the
appointment when Polonskii was arrested.[19] Meshcheriakov, who owed
his post to *kooptatsiia*, was a part of Polonskii's "family circle." He fell
with his boss. The target circles were beginning to widen.

Terror in Governing Institutions: The Unions of Party and State Employees

The Union of Political Education Employees and the Union of Employees
of State Institutions were politically sensitive as well as highly vulnerable
to repression because they included employees of party and state organizations, respectively. The purges in these unions revealed the complex
relationship between the VTsSPS, the Party, and the NKVD in promoting terror. Repression did not result from orders from Stalin or Ezhov,
but rather from a complex organizational dynamic between the Party (at
various levels), the NKVD, the unions' own central committees, and the

[16] GARF, f. 5451, o. 43, d. 69, "Postanovlenie sekretariata VTsSPS o rabote Nauchno-
issledovatel'skikh institutov okhranykh truda VTsSPS," "Dokladnaia zapiska o rabote
Institutov okhrany truda VTsSPS," ll. 158–159, 160–168.
[17] A. Thomas Lane, ed., *Biographical Dictionary of European Labor Leaders* (Greenwood
Press, Westport, CT, 1995), pp. 768–9.
[18] GARF, f. 5451, o. 43, d. 69, "Postanovlenie sekretariata VTsSPS," l. 148.
[19] GARF, f. 5451, o. 43, d. 72, "VTsSPS. Vypiska iz protokola zasedaniia sekretariata,"
l. 68.

VTsSPS. In both unions, VTsSPS investigations started the chain of events that resulted in arrests. Had the VTsSPS not been so zealous in demonstrating its own "vigilance," the destruction of union personnel might not have been so great.

The Union of Political Education Employees was one of the first to come under attack. The VTsSPS spearheaded an investigation, which led the Party to conduct its own review, which in turn involved the NKVD. By the end, the VTsSPS secretaries were terrified of the chain of events they themselves had set in motion. For a brief period, it looked as if they would be held responsible for the "enemies" the NKVD ultimately arrested. In June 1937, the VTsSPS launched its investigation of the union's leaders for cronyism and illegal spending on vacations and rest homes. The investigation, initially focused on finances, lacked a political edge. Union members, set to hold their congress that summer, had already elected forty-nine delegates when their leaders split in fierce fighting over the composition of the union's central committee. K. I. Nikolaeva, one of the five VTsSPS secretaries, reluctantly agreed to adjudicate the dispute. Nikolaeva, the daughter of a laundress and an unskilled worker, had helped organize the first National Women's Congress in 1918, and led the Zhenotdel (Women's Department) until its elimination in 1930.[20] Nikolaeva suggested that the current leadership remain intact until the congress, when the delegates could decide the issue by voting. This commonsensical decision, however, soon placed Nikolaeva in jeopardy.

Within a month, the Party Control Commission, drawn by the mudslinging among the union's central leaders, stepped in to launch its own investigation. The NKVD also entered the fray, bypassed both the Party Control Commission and the VTsSPS, and arrested several of the union's leaders. Two of the union's central committee leaders, Shumskii and Skripnik, had been arrested earlier. Efremov, one of the remaining central committee members, then brought N. Kolotilov into leadership, and Kolotilov, in turn, brought several of his own clients. Efremov was the next to be arrested, and his client, Kolotilov, followed him to prison. Kolotilov had served as party secretary of the Ivanovo regional committee during the great textile strikes in April 1932. By August, Kolotilov confessed to organizing the strikes in Ivanovo on orders from Tomskii, former head of the VTsSPS. The charges were of course absurd. Every worker in Ivanovo knew that Kolotilov had tried to suppress, not encourage, the strikes.

---

[20] Wendy Goldman, *Women at the Gates: Gender and Industry in Stalin's Russia* (Cambridge University Press, New York, 2002), pp. 37, 38, 55, 56.

And while his actions against the strikers had not been particularly bold or decisive, he certainly had not shown them any sympathy.[21]

The VTsSPS was now left with a terrifying mess. Nikolaeva had recommended that the union's leadership remain intact until the congress, but the NKVD had arrested most of them as "enemies of the people." She was now in the unenviable position of explaining why she had "protected" them. The Party Control Commission, moreover, weighed in with a report accusing the entire leadership of being part of "Shumskii's family group." It charged that they appointed rather than elected leaders, failed to hold meetings, covered up for each other, wasted the state's money, and engaged in personal corruption. The union's central committee had fallen like a row of dominoes: Efremov's arrest precipitated that of his client, Kolotilov, and Kolotilov's arrest resulted in the arrests of his own clients. Nikolaeva appeared to be next in line. When Ia. A. Iakovlev, deputy chairman of the Party Control Commission, sent Shvernik a copy of the investigation, Nikolaeva panicked. Arrests were already sweeping the VTsSPS. She wrote the other VTsSPS secretaries an urgent note. "I have no wish to protect this leadership," she said. "We must change it quickly." She disavowed her earlier suggestion, "These words are not mine," she said. "I don't know who said them." S. L. Bregman, a VTsSPS secretary, responded quickly, "We must make a quick decision on removing the current leadership before the congress." And he scrawled a frantic note over the message to Shvernik, "Comrade Shvernik, we need to discuss this immediately."[22] Everyone understood that they would be called to account for their management of the union's squabble.

The VTsSPS secretariat's response to the arrests of the union's leaders showed that even a simple organizational decision could lead to terrifying consequences. The VTsSPS was anxious to prove its vigilance to the NKVD, because each new arrest forced its leaders to explain why they had failed "to unmask" the purported enemy, a failure which was rapidly becoming a crime. Yet because it was impossible to determine who the next victim might be, VTsSPS leaders were continually caught off guard. Moreover, they understood that they were by no means personally protected

---

[21] On Kolotilov's role in the strikes, see Jeffrey Rossman, *Worker Resistance Under Stalin: Class and Revolution on the Shop Floor* (Harvard University Press, Cambridge, MA, 2005), pp. 54, 56–8, 235–6. Rossman notes that Kaganovich launched the purge of the Ivanovo party committee in August 1937 with Kolotilov's confession that he received orders from Tomskii to foment discontent and strikes (ibid., p. 235).

[22] GARF, f. 5451, o. 43, d. 69, "Tovarishchami Shverniku, Moskatovu, Bregmanu," "Tovarishchami Shverniku, Moskatovu i Nikolaevoi," ll. 183–184, 182.

from arrest. The secretaries, fearful that they might be charged with "protecting an enemy," hurriedly sought to protect themselves. Their attempts to stay one step ahead of the NKVD, typical of leaders in every institution, ensured the spread of repression. Herein was the peculiar amalgam of protection and risk offered by a position of leadership: one had the power to denounce others, but at the same time could easily be brought down with them. The secretariat, which headed a vast organization, not only provoked arrests, but was deeply fearful of becoming identified with those who were arrested. The secretaries were thus both perpetrators and potential victims, working overtime to affirm arrests by the NKVD, launching investigations to provoke new arrests, and, at the same time, quaking with fright with each new victim that disappeared. Very few leaders within the unions were capable of withstanding such intense psychological pressure. Many simply tried to protect themselves regardless of the cost to their colleagues. In so doing, they did deadly damage to others.

The charge that almost destroyed Nikolaeva, "protecting enemies," succeeded in destroying S. O. Kotliar, the head of the Union of Employees of State Institutions, which included 500,000 employees of the soviets and the Council of People's Commissars (SNK). Kotliar was one of a small number of leaders who attempted to halt the spread of repression and protect his staff. His union was particularly vulnerable because it was closely tied to organizations that were targets of intense investigation, including Osoaviakhim (the Society for Air and Chemical Defense), the soviets, and workers' training schools. Kotliar, as a result of his post, had close connections with several leaders who had recently been arrested. In 1936, for example, Kotliar had invited A. S. Kiselev, the secretary of the Russian Central Executive Committee of the Soviets and one of the most prominent members of the union, to give the keynote speech to the union's plenum. Kiselev was arrested within the year. Kotliar gave R. P. Eideman, an official of Osoaviakhim, money to build a rest home for its employees. Eideman was subsequently arrested as a spy, and shot in June 1937.[23] And Kotliar was closely tied to Ignatev and Shliapnikova, leading officials within the School of Soviet Construction, a training program for workers. Both Ignatov and Shliapnikova were arrested and accused of organizing "a whole nest of Trotskyists" within the school. Finally,

---

[23] Eideman was tried along with M. N. Tukhachevskii, L. E. Iakir, L. P. Uborevich, A. L. Kork, B. M. Fel'dman, V. M. Primakov, and V. K. Putna in June 1937 by the Military Council of the People's Commissariat of Defense for being a member of a military fascist organization, discovered by the NKVD.

Kotliar was linked to Gil'burg, the former head of the Union of Coke-Oven Workers. Gil'burg's brother, Rataichak, had been arrested and tried in the second Moscow show trial of the "Parallel Trotskyist Center" in January 1937. Kotliar helped Gil'burg retain his post after his brother was shot, although Gil'burg, too, soon disappeared into prison.[24]

Kotliar tried to save the leaders in his union by encouraging them to protect each other. He quickly recognized that each individual's terrified attempt to save him- or herself by demonstrating "loyalty" in denouncing others only increased the spread of repression. He tried to "circle the wagons." At the 6th VTsSPS Plenum in April 1937, he cautiously tried to halt the campaign for criticism and self-criticism, suggesting that it tarnished the reputations of union leaders before their members. Quickly perceiving the links between the campaign for democracy and the arrests, he attempted to slow the frenzy of mutual denunciation and name calling. Shvernik strongly rebuffed his efforts, but Kotliar was undeterred. Later that month, he spoke out again at a plenum of his union's Moscow regional committee. He made the serious mistake, however, of praising the union's Leningrad regional committee and its head, Nikitenko. That summer, almost the entire Leningrad regional leadership was arrested. Kotliar publicly defended Nikitenko in an effort to keep her out of prison, yet within several weeks she too had been arrested.[25] And when denunciations from workers threatened leading officials, Kotliar tried to quash them. Arrests in the School of Soviet Construction began with a denunciation by the head of the school's union committee, an older woman weaver, who demanded the removal of Ignatov, the school's director. Kotliar quietly attempted to protect Ignatov, by transferring the woman to another job. She refused and Kotliar's attempt backfired. He was accused of "an attempt to help an enemy of the people escape being unmasked."[26]

In the end, leaders of the union's Moscow regional committee, anxious to clear their own reputations, made Kotliar a scapegoat. Under fire themselves for tolerating "enemies" within the union, they blamed Kotliar for allowing "enemies" to flourish in Leningrad. In September, the Moscow regional leadership held a conference, which ultimately proved Kotliar's undoing. Kotliar, aware that his head was on the chopping block, gave a careful speech pieced entirely from current slogans about union

---

[24] "V Prokurature Soiuza SSR," *Trud*, January 20, 1937, p. 2; GARF, f. 5451, o. 43, d. 73, "Sekretariu VTsSPS. Tov. Shverniku, N. M. Zaiavlenie," ll. 31–33.
[25] "Sekretariu VTsSPS. Tov. Shverniku, N. M. Zaiavlenie," ll. 30–31.
[26] Ibid., l. 32.

democracy. He apologized for not recognizing the enemies in the Leningrad leadership and for protecting Nikitenko. "We did not succeed in unmasking her," he noted humbly. "This is my fault." Yet Kotliar still refused to denounce others or blame "enemies" for the union's problems. Rather, he blamed the union's lax approach to security, noting that its members in state institutions routinely filed secret documents in boxes with their "breakfast, dresses, and personal letters." Papers were scattered about offices. People took telephones, portfolios, and secret documents out of the office. And "this was considered business as usual."[27]

Yet the union's Moscow leaders were not interested in tightening up filing procedures in the state office buildings; they were out for blood. Kotliar's apologies and suggestions meant little. Margolin, the head of the union's Moscow regional committee, led the attack. He charged Kotliar with committing a serious political mistake in attempting to protect "enemies of the people" in the Leningrad organization. And he attacked Kotliar for focusing on organizational carelessness, when he should have explained why he "smoothed over" his ties with "the *über*spy, Eideman," in Osoaviakhim. "The conference should draw its own conclusions," he warned.[28] After four days of meetings, the conference delegates resolved to censure Kotliar for "praising enemies of the people in the Leningrad regional committee" and, more ominously, to send a copy of Kotliar's speech to the VTsSPS.[29] Shvernik received the speech soon after, with a note from Margolin asking him "to take the necessary measures."[30]

Two days after the conference ended, Kotliar made his strongest plea yet for limiting the accusations that were spreading terror within the union. He was now fighting for his life. At a plenum of the union's Moscow regional committee, he begged his fellow unionists to come to their senses, to stop the accusations and denunciations. He said, "Irresponsibility and slinging charges have splintered authority among us. As a result, we have poor relations among us. Within the union, we have insulted each other with strong words, we just keep spitting on each other. There are discussions now in every institution, and they abuse people on every sort of issue. They say, 'You are a formalist,' 'You have a formal approach,' and we have no other words except 'opportunist,' 'trade unionist,' 'antistate

---

[27] GARF, f. 5451, o. 43, d. 73, "Vypiska iz stenogrammy 1-i moskovskoi oblastnoi konferentsii," l. 51.

[28] Ibid., l. 41.

[29] GARF, f. 5451, o. 43, d. 73, "Vypiska iz protokola 1-i moskovskoi oblastnoi konferentsii Soiuza rabotnikov gosuchrezhdenii," l. 40.

[30] GARF, f. 5451, o. 43, f. 73, "Sekretariu VTsSPS tov. Shverniku," l. 39.

behavior.' Why?" Careful not to challenge the hunt for "enemies" or the campaign for union democracy, he asked the plenum to stop hurling accusations and exposing each other to the possibility of arrest. "We are scattered and not sticking together according to a principle of respect and mutual understanding. This is a product of our own, personal relations, *which we ourselves are guilty of creating.*"[31] Kotliar understood that his fellow unionists were fueling the terror with their own fear. Yet his plea fell on deaf ears. This speech, too, was sent to the VTsSPS as evidence of his continuing "enemy" sympathies.

At the end of September, Margolin, the head of the union's Moscow regional committee, and another member sent a vicious denunciation (*zaiavlenie*) to the VTsSPS chronicling all of Kotliar's mistakes. Claiming that his speeches and his ties with arrested "enemies" were not "accidental political mistakes," they requested a "serious investigation" of the union's central committee, and of Kotliar in particular. Couching their accusations in the language of union democracy, they denounced the union's leaders as "lickspittles, who stuck together in a circle of mutual protection."[32] The VTsSPS ignored such a communication at risk of being accused of "protecting an enemy." Within a week, the VTsSPS made the decision to remove Kotliar as head of the union, and he was arrested shortly thereafter.[33]

Kotliar was not brought down by orders from Stalin, the NKVD, the Party, or the VTsSPS, but by officials in his own union. Spurred partly by fear, members of the Moscow regional committee and the chairwoman of a local union committee actively sought his dismissal and arrest. They wrote to the VTsSPS, urged an investigation, sent "evidence" of Kotliar's "crimes," and repeatedly stressed his ties to people who had already been arrested. In other words, these people sought to demonstrate their own unassailable loyalty by actively seeking to destroy someone else.

Kotliar attempted to suppress criticism from below because he saw that it would only lead to more arrests. He recognized, more quickly than most, that each person who was arrested cast a deadly political shadow over their circle of intimates, colleagues, and acquaintances, who became suspect in turn for failing to "unmask" the "enemy" among them. Once failure to recognize and identify an "enemy" *before* their arrest became

---

[31] "Vypiska iz stenogrammy piatogo plenuma oblastnogo komiteta Soiuza rabotnikov gosuchrezhdenii," l. 36 (italics mine).

[32] "Sekretariu VTsSPS. Tov. Shverniku, N. M. Zaiavlenie," ll. 30–34.

[33] GARF, f. 5451, o. 43, d. 73, "VTsSPS. Vypiska iz protokola. Sov. sekretno," l. 29.

grounds for suspicion, the victim's colleagues, friends, and relatives were faced with a choice: to conceal their ties to the victim or to offer a full disclosure of the relationship. Those who kept silent were subject to exclusion from the Party, dismissal, and arrest for "concealing enemy ties." Those who reported their ties to the victim were subject to scrutiny, investigation, and further accusation. It was a devilish choice, and no small number of party members and others struggled with it.

A few people, like Kotliar, tried to negotiate this trap with some semblance of honor. Kotliar's strategy within the union was to promote mutual "protection." He tried to convince his colleagues that, if they stuck together and stopped flinging accusations of wrongdoing, they would limit the spread of repression. Yet the Party's Central Committee and the VTsSPS had already unleashed campaigns of democracy aimed precisely at destroying the "circles of protection" Kotliar invoked. Kotliar, in his efforts to promote human decency, became the perfect target of the campaign for union democracy: a mid-level official who attempted to protect his circle and suppress criticism from below.

Beheading the Unions

Throughout 1937, the terror spread through the upper reaches of the unions. Instructions for arrest did not always come directly from party leaders. In most cases, arrests were the result of a complicated interplay between the union, local and regional party committees, the VTsSPS, and the NKVD. In some unions, local party committees spearheaded the repression by expelling union leaders who were tied to regional party officials who had been purged. Many regions lost their entire union and party leadership. Expulsion from the Party then drew the attention of the NKVD, leading in turn to arrest. In other cases, the NKVD arrested a few highly placed leaders, which led to a raft of expulsions from the Party, and the subsequent loss of union or VTsSPS posts. Arrests and party expulsions also prompted the VTsSPS to launch its own investigations, which in turn led to more arrests. And, sometimes, VTsSPS investigations initiated the deadly chain, drawing party and NKVD attention to union leaders accused of malfeasance. Yet no matter which organization jumpstarted the process, the interaction among the Party, the NKVD, the VTsSPS, and the unions invariably widened the circle of arrests. The head of the Union of Workers in Municipal Services and Housing Construction, V. N. Krivikhin, for example, was fired by the VTsSPS and then expelled from the Party. V. A. Toshin, leader of the Union of Nonferrous Metal Workers, and K. E. Terent'ev, the head of the Union of Porcelain Workers, had the reverse experience: they were expelled from the Party and then fired from their union posts. Some leaders were fired after investigations revealed that they had hidden their "social origins." K. A. Trushin, the head of the Union of Fish Industry Workers of the South was discovered to be the "son of a kulak" who had "distorted a slogan of Stalin's." The head of the Union of State Farm Meat and Dairy Workers of Kazakhstan and Central Asia, Ablkhair Tspaev, also lost his job and party membership for hiding his "social origins."[34]

In many cases, the VTsSPS fired people who had already been arrested or shot. F. F. Kirdianov, the head of the Union of Oil Refinery Workers of the East, K. G. Evdokimov, head of the Union of Shipbuilders, and A. N. Riabov, the head of the Union of Construction Workers in Heavy Industry in the Central and Southern Districts, were all arrested and then fired by the VTsSPS. In other cases, the VTsSPS fired people who had already been shot by the NKVD, including K. A. Kabarava, the head of the Union of Primary and Middle School Employees in Georgia, B. N. Barkan, head of the Union of Tractor Industry Workers, A. Z. Zdobnov, the head of the Union of Motor Vehicle Workers, V. G. Savateev, head of the Union of Timber Cutters and Floaters of the North, K. K. Strievskii, the head of the Union of Heavy Machine Builders, M. G. Shlykov, the secretary of the Union of River Transport Workers, N. A. Basin, the head of the Union of Sawmill and Woodworkers of the North, Voltsit, the head of the Union of Electrical Workers, and Karklin, the head of the Union of Employees of Economic Institutions. The VTsSPS "fired" their corpses.[35]

Regional and local party committees and the NKVD combed through past minutes and records to uncover "enemies" and their associates. People were expelled from the Party and fired from their jobs because of a speech they had once made at a meeting, a vote for a pro-Trotsky resolution, a chance friendship or tie, a dusty, long-forgotten recommendation. P. S. Nikolaev, head of the Union of Employees of Electro-Communications, was dismissed from his post and expelled from the Party for his relationship with two "enemies of the people." M. M. Piterina, a leader of the Union of Dairy Workers, was thrown out of the Party and her

---

[34] The dismissals, expulsions, and arrests affirmed by the VTsSPS secretariat are listed as short documents with repeating titles: GARF, f. 5451, o. 43, d. 72, "VTsSPS. Vypiska iz protokola," "Zasedaniia sekretariata," "Postanovlenie sekretariata VTsSPS," ll. 64, 86, 39, 74, 225.

[35] Ibid., ll. 55, 65, 73, 82, 87, 89, 90. See same titles in GARF, f. 5451, o. 43, d. 73, ll. 162, 176, 182, 185, 190, 162, 176, 182, 185, 190.

job for voting for a Trotskyist resolution at a meeting in 1924. Divorced for five years, she was accused of "hiding" her relationship with her ex-husband, who had recently been shot as an "enemy of the people." At the end of August, the head of the Union of Medical Workers of Georgia, M. N. Mamardashvili, was expelled from the Party and dismissed from his job for giving aid to an "enemy of the people." The NKVD arrested the woman who replaced him, A. A. Pantsulaia, three months later. The head of the Union of Primary and Middle School Employees of Armenia, S. A. Makints, was fired after her husband was arrested as a "counterrevolutionary nationalist" and she tried to defend him. The VTsSPS secretariat wrote in defense of her dismissal, "If he is such a thing, it means she is also. Remove her." L. A. Mekhonoshina, the secretary of the Union of Primary and Middle School Employees of Russia, was thrown out of the Party and her job after her brother was arrested, and it was discovered she had once been active in the left Socialist Revolutionary Party. The leader of the Union of Coal Miners and Peat Workers of the Central Industrial Region, Shcherbakov, was fired for "loss of party vigilance." His crime? He once wrote a recommendation for a union official recently arrested for Trotskyism. D. N. Sokolov was expelled from the Party and his post in the Union of Iron and Steel Workers of the South for writing a recommendation for a man subsequently arrested as an "enemy of the people." M. M. Mashkevich was removed as head of the Union of Oil Refinery Workers of the Caucasus by the party group within the union for his associations with recently arrested "enemies of the people." He failed to inform his party group after a relative was arrested. The VTsSPS noted disapprovingly that he had been friendly with this relative up to the day of arrest. A. Ia. Margulis, the head of the Union of Garment Workers of the Southern Districts, was excluded from the Party for concealing that her husband had belonged to the Workers' Opposition after the Civil War, and for writing a recommendation for the head of the Garment Trust, who had been recently arrested. The head of the Union of Firemen was fired for failing to inform his party committee that his wife's brother, who shared his apartment, had been arrested. I. I. Sinchuk, head of the Union of Fish Industry Workers of the Far East, M. N. Steklov and P. P. Sokolov, leaders of the Union of Railroad Workers of the South, F. I. Fisenko and G. A. Raevskii, leaders of the Union of Grain Industry and Elevator Workers of the East, and A. F. Kuptsov, a leader of the Iron Ore Miners of the East, were all dismissed from the Party and their jobs because of ties with "enemies of the people." Some union leaders were charged with multiple "crimes." The head of the Union of Dining Hall Workers, Belakovskaia, was closely tied to another union leader who had already been arrested. In addition, she had provided a recommendation for the rector of the Institute of Public Catering, Mirskii, who had also been arrested. And, finally, she was discovered to be the "daughter of a noble." Belakovskaia was thrown out of the Party and fired from her post.[36]

The VTsSPS did not simply respond to action already taken by the NKVD or the Party. It removed many union leaders from their posts because they had failed to identify fellow officials as "enemies." I. A. Khaliavin, head of the Union of Workers in Heavy Industry of the Urals and Western Siberia, was thrown out of the Party and dismissed from his post because he failed to "unmask" union officials who were subsequently arrested. The VTsSPS noted that he was "not deserving of political confidence." Boldak and S. I. Zhibrov, leaders of the Union of Railroad Workers of Central Asia and the Union of Railroad Workers of the East and Far East respectively, also lost their jobs for "loss of Bolshevik vigilance."[37]

The arrests continued through 1937 and 1938. By the end of 1937, the VTsSPS had affirmed the dismissal of fifty-two union chairmen and secretaries as well as thirty other leaders.[38] These figures, in all likelihood incomplete, suggest that, at the very least, one-third of the unions were beheaded. The overwhelming majority of these leaders were arrested. The VTsSPS secretariat was responsible for affirming the removal of only the very top level of union leaders: union chairmen and secretaries, and heads of VTsSPS institutes and departments. The list of names provided here does not include lower-level officials or those removed and arrested in "batches," such as the entire Leningrad regional committee of the Union of Political Education Employees. If the names of all these officials were known, the total carnage would undoubtedly be many times greater.

How many arrests did it take to create "terror" among those who remained? There is no doubt that repression of this magnitude promoted great fear and transformed the daily work culture of the unions. Repression changed people's daily behavior, their relationships with colleagues, superiors, and staff, their banter, their attitudes, and their thoughts. In short, *everything* in their relationship to others was transformed by a

---

[36] Same titles, f. 5451, o. 43, d. 72, ll. 75, 76, 83, 84, 88; f. 5451, o. 43, d. 73, ll. 161, 183, 138, 186, 187, 209, 214, 230, 229.

[37] Same titles, f. 5451, o. 43, d. 73, l. 138; f. 5451, o. 43, d. 72, ll. 35, 32.

[38] On arrests and dismissals of VTsSPS Plenum members, see GARF, f. 5451, o. 43, d. 69, "VTsSPS vypiska iz prot. zased. prezidiuma," ll. 221–229.

culture of fear, denunciation, and arrest.[39] No one in the union staff was unaware of what was happening. Investigators cast a wide net, which encompassed former oppositionists, as well as their friends, mentors, workmates, relatives, and casual contacts. Anyone could become a victim. The VTsSPS secretariat met regularly throughout 1937 and 1938 to affirm the decimation of the union leadership, person by person. In November, a foreign workers' delegation arrived to celebrate the twentieth anniversary of the revolution. The VTsSPS secretaries paused briefly in their daily affirmations of arrests, shootings, and dismissals to plan the delegation's visit. They worked out a wonderful itinerary. The foreign workers went to the Bol'shoi theatre, toured the Volga canal by boat, visited factories, and marched in the great celebratory demonstration in Red Square. Shvernik, Lozovskii, and Moskatov, members of the VTsSPS secretariat, took time out to welcome their foreign comrades to the land of socialism.[40] Their split thinking as they showcased Soviet achievements can only be imagined. Yet the delegation's visit introduced no more than a pause in the grim business at hand. Within a few days, the secretariat was back at work, voting to affirm the arrest and repression of a seemingly endless list of unionists from every industry, institution, and corner of the country.

VTsSPS Investigations

The VTsSPS undertook its own investigations of the unions throughout 1937 and 1938, which led to numerous dismissals and propelled the NKVD into making more arrests. It employed a corps of investigators, who audited unions' financial records, reviewed officials, and reported on labor conditions. These *proverki*, initiated by personal denunciations, local newspaper articles, or unresolved squabbles within the unions themselves, were often published in newspapers. The investigators accused union leaders of personal corruption, work accidents, food shortages, and housing problems. Linking personal corruption with "enemy activities," the reports drew NKVD and party attention, and encouraged workers in other unions to make similar accusations against their own leaders.

The investigation of the Union of Railroad and Metro Construction, for example, typified this process. An initial VTsSPS investigation charged

---

[39] Robert Thurston, *Life and Terror in Stalin's Russia, 1934–1941* (Yale University Press, New Haven, 1996), pp. 137–63, argues that, for many, life was untouched by fear during the terror.

[40] GARF, f. 5451, o. 43, d. 72, "VTsSPS. Vypiska iz protokola zasedaniia sekretariata," l. 217.

that the union's chairman and secretary, Antropov and Shukhman, had disregarded enemies, engaged in corruption, and overlooked hazardous work conditions. Antropov hosted drunken parties in his apartment with union funds for officials whom he appointed. In the political parlance of the day, a small circle of leaders created an atmosphere of "family-ness" (*semeistvennost'*), cementing their bonds at regular drinking parties and suppressing criticism from below. At one drunken gathering in 1936, Antropov celebrated his new appointees to the union's central committee, and they in turn reelected him as chairman. As the party became more raucous, the union leaders "baptized" their new chair with alcohol. Later, during another drinking bout, this same inebriated group drafted the union's budget. Antropov extended the union's largesse to more than 100 officials from Likbez (Liquidation of Illiteracy School) at a restaurant party that cost the union 4,797 rubles, or more than two years' wages of the average union member. Unfortunately, the union's efforts to eradicate illiteracy did not extend beyond drinking with Likbez officials. Most importantly, VTsSPS investigators charged that the union ignored the railroads' abysmal safety record. In 1937 alone, 106 workers died in job-related accidents; the union did nothing to aid their families. On one construction site with 12,000 workers, there were more than 1,000 accidents in six months, including six fatalities. The report noted that former Trotskyists had been arrested up and down the railroad lines throughout Moscow, but the leaders ignored the "enemies" in their midst. The charges mingled political oppositionism, corruption, and disregard for safety in a direct appeal to workers. Investigators blamed the union leaders for dangerous and miserable conditions, thus mustering support for their arrests.[41]

Like Aladdin's discovery of the magic phrase "open sesame," workers soon realized the power of the words "enemy plot." If the Party cynically invoked "labor safety" to garner support for the arrest of former oppositionists, workers invoked "oppositionists" to improve labor safety. Officials ignored such allusions at their own peril. When approximately 200 adults and children in the Ivanovo textile region got sick after eating bread from the bakeries, one Comrade Nikolaevo sent the VTsSPS a denunciation claiming that they were deliberately poisoned by an "enemy" plot against the working class. Whereas in the past workers' complaints about spoiled food, chronic shortages, and irregular deliveries were often ignored, the claim of "deliberate poisoning" sent an electric

---

[41] GARF, f. 5451, o. 43, d. 73, "Prezidiumu VTsSPS. Dokladnaia zapiska," ll. 164–167.

shock through the VTsSPS leaders. They launched an immediate investigation, and implemented an entire series of health measures in the workers' dining halls as well the bakeries.[42]

The phrase "enemy of the people" proved useful to many groups. The VTsSPS used it to explain stubborn, seemingly intractable problems of food distribution. In shifting responsibility to "enemies" in the retail trade system, for example, they absolved themselves of responsibility. In July, almost the entire leadership of the Union of Cooperative Workers of Ukraine and Crimea was arrested, along with its chairman, Barkan. The decimation of the leadership was set in motion when the secretary of the union, Zlatopol'skii, was discovered to have concealed the arrest of his two brothers. VTsSPS leaders promptly removed him from his post, and launched an investigation of the union. Investigators uncovered the usual sins: "distortions of democracy," "familyness," "toadyism," "circles of protection," violations of wage policy, waste of social insurance funds, disregard of illegal overtime, and suppression of criticism from below. The union leaders had failed to provide work clothes, healthcare for children, and pensions for the elderly. Moreover, regional party leaders had connived in these corrupt practices.[43] The investigators blamed the complaints of the workers on "enemies of the people" within the union. One month later, at a meeting in Kiev in August, the remaining party and union officials tried to shift blame to the managers of the cooperative stores, blaming the empty shelves on "enemy managers." Everyone, high and low, now searched for "enemies of the people" to avoid responsibility for deep-seated organizational and economic problems.[44]

VTsSPS investigations often dovetailed with party and NKVD accusations against regional party officials. Although they appeared to be sparked from below, the chain of events was difficult to untangle. The leaders of the Union of State Farm Grain Workers and its head, Osipov, came to the attention of VTsSPS investigators after a journalist in a local workers' newspaper wrote a scathing denunciation of their conduct. Whether the journalist acted independently, perhaps on a tip from workers, or was prompted to initiate a purge of the union by party officials was unclear. The article, however, written in the wake of sweeping arrests within the Odessa regional party committee, led the VTsSPS to investigate

---

[42] GARF, f. 5451, o. 43, d. 73, "Postanovlenie," ll. 186–187.
[43] GARF, f. 5451, o. 43, d. 69, "Chlenam prezidiuma VTsSPS," ll. 197–198.
[44] GARF, f. 5451, o. 43, d. 69, "Postanovlenie soveshchaniia rabotnikov TsK soiuza s rabotnikami obkomov," ll. 199–203.

ties between union leaders and the regional and district party officials now sitting in prison. The union's leaders were charged with "political blindness." The arrests, which removed the leadership of Odessa's key institutions, were presented to the workers as a response to disgraceful labor conditions, fatalities, and injuries on the state farms. The VTsSPS charged Osipov, the head of the union, with creating an "atmosphere of toadying, protective circles, and suppression of criticism." It claimed Osipov fired anyone who criticized his leadership, and spent his time drinking with other officials. The arrests were presented as a long-overdue action against officials who had abused the trust of the people they were supposed to represent.[45]

Although the names, places, and details differed, the VTsSPS investigations all shared certain features. They charged union officials with the same "crimes," including indifference to the plight of their constituents, ties with "enemies," and corruption. They exposed miserable conditions in the industry, and they spread repression by prompting new NKVD inquiries. They functioned as an accelerant, sometimes initiating the terror, but more often spreading it through the unions. They also had a powerful populist element. VTsSPS investigators cast themselves as honest and avenging crusaders on behalf of an immiserated working class, righting the wrongs of corruption, ensuring that state money was properly spent, and remedying gross inequities and abuse.

The Dissemination of Repression in the Unions

The incendiary rhetoric, combining populism with the hunt for enemies, sparked a conflagration that soon engulfed the leadership of the unions from top to bottom. Officials responded angrily to any imputation of wrongdoing with vicious countercharges aimed at discrediting their attacker. Fear raised the stakes: a charge could result in not only disgrace, but the loss of a job, arrest, and even execution. Everyone cloaked their criticism or complaint in the language of democracy, using the same phrases to advance a multiplicity of interests. The slogans, deployed in a fierce struggle for position, advantage, and survival, were detached from any meaning. If language was currency, it was increasingly debased in the political hyperinflation of 1937–8.

---

[45] GARF, f. 5451, o. 43, d. 73, "Sekretariu VTsSPS – tov. Shverniku. Dokladnaia zapiska," ll. 156–158.

In the Union of Plywood and Matches Workers, based in Ufa, several members of the central committee accused its chairman, Pilinenok, and its secretary, Smirnova, of drunkenness, close ties to "enemies of the people," and "star syndrome." The issues, rooted in longstanding grudges and vendettas, were barely decipherable, although the accusations, based on the slogans of union democracy (*profdemokratiia*), were all too familiar. Lumber industry officials, too, took sides in the union's dispute. One former director of a large Ufa sawmill supported the charges against Pilinenok, but he was discovered to be nursing a personal grudge. When he was fired in 1935, Pilinenok had failed to support him. Pilinenok vigorously defended himself in precisely the same language used by his accusers. He charged that the central committee members who sought his removal were tied to the leadership of the plywood trust, an "enemy" group that had "ignored the signals of party and nonparty Bolsheviks," "failed to unmask enemies of the people" in the plywood factory and trust, and encouraged "enemy activities." The central committee thus split into two groups accusing each other of identical violations. Alerted by the fierce squabbling, the VTsSPS launched an investigation that soon spread beyond the union to encompass at least sixteen officials of the lumber industry. Yet not even the investigators could make sense of the mess of charges and countercharges. Two indisputable facts emerged: first, both sides repeatedly got drunk in the course of 1936 (often together). And, second, the union's department of labor protection was doing a poor job.[46] In other words, workers were losing fingers, hands, and other body parts to dangerous machinery and poor safety procedures, but neither Pilinenok nor his antagonists had made any effort to reduce the accident rate. This grubby knot of accusations landed on Shvernik's desk, with the implicit assignment to disentangle its threads and assign guilt. It was one of scores of cases that were sent to VTsSPS leaders for resolution, and it is no wonder that Shvernik, lacking the acumen and confidence of King Solomon, threw up his hands in disgust. Given that the charges on both sides involved associations with "enemies," Shvernik in all likelihood forwarded the compromising materials to the NKVD.

The fighting within the Union of Plywood and Matches Workers was replicated in many unions. Leaders reframed personal grievances, internal struggles for control, and institutional animosities in the language of the day. High accident rates, drunkenness, and corruption were automatically

---

[46] GARF, f. 5451, o. 22, d. 64, "Sekretariu VTsSPS, tov. Shverniku, N. M., tov. Bregmanu, S.," ll. 204–2040b.

equated with "enemy activities." Once problems were framed as treason, they drew the attention of investigatory bodies, which in turn uncovered more unsavory behavior and "enemy" ties. VTsSPS and party officials responded with alacrity to any charge involving "enemies" for fear that they might be accused of concealment. The whirl of denunciation and investigation also captured the attention of the NKVD, which did not hesitate to arrest anyone tarred by the brush of accusation.

In this way, terror moved outward to encompass one union after another, and downward through each union's hierarchy. About 200 miles east of the Union of Plywood and Matches Workers, the Union of Timber Cutters and Floaters, headquartered in Sverdlovsk, was also involved in vicious infighting in the wake of elections. The leadership of the union literally consumed itself in the process of "criticism and self-criticism." In the fall of 1937, after elections unseated a few of the old leaders, *Trud* published an unflattering article about the new leadership. The article spurred one Nifetov to write a lengthy denunciation of the presidium of the union's regional committee to the VTsSPS. Nifetov accused the newly elected presidium of abusing its position by not meeting regularly. As Nifetov explained, the seven-member presidium was in disarray. Rubel, its new chairman, had recently been expelled from the Party and his union post for "a tie with an enemy of the people," another member for "systematic drunkenness and scandal," and a third for "drunkenness and beating his wife who also happened to be a Stakhanovite." A fourth member was sent to supervise prisoners in an NKVD timber camp, and a fifth had left Sverdlovsk. Although the two remaining members continued to meet, they were hardly a substitute for the full presidium. Members of the larger regional committee, including the labor inspector and the physical culture instructor, had been arrested. Nifetov bore a serious grudge against Pestov, one of the remaining members, who had become the presidium chairman. He complained that Pestov held three positions, including "instructor," a post that paid him 700 rubles a month to read the newspaper aloud to workers.[47] (Pestov may have picked up these additional jobs when members of the union's paid staff were arrested.)

According to Nifetov, Pestov was also guilty of "violations of union democracy." Part of the old leadership, he had tried to rig the union elections by convening the Sverdlovsk delegates to prepare a list of candidates in advance. Pestov had allegedly told the delegates: "We must discuss and

---

[47] GARF, f. 5451, o. 22, d. 64, "Otvetstvennomu redaktoru gazety 'Trud' tov. Popovu," ll. 122–126.

decide who we will put up for candidates to the plenum and who we will vote for." And Pestov had attempted to stack the union's congress by instructing a workers' committee to organize a by-election to overturn the results of an earlier vote for delegates. Nifetov wrote furiously, "The regional committee was transformed in a backroom deal."[48]

And Nifetov was not the only person hurling accusations. A safety inspector also accused Pestov of violating election rules, and demanded he write up an honest report of the union's congress. Pestov refused and promptly fired him for "political mistakes." The safety inspector demanded an explanation; Pestov refused to provide one. When Nifetov stepped in to defend the safety inspector, Pestov withdrew the charge, rehired the safety inspector, and sent him on a vacation. Nifetov promptly charged Pestov with "suppression of criticism." After pages of charges, Nifetov ended his denunciation: "Considering the adverse state of the leadership of the regional committee, I want to interest and involve the central committee of the union and the VTsSPS in this business and publish this material in *Trud* and also to end Pestov's scorn for the officials of the regional committee and end violations of union democracy and consider the possibility of terminating Pestov's tenure in the union's regional committee."[49] Thus Nifetov built his denunciation of Pestov, layering each charge between the handy slogans of union democracy.

In his second denunciation, Nifetov's rhetoric became even harsher. "When will Pestov, the chairman of the Sverdlovsk union regional committee, finally be unmasked?" he demanded impatiently. "This swindler, double-dealer, and lickspittle has trampled on union democracy, and surrounded himself with a collection of swindlers, aliens, degenerates, even up to and including that counterrevolutionary physical culture instructor." He went on to describe Pestov as the "main lickspittle" of Rubel, the former chairman of the union regional committee, who had been thrown out of the Party for a counterrevolutionary conversation about Stalin. Pestov knew about this conversation! Pestov tried to defend Rubel! Pestov had written Rubel a recommendation, which claimed that such a conversation never occurred! Nifetov recounted with rising hysteria that he had exposed everything, informed on them all. The letter ended with a barely veiled threat to the VTsSPS: "Don't you think that nothing has changed. Comrade Stalin teaches us to work in a new way."[50] Phrases from the Central Committee and VTsSPS Plenums littered Nifetov's denunciations

---

[48] Ibid., ll. 123–124. [49] Ibid., ll. 122–126.
[50] GARF, f. 5451, o. 22, d. 64, "Redaktsii gazety 'Trud', tov. Popovu," ll. 127–129.

of Pestov: "violations of union democracy," "toadies, lickspittles, corrupt degenerates," "gross political mistakes and violations of secret-ballot elections." Yet the letters were also fueled by what appeared to be a deep personal grudge.

A. P. Sholmov, the 37-year-old head of the Union of Timber Cutters and Floaters, tried to put an end to the affair in a reasonable letter to Bregman, the former head of the Union of Shoe Workers who had vaulted into the post of a VTsSPS secretary. He explained that the newly elected presidium of the regional committee had been decimated over the fall. It was left with four people, two of whom were not in Sverdlovsk. It had been difficult to meet regularly, but elections had been held again, and Pestov had been fairly elected as chairman. A local union investigation had cleared him of all accusations. According to Sholmov, Pestov was a reliable and able official.[51] Yet whose interests did Sholmov have at heart? A recent graduate of the Technical Forestry Academy in Leningrad, he had become secretary of the union in 1936, his first union job. He had never sawed a tree or floated a log in his life, and his meteoric rise through the ranks of the union was the direct result of the removal and imprisonment of an entire layer of leadership.[52]

It is difficult to understand exactly what motivated the charges and countercharges, but they seem to have emerged from a local struggle for power after the elections.[53] The old union leaders had tried to protect their positions by organizing bloc voting and overturning unfavorable election results. They were successful to a limited extent. The NKVD then moved in, made arrests, and removed Rubel, the regional committee chairman. Pestov, one of the few officials associated with the old leadership who was reelected, moved into several vacated positions. Accused by Nifetov of various misdeeds, he fought to clear his name and maintain his position. Both sides in this ugly fight claimed to be representing union democracy. Which side, however, was the true defender of democratic principles was far from clear. Was Nifetov an honest man trying to reform the regional committee and eliminate abuses of power? Was he a member of a rival clique for power, in league with the safety inspector and others, eager to unseat Pestov in order to install his own people? Or was he a deranged

[51] GARF, f. 5451, o. 22, d. 64, "Sekretariu VTsSPS tov. Bregmanu," l. 120.
[52] GARF, f. 5451, o. 43, d. 73, "Postanovlenie sekretariata VTsSPS," l. 160.
[53] The union had been in turmoil for more than a year. Its first secretary, V. V. Chernyshev, had been removed in June 1936 for political mistakes, self-importance, rudeness, and bureaucratism. Rubel, who had pushed for his removal, was then arrested: GARF, f. 5451, o. 43, d. 71, "Postanovlenie sekretariata VTsSPS," l. 123.

individual irrationally obsessed with Pestov for personal reasons? And what about Pestov? Did he cynically collect four union salaries while the workers stood waist-deep in icy rivers, rafting logs to the lumber mills for a paltry 250 rubles a month? Or did he try hard to keep the union functioning, assuming extra jobs after the union staff was decimated by arrests? Was Sholmov a quiet man of reason or a careerist "lickspittle" protecting Pestov? And what of the outcome? Did the NKVD eventually arrest Pestov and his circle, and laud Nifetov for advancing "union democracy" in Sverdlovsk? Or did Nifetov end up raving about the "alien clique" from the locked ward of a mental asylum? The shifting, subjective perspectives of the drama's actors obscure the "objective" truth. Yet regardless of where "truth" lay, Nifetov's ability to couch his obsessions in the language of the day ensured that he received a full hearing. His charges, real or imagined, had consequences, and ultimately launched a serious investigation of the regional committee.

The Party, the VTsSPS, the unions, and the NKVD were flooded with denunciations like Nifetov's. On countless stages from Kiev to Khabarovsk, local actors played in petty dramas packed with political accusations, trivial details, personal grudges, and ugly entanglements. Charges and countercharges flew back and forth, dense with the rich trivia of daily life: who drank with whom, who earned more than his due, who made an improper political remark. This was not a story of one villain and many victims, but a far richer drama in which political repression became a convenient expression for resentment toward officials, organizational rivalries, and personal ambitions. Daily workplace gossip turned deadly, creating an ugly mess that the NKVD was all too eager to "investigate" under the watchwords of democracy. There was no dearth of villains or victims: officials in every union were soon caught up in the deadly game. Few leaders acted like Kotliar. The vast majority, terrified of prison and execution, picked up the double-edged sword of terror and democracy and began swinging wildly at each other. Meetings had turned into cunning and deadly games of slogan-wielding gladiators. Yet the game of survival was becoming increasingly complex.

Halting the Madness?

In January 1938, the Central Committee met to consider the wholesale expulsions from the Party. Stalin, concerned about their effect, criticized the "false" vigilance that produced them. Many party committees had disappeared or ceased to function, organizations were stripped of leadership and roiled by internal strife. Stalin's criticism led to a surge of expellees seeking redress and reinstatement. In the months that followed, expulsions from the Party slowed, many ex-members were readmitted, and recruitment of new members began for first time since 1933.[54] At the same time, the arrests continued. These two powerful and opposing currents of people – the victimized and the exonerated – created havoc within the unions. As one group was marching off to prison, the other was struggling to return to work. In a grim organizational logic all its own, officials in the NKVD, the Party, economic trusts, and the VTsSPS found themselves at cross-purposes. Paralyzed by fear, lacking laws or procedures, officials overturned, overrode, and contradicted each other.

Party members who believed they had been wrongly accused, reprimanded, or expelled had the right to appeal their cases. In many cases, decisions of expulsion were overturned. The VTsSPS was then responsible for restoring the victim's job and union membership. Yet many factory directors, officials in the economic trusts, and shop-floor bosses refused to sign the forms to put the "reinstated" back to work. Given the unpredictable political climate, it was impossible to know whether today's exonerated victim would be tomorrow's newest arrest. No one wanted to commit to paper any act that might later "prove" that they had "aided" or "covered for" "an enemy." As a result, officials refused to act, and all personnel actions ground to a halt. Thousands of people, cleared of charges, were left in limbo. Fired from jobs and stripped of union membership, they were reinstated in the Party but unable to find work. They escaped prison only to starve in the streets. The unions dealt with hundreds of people who had been "unfairly" fired and now sought to regain their jobs. People shuttled anxiously between VTsSPS headquarters, union central committees, and the economic trusts in search of the signatures that could restore them to work. Union leaders wrangled with the Party, the economic trusts, and other institutions over reinstatement. No one was sure what procedures to follow, and everyone was frightened of making a mistake.

Just as the VTsSPS had replicated the Party's emphasis on party democracy at the February–March 1937 Central Committee Plenum in its own campaign for union democracy, it once again copied the January 1938 Party Plenum. Shvernik opened the VTsSPS Plenum that same month

---

[54] See *Pravda*, January 19, 1938, for the Central Committee Plenum resolution; J. Arch Getty and Oleg Naumov, *The Road to Terror: Stalin and the Self-Destruction of the Bolsheviks, 1932–1939* (Yale University Press, New Haven, 1999), pp. 491–9.

with a summary of Stalin's speech. The Party's new focus on "mistakes" and "excesses" provided an opening to the assembled union leaders, who were confused, fearful, and anxious to end the uncertainty that threatened the positions they had so recently assumed.[55] The delegates to the VTsSPS Plenum used Stalin's speech to criticize "excessive caution [*perestrakhovka*]" a shorthand term for the official paralysis that had brought all business to a standstill. Union leaders offered numerous examples of people who had lost their jobs as a result of accusations. Yet when the accusers were subsequently "revealed as enemies," no one would assume the responsibility of reinstating their victims. Strievskii, the head of the Union of Heavy Machine Builders, had gathered "compromising materials" on another leader, M. L. Kaganovich, based on a denunciation someone sent to union headquarters. Kaganovich was rumored to be connected with a group of Trotskyists and guilty of "an entire series of sins." As a result, union leaders decided not to bring Kaganovich onto the union's plenum. Strievskii himself was then arrested as an "enemy." A subsequent investigation showed the accusations against Kaganovich to be baseless, and the case fell apart. The VTsSPS hired Kaganovich to work in its Wage Department. Yet he had clearly been harmed by the rumors and the union's refusal to act on his exoneration.[56]

Pogrebnoi, the new head of the union, who had replaced Strievskii after his arrest, told the plenum that Kaganovich's experience was common. The union was inundated with complaints from people who had been fired because "their relatives were revealed to be enemies of the people, or they themselves were excluded from the Party, or they were abroad or knew someone abroad." The union could not get machine-trust officials to sign the papers necessary to send these people back to work. "They will speak on the phone," he said. "But they will not put anything in writing." Pogrebnoi offered several examples of people who had been wrongly dismissed. One woman, who was seven months pregnant, lost her factory job after her husband was arrested as an "enemy of the people." "They threw her out of the factory," Pogrebnoi explained, "and excluded her from the Komsomol." When Pogrebnoi appealed the case to the VTsSPS, Moskatov, one of the secretaries, told him, "Rehire her, and forget about the necessary signatures." Yet the party committee in the factory then stepped in, and threatened to punish anyone who hired a

---

[55] GARF, f. 5451, o. 43, d. 69, "Stenogramma soveshchaniia chlenov prezidiumov TsK soiuzov i otvetstvennykh rabotnikov VTsSPS," ll. 262–352.
[56] Ibid., l. 264.

worker without completing the necessary paperwork. They claimed that "Trotskyists" were being put back to work. The union was thus at cross-purposes with the trust and the party committee, neither of which wanted to take responsibility for rehiring a potential "enemy."[57]

To further complicate the issue, many people were fired by managers who were subsequently "unmasked" and arrested. Were the decisions of those subsequently found to be "enemies" still valid? In Uralmashzavod, a machine-building factory, for example, one Karpelevich was excluded by his district party committee for spying early in 1937 "when the unmasking began." The union's factory committee promptly followed suit, stripping him of his job and union membership. However, the district party leader and factory director were then arrested, casting doubt on Karpelevich's removal. Karpelevich petitioned the union's central committee to review the decision of the union's factory committee. It affirmed the lower decision, and Karpelevich took his case to the VTsSPS secretariat. Pogrebnoi explained, "Here, comrades, the situation became completely incoherent." The secretariat affirmed the union, but suggested at the same time that Karpelevich be reinstated as a union member, an utterly contradictory decision. Pogrebnoi complained, "A person is excluded for spying, for engaging in diversionist activities. Nine months pass, and he suddenly becomes honest. The evidence was obviously absurd." Shvernik interrupted Pogrebnoi, and cut to the essence of the business: "Is he free?" he asked. Shvernik understood that the NKVD was the ultimate arbiter of guilt or innocence. If Karpelevich was in prison, the VTsSPS had a serious problem on its hands. The secretariat would have to answer for recommending the reinstatement of an enemy. Pogrebnoi shrugged. "He comes and goes, and he works." Shvernik was relieved. But the rules were still unclear.[58]

The VTsSPS, moreover, had lost its authority over the unions. Union officials flouted VTsSPS recommendations and refused to reinstate people. Voronina, who had offered a spirited defense of workers' rights at the VTsSPS Plenum less than a year before, now headed the VTsSPS's Bureau of Complaints. Dealing with hundreds of cases of reinstatement, she contended that the unions had lost all direction under the pressure of terror. Elections and arrests ensured that new people now staffed the unions' central committees. "We no longer know who these people are," Voronina said. When the Bureau of Complaints ordered union leaders to reinstate people, it was ignored. The Union of Printers, for example, told

---

[57] Ibid., ll. 264–265.   [58] Ibid., ll. 265–266.

Voronina, "Don't come crawling to us. It is impossible. We are unmasking, we are purging now." The Union of Defense Metal Workers responded in the same way, warning her not to interfere in a military organization. "And the aviation industry is even worse," she said. "Terrible things have happened there. They told us, 'You are absolutely not to make a political investigation of this case. We request that you do not interfere.'" Shvernik asked her, "Did you interfere in the aviation case?" Voronina replied that the bureau had tried, but the Union of Aviation Workers had informed her, "We are restoring people ourselves." Voronina was furious, and quoted Stalin, "What does this say? It says that people don't pay any attention to living human beings."[59]

The unions, commissariats, and trusts refused to take orders from the VTsSPS; the unions' factory committees were at war with their central committees, and higher party decisions on reinstatement added another layer of complication. Voronina complained that the commissariats had no right "to rule over the unions" or "to bully our members." If the union reinstated someone, the commissariat could not refuse to employ them. Could the unions order managers to take someone back? Could the VTsSPS order the unions? Could both order the local party committee? No one had any answers. One editor of Iaroslavl's newspaper, *Severnyi Rabochii*, confessed after his arrest to participating in a counterrevolutionary group that included the head of the party committee and other employees. The procurator arrested the entire group, but then he himself was revealed to be a spy. The head of the party committee appealed the case, but his appeal was ignored and he was thrown out of his apartment. Finally everyone, with the exception of the procurator, was reinstated in the Party. The union was suing for back pay for lost work time. Osiannikova, the head of the Union of Press Employees, asked, "How can we correct all these mistakes and violations of labor legislation?" The newspapers had instructed people how to "unmask enemies," but no one knew how to reinstate them. Moreover, nonparty people received compensation for wrongful dismissal, but party members received nothing. Shvernik interjected, "There should be the same law for all."[60]

Denunciations no longer served to "unmask enemies" or demonstrate vigilance, but had become the automatic response to any perceived slight or argument. When the VTsSPS refused to restore a timber official accused of corruption, he immediately wrote to the Central Committee of the Party, denouncing Voronina as a "Trotskyist, Bukharinist, Zinoviev'ka."

[59] Ibid., ll. 271–273.   [60] Ibid., ll. 279, 280–284, 300.

People hurled accusations with no sense of their meaning. Names that had once represented alternative political programs became empty terms of abuse. A foreman and a cashier in a Kharkov factory got into an argument because the cashier refused to make change. "Go to the devil," the foreman yelled. "Go to the devil yourself," replied the cashier. The argument quickly escalated and soon the two men began cursing each other, each calling the other "devils" and, finally, "Trotskyists." With this last epithet, however, the argument assumed a political dimension. The cashier was ultimately fired for being "an enemy of the people." Osiannikova admitted that the February–March 1937 Central Committee Plenum had let loose legions of slanderers and "unmaskers." "It is a fact," she said, "that honest, well-intentioned, totally innocent people were out of work for a long time."[61]

Many cases of dismissal highlighted the absurdity of the reigning madness. In some factories, people had been fired and deprived of union membership "in batches." Women frequently lost their jobs when their husbands were arrested. People were fired because they went abroad for medical treatment, or had a relative living abroad. In one case, a man sent a private telegram costing four rubles at his employer's expense. He was fired and brought to court, and his wife was fired as well. People were given negative recommendations from former employers, ruining their prospects for future employment. Kozmin, head of the Union of Employees of the Northern Sea Lanes, noted, "All this is extraordinarily difficult for us." He was concerned that the atmosphere of wild rumor and slander was turning "people against the Party and Soviet power." Kozmin gave an odd twist to the hunt for enemies by defining "enemy disruption" in a new way. In a concluding statement that foreshadowed the arrest and repression of Ezhov himself, he noted that enemies were fomenting the repression of honest people. "We should tear out these people by the roots," he said, suggesting that the time had come to arrest those who had been so busy accusing others. Another delegate boldly noted that the VTsSPS itself prompted many arrests and dismissals with its aggressive investigations of union leaders, and had "made many mistakes." "We have forgotten that behind every denunciation there is a living human being," he said. Another noted, "We have shown a heartless attitude toward people . . . There was a lot of 'self-protection' and innocent people were hurt for no good reason." In suggesting that the VTsSPS had created

[61] Ibid., ll. 296–298.

much needless suffering, the delegates acknowledged its role in destroying the unions.[62]

Delegates were fearful of criticizing the terror outright. No one would say that "enemies of the people" might have been innocent. Yet by highlighting cases of "simple workers wronged by authorities," they exploited the opening created by Stalin's speech at the January 1938 Central Committee Plenum. Voronina related the case of a railroad worker, Ryzhkov, who worked for sixteen years in a steam-engine shop. Railroad workers had a long tradition of political activism, and their unions had been decimated by arrests of workers and officials. Ryzhkov, a worker without any history of oppositionism, incurred the wrath of managers for criticizing welds on the steam boilers. They accused him of drunkenness and fired him. He in turn wrote a denunciation stating that his shop was "a scandalous mess." Investigators ruled in Ryzhkov's favor, and suggested he be rehired. Management refused, and produced ten new accusations. Voronina cited this case because Ryzhkov's story fit easily into the politically acceptable tale of an "honest worker," who tried to produce a better product, but was victimized by "corrupt officials." Ryzhkov's experience illustrated her larger point that loyal people had been victimized and were struggling to be rehired. She cleverly turned the terror's stock theme of crusading workers and corrupt officials to a new purpose: not to denounce officials but to draw attention to those who had been falsely denounced.

Voronina cited several similar examples, all showcasing workers with long seniority and impeccable political credentials. One case featured Luk'ianova, a member of the VTsSPS Plenum and textile worker with thirty years' seniority in an Ivanovo textile factory. In 1929, Luk'ianova had visited a relative and drunk a toast with a Polish visitor who dropped by. Eight years later, the Pole was arrested as a Trotskyist, and Luk'ianova was thrown out of work, the union, and the plenum for consorting with an "enemy of the people." Her daughter was expelled from the Komsomol. Luk'ianova, in despair, went home and put a noose around her neck, but the neighbors rushed in and saved her. Her son petitioned the union's central committee, which restored her union membership, but the factory committee refused to readmit her. Finally, the VTsSPS interfered. Voronina noted that so many people had been fired for all kinds of slander that workplaces were shorthanded: "if we do not have three times more people on the job, we'll be pulling people out of court!"[63] Many workers, with

[62] Ibid., ll. 265–266, 268, 269–270, 288–289, 291, 293.
[63] Ibid., ll. 275–276, 278.

no relationship to opposition politics, undoubtedly were victimized by a stray remark, casual contact, or misplaced criticism. Yet the delegates used these particular stories not simply to right a wrong, but to offer a subtle critique of the terror. Unable to speak out directly, they employed the sacrosanct figure of the wronged worker to try and stem the madness. The stories, strategically selected, also revealed the limits of criticism. It was possible to defend a worker innocent of opposition politics; it was not possible to suggest that "enemies" were invented phantoms or that former oppositionists were not "enemies."

The delegates interpreted Stalin's speech as a signal of the return to normality. Not daring to criticize the hunt for "enemies" directly, they offered numerous examples of baseless slander and sought clear, enforceable procedures to correct mistakes. Yet they had misinterpreted the signal. Despite their criticism, the delegates were unable to halt or even slow the repression. In fact, they continued to collude in its wider dissemination. The VTsSPS continue to launch investigations in 1938, involving many unions in precisely the same practices the delegates had criticized. The Union of Textile Workers was drawn into a huge controversy, and arrests decimated the Union of Railroad Workers of the East and Far East. In this union alone, a total of 239 officials were fired, arrested or excluded from the Party. One report noted simply, "This is the entire leadership of the union, everyone in a leading position from the line committees to the central committee."[64] The NKVD scarcely missed a beat. From January to December 1938, fifteen more union leaders were arrested and dismissed from the VTsSPS Plenum, a body that included the heads of the unions. The new leaders who had replaced those arrested in 1937 were now being arrested.[65]

On January 4, 1938, the VTsSPS launched its own purge of the union press, beginning with an investigation that deemed the press "unsatisfactory." According to the investigator's report, the editorial staff of *Trud*, the national labor newspaper, was "blocked up with foreign and dubious elements." Its current circulation of 100,000 was too small to include all the factory committees, let alone all union members. The labor journals had failed to meet the needs of activists, and the ten newspapers published by individual unions were "totally unsatisfactory, apolitical, and toothless." They needed to be shut down. The investigative report charged that

[64] GARF, f. 5451, o. 43, d. 69, "Sekretariam VTsSPS. Dokladnaia zapiska," "Spisok. Razoblachennykh vragov naroda i sniatykh s profraboty po drugim prichinam po DK, LK, i MK zh.d. vostoka i dal'nego vostoka," ll. 376–378.

[65] See announcements in GARF, f. 5451, o. 43, d. 69, in documents titled "Postanovlenie sekretariata VTsSPS," "Postanovlenie prezidiuma VTsSPS," ll. 405–470.

the Union Publishing House (Profizdat) had virtually stopped publishing books, and had made "serious political mistakes" in several pamphlets. Its staff was riddled with "enemies." More than sixty staffers were revealed to have once been members of other parties, antiparty groups, or former elites, including nobles and clerics. Many had ties to people abroad. The report urged that they all be fired immediately. Forty-one of these, listed by name, were to be investigated further. A brief survey of their backgrounds revealed the "crimes" that put them at risk: briefly living abroad or in White territory during the Civil War, having relatives who lived abroad, or receiving a higher education under the old regime. Several Jewish staff members had once been members of the Bund; others had once belonged to the Socialist Revolutionaries (SRs). Of the party members, almost one-quarter had joined during the Civil War. The VTsSPS thus discovered that its publishing house, not surprisingly, employed a mix of highly educated former elites and politically sophisticated, older revolutionaries. It was a group of former Whites and older Reds working side by side: in a nutshell, precisely the group to draw suspicions of opposition.[66]

The Party's Central Committee, hypersensitive to "enemies" in any institution of mass communication, immediately got involved in the case. It fired the head of the Union Publishing House, E. O. Lerner, and threatened remaining staff members that if they did not "meet Bolshevik standards" within twenty days, they, too, would lose their jobs. It informed the VTsSPS that the union press was "deficient," and its staff needed to be replaced. It ordered the union newspapers to develop a group of worker correspondents (*rabkory*) from the ranks of Stakhanovites and shock workers and censured the union journals for their lack of practical relevance to activists in the shops. The Party shut down the individual union newspapers, increased *Trud*'s print run to 250,000, and renamed several journals.[67] It thus eliminated the autonomy of the smaller union newspapers and centralized the efforts of the union press in *Trud*.

In launching the purge of its own press, the VTsSPS thus demonstrated the schizophrenia characteristic of many organizations and individuals during the terror. At the very moment of its plenum, when its leaders could barely conceal their disgust with the endless round of dismissals, exclusions, and arrests, they issued a report guaranteed to provoke a

---

[66] GARF, f. 5451, o. 43, d. 69, "O rabote Profizdata i Profsoiuznoi pechati," "Rabotniki Profizdata, zhurnalov i gazet trebuiushchie proverki i zameny," ll. 421–427, 429. The union journals included *Voprosy Profdvizheniia, Voprosy Strakhovaniia, Klub, Gigiena Truda, Tekhnika Bezopastnosti,* and *Zhizn' Glukhonemykh.*

[67] GARF, f. 5451, o. 43, d. 69, "Postanovlenie prezidiuma VTsSPS," ll. 414–418.

new bloodletting in a key organization under their auspices. How can we explain this "dual-mindedness," this mindset that continued to fuel the terror and, at the same time, fully recognized the great damage it was doing?

Conclusion

The leaders of the VTsSPS and the unions were not helpless victims of repression. They were not isolated individuals, naïve youngsters, or hapless innocents struggling to understand an inexplicable social phenomenon. They were, in fact, active agents embedded in powerful institutions and deeply implicated in the organizational dynamics of the terror. They were both victimizers and victims at the very same time. Without their willing, even eager assistance, the number of victims would have been far smaller. In fact, one might argue that, if it had not been for the active engagement of union and VTsSPS leaders, there would have been no repression in the union movement. No social phenomenon exists apart from human agents, and the agents of repression in the VTsSPS and the unions were the organizations' own officials. No hard and clear line divided the denouncers from the denounced, the purgers from the purged, or the guilty from the innocent. While some people were more zealous than others in pursuing their colleagues, all outwardly adhered to the slogans and practices that comprised the terror. What does this chapter tell us about how organizations and individuals reacted? What can it tell us about the pathways of terror in the unions?

The terror in the unions began slowly in 1936 in connection with the arrest of former Trotskyists. It spread outward through the fall of 1936 through interlocking party and union circles of staff, mentors, relatives, and friends. Many people were caught up in these organizational wheels, with each fresh victim serving as a hub for new spokes, and new wheels. Repression of top leaders pulled down many "clients" and repression of local and regional officials threatened their patrons at the top. Yet the arrests were still largely confined to former oppositionists and their circles. The February–March 1937 Plenum and the campaign for union democracy launched by the 6th VTsSPS Plenum introduced a qualitative shift in the pattern of repression. The campaign for democracy created power struggles among union leaders that easily lent themselves to denunciations and accusations. The popular appeals to workers – recasting charges in the language of democracy, invoking wrecking to explain shortages of food and housing, blaming high accident rates on "enemies" – all drove the furious hunt for "enemies" at lower levels. The blame game took new and complicated forms as charges prompted identical countercharges. The VTsSPS added fuel to the fire by launching its own investigations, which drew in the Party and the NKVD. Muckraking articles or denunciations prompted the investigations, which, once published, were responsible for a fresh spate of denunciations. VTsSPS leaders aggressively pursued staff members and union leaders for fear they would be seen as "concealing" enemies. Union leaders cast aspersions on the VTsSPS. Officials and workers did not hesitate to hurl dangerous political charges against each other. Such charges had consequences.

The process of purge was chaotic, and did not follow a clear set of steps. By the time repression came to engulf the unions, the great bureaucratic mazes of the NKVD, the Party, the unions, and the VTsSPS contained many paths to prison. People were arrested by the NKVD, convicted of counterrevolutionary activity or other political charges, and then excluded from the Party and their union posts. Party committees, unions, and the VTsSPS merely ratified decisions that had already been made by the NKVD. In other cases, union officials who were also party members were excluded from the Party, and then lost their union posts. These cases, too, were frequently remanded to the NKVD. Others were victimized by the VTsSPS, which subsequently turned over compromising materials to the NKVD. For some, repression proved a lengthy process, moving in painful and uncertain stages. Others were imprisoned immediately, and the unions, the Party, and the VTsSPS moved hurriedly to strip them of their membership and posts. The unions fired people who had already disappeared or been executed. The process created a surreal and macabre confusion, as leading bodies in the Party, the VTsSPS, and the unions met repeatedly with the sole agenda of expelling or firing people who had already ceased to exist.

For a brief moment in January 1938, union officials thought that the Central Committee had called a halt to the frenzy of expulsion, denunciation, and slander that had ripped apart the unions and the Party. Tentatively, they criticized the most egregious excesses of the terror, using the figure of the "wronged and honest worker" to endorse a halt. But the January 1938 Central Committee Plenum only added a new layer of complication. Arrests continued as reinstatements began, a situation that created great confusion, and further paralyzed frightened officials. It was now thoroughly impossible to tell the "enemy" from the innocent. Chaos reigned.

11. Aleksandra V. Artiukhina, head of the Union of Cotton Textile Workers in Moscow and Leningrad. Courtesy of www.cultinfo.ru

12. Nikolai M. Shvernik, head of the All Union Central Council of Unions. Reproduced from *Voprosy profdvizheniia* 9–10 (May 1937), p. 6

6

Rituals of Repression in the Factories

"Enemies of the Party know how to mask themselves. Yet however they may mask themselves, our task is to rip the masks from their faces."
– Budanov, member of the party committee in Likernovodochnyi factory, 1938[1]

"They're shooting all the intelligent ones and leaving all the fools."
– Margolin, member of the party organization in Dinamo factory, arrested[2]

"Take the active Komsomol'tsy and knock out Margolin's teeth."
– Starichkov, secretary of the party committee in Dinamo[3]

By 1937, the easy tolerance that prevailed in the local party committees (*partkomy*) in the factories had disappeared. In the words of Starichkov, the party secretary in Dinamo, a large machine-building factory, "We don't need this good nature. We need revolutionary vigilance."[4] Throughout the fall of 1936, party officials had hectored the *partkomy* to hunt more actively for enemies in their ranks. The Kemerovo and Piatakov trials, the February–March 1937 Central Committee Plenum, and the campaign for union democracy (*profdemokratiia*) all served to popularize and democratize repression. Party leaders urged the rank and file to become

---

[1] TsAODM, f. 428, o. 1, d. 1, "Stenogramma obshchego otchetno-vybornogo zakrytogo partsobraniia moskovskogo Likerno-vodochnogo zavoda," April 19–21, 1938, l. 64.
[2] TsAODM, f. 432, o. 1, d. 179, "Protokol zasedaniia plenuma partkoma zavoda 'Dinamo im. Kirova,'" June 18, 1937, l. 145. On the subsequent arrest and exclusion of Margolin, see TsAODM, f. 432, o. 1, d. 188, "Stenogramma otchetno-vybornogo zakrytogo partiinogo sobraniia partorganizatsii zavoda Dinamo im. Kirova," April 8, 1938, ll. 26–27.
[3] "Protokol zasedaniia plenuma partkoma zavoda 'Dinamo im. Kirova,'" June 18, 1937, l. 145.
[4] TsAODM, f. 432, o. 1, d. 176, "Stenogramma otchetnogo partiinogo sobraniia," April 8–10, 1937, ll. 3, 8–9.

involved in "unmasking enemies," to find hidden enemies *before* they were arrested by the NKVD, and to expose corrupt and abusive officials. The *partkomy* were soon caught up in a complicated psychological and organizational process, which required them to find and "unmask" the hidden enemies among them. Party members turned against each other, becoming active agents in the repression. Deeply engaged in scrutinizing, interrogating, and expelling each other, they wrote denunciations to their primary party organizations, shop, factory, district, and city committees, and various branches of the NKVD. Many cases that came before the *partkomy* began with internal denunciations or letters to the factory newspapers. The process was uneven, and some *partkomy* were sucked in more rapidly and completely than others. Serp i Molot's *partkom*, for example, which represented more than 700 members, was completely taken up with mutual denunciations despite the fact that P. F. Stepanov, the director, tried repeatedly to slow the process, maintain some semblance of rationality, and focus on production. In Trekhgornaia Manufaktura, a textile factory, the process of "unmasking" gained momentum more slowly, despite the arrest of its director at the beginning of 1937.[5]

The issues that got party members into trouble fell roughly into four categories: social origins or prior political activities; ties to family members, friends, or mentors who were arrested; ideological mistakes; and accidents, safety violations, and problems with production. The *partkomy* in all the factories shared certain procedures that created similar organizational dynamics. Party members were required, for example, to issue a declaration (*zaiavlenie*) if they suspected "enemy" activities or wrecking, overheard a suspicious conversation, learned of the arrest of a relative, friend, or mentor, or received compromising information. A *zaiavlenie* could be about oneself or others, and take the form of a personal confession, denunciation, rumor, or even mere suspicion. There were no consequences to writing a *zaiavlenie* without evidence, although there were consequences to *not* writing one. The failure to report the arrest of a relative, for example, was itself grounds for expulsion and even arrest. There was thus strong impetus to denounce, if only to protect oneself from the failure to have denounced. Throughout 1937-8, flurries of such "informational declarations" blanketed the NKVD and the Party at every level. In the factories, party organizations were completely occupied with investigating *zaiavleniia*.

5 TsAODM, f. 369, o. 1, d. 171, "Stenogramma otchetno-perevybornogo partiinogo sobraniia," March 30–31, 1937, l. 155.

Party members in the factories were organized in a pyramidal structure, with the primary party organizations and shop committees at the base. The *partkom*, an elected body of ten to fifteen people, was the apex of the pyramid, representing all the factory's party members. Party membership cut vertically through the factory, and included workers, shop heads, managers, and the director. Party meetings, from the *partkom* to general, factorywide meetings, ranged in size from ten members to hundreds, and encompassed different, even opposing interests. In the large and important factories, there were hundreds of party members; in many smaller ones, none. Dinamo, a machine-building factory with almost 7,000 workers and eighteen shops, had more than 700 party members and candidates; Trekhgornaia Manufaktura, more than 500.

Both party shop organizations and *partkomy* discussed *zaiavleniia* in highly ritualized meetings that resembled court trials.[6] Members in the shop committees considered the charges first and decided what action to take. The *partkom* then reviewed their decision, often with additional testimony and "evidence." The secretary of the *partkom* presented the charges, the accused defended him- or herself, other members asked questions, the accused responded, the party secretary gave his opinion, and the members voted on the outcome. No rules, however, governed the presentation of evidence. Hearsay was a mainstay of the proceedings, and members' questions were often openly prejudicial and belligerent. Moreover, as one "trial" followed another, a tangle of animosities and alliances developed among party members who found themselves in the successive roles of juror, procurator, and accused. Each new arrest by the NKVD spurred the *partkomy* into new investigations of the victim's workmates, subordinates, and superiors. Yet, by 1937, the process was also propelled from within. The "terror" in the factories became a self-generated and self-replicating process.

This chapter is based on stenographic reports of *partkom* meetings from 1937 to 1939 in five Moscow factories: Dinamo, a machine-building factory, Serp i Molot, an iron and steel plant, Krasnyi Proletarii, a small machine-tool factory, Likernovodochnyi factory, a liquor and spirits factory, and Trekhgornaia Manufaktura, a textile factory. It examines the organizational dynamics by which people moved collectively into a

---

[6] For a fascinating history of staged trials as political education, see Elizabeth Wood, *Performing Justice: Agitational Trials in Early Soviet Russia* (Cornell University Press, Ithaca and London, 2005).

phantasmagorical world peopled by enemies and wreckers.[7] The stenographic reports, which captured every word of their meetings verbatim, make it possible to eavesdrop on people long dead, observe their changing interactions, and trace their fates. The meetings provide insight into the conflicts, friendships, and grievances that constituted daily life and political culture in the factories. They show how party members moved through stages, from charge to countercharge, and from individual expulsions to collective chaos and hysteria. They reveal, in other words, people both actively shaping and reacting to a process that was simultaneously of their collective making and beyond their individual control.

Deviations from the "Heroic Biography"

In the spring of 1937, party members in the factories began scrutinizing biographical records and minutes of old meetings in an effort to "unmask the enemies" among them. As late as fall 1936, even past oppositional activity had not constituted sufficient reason for expulsion. Many members had been active in earlier oppositions, and some had even been expelled and reinstated. Now evidence of past oppositional activity ceased to be a questionable marker, and became a definitive criterion for expulsion. Party members measured each other against an implicit "heroic biography" defined by working-class or poor peasant origins, a complete absence of political opposition, and "pure" relatives who could boast similar origins and politics. Anyone who deviated from the rigid conventions of this biography, no matter how loyal, productive, or self-sacrificing, was subject to expulsion and arrest. The longer a person had been in the Party, however, the more difficult it was to construct an "untainted biography." The *partkomy* began scrutinizing Civil War activity as well as experience with other political parties such as the Bund (Jewish Workers' Party) or the Socialist Revolutionaries. Although many Jewish party members had once belonged to the Bund, and the Bund officially merged with the

---

[7] Unfortunately, it was impossible to obtain a full run of meetings for each factory. The years include: Dinamo 1937–8; Krasnyi Proletarii 1935–6, 1938–9; Serp i Molot 1935–8; Likervodochnyi 1937–8; and Trekhgornaia Manufaktura 1935, 1937. On the history of Serp i Molot, see Kevin Murphy, *Revolution and Counterrevolution: Class Struggle in a Moscow Metal Factory* (Berghahn Books, Oxford and New York, 2005); Kenneth Straus, *Factory and Community in Stalin's Russia* (University of Pittsburgh Press, Pittsburgh, 1997); Andrei Sokolov and Andrei Markevich, *Magnitka bliz Sadovogo kol'tsa: stimuly k rabote na moskovskom zavode "Serp i molot," 1883–2001* (ROSSPEN, Moscow, 2005).

Bolsheviks in 1920, early Bund membership now became suspect. In fact, any of the following experiences or contacts cast suspicion on a party member:

(1) time spent abroad or in White territory during the Civil War;
(2) relatives living abroad;
(3) correspondence with people living abroad, including relatives;
(4) relatives who had been kulaks, clergy, traders, businessmen, or landowners;
(5) sponsors for party membership, relatives, friends, mentors, or even casual acquaintances who had been arrested;
(6) participation in oppositional groups in the past or contact (even of the most casual type) with those who participated in oppositional activities.

Party members were required to submit a *zaiavlenie* if they were affected by any of these "compromising circumstances." If they heard that a relative or friend had been arrested, for example, they were required to report it to the *partkom* immediately. Entire meetings were spent listening to members' *zaiavleniia*, which once investigated, produced new fodder for further meetings. In 1938, the *partkom* of Likernovodochnyi factory admitted that it had been completely occupied with denunciations and "unmasking" since the beginning of 1937. Gul'bis, an old party member, came under fire when the *partkom* uncovered evidence that White soldiers had briefly taken him prisoner during the Civil War. The Whites apparently saw his party card, but did not arrest or shoot him. Why not? Gul'bis explained that a kindly White Guard had taken pity on him and allowed him to escape. The *partkom* found this story suspicious, and peppered him with questions. Perhaps Gul'bis performed some service for the Whites, which they rewarded by releasing him? Perhaps he was a double agent? Gul'bis's failure to account plausibly for his release now resulted, almost twenty years later, in his expulsion from the Party for "muddling his autobiography" and subsequent arrest.[8] By the late 1930s, the tumultuous history of the revolution and Civil War had been reduced to a mechanical script with cardboard villains and heroes. It had no room for people who deviated from "type," not for a White Guard who might have acted from pity, and certainly not for a Red Guard who might have committed a dubious act to save his life. The case, moreover, did not end with Gul'bis, but poisoned relations within the Party as it rippled outward to involve his friends and workmates.

---

[8] "Obshchego otchetno-vybornogo zakrytogo partsobraniia moskovskogo Likerno-vodochnogo zavoda," April 19–21, 1938, ll. 120b, 15, 110b.

Geche, a member of the *partkom*, had been close to Gul'bis before his arrest. His fellow workers, expecting that he would soon follow Gul'bis into prison, treated him like a pariah. Geche complained, "I consider the behavior of certain communists to me incorrect. I am a member of the party organization but they will not sit with me because I worked with Gul'bis. I went to the club, and everyone sitting around me got up and left." When Geche appeared in the party office, the two members sitting there greeted him with silence. Geche related the conversation: "I say, 'Hello.' They are silent. I repeat it. 'Hello,' they answer. This shows that I am allegedly on the outs, I do not exist." When he went to the factory courtyard, people asked him with mordant humor, "You're still alive?" Finally, unable to stand being shunned any longer, Geche went to see the party secretary. Referring to his Latvian background, he said in desperation, "If there is suspicion, take me away, if I am a Lettish Nazi, take me away. If something is wrong, tell me. But, here, people just try to get farther away from me."[9]

In July 1937, the Politburo signed a series of orders, which resulted in hundreds of thousands of arrests. "Order 00447" for "mass operations" in July 1937 set target numbers for the imprisonment or execution of criminals, clergy, religious activists, former kulaks, and other "hostile elements." It was followed by "Order 00485," which led to the mass roundup of Polish nationals, and "Order 00486," which mandated the arrest of wives of men convicted of counterrevolutionary crimes.[10] People without passports were rounded up and arrested in the cities, and thousands of peasants who had returned from exile were arrested in the countryside. The "mass operations" were aimed at "marginal elements," but reverberations from these arrests affected workers and party members. Many had relatives who had been dekulakized or had fled the villages. No matter how "pure" a party member's biography, their relatives often had spottier histories. By fall 1937, the fallout from these mass operations reached the

---

[9] Ibid., ll. 120b, 76.

[10] J. Arch Getty, "'Excesses Are Not Permitted': Mass Terror and Stalinist Governance in the Late 1930s," *Russian Review*, 61 (January, 2002), pp. 113–38; Paul Hagenloh, "Socially Harmful Elements and the Great Terror," in Sheila Fitzpatrick, ed., *Stalinism: New Directions* (Routledge, London and New York, 2000), pp. 286–308; Barry McLoughlin, "Mass Operations of the NKVD, 1937–1938: A Survey" (pp. 118–52), Nikita Petrov and Arsenii Roginskii, "The 'Polish Operation' of the NKVD, 1937–1938" (pp. 153–70), and David Shearer, "Social Disorder, Mass Repression and the NKVD During the 1930s" (pp. 85–117), all in McLoughlin and Kevin McDermott, eds., *Stalin's Terror: High Politics and Mass Repression in the Soviet Union* (Palgrave, Basingstoke and New York, 2003).

factories, and party members began presenting *zaiavleniia* about arrested relatives. In November, P. M. Larkin, a member of the *partkom* in Serp i Molot, gave a *zaiavlenie* that his father, a 63-year-old collective farmer, had been arrested. Larkin learned of the arrest from an old friend from his village. "What do you think he could have been arrested for?" a fellow party member asked. Larkin answered miserably, "For what, I don't know. He didn't owe taxes. I saw him last in 1933. He was never mixed up with anything, anywhere. The leaders of the collective farm were sentenced for drinking up the harvest and ruining the garden. But my father was not involved in this business." The *partkom* vowed to investigate the case further.[11]

In Trekhgornaia Manufaktura, party members also reported arrests of rural relatives. Iarkin, a party member since 1919, presented a *zaiavlenie* about his cousin who worked on a state farm in Bashkiria. After the cattle got sick, his cousin was charged with wrecking. Iarkin had not seen his cousin since 1921. One party member asked tendentiously, "How can you help the Party uncover your tie with your cousin?" Another added nastily, "I worked with Iarkin and I never heard he had a cousin on a state farm." After numerous questions, Pavlov, a worker in the factory garage, mercifully put an end to the discussion. "To investigate relations between cousins is difficult. I think Iarkin's *zaiavlenie* should be accepted as information."[12] Yet Pavlov's timely intervention may have been prompted by his own biographical secret. A month later, he presented a *zaiavlenie* that his brother-in-law had been arrested on a collective farm near Riazan. After harsh questioning, Pavlov revealed that his brother-in-law's family, exiled as "kulaks" during collectivization, had returned once their term of exile expired. Pavlov swore that, although he visited the collective farm during vacations, he knew nothing about his brother-in-law. The questioning became sharper:

"Why didn't you say that you had a relative who had been dekulakized?"
"I somehow didn't attach any significance to this fact."
"What was your brother-in-law's mood?'
"I never noticed."
"What kind of household did you come from in the countryside?"

---

[11] TsAODM, f. 429, o. 1, d. 223, "Protokol no. 38 zasedaniia partiinogo komiteta zavoda 'Serp i molot,'" November 11, 1937, l. 91.
[12] TsAODM, f. 369, o. 1, d. 173, "Protokol no. 31 zasedaniia plenuma partkoma," November 22, 1937, ll. 50–51.

"Before callup into the army I was a peasant in my grandfather's household, then
I became a seasonal worker, and in 1925 I began to work in Trekhgornaia."
"How is it that up to this time you had no interest in your dekulakized relatives in
the countryside?"

The questions continued. Finally, the *partkom* agreed to investigate
Iarkin's relations further.[13]

Politically compromised relatives were just one of many factors marring
otherwise "pure" biographies. A number of party members found themselves answering uncomfortable questions about their relationship to the
left opposition in the 1920s. Ia. I. Sokol, a 28-year-old party member in
Serp i Molot, was part of a generation that experienced great upward
mobility under Soviet power. Too young to participate in the revolution,
he came of age in the late 1920s, a time of exciting political debate. He
joined the Komsomol while working at a factory in Kiev, and then joined
the Party in 1930. The Party promptly sent him to a technical institute to
become an engineer, and then to Serp i Molot. By 1937, he was the head of
the department of technical control in the calibration shop. When rumors
reached the *partkom* that Sokol had been part of a Trotskyist group in
Kiev in his youth, it sent Petrov, one of its members, to ferret out material.
Based on this information, the *partkom* charged Sokol with Trotskyism.
Sokol, brought before the *partkom*, tried to answer the charges. He
explained that a Trotskyist group, composed of young workers in the
Komsomol, existed in Kiev at that time. It distributed leaflets in the factory and even in the Komsomol district office. When Sokol became head of
the factory's Komsomol, he broke the group up. "I smashed this group,"
he explained. "You can check this. I entered the Party there. I passed
through the purge of 1929. The guys were workers. The Trotskyists organized them in apartments, not the factory. Earlier we were all comrades.
After excluding them from the Komsomol, I had no contact with them."
Ask to name the young workers who had been active in the group, Sokol
promptly complied. One now worked in Elektrostal, an electrical factory
southeast of Moscow. Sokol's list broadened the case and prompted a
torrent of new questions. "Did you inform anyone that an oppositionist worked in Elektrostal?" "How many of the people you named have
been arrested?" "Did you know Klinkov, the provincial Komsomol and
district party secretary?" "When did you meet with him?" Klinkov, who

[13] TsAODM, f. 369, o. 1, d. 173, "Protokol no. 32 zasedaniia plenuma partkoma," December 9, 1937, ll. 55–56.

had risen to a prominent position in Kiev's city government, had already been arrested. Sokol argued that he met with the young Trotskyist workers solely to convert them. The secretary of Serp i Molot's *partkom* then pulled out the minutes of a party meeting in 1927. "You spoke there," the secretary insisted. "What did you speak about?" Frightened, Sokol began to stutter, "I was not so literate as I am now. Maybe I was mistaken." The minutes showed that Sokol had defended the opposition. Sokol pleaded with the *partkom* to take the political context into account: "In 1927, there was a lot of argument about whether to believe the Central Committee or not." Finally, Petrov summarized the results of his visit to Kiev: "According to the research I did, in 1927 the Trotskyist guys were openly active, although a few were concealed. Ernyshev and Rozenberg were the base of the opposition. Rozenberg was Sokol's closest friend. The party organization investigated the whole business. There were a whole series of meetings that Sokol did not mention. Klinkov spoke out publicly against the group, but he was a double-dealer because he also met with them at his apartment. Rozenberg was the leader. Sokol helped him. Klinkov recommended Sokol to the party. I spoke with many workers who said Sokol was very close to Rozenberg. Rozenberg was expelled from the party in 1933 ... The *partkom* of the Komsomol at that time were all Trotskyists." Sokol, initially bewildered and frightened by the charges, soon understood what had happened. Klinkov, the second secretary of the central committee of the Ukrainian Komsomol, Rozenberg, and several workers from the Kiev factory had recently been arrested. *Partkomy* throughout the country were now investigating the intricate friendship, work, and party ties that originated in this young group in the 1920s.[14]

Larkin, who had given a *zaiavlenie* about his father's arrest only one month before, was eager to demonstrate his own vigilance. "You retained your tie with a Trotskyist," he told Sokol. "Sokol participated with these people in meetings. Exclude him for concealing his participation in the Trotskyist opposition." The meeting now lost all semblance of order, as party members began yelling out, "Exclude him from the party. Remove him from responsible work!" "He made a counterrevolutionary speech in 1930!" "I was in Ukraine in 1926 and 1927. There were many Trotskyists operating there. Voikov was murdered in Poland with Trotskyist help. There were kulak uprisings ... He can't stay in the party." Petrov, raising his voice over the hubbub, demanded that Sokol's testimony be sent back

---

[14] TsAODM, f. 429, o. 1, d. 223, "Protokol no. 40 zasedaniia partkoma zavoda 'Serp i molot,'" December 8, 1937, ll. 111–115.

to the Kiev party organization so they could hunt down all the original oppositionists. Finally, Petrov delivered the final blow, "Many workers said Sokol was a careerist. He had nothing in common with the factory, and he only wanted to crawl into the party and the institute." The *partkom* voted to expel him for concealing his tie to known Trotskyists, and for his "counterrevolutionary speech" at a party meeting in 1930.[15] The case against Sokol was similar to many others. Although Sokol appeared to be a dedicated engineer, a young worker educated by the party, his biography turned out to be considerably more complicated.

Thousands of people were tarred with the brush of "Trotskyism," either through their own participation or contact with a relative, mentor, or friend. A. S. Fomin, the head of the fourth machine shop, began work in Dinamo in 1923 as a mechanic in a shop sympathetic to the left opposition. He worked briefly in an administrative post in the controller's office, and eventually became a shop head. When the head of the controller's office and several old shopmates were arrested for Trotskyism, Fomin got into serious trouble. Razin, one of the *partkom* members, charged that Dinamo was "run by Trotskyists" in 1926–7. "They distributed proclamations in every worker's box, and left leaflets on the machines." Fomin, a candidate member, had developed a "bad attitude at the time." He had stopped paying his dues, and dropped out of the Party. In 1929, Razin had a long conversation with Fomin to determine how he felt, and "he [had] answered that he looked at things differently now than in 1927." Razin recommended that he reenter the Party. Fomin's trouble did not stem from anything he had done or said. His main failing was that he was close to several people in the factory who were subsequently arrested as "Trotskyists." As shop head, he had also rehired one Itkin, who was fired for "going on strike every time they raised the norms." Fomin's "Trotskyism" differed from Sokol's. He had not been involved with a left opposition group or actively propounded Trotskyist ideas. In defending himself, Fomin stressed his loyalty, offering a list of people he had previously denounced. The *partkom* expelled him anyway, declaring: "He had a close tie with Trotskyists who have now been arrested. They met regularly and invited him. He did not help the party organization to unmask them. He never gave a *zaiavlenie* about any of them."[16] Fomin's essential mistake thus lay in not exposing friends who were subsequently arrested.

---

[15] Ibid., ll. 115–116.
[16] TsAODM, f. 432, o. 1, d. 179, "Protokol zasedaniia plenuma partkoma zavoda 'Dinamo im. Kirova,'" March 18, 1937, ll. 75–80.

Cases like Fomin's heightened the atmosphere of fear and denunciation. If a person could be expelled or arrested simply for the failure to denounce someone who had not yet been revealed as an enemy, the only response guaranteeing protection was to write *zaiavleniia* about everyone.

The most common subjects of *zaiavleniia* were party members in positions of authority. By spring 1937, the *partkom* of Serp i Molot had received more than thirty *zaiavleniia* about P. F. Stepanov, the factory's director, charging him with "enemy ties," embezzlement, wrecking, and a variety of other crimes and misdemeanors. The *partkom* spent almost all of July investigating and grilling Stepanov, leaving him little time to run the factory. On the surface, Stepanov appeared to have impeccable biographical credentials. The son of a poor worker, he led a factory committee in the heady days of the revolution, joined the Party in 1918, and rose to a powerful position. Yet under close questioning, Stepanov, the trusted director of Moscow's largest iron and steel plant, revealed a far more ambiguous and complicated history.[17]

Stepanov's father, the son of serfs, was an alcoholic who worked sporadically as a worker and petty trader. He abandoned the family when Stepanov was eight. The boy's youth was marred by horrible poverty, alcoholism, and political confusion. In a long torturous interrogation, the *partkom* dwelled on Stepanov's relationship to the workers' movement after the 1905 revolution. "What were your politics up to 1917?" demanded Bubnov, the secretary of the *partkom*. "I was demoralized and I demoralized others," Stepanov admitted. "That's not a political answer," Bubnov replied tartly. Another member added, "Perhaps you want to say that you were *politically* demoralized and you demoralized others *politically*?" Stepanov repeated grudgingly, "I was demoralized and I aided the demoralization of the proletariat." Under continued prodding, Stepanov admitted that he had joined a church choir. He added, hopefully, that they had sung "Stenka Razin," a song about a peasant rebel. "We're not interested in what songs you sang," another member replied sharply; "Who used you? What kind of organization? Give a political evaluation of this business." Stepanov was silent. The *partkom* asked him again about the organization that sponsored his choir. Was it the Black Hundreds, a notorious anti-Semitic organization, or the Zubatovtsy, a union organized by the police? After a long uncomfortable silence, Stepanov

---

[17] TsAODM, f. 429, o. 1, d. 269, "Stenogramma zasedaniia partiinogo komiteta zavoda 'Serp i molot,'" July 22, 1937, ll. 69–109; TsAODM, f. 429, o. 1, d. 269, "Stenogramma zasedaniia partiinogo komiteta zavoda 'Serp i molot,'" July 25, 1937, ll. 111–136.

whispered shamefacedly, "The Black Hundreds." With heavy sarcasm, Bubnov said, "The aim of the Black Hundreds was not just to organize the lumpenproletariat to sing in the choir. What did you do?" "I sang." "Were there people who participated in pogroms?" Bubnov asked. "There were." Stepanov admitted that, by 1909, he had become a sodden alcoholic, his singing voice had deteriorated, and even the Black Hundreds had lost interest in him. "I was ashamed of myself," he explained. "All my comrades stopped greeting me." One night, he wandered into a theatre and saw a play, *Poverty Is Not a Vice*. "This play had a strong effect on me," Stepanov recounted. "I immediately stopped drinking." He began work at the Bromlei factory (later renamed Krasnyi Proletarii), a hotbed of unrest, and became involved in the workers' movement. In Bromlei, the Mensheviks and the Bolsheviks worked together. Like many workers at that time, Stepanov perceived little difference between them. This angered several *partkom* members who demanded to know which faction he joined. "I don't understand how you could not know which tendency you joined," said one. "There was confusion," Stepanov replied. "How did the workers know you?" asked another. The *partkom* had gone to the trouble of soliciting statements from workers who had remained at Bromlei. Bubnov said, "Bogdanovich writes that he knew you as an active Menshevik. We have a report from him."[18]

Stepanov's biography revealed the ambiguous shadings of a history filled with confusion and contingency. Stepanov, "a true son of the people," had at one time been a hopeless and demoralized alcoholic, a participant in an anti-Semitic organization, and a revolutionary worker who was neither Bolshevik nor Menshevik. His social origins, too, defied neat categorization. His father had been a peasant, a worker, a trader, and a drunk who abandoned his family. By any generous accounting, Stepanov had been a poor worker who participated actively in the revolution and benefited greatly from its victory. Yet, by 1937, the *partkom* measured Stepanov against criteria that had been stripped of all connection to the real, human history of the revolution.

The need for impeccable biographical credentials took a heavy toll not only on individuals but, ultimately, also on the ability of the *partkomy* to function. Few members could withstand the rigorous grilling that preceded selection for higher office. By 1938, the *partkom* in Liker-novodochnyi, for example, could not find enough sufficiently "pure"

---

[18] "Stenogramma zasedaniia partiinogo komiteta zavoda 'Serp i molot,'" July 22, 1937, ll. 69, 81–94.

candidates to represent it on the district committee. The factory had 114 party members, 27 candidates, and 47 "sympathizers."[19] Nominees for higher party posts were subject to grueling review by their fellow members. The *partkom*'s examination of Kulikova, a woman who joined the Party in 1929, was typical of the screening process. Kulikova came from a working-class family, and had worked in factories since the age of thirteen. She and her father had lost their jobs during the Civil War, when many factories closed for lack of fuel and materials. Like many desperate city dwellers, her father had begun trading in the market to keep the family from starving. In the 1920s, a period of high unemployment, the old man found it difficult to get rehired and continued to work as a trader. In reciting the basic elements of her biography, Kulikova did not conceal her father's activities. Her fellow party members quickly focused on her social origins. Was she the daughter of a worker or a trader? The questions came hard and fast:

"They say you yourself traded."
"Everyone knows I did not trade."
"What did your father trade?"
"Candy. He was sixty-five and unemployed. The manufacturer said, 'Take the candy.' He tried to get a pension, but he did not succeed and I was not able to make him do it. Then I split up with my husband, and it was hard."
"They say your father was dekulakized."
"No. We never had a farm. I lived in the same house since I was fourteen. He was deprived of voting rights in 1929 because of squabbles, but then his rights were restored."
"Did your father trade in the market with a basket or did he have a stall?"
"He had a stall."
"Where is your husband?"
"He lives with me."
"I have information that the Kulikovs were in trade."
"The Kulikovs in Rogozhskii district were traders but my father's name is Egorov."
"Your husband was connected to enemies of the people who were arrested. I refer to Eideman [an official in Osoaviakhim]. Were you ever a guest in his home or not?"
"This is some kind of foolishness. My husband worked in the Bauman district branch of Osoaviakhim as a simple official. He was not personally familiar with Eideman. He knew him only as a boss."[20]

The *partkom* in Likernovodochnyi carefully reviewed all its members, but few could withstand the scrutiny. Vikulov, the factory's deputy

---

[19] "Obshchego otchetno-vybornogo zakrytogo partsobraniia moskovskogo Likerno-vodochnogo zavoda," April 19–21, 1938, l. 15.
[20] Ibid., ll. 116–117.

director, was closely associated with a recently arrested "enemy of the people" in the transport department. Borisova, a daughter of poor peasants, had cut peat and worked for room and board in a monastery as a child. "I heard she was a nun," someone claimed. Petty nastiness infused the exchanges between party members. Borisova had divorced her husband in 1923 and had lived apart from him for fourteen years. When he was arrested for drunkenness, a female party member exclaimed, "My husband drinks but they didn't arrest him!" Another noted maliciously, "Everyone says that she fights constantly with her husband because he drinks. The last time he drank, he didn't work for three months. Maybe that's why they arrested him." Borisova reiterated wearily, "I haven't lived with him since 1923."[21]

From 1937 to 1939, the *partkomy* went to great lengths to uncover material from the past. Meetings witnessed a parade of fearful members presenting *zaiavleniia*, followed by "unmasking" sessions, in which they were grilled by eager comrades. Very few people had no weak spot. Yet such "weak spots" frequently made people publicly less, not more, sympathetic. Their need to demonstrate "vigilance" broadened the investigations, which in turn increased the number of victims. Self-protection was thus ultimately a self-defeating strategy. In the short run, it provided "cover" for the individual. In the long run, it heightened the risk for all.

"Family Circles" and Geometric Progressions

Many party members were expelled or arrested because they were connected to a relative, patron, friend, or workmate who had been arrested. As the atmosphere became increasingly tense and hysterical, ties to a so-called enemy of the people became grounds for expulsion. Such ties opened party members to lengthy and uncomfortable interrogations about the nature and frequency of their contact with the victim. When managers were arrested, and the *partkomy* began investigating their "circles," the victim served as a hub with multiple spokes to a wheel of contacts. As more compromising material was uncovered, the initial investigations expanded. The wheels, moreover, were not self-contained: any particular point on the rim was itself a hub with its own spokes. In this way, incrimination by association spread rapidly to encompass ever more people.

Bystritskii, an engineer and party member in Dinamo, was an excellent example of this process. He first came under investigation by the *partkom* because he worked with several managers who had been arrested. The questioning, however, quickly revealed additional harmful details. Party members testified that Bystritskii received money from his parents who had fled abroad after the revolution. Bystritskii claimed his father was a worker, but a member of the *partkom* quickly retorted, "We know that workers had no reason to leave. And we know that workers abroad earn almost nothing. Here it seems that capitalists pay well. Exclude him." Then the party secretary dropped an unexpected bombshell. He announced that he just received information that Bystritskii's brother had been arrested. Bystritskii was in shock. "They are saying a lot of things that are very farfetched," he said softly. "I didn't know that my brother had been arrested. I just learned about this now. They want me to say that my father was a capitalist, but I know he was a worker because I worked with him from the age of thirteen." But Bystritskii had too many strikes against him: close ties to a "family circle" of managers and engineers who were arrested, a brother who was recently arrested, and two parents abroad who tried to help him. The *partkom* voted to exclude him. Bystritskii himself was arrested two months later.[22]

In every factory, "batches" of people were expelled and arrested in the wake of the arrest of a common acquaintance or colleague. In Dinamo, for example, a few key arrests pulled down multiple people. Prokhorov, head of the factory's experimental station, Kreitsberg, head of the second machine shop, Tolchinskii, the technical director, and Zhailov, head of the Bureau of Locomotive Prototypes, all worked on production of an experimental electric locomotive. When these four men were arrested for Trotskyism, the *partkom* began investigating their protégés, friends, and mentors. Zhailov's arrest led the *partkom* to investigate Menis, Khvedchen, and Korneev, all working on the locomotives. When Korneev's sister, a young Komsomol and worker, defended her brother to an acquaintance, this person in turn wrote a *zaiavlenie* about Korneeva's comment, which resulted in her expulsion from the Komsomol. Aftershocks of the initial arrests thus spread downward to the workers. They also spread upward. The victims, shop heads and managers, were closely linked to M. E. Zhukov, the factory director. Zhukov, a party member since 1918, was blamed for allowing "enemies" to "rule over" the factory and "personally supporting" and "surrounding himself with enemies of the

---

[22] TsAODM, f. 432, o. 1, d. 194, "Informatsiia v proletarskii raikom VKP (b) o proshedshem otkrytom partiinom sobranii," February 1, 1938, ll. 22–24; TsAODM, f. 432, o. 1, d. 188, "Stenogramma otchetno-vybornogo zakrytogo partiinogo sobraniia partorganizatsii zavoda 'Dinamo im. Kirova,'" April 8, 1938, l. 11.

people."[23] Expelled from the Party, he also lost his job. After a fire in the factory, Zhukov's protégés Sheinin, deputy director of financial administration, Kliupov, head of the scrap shop, and Romanov, the head of the research bureau, were arrested for wrecking.[24] A stream of *zaiavleniia* poured in, naming all *their* friends and workmates, including Agureev, a manager, who was then linked to Fomin, the head of the fourth machine shop, and Marek, the shop's technician.[25] After being investigated and expelled by the *partkom*, the group fell like dominoes into the hands of the NKVD.[26] The shop and *partkomy*, the NKVD, and countless anonymous *zaiavleniia* together created a grim synergy, which exponentially expanded the circles of arrest. The repression at Dinamo did not end with Zhukov's arrest. Iasvoin replaced him as the new director, but Iasvoin, too, was shortly arrested and replaced.

Party members spoke constantly about "total honesty before the Party," "not concealing anything from the Party," "sincerity in relation to the Party." This insistence on total disclosure placed many members in a terrible bind. If they reported dubious biographical elements or connections, they were subject to sharp interrogation and further investigation. On the other hand, if they did not write a complete and timely *zaiavlenie*, they were subject to expulsion for dishonesty or concealment. Yet full disclosure was hardly a guarantee of safety. When Margolina, a party member in Trekhgornaia Manufaktura, received a cryptic postcard from her brother stating that her married stepsister was "alone," she promptly reported it to the secretary of the *partkom*. He sternly warned her not to respond. Several months later her brother wrote again, informing her that their stepsister's husband had been arrested. The *partkom* then took up the case. "Why such caution in receiving a postcard?" a *partkom* member asked disingenuously. After a lengthy interrogation, the *partkom* vowed to write to all the corresponding organizations – including the NKVD and the respective party organizations of her stepsister, brother-in-law, relatives, and the friend who helped her find work in the factory – to inform them of the arrest and solicit further information.[27] A case like Margolina's

---

[23] TsAODM, f. 432, o. 1, d. 179, "Protokol zasedaniia partkoma zavoda 'Dinamo im. Kirova,'" May 12, 1937, ll. 114–117.

[24] Ibid., l. 117.

[25] See TsAODM, f. 432, o. 1, d. 179, "Protokol zasedaniia plenuma partkoma zavoda 'Dinamo im. Kirova,'" February 16, 1937, ll. 39–56, on interlocking circles in the factory.

[26] TsAODM, f. 432, o. 1, d. 179, "Protokol zasedaniia plenuma partkoma zavoda 'Dinamo im. Kirova,'" May 21, 1937, ll. 123–131.

[27] TsAODM, f. 369, o. 1, d. 173, "Protokol no. 30," November 17, 1937, ll. 41–44.

turned many honest people into liars. They chose not to "confess" their knowledge of arrests for fear that the ensuing interrogation would wreak havoc on their lives and others. They concealed the existence of relatives with "dubious" backgrounds, stopped writing letters, developed short-hand methods of communication, and built up elaborate defenses even with close friends and family, deepening the atmosphere of "guilt" and suspicion. The atmosphere made it impossible to be honest.

Party members were warned to sever contact with the families of those who had been arrested. Arrests devastated thousands of families, leaving children, wives, and elderly parents without support. Was it really possible to turn away a hungry, devastated child, a haunted, suffering mother, a frightened elderly neighbor? Many party members were caught between the desire to help friends and relatives and their "loyalty" to the Party. Gringauz, a party member in the assembly shop in Krasnyi Proletarii, lived with his sister and brother-in-law, Denisov. After Denisov was expelled from the party and his job, Gringauz helped him find work in Krasnyi Proletarii. Denisov was then arrested as a spy. Gringauz was subject to sharp questioning by the *partkom*: "You arranged for Denisov to work in the factory after his exclusion from the party, and you were not interested in his political face. In essence, you placed a spy in the factory." They asked, "Who visited you in your apartment?" Gringauz in turn named four people. The *partkom* grilled him about political conversations. Gringauz pled ignorance, but no one believed him. One party member declared, "Gringauz is confusing everything, and he doesn't tell the truth. Instead he shows help to the enemy, and pretends that he is a Philistine, telling us he only discussed daily trivia with Denisov. Of course, they discussed politics." Accused of "failure to unmask in a timely manner," close ties to an enemy, helping an enemy gain access to the factory, and dishonesty, Gringauz was expelled from the party.[28] Gringauz's case was not unusual. His link to his brother-in-law sealed his own fate, and his naming of others ensured new investigations and interrogations.

As arrests and expulsions multiplied, the hysteria intensified. The demands for loyalty grew ever more fantastic, producing in turn more prevaricators who needed to be "unmasked." The terror had become self-generating, manufacturing ten new "sinners" with the "unmasking" of each one. Some circles were confined to the factory, but many extended outside it. And circles originating outside the factory also extended into it,

[28] TsAODM, f. 412, o. 1, d. 87, "Protokol zakrytogo zasedaniia partiinogo komiteta zavoda 'Krasnyi proletarii,'" August 16, 1938, ll. 36–39.

encompassing factory members in the outer reaches of other "nests" and groups. Arguably, every citizen was part of a pattern of interlocking circles that overlaid the entire country. Forged from the cataclysmic events of the past two decades, the circles linked managers to working-class relatives, workers to former "oppositionists," oppositionists to peasant relatives, peasants to "kulaks," and "kulak" fathers back to manager sons.

Ideology and Political Catechism

The increasingly rigid constructions of loyalty and biography were accompanied by decreasing tolerance for ideological mistakes. An "incorrect" formulation or explanation proved the undoing of many an organizer and instructor. Fellow party members, overhearing an untoward remark in a dining hall, study circle, or dormitory, were quick to write a *zaiavlenie*, construing ideological confusion as enemy propagandizing. Stalin's famous slogan "socialism in one country" proved the undoing of more than one party member. Stalin had coined his phrase in 1924 in debates with the left opposition after the failure of revolution in Germany. Trotsky argued that, although it was possible to work toward building socialism, a fully socialist system could never be achieved in a backward, peasant country encircled by hostile powers. Stalin, ever the artful propagandist, twisted Trotsky's words and charged him with "defeatism." It was possible, Stalin claimed, to build and realize socialism under conditions of capitalist encirclement.[29] In the debate, which was initially "political" in the narrowest sense, each side dusted off quotations from Lenin's early writing to discredit the other. Although the debate was broadly connected to differences over the tempo of industrialization and the role of the peasantry, it did not affect the commitment of either leader to building socialism in the Soviet Union. Stalin's caricature of Trotsky's position, however, assumed a hallowed fixity after the demise of the left opposition. Many an organizer subsequently stumbled over the issue.

Workers seemed to delight in catching party organizers off guard. Bored in mandatory study circles, they would ask innocently, "Is the state 'withering away'?" "Can socialism be built in one country?" So many people were tripped up that many claimed they were too ignorant to be instructors. Better to be thought a fool than an enemy. Katyshev, a party

[29] Leon Trotsky, *The Challenge of the Left Opposition, 1923–1925* (Pathfinder Press, New York, 1975); Joseph Stalin, *On the Opposition* (Foreign Languages Press, Peking, 1974), pp. 476–92.

propagandist in Dinamo, was hauled before the *partkom* for propounding "Trotskyism." According to Katyshev, a worker had approached him during dinner break and asked whether it was possible to build communism in the Soviet Union. Katyshev answered, "No." He later said, "I committed a deep mistake, in essence expressed in Trotsky's theory. I didn't think this question through, and just answered." Then, attempting to navigate the narrow straits of this theoretical channel once again, he explained, "I thought it was possible to build communism only when there will be no government, army, and other organs of force. It was my mistake that I was not prepared." After swearing to the *partkom* that he had carefully reviewed Stalin's *Collected Works*, Katyshev escaped with a reprimand.[30] But Katyshev was not the only one to smash against these dangerous rocks. Two other party members in Dinamo also were cited by the *partkom*, one for announcing that it was impossible to build socialism in one country, and the other for declaring that, under communism, the dictatorship of the proletariat would not "wither away."[31]

The contradictions between early Bolshevik ideology and Stalinism proved particularly difficult for party members to master. Older revolutionary ideas and slogans, such as the promised "withering away of the state," could not be directly repudiated, yet were an indictment of current realities. Lenin argued in *State and Revolution*, for example, that the state would "wither away" under socialism. The book guided the construction of civil, family, and criminal law codes in the early 1920s. By 1937, however, the trend in law as in ideology had reversed to favor a strong state with vastly expanded powers. Stalin explained the reversal in terms of "dialectics": as the enemies of the state grew more embattled, they became more dangerous, thus forcing the state to expand its powers. Once these enemies were vanquished, however, the state would no longer be necessary. Its growing power was thus part of the very process by which it would "wither away."[32] These sophistries, however, left many workers and party organizers scratching their heads in confusion. Was the state

---

[30] TsAODM, f. 432, o. 1, d. 179, "Protokol zasedaniia plenuma partkoma zavoda 'Dinamo im. Kirova,'" February 16, 1937, l. 52.

[31] "Stenogramma otchetnogo partiinogo sobraniia," April 8–10, 1937, l. 11.

[32] V. I. Lenin, "The State and Revolution," in *Selected Works*, vol. II (Progress Publishers, Moscow, 1970), pp. 352, 353, 317. See Wendy Goldman, *Women, the State and Revolution: Soviet Family Policy and Social Life, 1917–1936* (Cambridge University Press, New York, 1993), pp. 1–58, 185–213, on the "withering away" of the state and law.

getting stronger or weaker? Was Lenin wrong or right? What *was* going on, and how could one possibly explain it to someone else?

D. Sagaidak, a party member and the head of the cold rolling mill in Serp i Molot, was excluded by the *partkom* and subsequently arrested for wrecking and poisoning workers. He first came to the attention of the Party, however, with a small "theoretical error." While leading a factory study circle in 1936 on the new Stalin Constitution, Sagaidak answered a seemingly innocent question posed by a woman worker: "Do you think the state is now 'withering away'?" Sagaidak, quoting from Lenin's *State and Revolution*, answered affirmatively. His answer, conscientiously noted in a *zaiavlenie* from a fellow party member at the study circle, soon returned to haunt him. He was forced to repudiate it twice, once before the study circle, and again in a lengthy written "confession" in *Martenovka*, the factory's newspaper. At the *partkom* meeting to decide his expulsion, one party member asked Sagaidak, "How can you even mention the 'withering away of the state' at the very moment of cruel onslaught by enemies against the dictatorship of the proletariat, against the working class, when all these bastards, these Trotskyist bands are attempting to penetrate the territory of the Soviet Union?" His statement could only be "the sally of a class enemy," "an attempt to carry on counterrevolutionary work."[33]

Given the prevailing atmosphere, propagandists, leaders of study circles, librarians, and organizers in official contact with workers were at particular risk. Many organizers had their words twisted out of context. Ia. I. Menis, the head of Dinamo's research bureau, also led study groups among workers. The son of workers, Menis had joined the party in 1917, at the age of eighteen. He was expelled by the *partkom* for propounding Trotskyist ideology. The evidence? Menis had told the workers, "It is a shame that you cannot read what Trotsky writes because you would be convinced of his treachery." The *partkom* claimed that Menis encouraged the workers to read Trotsky's writing! He was arrested on several charges in early 1937.[34] By April 1937, most of the leaders of study circles in Dinamo had been arrested. Starichkov, the *partkom* secretary, noted,

[33] "Posledam vystuplenii Martenovki. Obshibki propagandista Sagaidaka," *Martenovka*, February 2, 1937, p. 2; TsAODM, f. 429, o. 1, d. 269, "Stenogramma partiinogo komiteta zavoda 'Serp i molot,'" March 4, 1937, ll. 6–8, 18–19, 20.
[34] "Protokol zasedaniia plenuma partkoma zavoda 'Dinamo im. Kirova,'" February 16, 1937, ll. 55–56.

"Here we had an absolute majority of enemies of the people."[35] Ideological instructors also came under fire in Serp i Molot. V. G. Schetchikova, a woman from a revolutionary family who joined the Party at the front during the Civil War, headed the factory's library. The *partkom*'s review of her small staff revealed two staff members with suspicious social origins. Both were good, literate employees, educated before the revolution. When Schetchikova fired the daughter of a worker because "she was too uneducated to give out the books," she received a strict reprimand from her party organization for "littering the library staff with anti-Soviet elements." Schetchikova explained. "I tried to get qualified people onto the staff, but it was hard." After a long, painful discussion, the *partkom* removed Schetchikova's reprimand, but ordered her to "hire some better people."[36] In Serp i Molot, too, most of the people responsible for education and training were arrested, including the staff of the factory's training institute. The head of the institute's library was charged with "distributing counterrevolutionary literature," and its director and dean with "Trotskyism." They were all part of a "family group" led by one Zaitsev, who had already been arrested.[37]

Party instructors were not the only victims of a political catechism that had become increasingly rigid and incomprehensible. Many workers who spoke out about conditions or voiced opinions that were at odds with the "party line" found themselves under investigation. Starichkov, the head of Dinamo's *partkom*, noted that workers made "all kinds of slanderous declarations about the collective farms." Despite heavy propaganda about collective farm successes, workers with rural relatives insisted that the collective farmers lived poorly.[38] And honest answers to questions also proved the undoing of many. When a worker asked a party engineer, "Why didn't they physically eliminate Trotsky in 1929?," the engineer replied, "Trotsky had authority then." This small admission – that Trotsky had been an important leader – got the engineer into serious trouble.[39] Party members, terrified of petty slips in conversation, rushed to confess their "mistakes." Among endless *zaiavleniia* presented at party meetings were many foolish, petty confessions. One party member in Krasnyi Proletarii

[35] "Stenogramma otchetnogo partiinogo sobraniia," April 8–10, 1937, ll. 31–32.
[36] "Protokol no. 38 zasedaniia partkoma zavoda 'Serp i molot,'" November 11, 1937, ll. 87–88.
[37] TsAODM, f. 429, o. 1, d. 223, "Sekretariu partkoma zavoda 'Serp i molot,'" December 21, 1937, ll. 144–147.
[38] "Stenogramma otchetnogo partiinogo sobraniia," April 8–10, 1937, ll. 7, 8.
[39] Ibid., ll. 10–11.

confessed that he had deemed a recently arrested "enemy" "an excellent orator." "I recognize my mistake," he said humbly.[40] The theoretical nit-picking, the refusal to acknowledge obvious contradictions between early revolutionary ideals and current realities, and the construction of every error as intentional counterrevolutionary propaganda made party members keenly aware that a single slip of the tongue could ruin a lifetime of commitment.

Wrecking

By the late 1930s, the Soviet Union had achieved, in less than a decade, an unprecedented industrial growth rate. Yet despite the great successes, the very rapidity of the process created organizational and economic tensions, which contributed to the strained atmosphere in the factories. Each factory and shop, part of larger industrywide and regional plans, had its target figures. Managers and shop heads were under intense pressure to meet goals set in Moscow. Faulty, old machinery in textile factories such as Trekhgornaia Manufaktura broke down often, frustrating workers and managers alike. In heavy industry plants, such as Dinamo, Serp i Molot, and Krasnyi Proletarii, managers and workers struggled to integrate new and expensive technologies imported from abroad. Shops ran a lot of waste and were unable to fill orders. Machines were often misused in order to increase capacity; motors burned out, expensive new equipment broke. Shops alternated between "storming" and lulls in production. There were chronic shortages of machine parts, fuel, and raw materials. Economic development lurched forward unevenly, lacking balance and integration. Shops overflowed with garbage and waste products, ventilation was poor, safety sacrificed to production. Lack of housing led to persistently high rates of labor turnover. Pressure to meet the plan encouraged shop chauvinism or *tsekhovshchina*, whereby shop heads stubbornly defended their own records and blamed other shops for problems. Directors continually mediated between shop heads in an effort to get them to work in the interests of the factory as a whole.

In February 1937, Moscow party officials organized huge, freewheeling party forums in the factories with no set agenda. In Dinamo, at least 700 party members and candidates attended; in Trekhgornaia Manufaktura, at least 500. Moscow party committee officials encouraged the rank and

---

[40] TsAODM, f. 412, o. 1, d. 87, "Protokol zakrytogo zasedaniia partiinogo komiteta zavoda 'Krasnyi proletarii,'" October 13, 1938, ll. 77–78.

file to voice their grievances against party leaders and the factory administration. The meeting in Dinamo stirred up a hornets' nest. Party members
provided numerous examples of wrongdoing, and scores of people fired
off *zaiavleniia* filled with accusations, slander, and rumors after the meeting. A commission was established to investigate all the new allegations.[41]
A deadly political fog crept into the factories, shrouding every subject in
accusation. *Partkom* members construed shop rivalries, production problems, accidents, and even personal animosities as "enemy activities." Frustration with difficult conditions encouraged workers and party members
to level political accusations in the hope of redressing production problems. In Trekhgornaia Manufaktura, for example, Fedulov, an elderly
party member, spoke angrily on behalf of the workers in the weaving factory. Discarded bobbins were scattered about the floor, workers could not
reach the water faucets, and the rooms were filled with poisonous coal gas.
Women workers crouched "in a permanent stoop" in an attempt to lift
the bobbins. Fedulov noted that he had already written several *zaiavleniia*
about the problem but had received no response.[42] Frustration frequently
led to charges of "wrecking." In a shop in Likernovodochnyi, boxes with
wine bottles were piled up everywhere. The workers protested but the
foreman ordered them to continue stacking. When the boxes finally came
crashing down, one party member noted, "Luckily, only the wine bottles
were broken, and they did not kill anybody." Yet, she added ominously,
"What if a person had been killed, who would answer for this? It is possible to ascribe this business to wrecking."[43]

Accidents were common throughout the factories, a combination of
unfamiliar machinery, unskilled workers, pressure to meet the plan, and
a shortage of timber for mine supports, railroad ties, and construction
scaffolding. In Dinamo, poor maintenance and a shortage of ties and rails
resulted in a series of accidents on the branch lines of the railroad leading
to the plant. The loading platforms were collapsing, and the transport
department was staffed with unskilled workers.[44] Yet the politicization of
production required a scapegoat. Party members, like Freudians, operated

---

[41] "Protokol zasedaniia plenuma partkoma zavoda 'Dinamo im. Kirova,'" February 16,
1937, ll. 48–51.

[42] "Stenogramma otchetno-perevybornogo partiinogo sobraniia," March 30–31, 1937,
l. 67.

[43] "Stenogramma obshchego otchetno-vybornogo zakrytogo partsobraniia moskovskogo
Likerno-vodochnogo zavoda," April 19–21, 1938, l. 62ob.

[44] TsAODM, f. 432, o. 1, d. 179, "Protokol zasedaniia plenuma partkoma zavoda 'Dinamo
im. Kirova,'" April 2, 1937, ll. 90–92. Accidents on spur lines were common. See also
TsAODM, f. 412, o. 1, d. 72, "Protokol zasedaniia partiinogo komiteta zavoda 'Krasnyi
proletarii,'" April 17, 1935, ll. 13–15.

on the assumption that there were no "accidents." What one group viewed as a manifestation of unconscious desires, the other viewed as the result of conscious political acts. One party member in Trekhgornaia Manufaktura declared, "Every physical injury is tied first to wrecking and then to our political nearsightedness."[45]

A large fire in Dinamo in the dead of winter in 1937 resulted in the expulsion and arrest of the factory's leading engineers and managers. The fire, which started in a wooden structure covering a warehouse, quickly spread to the tool and scrap shops, destroying 300,000 rubles' worth of goods, special orders, and factory stock. An investigation revealed that neither the electrical system nor a carelessly discarded cigarette had caused the fire. The fire, the director noted, could not have "started by itself." Moreover, the warehouse was piled with goods that someone had failed to deliver. The director flatly told the *partkom*, "The reason for the fire was connected to arson. This was a sally of the class enemy." All signs pointed to deliberate wrecking.[46]

The *partkom*'s ensuing discussion, however, revealed sheer disorganization as a far likelier explanation. Goods, including consumer items for workers, had piled up in the warehouse due to the shortage of transport. The tool shop was housed in a ramshackle old firetrap because there were no construction materials to build a new structure. There were too few factory guards because there was no place to house them. Poor, homeless people, including workers' relatives, were living in makeshift shelters all over the factory's grounds. Yet the *partkom*'s immediate impulse was not to solve the underlying problems, but to find someone to blame. One party member declared, "There are facts of wrecking. We have a group of wreckers. The materials that burned were to be delivered to the defense industry." He added that shavings had been found in wheel bearings, the rubber around packaged magnets had been sliced up, and the special castings shop was running nothing but waste. The *partkom* immediately reported the fire to the NKVD. Several leading managers, including the head of the scrap shop, were arrested and charged with arson and Trotskyism. A large group of their associates soon followed them into prison.[47]

Party members easily attributed spectacular fires and serious accidents to wrecking, but shop heads began to blame wreckers for daily production problems as well. Under tremendous pressure to meet production

---

[45] "Stenogramma otchetno-perevybornogo partiinogo sobraniia," March 30–31, 1937, l. 63.

[46] TsAODM, f. 432, o. 1, d. 179, "Protokol zasedaniia plenuma partkoma zavoda 'Dinamo im. Kirova,'" January 24, 1937, l. 20.

[47] Ibid., ll. 21–22.

quotas, shop heads often faced circumstances beyond their control: labor turnover, machine breakdowns, lack of raw materials. They commonly counted poor-quality products or waste toward their quotas, a method that helped them meet the plan, but created new headaches for shops that relied on their products. Starichkov, the head of Dinamo's *partkom*, noted that the factory had a serious problem with "whitewash." Shops routinely passed off unfinished, poor-quality items to others, provoking terrible fights between party members, who defended their own "shop" interests. Some shops were so skilled at "whitewash" that it had become an entire "system." The tool shop was particularly adept at producing and passing off useless tools. "Today, mutual relations between communists are not normal," Starichkov noted. Shop heads and party members were busy collecting information and informing on each other, all in an effort to defend their own production records. Rather than clean up the mess in their own shops, they blamed others.[48] After Dinamo's first director was fired and expelled, Iasvoin, his successor, begged the *partkom* for help. "The heads of the shops think only about their own shops," he said, "although all the shops here are tied to each other."[49]

Conflicts over technology and design were also recast in political terms. In Dinamo, for example, the design bureau, electrical shop, continuous current machine shop, foundry, and locomotive body shop were involved in developing and testing prototypes for an electric locomotive that could operate above ground and in the mines. Engineers, technicians, and party officials hotly debated which prototype to put into production. The debate reached all the way to G. K. Ordzhonikidze, the commissar of heavy industry. When a locomotive ordered by Italy turned out to be useless, the resulting scandal led various engineers to accuse each other of wrecking.[50] The heads of several shops were arrested, one for cosigning a denunciation with a colleague who was subsequently arrested as a Trotskyist![51]

The chaos and tempo of the industrialization drive demanded a special type of manager. These men, mostly party members, were for the most part energetic, hard-driving, highly intelligent individuals with scant

---

[48] TsAODM, f. 432, o. 1, d. 179, "Protokol zasedaniia plenuma partkoma zavoda 'Dinamo im. Kirova,'" January 31, 1937, ll. 27–31.

[49] TsAODM, f. 432, o. 1, d. 179, "Protokol zasedaniia partkoma zavoda 'Dinamo im. Kirova,'" April 22, 1937, l. 108.

[50] "Protokol zasedaniia partkoma zavoda 'Dinamo im. Kirova,'" May 12, 1937, ll. 114–117.

[51] "Protokol zasedaniia partkoma zavoda 'Dinamo im. Kirova,'" May 21, 1937, ll. 123–130.

formal education or social graces. They virtually lived in the factories, ruling vast construction empires that included housing, hospitals, day-care centers, and food distribution as well as production. They worked long hours, installing expensive equipment, solving supply and production bottlenecks, and procuring needed materials. They bullied, bribed, begged, and traded in "grey markets" to get the inputs they needed. They were brusque, even brutal, toward the people who worked beneath them. Under tremendous pressure, they tended to overlook factors that were not essential to the production process, including hazardous conditions, the needs of their workers, and routine maintenance on machinery. Many were roundly hated, but they got the job done.

D. Sagaidak, a party member and the head of the cold rolling mill in Serp i Molot, was typical of the mid-level managers who fell victim to the politicization of production. The son of a railroad worker, Sagaidak came from a family of eight children, all of whom benefited immensely from Soviet power. One brother became an engineer, another worked for the NKVD, the third joined the Party and became a pilot. Sagaidak's wife was an engineer and party member, and many of her relatives were party members in leading posts. Sagaidak began work at Serp i Molot in 1929. Within two years, the director sent him to Germany to master the processes of hot and cold rolling steel. In 1933, he became the head of the new cold rolling mill, producing specialized stainless steel for the aviation industry. The cold rolling mill, too, was typical of the new industrial enterprises. Constructed with imported technology during the first five-year plan, it was called "the child of the factory" by the proud director. Six engineers, managers, and workers began the start-up. Working sixteen-hour days, sleeping in the mill, they struggled to master the new technology. Initially, output was low, and the mill did not produce according to plan. Production slowly increased, and Sagaidak was assigned the job of ensuring the mill met its output targets. Like many managers, he did not spare himself and was demanding of his subordinates. When a young engineer stumbled home after working twenty-four hours straight on tempering the steel, Sagaidak gave him a strict reprimand for leaving work without permission. Sagaidak struggled with numerous problems, including a lack of raw materials, malfunctioning rollers, and an inexperienced workforce. Yet he got results, and even received a special commendation for producing the factory's first order of specialized stainless steel.[52]

---

[52] "Stenogramma partiinogo komiteta zavoda 'Serp i molot,'" March 4, 1937, ll. 8–9, 13–14, 54, 15–16, 50–51.

Sagaidak, as previously noted, made his first serious political mistake when he gave a "harmful" answer to a worker's question about the "withering away" of the state under socialism. Sagaidak publicly confessed his "theoretical error," and the small squall seemed to pass. Yet his "slip" provided the opening for a new set of charges. Later that month, an anonymous worker wrote an article in the factory's newspaper charging Sagaidak and his assistant with responsibility for accidents, broken rollers, stoppages, and defective production in the cold rolling mill. The worker claimed that Sagaidak "sped up" machines until the motors burned out, ignored the steel's chemical "bath" timetable, failed to repair machine parts, and suppressed workers who criticized his leadership.[53] A day later, a second anonymous article, even more ominous in tone, appeared. "Machines don't break themselves and boilers don't explode on their own. Behind every case is a human hand. Is it the hand of an enemy?" It went on to detail all the problems in the cold rolling mill, blaming them on "the enemy Sagaidak." Workers in the chemical baths had been poisoned by acid steam, and burned by the dripping pails of acid they carried across the slippery shop floor. One worker got acid in his eyes. "Was Sagaidak distressed?" the article asked. "Not at all." Sagaidak padded production figures and passed off poor-quality steel. When caught, he allegedly declared, "Everyone lies. Deception is one of the principles of technical production." The article ended with a pointed message to the party organization: "An enemy covered by a party card should be unmasked."[54] The following day, a third article appeared, once again excoriating Sagaidak for running waste and passing it off as quality steel.[55]

In a marathon meeting of the rolling mill's party organization, Sagaidak's accusers confronted him with a long list of technical and political "sins," including but not limited to those already plastered across the pages of the factory newspaper. Sagaidak was also charged with deliberately concealing the true productive capacity of the mill, abusing workers, and encouraging "lickspittles."[56] Many of the accusations were contradictory. Workers attacked him for highhandedness, managers for his inability

---

[53] Val'tsovshchik, "Kak proiskhodiat avarii v kholodnom prokate," *Martenovka*, February 27, 1937, p. 2. The practice of using a stick to keep a motor from cutting off after it became overheated was common.

[54] "Na ruku vragu," *Martenovka*, February 28, 1937, p. 3.

[55] S. Levashev, "Pod vidom 'opytnoi' produktsii," *Martenovka*, March 1, 1937, p. 1.

[56] "Segodnia – partiinoe sobranie v tsekhe kholodnogo prokata," *Martenovka*, March 3, 1937, p. 1.

to impose discipline. But consistency was hardly the issue.[57] During the meeting, new and explosive "evidence" emerged that he had poisoned workers in the chemical bath (*travil'ka*). After lengthy discussion, the party organization voted to expel him.[58]

The *partkom* heard the case the following day. Somov, the secretary, briefly summarized the charges. In his defense, Sagaidak offered a rational, technical refutation of the charges. Statistics showed that the shop failed to meet the 1936 plan because it "never received the 500 tons of metal that we were supposed to receive that year." "This is known not only by the workers in the shop," Sagaidak said, "but by the whole factory." Yet overall, production had risen steadily, and the mill was handling larger orders. In fact, the mill's productivity had almost doubled in 1936. "I gave all my strength, all my time to the factory," Sagaidak said. "I tried to master new brands of steel to better the quality and quantity of production. We had only one machine in the shop for stainless steel. The shop did not go backwards, but forwards." He pleaded with the *partkom* to recognize that it was impossible to meet targets without inputs. "Comrades," he said, "I produce from real resources."[59]

Sagaidak, however, was also charged with "poisoning the workers." Fourteen bottles of nitric acid, rather than the required hydrochloric acid, had spilled into the chemical bath. The resulting fumes had sickened several workers. Sagaidak was at a loss to explain what had happened, but he strongly protested the charge of deliberate poisoning: "To say that I consciously poisoned workers is a heavy and incorrect accusation. It is possible to say that I did not give sufficient attention to this sector, or that I did not fully involve myself in this business." He begged the *partkom* to admit what everyone implicitly understood: "The insufficiencies that we have in the shop should not be a basis for thinking that I consciously wrecked." Sagaidak ended his defense by invoking his loyalty to the factory, the working class, and the Party. He admitted to personal failings, and pled for mercy: "Beyond my shop and my home, I know nothing. Work was everything to me. The problems we had in the shop were not

[57] "Stenogramma partiinogo komiteta zavoda 'Serp i molot,'" March 4, 1937, ll. 1–68.
[58] L. V. Marmorshtein, "Fakty i vyvody," *Martenovka*, March 5, 1937, p. 2; "S partiinogo sobraniia v tsekhe kholodnogo prokata," *Martenovka*, March 6, 1937, p. 1; TsAODM, f. 429, o. 1, d. 269, "Stenogramma zasedaniia partiinogo komiteta zavoda 'Serp i molot,'" March 4, 1937, ll. 1, 2, 5.
[59] "Stenogramma partiinogo komiteta zavoda 'Serp i molot,'" March 4, 1937, ll. 2, 4, 3, 8, 5. The mill produced 158 tons of stainless steel in 1936, and 257 in 1937.

the result of wrecking, but of a series of personal shortcomings, a result of my presumptuousness and not listening to the voices of the workers, engineers, and technicians." Finally, he cited his class background: "There never was and never will be any wrecking from me. I have never been and never will be an enemy of the working class . . . I myself come from a family of workers."[60]

Sagaidak's defense was sensible and well reasoned. Yet as the meeting wore on, it became clear that rational explanation was irrelevant to the business at hand. One party member stated baldly, "By the study of Marxist dialectics, we know that accidents do not occur without a reason." Party members met Sagaidak's explanations with hostile disbelief, peppering him with aggressive questions: "Perhaps you remember delaying the steel for aviation?" "You spoke about fulfilling the 1936 plan, but not about the failures; you didn't say what they asked you to produce, only what you produced." "You say you weren't guilty of poisoning the workers, but how do you view the fact that they were systematically poisoned?" "What kind of measures did you take to improve safety in the chemical bath?" "How did it happen that fourteen bottles of nitric acid spilled into the chemical bath?" The questions dragged on and on.[61]

Sagaidak struggled to maintain his composure in the face of the group's suspicion and hostility. He answered every question, no matter how tendentious, in great technical detail. Yet few of his fellow party members showed him any sympathy. Several used the meeting for political grandstanding and posturing. One member said piously, "We are proud of our aviation. Why did he delay the deliveries when he knows that our country needs every kilogram of aviation steel?" Stepanova, a worker in the cold rolling mill, made a long speech filled with insinuations and petty grievances. She charged that the white-collar employees in the mill "had unhealthy relations with the workers." After an accident, Sagaidak scolded the worker who caused it. "Is this how a Soviet engineer should speak to a worker?" she asked; "A worker who takes every breakdown deeply to heart?" Her speech became increasingly vituperative, her charges absurd: Sagaidak compared productivity in the Soviet Union and in capitalist countries. Sagaidak spoke roughly to workers for rolling defective steel. Sagaidak "put all the blame on the shoulders of the workers." Sagaidak claimed that the counterrevolutionary Trotskyist-Zinovievites were once Bolsheviks. She even accused Sagaidak of caring too much about production. "We have party meetings in the mill. All

[60] Ibid., ll. 5, 9, 8.   [61] Ibid., ll. 52, 9–11.

the members of the party gather, but Sagaidak goes back to the shop." She noted that she had repeatedly informed the *partkom* about her suspicions. "Sagaidak," she concluded, "is not one of us."[62] Several other party members also mentioned that Sagaidak treated the workers too harshly. Mikhailov, the head of the electrical shop, told a long story about a flood in the shops: "When Smirnov told Sagaidak that the workers were forced to swim, that the shop was under water, he answered 'Let the workers swim.' When they called him to see the director, he began to twist like a fox. This is his approach toward the workers, the equipment, and preserving his own position." Mikhailov concluded that Sagaidak did not belong in the ranks of the Party. "He did not consider the people he worked with as people." Yet the denunciations of Sagaidak were not prompted solely by his highhandedness. Mikhailov, for example, was furious that the workers in the cold rolling mill were bypassing the cut-off switches on the motors, and Sagaidak had barred the electricians from entering the mill. Mikhailov finally told the factory director that he would not be responsible for the equipment if electricians were not permitted to enter.[63] Here was a typical shop rivalry: Sagaidak's output quotas conflicted with Mikhailov's responsibility to maintain the motors.

The discussion over Sagaidak quickly broadened to include charges against others. One asked, "Why did the *partkom* allow him to continue leading a study circle? There was a strong lapse of Bolshevik vigilance." Brun, the secretary of the Komsomol, stated that some party members in the cold rolling mill were "too liberal toward Sagaidak." Karmanian, for example, had advocated only a "strict reprimand" rather than expulsion. The party organization in the cold rolling mill needed to investigate why Karmanian had said this. And Sagaidak was not the only enemy in a position of authority. Other shops needed to be reviewed as well. Brun asked, "Was it accidental that Comrade Bogoliubskii messed up the aviation wire? There were many denunciations from workers and shift bosses, but the *partkom* does not care about this." Angrily, he stressed that *every* denunciation and allegation of the workers had to be fully investigated. Polukarov, the deputy secretary of the *partkom*, summed up the case, "Did he poison people? He poisoned them. Did he break equipment? He broke it. Did he burn out machines? He burned them out." "Why did this all happen?" Polukarov asked. "Because Sagaidak is a Trotskyist and an enemy." Polukarov perfectly captured the prejudicial nature of the proceedings in his concluding words, "Sagaidak defended himself. But what

[62] Ibid., ll. 21, 17.　　　　　　[63] Ibid., ll. 26–28.

should he say? He should admit he is obviously a Trotskyist, an enemy, and not say anything else."[64]

In the end, Stepanov, the director, decided the case. Stepanov, unlike many party members, tried to contain the wild fires of accusation that threatened to engulf the factory. He adamantly refused to equate every mistake or accident in the shops with wrecking, and even praised Sagaidak's efforts in the cold rolling mill: "Sagaidak in his time gave his blood for the shop." He dismissed the idea that Sagaidak was guilty of intentional wrecking. "Young engineers make mistakes," he said. Stepanov, however, willingly sacrificed Sagaidak. Recognizing that it was too late to save him, Stepanov tried to limit the damage by blaming Sagaidak solely for his political error. "It is impossible to ascribe mistakes and accidents in every shop, in every place to wrecking," he said firmly. "But if there is also a political angle, then it is possible to say yes, there is a problem." He asked, "Where did Sagaidak get the thought about the withering away of the state when we are spending 20 billion on the defense of our country? All of us have made mistakes. I have worked as the director for twelve years and not without mistakes. But there is no mercy if the director makes a political mistake." And then he added his voice to those calling for Sagaidak's expulsion. Sagaidak had the last word. "Comrades," he pleaded, "before those who will make the decision, I want to say one more time that I was not a wrecker, I did not wreck, I had no tie to Trotskyism, I did not and never have had. I never in my whole life betrayed the working class, never in my thoughts did I consider wrecking anywhere." Sagaidak had become the scapegoat for everything that was wrong in the cold rolling mill and associated shops: poor safety conditions, delayed orders, failure to meet the plan. The workers resented the dangerous conditions; the engineers, his tactlessness; the communists, his absorption in production; the electricians, his disregard of the motors. Sagaidak was expelled by the *partkom* and arrested soon after.[65]

Many of the party members who denounced Sagaidak were also arrested within the coming months. L. V. Marmorshtein, the head engineer, had written a nasty article about Sagaidak.[66] He was arrested along with a large circle of allied engineers and managers. Zhidkova, who attended the study circle where Sagaidak made his fatal political slip, was expelled from the party in 1938. One of the more righteous party members, Zhidkova wrote numerous denunciations throughout 1937 to

[64] Ibid., ll. 22–3, 43, 37.   [65] Ibid., ll. 54, 55, 56–58, 67.
[66] Marmorshtein, "Fakty i vyvody," p. 2.

the factory and district party committees and the NKVD. It is likely that she first brought Sagaidak's "error" to the attention of the party organization. Her denunciations resulted in the expulsion of Somov, the party secretary, in 1938, and the arrest of his Polish communist girlfriend in 1937. She herself was interrogated after her brother, an old Bolshevik, was arrested. Insisting that the NKVD had made a mistake, Zhidkova maintained her brother's innocence. His arrest precipitated a psychological crisis. Beginning as the staunchest of true believers, she denounced and prosecuted others, until her faith in her beloved brother made it impossible for her to retain her blind faith in the NKVD.[67]

Stepanov's attempt to draw the line between honest mistakes and wrecking was largely unsuccessful. Within four months, his head was on the chopping block. At another long and painful meeting, the *partkom* grilled Stepanov about his biography, but its main accusation was that he had tried to protect Sagaidak and other managers. Party members fired a round of hostile questions at their director: "Why is the administration of Serp i Molot littered with foreign elements?" "Did you know that fifteen people in the factory were removed for wrecking?" "Why did you protect Sagaidak?" Stepanov nimbly dodged the questions: "I never protected him." "All the information was immediately passed on to where it was needed." Stepanov thus admitted that he had sent the allegations against Sagaidak to the NKVD. Bubnov probed further, "Is there wrecking in the factory?" "Yes," Stepanov answered. Bubnov asked craftily, "Whom do you distrust?" This question was a trap. If Stepanov said, "No one," he opened himself to a charge of lack of vigilance. If, on the other hand, he named names, he widened the investigation. Stepanov, however, was well practiced at games of thrust and parry. "One must be on guard against everyone," he replied, looking steadily at Bubnov. Even under fire, Stepanov refused to equate production problems with wrecking. He implicitly understood that, if every problem was ascribed to wrecking, the entire workforce would end up in prison, and the factory would collapse. He told the *partkom*, "The pipes fell down in the cutting department, the workers pour oil into the drains," and "the shop bosses try to hush it all up." He admitted honestly, "It is difficult to decide who is innocent and who is guilty." Another party member approached the question from

---

[67] See case of Somov in "Protokol no. 40 zasedaniia partkoma zavoda 'Serp i molot,'" December 8, 1937, ll. 117–118, and TsAODM, f. 429, o. 1, d. 261, "Stenogramma obshchego zakrytogo partiinogo sobraniia," January 11, 1938, ll. 24–42. Somov mentioned Zhidkova's role in "unmasking Sagaidak" (l. 39). On Zhidkova's case, see "Protokol no. 40 zasedaniia partkoma zavoda 'Serp i molot,'" December 8, 1937, ll. 138–141.

a different angle. "Were there signals or denunciations about wrecking, about officials who worked in the factory?" But Stepanov again refused to take the bait. "There were many signals that there was wrecking," he answered. The party member pressed on, "About whom?" "About many," replied Stepanov calmly. "But there were no facts."[68]

Stepanov was unusual in his forthright refusal to be bullied or trapped into incriminating others. At a time when few party members maintained their integrity, he stood firm. The following excerpt of his interrogation by the *partkom* gives a sense of how cleverly he evaded their insistence that he blame others:

"You said that no one could force you to accept that this work was the actions of wreckers, yet you were surrounded by wreckers."

"I was not."

"How could you have such people around you, people of such character?"

"We have thousands of commanders and there is a percentage that are bastards, but the command is in essence devoted."

"Why were there wreckers in all the main sectors?"

"Many good commanders were selected, among them you and others. But now you say that everything good has nothing to do with me, and everything bad is my fault."

"I am asking you why wreckers ended up in the factory. You should be vigilant and oriented toward unmasking wreckers. But you are a cock with his comb [*petushki da grebeshki*]. How do you explain your insufficiently sharp approach to wrecking?"[69]

Stepanov was one of the very few who managed to withstand such interrogations. In part, his privileged position as director allowed him to trump pushy questioners by quietly insinuating that he had been privy to information about them as well. In the end, the *partkom* did not expel Stepanov. Unfortunately, few demonstrated his principled strength.

Managers and Workers

The hunt for "enemies" and "wreckers" severely undercut the lines of authority of the factories.[70] Directors spent endless time in meetings

---

68 "Stenogramma zasedaniia partiinogo komiteta zavoda 'Serp i molot,'" July 22, 1937, ll. 100–102. For the interrogation of Stepanov, see ll. 69–108 and "Stenogramma zasedaniia partiinogo komiteta zavoda 'Serp i molot,'" July 25, 1937, ll. 111–136.

69 "Stenogramma zasedaniia partiinogo komiteta zavoda 'Serp i molot,'" July 22, 1937, ll. 106–108.

70 Sheila Fitzpatrick, "Workers Against Bosses: The Impact of the Great Purges on Labor-Management Relations," in Lewis Siegelbaum and Ronald Suny, eds., *Making Workers Soviet: Power, Class and Identity* (Cornell University Press, Ithaca, 1990), pp. 311–40,

defending themselves and their subordinates from political, biographical, and technical charges. Stepanov managed to retain his position, but Dinamo had three directors in a little more than a year. Zhukov, the first, was expelled from the Party and replaced by Iasvoin, who was immediately attacked for poor organization of the shops, financial irregularities, eliminating wage bonuses, and failure to restore order. He found himself in an impossible position. If he "restored order," a demand of the managers, he was subject to charges of "suppressing criticism." If he restored wage bonuses, a demand of the workers, he was forced into overspending the wage fund. The head of the *partkom* admitted that there was a sharp drop in labor discipline among workers and managers. Yet the *partkom* was partially responsible. It systematically undermined Iasvoin's authority, refusing, for example, to allow him to hire. Forced to apologize for hiring a deputy director, Iasvoin admitted, "I didn't know who was supposed to select cadres, me or the *partkom*." Wielding little authority, but assuming all the blame, Iasvoin was paralyzed by fear and depression. The *partkom* censured him: "First of all, he must eliminate his pessimistic attitude toward work." Yet Iasvoin's pessimism was justified: he too was soon expelled and arrested.[71]

Authority broke down in the shops as well. It became impossible for a shift or shop boss to criticize or dismiss an employee without opening himself to charges that he was "an enemy of the people." When Korostelin, a party member in Likernovodochnyi, was accused by Tynkov, the head of his shop, of overspending thousands of rubles in state funds, he immediately took the political offensive against his boss. He launched a campaign to get Tynkov arrested as a "Trotskyist enemy." He wrote to the factory director, charging that Tynkov tried to fire communists in the shop, "devoured" people, forced older workers to leave, and paid workers large bonuses to ensure their support. The director ignored such charges at his own peril. He established an investigative committee, which upheld Tynkov, the boss of the shop, against Korostelin. At this point, the *partkom* tried to wash its hands of the whole affair. Korostelin, charged with mismanagement, ended up in court. Yet he continued to write denunciations to the party and district committees, claiming that Tynkov was an "enemy of the people." The court found Korostelin guilty, but the NKVD

---

and Robert Thurston, *Life and Terror in Stalin's Russia, 1934–1941* (Yale University Press, New Haven, 1996), make similar arguments.
[71] "Protokol zasedaniia partiinogo komiteta zavoda 'Dinamo im Kirova,'" June 18, 1937, ll. 150–151.

"ruled" in his favor. He was saved from his court-ordered sentence by the timely arrests of both Tynkov and an engineer who served on the director's investigative committee.[72]

Korostelin was still not satisfied. The arrest of Tynkov and the engineer now allowed him to present himself as a victim. He indignantly lectured the *partkom*, "I have been in the Party fifteen years, and I worked in this factory for twenty-five. My party card was put at risk. I was betrayed by the court. Who is guilty? An enemy of the people. But the *partkom* said, 'You are guilty. You must answer for this.' If I had not gotten so excited about this, I would have sat in prison for a long time." Korostelin berated the party secretary, "I wrote to you several times that Tynkov was an enemy of the people. What do you want, that he should come in and tell you that he's an enemy of the people?" He was furious that his denunciations had not resulted in immediate action, that he was forced to go to court. Several members of the *partkom* tried to explain to Korostelin that it was impossible to arrest people without proof, on the basis of a single denunciation, but to no avail.[73] Korostelin then redirected his anger at the entire *partkom*. He sent an accusation to the district committee that his *partkom* failed to help him unmask enemies. The district, fearful of being tarred by a similar accusation, launched another investigation. Party members turned against each other. The secretary of the *partkom* admitted her lack of vigilance, but refused to support Korostelin: "You are not the hero here," she cautioned Korostelin. "The NKVD did its job, and you don't deserve any laurels."[74]

Korostelin's case showed how easily an accusation of waste, poor management, or embezzlement could be transformed into a "political" case. When Tynkov, the head of the shop, blamed Korostelin for fraud, Korostelin fought back with every weapon in the political arsenal, charging Tynkov with obstructing party meetings, bribing workers, and "Trotskyism." His denunciations, a direct response to his own endangered predicament, ultimately resulted in his boss's arrest. By the time the affair was over, Tynkov was in prison and the *partkom* members were under investigation for their "failure to unmask." The case sent a clear message: any manager who tried to discipline wrongdoing had better be prepared to brave an onslaught of counteraccusations.

---

[72] "Obshchego otchetno-vybornogo zakrytogo partsobraniia moskovskogo Likerno-vodochnogo zavoda," April 19–21, 1938, ll. 48–50ob.

[73] Ibid., ll. 161, 163–164.   [74] Ibid., ll. 160ob–162, 163–164.

Vikulov, the deputy director of Likernovodochnyi, found himself facing numerous charges when Mongert, a demanding foreman he appointed and supported, was arrested. The workers, unhappy with Mongert's strict discipline, claimed a victory in the arrest: the NKVD arrested Mongert because he had fired "the old, good workers." Vikulov had a very different perspective. He defended Mongert for struggling against the workers' drunkenness and petty thievery. In a party meeting, Vikulov refused to admit that he had hired an enemy. Prompted either by a stubborn commitment to the truth or fear of incrimination by association, Vikulov refused to denounce Mongert. Efteev, an official from the district party committee, upbraided Vikulov:

EFTEEV: "You said that Mongert demanded, pushed, and fought against thievery."
VIKULOV: "Perhaps he was too rule-bound."
EFTEEV: "Precisely. He was too rule-bound, he pushed the workers, and he tried to present himself as an active Soviet person."
VIKULOV: "Possibly."
EFTEEV: "But he was an enemy, and you overlook that and praise him."
VIKULOV: "I told it like it was."
EFTEEV: "I would not say that he fought and pushed. You need to say, 'Excuse me, I was a party member who overlooked this bastard.' You don't need to praise him."
VIKULOV: "I didn't praise him."

Several party members used Mongert's arrest to strike back against Vikulov. Old grievances between the transport department and other shops tumbled out. Shop heads complained that the transport department refused to ship materials that were not properly packed. Vikulov, not wanting to take up precious boxcar space with nonessential items, had refused to ship baskets to the factory store as part of the October revolution celebration. Vikulov curtly told the party organizer, "Hire a taxi!" Others charged that Vikulov and Mongert set workers and party members against each other, and fired old workers. Vikulov defended himself against the accusations. At least one of those workers, he explained angrily, was a chronic drunk. "How many times did he get drunk at the factory?" Vikulov demanded. "Yesterday he spoke at our meeting and he was drunk." Mongert's arrest opened Vikulov to a host of grievances. Politics and production had become so closely intertwined that it was no longer possible to censure a drunk, refuse a shipment, or discuss factory business with any semblance of rationality.[75]

[75] Ibid., ll. 149–152.

"Bawlers" and Organizational Chaos

By 1938, the *partkomy* were completely occupied with *zaiavleniia* and investigations. Scarcely a soul remained who could not be found "guilty" of something, be it a tie with an "enemy," a tainted biography, a technical mistake, an accident, or a theoretical error. The democratization of repression had taken the hunt for enemies far beyond the target group of former oppositionists. Party meetings were transformed into a war of each against all, in which it was impossible to extract the truth of any particular case from the muck of charges, grudges, and vendettas. The remaining members, now well schooled in the hunt for enemies, were quick to parry any insinuation with a countercharge. Eager to protect themselves, they denounced others in preemptive strikes. They became known, in party parlance, as "bawlers [*krikuny*]." Like a snake swallowing its tail, the *partkomy* could devour themselves no further when "bawlers" themselves were arrested for "bawling."

The *partkomy* were under intense pressure to "unmask" enemies before they were arrested by the NKVD. Anticipating the NKVD, however, was impossible. The *partkomy* often had no idea why someone was arrested. After an arrest, they tried to atone for their failure by finding someone to blame for "overlooking the enemy," an exercise that invariably resulted in more victims. In Trekhgornaia Manufaktura, for example, the arrest of Polozkov, the factory director, initially shocked the *partkom*. Yet the need to affix blame rapidly superseded shock. "These wreckers sat among us, and no one saw them," one member declared. "Where was our triangle [director, *partkom* secretary, union head] that it couldn't see what these wreckers were doing?" The *partkom* soon shifted to an attack on its own secretary, Severianova, accusing her of surrounding herself with "toadies" and "lickspittles." "How else can we explain enemies like Polozkov in the *partkom*?"[76] Another secretary replaced Severianova but, again, little changed. The *partkom* then refocused its attention on Severianova's remaining allies. The process, allegedly aimed at finding enemies, had by this time developed its own self-destructive dynamic: each new victim was blamed in turn for "failure to unmask" the previous group. Months later, the *partkom*, still embroiled in the fallout over Severianova's removal, split into warring factions over a slur in the factory's newspaper. One party member protested the insult; the editor of the paper refused to retract

---

[76] "Stenogramma otchetno-perevybornogo partiinogo sobraniia," March 30–31, 1937, ll. 22, 30, 34, 82–3.

it. The issue had no more substance than a schoolyard squabble: who was correct to call whom a "lickspittle." Eventually the *partkom*, unable to resolve its differences, placed the squalid mess of charges and counter-charges before the district party committee.[77] Conditions at Trekhgornaia were unchanged, but the district committee was occupied in determining the true "lickspittle."

In Serp i Molot, the *partkom* processed so many cases of arrest and exclusion that its remaining members were all in some way connected to the victims. The tragic roster included Zaitsev, the deputy director, Sagaidak, the head of the cold rolling mill, Malyshev, head of the crane sector of the electrical shop, Piguzov, the head of the department of capital construction, Somov, the secretary of the *partkom*, Perversev, a turner in the casting foundry, Perverseva, his wife, Kachurin, her brother, Diat-lovitskii, a research engineer in the rolling mill, Sokol, the head of the department of technical control (OTK), Mironov, Sokol's replacement, and numerous others. By 1938, the interlocking circles had become so tangled that charges against Mironov, the newly appointed head of the OTK, threatened to bring down the entire *partkom*. The process of purge in Serp i Molot had reached the point of absurdity: there had been so many arrests that everyone who remained had some tie to an "enemy."

Mironov was a 47-year-old former revolutionary who had begun factory work at the age of sixteen. He spent time in tsarist prisons and joined the Bolsheviks in 1917. Having entered Serp i Molot in 1923, he was promoted to head the OTK after Sokol, his predecessor, was arrested. Mironov, too, soon got into trouble when the connections that had helped his meteoric rise proved his undoing. In January 1938, Mironov was charged with a close tie to Filatov, a former secretary of the *partkom*. Filatov had been expelled from the Party and the factory earlier for ties to the right opposition. Yet when the *partkom* took up Mironov's case, it quickly became apparent that everyone at the meeting was in some way tied to "the enemy Filatov"! As former party secretary, Filatov had wide contacts with shop heads, managers, and even the director. "I was not the only one," Mironov said. "Perhaps there are party members here brave enough to admit that they, too, were no less and perhaps even more friendly with Filatov than I was." Someone yelled out from the floor, "Who exactly?" Mironov did not hesitate to name names, and the list comprised a "who's who" of managers. More than 100 people had attended a going-away party in the factory for Filatov when he went off

[77] "Protokol no. 31 zasedaniia plenuma partkoma," November 22, 1937, l. 51.

to do his army service, including Stepanov, the director, Bogoliubskii, the head of the sheet-rolling shop, Pogonchenkov, Korotin, Romanov, and other managers living in the House of Shock Workers at the time. When Filatov came home on leave, the factory's leaders met again at Mironov's apartment to welcome him. "I don't see anything wrong with the fact that I, as a party member, gave the chance to our officials to gather in my apartment," Mironov declared.[78]

Mironov, however, was not charged with throwing parties, but with engaging in "counterrevolutionary conversations." Well schooled by now in defensive tactics, he slyly told the *partkom*, "Many of *you* knew Filatov. Perhaps one of you can say that you *heard* a counterrevolutionary conversation." Mironov knew that anyone who admitted to hearing such a conversation would also have to explain why they failed to report it at the time. Naturally, no witnesses came forward. Emboldened by the silence, Mironov added, "Stepanov [the director] was more friendly with him than I was. Does this mean that Stepanov as a member of the *partkom* voted to exclude me for a friendship with someone who was also *his* friend?" Various party members then spoke about visits, parties, and drinking bouts with Mironov and Filatov. No one could remember any "counterrevolutionary conversations." One party member asked, "Why is Mironov accused of a connection to Filatov, when Stepanov drank with Filatov more than Mironov?" Everyone began to laugh. Another party member, annoyed at the frivolity, angrily intervened, "We have listened to a flippant group of comrades, who have not treated this business seriously, and not only the drinking parties . . . what about the accident rate?" No one wanted to discuss the accident rate. Once again, the comrades reverted to a merry discussion of past drinking bouts. The party secretary tried to call them to order. "I consider it incorrect when a party meeting begins to conduct itself unseriously. It is impossible to resolve the case amid this laughter and fooling around." Chastened, several party members returned to the attack: Mironov had gotten his brother, a priest, a job in the factory. The workers did not want him to head the OTK. He had allowed the shop heads to ship out poor-quality products. The "evidence" against him, a mixture of rumors and slander, piled up. Finally, someone suggested that every person who had ever drunk with Mironov should testify whether they had had a "counterrevolutionary conversation." This ridiculous suggestion would have required hours, if not days, of additional testimony, involving almost every party member, shop head,

---

[78] "Stenogramma obshchezavodskogo zakrytogo partiinogo sobraniia," January 11, 1938, ll. 42–44.

and manager. At this point, someone impatiently called for a vote. The *partkom* split in half: 157 for exclusion, 154 for reprimand. The secretary called for a recount, and the numbers reversed. Mironov would remain in the Party.[79] Mironov's case illustrated how absurd the hunt for enemies had become. Party members recognized that everyone was tied to someone who had been arrested. Who had not raised a glass with Mironov, gotten drunk with Stepanov, or attended Filatov's goodbye party? The process of tracing ties and friendships, so zealously pursued in 1937, had become a hopeless muddle. The hunt for "enemies" finally reached its logical conclusion: the hunted and the hunter recognized each other as one and the same.

In January 1938, the Central Committee tried to slow the process of expulsions. The Politburo and Stalin in particular were concerned that the Party was destroying itself. But the message the Central Committee sent was mixed: it criticized wholesale expulsions, but urged party members to continue their hunt for enemies. Its acknowledgment that some "innocent" people had been wrongly accused was not synonymous with a halt to repression.[80] A candidate member of the Party in Dinamo summed up the prevailing mood after the January plenum: "In our party organization many were unmasked as enemies of the people and their helpers, but there are still many remaining to be unmasked." A major contributor to the factory's wall newspaper, he had made of career of unmasking others.[81] The January 1938 plenum further complicated the organizational dynamic: party members who had been charged and cleared now felt justified in retaliating against those who had denounced them. In fact, the hatred of the exonerated for their former accusers introduced an even greater element of instability.

In Dinamo, the process of "unmasking" deteriorated into chaos. Here, too, a large cluster of people had been expelled and arrested. Khorikov, the third director, noting a "full renewal" of the managerial staff, suggested that scarcely a single manager remained in his former position. Resentments of old accusations now shared the agenda with new ones. At a large party meeting in January 1938, one member complained that,

---

[79] Ibid., ll. 44–64 (italics mine).

[80] For the resolution, see *Pravda*, August 7, 1938; J. Arch Getty and Oleg Naumov, *The Road to Terror: Stalin and the Self-Destruction of the Bolsheviks, 1932–1939* (Yale University Press, New Haven, 1999), pp. 491–8. Repression continued after the January 1938 plenum. More than 638,000 people were arrested, compared with 936,000 in 1937, the majority for counterrevolutionary crimes (ibid., pp. 496–7).

[81] TsAODM, f. 432, o. 1, d. 194, "Informatsiia v proletarskii RK VKP (b) o proshedshem obshchem zakrytom partsobranii ot 6 i 7 ian. 1938 na zavode Dinamo," ll. 1–8.

when he went to Starichkov, the party secretary, to inform him of his brother's arrest, Starichkov asked him, "What for?" He replied that he did not know. Starichkov responded, "You're not a boy who doesn't know what for. It's clear he's an enemy of the people." His brother was eventually exonerated, but Starichkov's comment still rankled. He said bitterly, "Thanks to this, I went to a sanitarium for a nervous breakdown." Other members were furious that they had once been accused of being enemies. Kruk, a party member, attacked Starichkov for sending accusations about him to the district committee. Another member responded, "It's impossible to say that you were pure, Comrade Kruk. Your speech is aimed at freeing yourself from blame and dumping it others. You're supposedly innocent, a little sheep, felled by a blow from Starichkov." Kruk stormed out of the meeting in a fury. The meeting became a free-for-all. Khromogin yelled that he, too, had been defamed, called a "bawler," when in fact enemies who were later arrested had tried to denounce him. Other people named other "bawlers." One member announced that the factory newspaper "is occupied only with the defamation of communists."[82]

Three months later, an official from the Moscow city committee visited Dinamo to introduce some order. He reprimanded the *partkom* for its obsessive focus on wreckers. "It is impossible to be occupied only with this all the time," he said. The accusations had gone too far. Even Kaganovich, a Politburo member and Stalin's close supporter, had noted, "You begin work today and, within twenty-four hours, they blame you for something." He urged the *partkom* to redirect its attention to problems in the factory. Yet his message was contradictory. "Your main mistake," he explained, "was that eighteen enemies of the people were arrested whom you failed to unmask. You need to ask why the people who worked with these enemies failed to unmask them." He thus commanded the *partkom* to investigate everyone who worked with the victims, an order that would keep them busy for months with eighteen new circles of workmates, friends, and mentors. Why had the *partkom* failed to recognize that these people were enemies? The official's advice now entered the realm of psychological absurdity. He urged them to search their memories. "If you think back and analyze this," he told them, "you will see that you know why these people were arrested."[83]

[82] TsAODM, f. 432, o. 1, d. 194, "Informatsiia v proletarskii RK VKP (b) o proshedshem obshchem zakrytom partsobranii ot 26 ian. 1938 na zavode Dinamo," ll. 16–18, 20.
[83] TsAODM, f. 432, o. 1, d. 189, "Stenogramma otchetno-vybornogo zakrytogo partiinogo sobraniia," April 9, 1938, ll. 40–42.

Conclusion

By 1937, party members in the factories had become important participants in Stalinist repression. Responding to pressure from above to search for hidden enemies, they became active agents in the expulsion and repression of their own comrades. They took up the hunt for enemies alongside the NKVD and began actively "unmasking" their own ranks. Party leaders encouraged workers and party members not only to "unmask" enemies, but to denounce abuses by managers and party officials and to recast accidents and production problems in political terms. The "powerless" were urged to expose officials who exercised power directly over them. The mass meetings organized from above in the factories in February 1937 jumpstarted this process. They were purposely and tellingly designed without a set agenda, and resulted in a flood of *zaiavleniia*.

The center pushed the party rank and file to participate, but quickly lost control of the process. Within a year, the *partkomy* were devouring themselves. It is difficult to know how many people were expelled or arrested in the various factories, but data from Dinamo seem typical. In April 1937, Dinamo had 561 party members and 178 candidates in a factory of 6,991 workers. Of these party members, 163 were workers. One year later, the party had 532 members and 229 candidates. The party had excluded 64 members as "enemies," of which 44 were arrested and 11 restored by a higher party organization. An additional 18 had been arrested and then excluded. Thus, of 561 members, a total of 62 were arrested, or 11 percent.[84] Although the statistics suggest considerable disruption, they only hint at the prevailing atmosphere. In 1937–8, Dinamo had three directors in rapid succession: two were expelled from the party, and one arrested. Stenographic reports of *partkom* meetings show that it was occupied almost solely with *zaiavleniia*, accusations, countercharges, and expulsions.[85]

Although purges or *chistki* had always been a regular feature of party organization, what happened in 1937–9 was qualitatively different in terms of scale, aim, atmosphere, and consequence. "Unmasking" differed from earlier purges in that it was not a routine means of eliminating the

[84] "Stenogramma otchetnogo partiinogo sobraniia," April 8–10, 1937, ll. 6–9; "Stenogramma otchetno-vybornogo zakrytogo partiinogo sobraniia partorganizatsii zavoda 'Dinamo im. Kirova,'" April 8, 1938, ll. 1–9.

[85] "Stenogramma otchetno-vybornogo zakrytogo partiinogo sobraniia partorganizatsii zavoda 'Dinamo im. Kirova,'" April 8, 1938, ll. 6, 9, 14. In 1937–8, the *partkom* heard more than fifty cases of expulsion, arrest, and denunciation.

malfeasant, alcoholic, or passive. Nor was it aimed at members with real political differences with party policies. It was a hunt for a "masked" or a literally invisible enemy, conducted in an increasingly self-destructive atmosphere. In the past, expulsion was not linked to arrest unless there was criminal wrongdoing. Beginning in 1937, arrest and expulsion were closely linked. In Dinamo, for example, 69 percent of those excluded from the Party were arrested. Not all members were arrested after being expelled, and a small percentage successfully appealed their cases and were reinstated. Yet, for many, expulsion was either the prelude to or the consequence of an arrest that rippled out to destroy family, friends, and workmates.

Who was most at risk in the factories? Did repression cut across hierarchical lines? Managers and bosses were certainly at high risk, and their tendency to staff positions with "family circles" resulted in multiple arrests. Yet many of these circles had their origins in the complicated politics of the 1920s, and cut across hierarchical lines. Investigations of managers uncovered ties to workers and managers in distant towns. Managers, shop bosses, and engineers were more likely to be charged with responsibility for accidents and production problems, yet workers were not immune to such charges. Sharova, a woman worker and party member in Trekhgornaia Manufaktura, for example, explained to the *partkom* that her husband, a railroad signalman, had been arrested after a train crashed in a dense fog. The NKVD searched their apartment and confiscated his letters and books. Sharova, asked to describe the books by the *partkom*, admitted, "I don't know. I am barely literate."[86] Rapid upward mobility ensured that most managers had working-class and peasant relatives. Even if a worker or collective farmer was less likely to be targeted, the arrest of a manager left working-class or peasant families devastated. Moreover, a worker was as likely as a manager to have a peasant relative arrested, a "kulak" past, or links to a Trotskyist workers' group from the 1920s. By 1938, the lines of attack had become completely blurred. Everyone wrapped themselves in the banner of "the workers' interests," the Soviet equivalent of modern-day patriotism or the flag. Meetings turned into a "war of each against all." No one was impervious to smear, from the director to the shop foreman to the turner in the calibration shop. The process, popularized by a campaign that encouraged "little people" to speak out against their bosses, quickly subsumed the distinction between "little" and "big."

[86] "Protokol no. 32 zasedaniia plenuma partkoma," December 9, 1937, ll. 54–55.

By 1938, "unmasking" had developed an internal, self-generating organizational dynamic. Party members who failed to inform their organizations immediately of biographical shortcomings, arrests of close friends or relatives, or suspicions of "enemy" activity could be punished for concealing information. Fear of punishment impelled numerous party members to write *zaiavleniia*, prompting investigations, which uncovered ever more enemies. Officials were compelled to investigate these *zaiavleniia* no matter how nonsensical or unreasonable. The failure to investigate, termed "overlooking enemies," "smoothing over enemy activity," or failing to "unmask the enemy among us," was itself grounds for expulsion and arrest. Many sensible, well-meaning officials thus lost their last bulwark of defense against the madness: the choice to ignore it. Unable to disregard even the most preposterous claims, officials helped fuel an ever-quickening dynamic of purge independently of signals from above or NKVD arrests. Party members quickly learned to parry an accusation with a counterthrust. Some sought to cover their own secrets with loud, aggressive denunciations of others. Each party organization went through a painful process in which its members righteously, even enthusiastically, attacked, tormented, and ultimately devoured each other. Individual strategies of defense served only to intensify and spread the terror within the group. In the end, everyone was guilty of some transgression: a biographical weakness, an "enemy" relative or friend, or just the simple failure to "unmask" a workmate later revealed to be "an enemy." The Party's quasi-religious insistence on "total honesty," and the investigations which followed even the smallest "confessions" turned everyone into secret "sinners." The process reached its own dead end when it had transformed all its participants into potential "enemies."

13. P. F. Stepanov, director of Serp i Molot, 1933. Courtesy of RGAKFD

14. Workers in the Likernovodochnyi (Spirits and Vodka) factory pouring vodka into bottles, 1937. Courtesy of RGAKFD

15. Workers in Krasnyi Proletarii listen to a speech by a party organizer, 1939. Courtesy of RGAKFD

16. Meeting of workers in Serp i Molot, 1939. Courtesy of RGAKFD

Conclusion

The history of repression in the unions and the factories shows that the terror cannot be construed solely as a series of orders issued by Stalin and Ezhov against a helpless population. Nor can the terror be seen as a spontaneous eruption of working-class resentment against managers and officials. Events in the unions and the factories reveal instead a dynamic interplay, evolving over time, between the actions of central party leaders and the responses of workers and officials. The terror involved orders and signals, but also millions of active human agents who translated them into action. Most importantly, people had interests of their own, which encouraged them to adopt the language of the terror: to "unmask enemies," to accuse "wreckers," and to denounce their colleagues, bosses, and fellow party members. Over time, the terror came to involve a self-generating dynamic that affected both individuals and organizations. Specific rituals set in motion self-protective responses, including destructive demonstrations of "loyalty," preemptive accusations, and counter-denunciations. Leaders of organizations purged their own departments; party and union members devoured each other. As the process came to a slow and shuddering halt at the apex of the party and union hierarchies, it hit a dead end within the unions and party committees as well. The snake, devouring its tail, reached the point where its mouth swallowed its head. This imaginary point, almost impossible to visualize, was in fact a real moment in time that occurred when the "bawlers," or the mouths of denunciation, were themselves denounced and arrested for "bawling."

Grasping the tensions and grievances of the industrial workplace is indispensable to understanding the development of the terror. The rapid tempo of industrialization coupled with the unforeseen consequences of collectivization created a crisis in provisioning. Millions of peasants entered the workforce, and shortages of food, housing, consumer goods, and services were ubiquitous. Real wages fell by half. Managers faced intense pressure to meet output targets set in Moscow, shop heads struggled with new and unfamiliar technologies, and accident rates soared. In 1929, the unions were purged of "rightists" and reoriented "toward production." Workers had no official outlet to redress grievances. Once a mainstay of support for the Party, they were increasingly alienated by the sacrifices industrialization required. Working-class party members and union activists found it difficult to build support for party policies. Former oppositionists, scattered in factories, unions, and economic administration, were filled with doubts but did not pose an alternative to Stalinist industrialization. The few who were still politically active were appalled by the bitter anti-Soviet mood of recent peasant migrants and hesitated to make common cause with them. Party leaders understood that collectivization and the decline in living standards had hurt their standing with peasants and workers. Yet, in 1934, they believed that they had weathered the worst of the storm. They had successfully vanquished all organized opposition, and were reasonably confident that their strategy would create a firm base for further economic development.

The Kirov murder shook this precarious sense of security. Initially, party leaders were unsure of how to interpret the assassination. Ezhov's view, that the Party was honeycombed with hidden enemies, gradually gained predominance, and the search for Kirov's assassins widened into a larger attack against former supporters of Zinoviev and Trotsky. Each new victim of arrest implicated others under the duress of interrogation, buttressing Ezhov's notion of a wide, hidden conspiracy against the state and the Party. The process culminated in the August 1936 trial of the "United Trotskyist-Zinovievite Center," which targeted former members of the left opposition and hinted at the participation of former rightists as well. On the local level, however, people were relatively untouched by the rising hysteria of party leaders. Workers and party members participated in the mourning rituals for Kirov, closely followed the trial, and attended mass rallies designed to whip up public opinion against the defendants. But they disregarded the Party's calls for increasing vigilance. The trial was a spectacle that had little to do with their daily lives and problems. They had no personal connections to the defendants, prominent former revolutionaries, or their intended victims, Stalin and other leaders. They did not quarrel with the Party's insistence on hidden enemies, but they were not moved to search for them. In private, older workers spoke positively about Trotsky, and recent migrants railed against all Bolsheviks, making little distinction between Stalin and his opponents. In the factories, some former oppositionists were arrested, but workers and party members were not overly concerned.

By fall 1936, party leaders had become increasingly frustrated with the lackadaisical approach of the *partkomy*. Local leaders had used the *proverka* and *obmen* to expel "passives," not "politicals." At this point, party leaders made a concerted effort to popularize the hunt for enemies. They exerted sharp pressure on the *partkomy* and district committees to comb their records and review their members for past opposition-ism. They staged a highly publicized trial of mining officials and former oppositionists for an explosion in the Kemerovo mines, which raised the issue of wrecking in every factory. And they held a second, larger trial in January 1937, which again linked managers to former Trotskyists, and wrecking in Kemerovo to the chemical industry and railroads. The new campaign spread quickly through the factories. Workers used the charge of wrecking to bring attention to safety problems, ventilation, and poor work conditions. Shop heads used it to defend their records against other shops. Managers and union officials used it to excuse problems beyond their control. Its unparalleled utility and versatility assured its spread. The factories became hotbeds of accusation and denunciation. Finally, the February–March 1937 Central Committee Plenum added one more element to the explosive mix. Party leaders introduced democratic, secret-ballot, multicandidate elections to the Supreme Soviet, the Party, and the unions. They encouraged "little people" to speak out against abusive offi-cials and bureaucrats, to take back their unions, and to hold their leaders accountable for problems at work. Party leaders saw terror and democ-racy as complementary: they hoped to remove former oppositionists and renew ties with the rank and file. What better way to achieve both these aims than to embolden the base to attack the "family circles" that pro-tected former oppositionists?

The campaign for union democracy spread repression throughout the unions. Workers briefly gained some power; they swept out the old lead-ership in elections, and forced the unions to address safety problems. On other fronts, however, workers were less successful. In many unions, the new leadership proved more inefficient, corrupt, and disinclined to sobriety than the old. At the upper levels, officials played a "lateral leapfrog," moving back and forth between managerial and union posts, one jump ahead of the NKVD. Most importantly, the elections did not alter the unions' basic role as cheerleaders for production. Union leaders fought bitterly in the wake of elections. Using the language of repression – "wreckers," "toadies," "lickspittles," "enemies," and "family circles" – to advance their personal and narrowly political interests, they quickly drew the attention of the NKVD.

The damage to the unions was great. Fragmentary evidence suggests that at least one-third of union heads were arrested. Yet arrests were not simply the result of orders from central party leaders, but rather a grim interplay between the Party (at all levels), the unions, the NKVD, and the VTsSPS. The unions and the VTsSPS were active participants in their own destruction. The paths to prison were many. Leaders were expelled from their local party organizations and then arrested. VTsSPS investigators found evidence of malfeasance that captured the attention of the Party and the NKVD. Union leaders denounced each other and were denounced by their members. And the NKVD targeted any number of leaders for reasons of its own. A few principled union leaders tried to protect their staff, begging officials to stop denouncing each other. Yet they were promptly accused of the very practices that the terror aimed to eradicate: "suppression of criticism from below" and "building circles of family protection." Their efforts proved in vain. The vast majority of union leaders made little effort to halt the madness. In an attempt at self-protection, they countered one accusation with another, a strategy that served only to increase the number of victims. In the end, VTsSPS and union officials proved to be the willing instruments of their own destruction.

In the *partkomy* in the factories, the process was much the same. Local party leaders requested records and minutes from distant party organizations, mining the past for compromising information on each other. Few were able to withstand such rigorous biographical review. The growing number of arrests ensured that ever-larger circles of people were subject to interrogation about their ties to "enemies of the people." Interlocking circles of friends, mentors, and workmates were pulled into the vortex of terror as more and more people were arrested and interrogated. The practice of *kooptatsiia*, so popular in staffing positions, proved fatal to entire circles of managers. Denunciations from workers in factory newspapers brought down managers and shop heads as production problems and accidents became increasingly politicized. The process of "unmasking" ended in absurdity. The survivors, left standing amid the ruin they had wrought, were all tied to the "enemies" they had so self-righteously dispatched. By the terror's own iron logic, everyone was now guilty of something.

Workers, too, were not immune from arrest. Mass operations in the summer of 1937 targeted foreign nationals, former kulaks, priests, homeless people, and other marginal groups. Workers and their relatives also disappeared in these massive sweeps.[1] Although managers were more likely to be the target of arrest, they were embedded in families of workers and peasants. These family members were the people who stood in line at the prisons, lost jobs and educational opportunities, and suffered the consequences of a tie to an "enemy of the people." In a period of rapid upward social mobility, class analysis of the victims alone tells us little about the effect of terror on families or the general population.

The first signal that the terror was waning occurred when party leaders in the January 1938 Central Committee Plenum admitted that many members had been erroneously expelled. VTsSPS officials used the plenum's pronouncements in a cautious effort to halt the madness, but they had little influence. In fact, reinstatements coupled with continuing repression created a huge organizational mess that stymied union officials, managers, and party members. Organizations worked at cross-purposes: no one knew who was in charge or what rules to follow. In March 1938, Bukharin, Rykov, and nineteen other defendants were sentenced in a trial of the "Anti-Soviet Bloc of Rightists and Trotskyists," the last of the three great Moscow show trials. The charges, a reprise of the two earlier show trials, included the assassination of Kirov, wrecking, sabotage, and collaboration with fascist powers. In April, Ezhov received a second appointment as head of the Commissariat of Waterways and, in August, L. P. Beria was appointed as deputy commissar of the NKVD. Both moves signaled that the terror was waning. In the fall, the Central Committee passed a series of measures limiting the power of the NKVD. In November, Stalin decreed an end to the mass operations and shifted control for sentencing from the NKVD back to the courts. Ezhov was removed and replaced by Beria. Ezhov made his last official appearance in February 1939. Arrested soon after and charged with "leftist overreaction," he was

---

[1] Oleg Khlevniuk, *The History of the Gulag: From Collectivization to the Great Terror* (Yale University Press, New Haven, 2004), p. 306, notes that many victims of the mass operations were not "pauperized elements" but ordinary citizens who had forgotten their identification cards; Valerii Vasiliev, "The Great Terror in the Ukraine, 1936–1938," in Melanie Ilic, ed., *Stalin's Terror Revisited* (Palgrave, Basingstoke, 2006), p. 158, notes that in Donets province almost half of the repressed were manual workers.

convicted and shot in 1940.[2] From the perspective of high politics, "the terror" was officially over.

In the factories and the unions, however, no definitive signal ended the terror. Stalin never blew a mighty horn that sounded the all-clear. No piercing factory whistle marked the end of this "graveyard shift." In September 1938, at the same time as the Party was beginning to rein in the NKVD, the VTsSPS ordered the Union of Retail Clerks to "root out enemies" in the trade organizations, producing a new round of arrests for wrecking.[3] Arrests slowed, but they did not stop. As the international situation worsened, however, Party leaders attempted to stabilize the unions and the *partkomy*, reinstitute labor discipline, and prepare for war. By 1938, fascism was triumphant in Italy, Germany, and Spain, Hitler's army was on the march, and Britain and France had repeatedly rejected Soviet offers of collective security. In December 1938, the state passed harsh new legislation aimed at reducing absence, lateness, and idleness in the workplace.[4] Party leaders moved to restore the authority of union officials. The campaign for union democracy had encouraged workers to criticize officials and oust "bureaucrats." By 1939, the unions were so discredited that one newspaper called union officials recently dismissed in a curtailment of staff "an entire army of free loaders and good-for-nothings." The article prompted a former union official to write a letter to Stalin complaining that the unionists had been fired not because they worked poorly, but because their jobs had been eliminated. He noted that union officials had little authority and were routinely derided as "idlers." People cast these aspersions "not only as a joke, but seriously."[5] If union officials were to

---

[2] Wladislaw Hedeler, "Ezhov's Scenario for the Great Terror and the Falsified Record of the Third Moscow Show Trial" (pp. 49, 50–2), and Barry McLoughlin, "Mass Operations of the NKVD, 1937–1938: A Survey" (pp. 132, 138–40), both in McLoughlin and Kevin McDermott, eds., *Stalin's Terror: High Politics and Mass Repression in the Soviet Union* (Palgrave, Basingstoke, 2003); Boris Starkov, "Narkom Ezhov," in J. Arch Getty and Roberta Manning, eds., *Stalinist Terror: New Perspectives* (Cambridge University Press, New York, 1993), pp. 38–40; Getty and Oleg Naumov, *The Road to Terror: Stalin and the Self-Destruction of the Bolsheviks, 1932–1939* (Yale University Press, New Haven, 1999), pp. 527–9.

[3] GARF, f. 5451, o. 22, d. 72, "Stenogramma sobraniia profaktiva gor. Moskvy po voprosu o resheniiakh VII Plenuma VTsSPS," l. 37.

[4] "O meropriiatiiakh po uporiadocheniiu trudovoi distsiplinu," *Pravda*, December 29, 1938, p. 1. The decree stipulated that workers who were absent more than once in a single month or more than twenty minutes late without a valid reason would be fired and evicted from factory housing. See Donald Filtzer, *Soviet Workers and Stalinist Industrialization: The Formation of Modern Soviet Production Relations, 1928–1941* (M. E. Sharpe, Armonk, NY, 1986), pp. 233–4.

[5] GARF, f. 5451, o. 43, d. 91, "Dorogoi tovarishch Stalin!," l. 62.

resume their role in promoting productivity, party leaders had to quell the fires that raged below.

In spring 1939, union and party leaders stealthily reversed the campaign for union democracy. The Moscow party committee called a joint meeting of heads of the *partkomy* and factory committees. Shvernik, the head of the VTsSPS, explained that the Moscow party committee would "oversee" the upcoming union elections. New rules abolished direct elections. Instead, workers would vote for "electors," who would in turn select candidates in consultation with the *partkom* and the factory committee. Workers would not be permitted to add independent candidates to the list. The unions now had two tasks: elections and the "fulfillment and overfulfillment" of the plan. Every union had to reorient itself to enforce labor discipline and increase productivity. Trial elections for the factory committees would be held in two or three workplaces. Based on this experience, other workplaces would begin the process. The districts gave out careful instructions: elections were to be tightly linked to campaigns to increase productivity. Members of the factory committees would account for their activities to the workers. Shvernik provided clear topic headings for the account, and explained how factory committee members were to answer questions from the workers.

Workers were not directly informed of the shift in policy. The accounting meetings, the prelude to elections, drew thousands of workers, still inspired by the union democracy campaign of 1937. In the giant Stalin motor vehicle factory, almost 26,000 workers (of a workforce of 40,000) came to lively meetings, which lasted for hours. They sharply questioned the factory committee about housing, poor-quality output, the absence of work gloves, and consumption. In some places, workers accused union officials of wrecking and posed sharp questions they could not answer. In the engine depot of the Moscow-Savelovsk railroad, workers protested the new norms, stoppages, and wage decreases. Demanding that the union line committee fix the problem, they slyly inquired, "Perhaps there has been some kind of wrecking?" But the days of unbridled rank-and-file criticism were over.[6] The 1939 union elections, carefully managed from beginning to end by the Party, would bring no surprises from the workers.

Shvernik was at pains to disguise the new role of the *partkomy* and electors in controlling the elections. He overheard a group of workers leaving an election meeting talking among themselves: "Everything was

---

[6] GARF, f. 5451, o. 23, d. 22, "Stenogramma partiinogo i profsoiuznogo aktiva g. Moskvy o khode vyborov profsoiuznykh organov," ll. 37, 1–92.

fine, but when they began to discuss the candidates, they put forth their own." "Yes," another replied. "They already had a list. This means they decided it beforehand." Shvernik counseled union officials to prepare a list of candidates in advance, but then to instruct the electors to present their lists as individuals.[7] In other words, officials were instructed to disguise the fact that voting by list, a practice banned in 1937, was reinstituted. The campaign for union democracy had been linked at its inception to democratic national elections to the Supreme Soviet. The ill-fated experiments in democracy were also twinned in their demise. Shvernik noted that Moscow party officials had decided to abolish direct union elections based on their experience with elections to the Supreme Soviet. *Profdemokratiia* – union democracy – the great rallying cry of 1937, was dead.

Conditions worsened as party leaders began preparing for war. Fuel and food shortages wracked the country. The VTsSPS was inundated with letters from union leaders pleading for help. The head of the Union of Iron Ore Miners in the Krivorozhskii basin begged Shvernik to send coal to heat the freezing dormitories and communal baths. The head of the Union of Bath, Laundry, and Hairdressing Workers noted that the public baths in Omsk had closed for lack of fuel. Only ten workers could cut wood on the plot allotted because of a shortage of warm clothing. The temperature in the baths was 40 degrees below zero, and the pipes had burst. Public baths in Gorky and Moscow were also on the verge of closing. Bread lines were everywhere. Devoid of solutions to seemingly intractable problems, union activists begged the VTsSPS and union central committee officials to send food or fuel, visit the shops, and tell them what to do.[8] Workers once again tightened their belts, and the Soviet people readied themselves for war.

Repression did not end with Ezhov's removal. In June 1940, a new decree criminalized quitting and absenteeism. Leaving a job without permission of the director became punishable by two to four months in prison; absence or lateness without a valid reason, by up to six months

---

[7] GARF, f. 5451, o. 23, d. 23, "Stenogramma soveshchaniia predsedatelei moskovskikh oblastnykh komitetov soiuzov po voprosu o vyborakh fabrichno-zavodskikh i mestnykh komitetov," ll. 63–64.

[8] GARF, f. 5451, o. 43, d. 101, "Sekretariu VTsSPS tov. Shverniku, N. M.," l. 393; GARF, f. 5451, o. 22, d. 72, "Stenogramma sobraniia profaktiva gor. Moskvy po voprosu o resheniiakh VII Plenuma VTsSPS," ll. 1–37; GARF, f. 5451, o. 22, d. 82, "Dokladnaia zapiska," "Narodnomu komissaru putei soobshcheniia tov. Kaganovichu," "V prezidium VTsSPS. Lichno tov. Shverniku," ll. 2, 15, 29–30.

of corrective labor at the existing place of work with a 25 percent deduction in salary. The working day was extended by up to two hours, but wage rates and salaries remained the same. The decree resulted in more than 2 million convictions.[9] Local judges, drawing on the political experience of the terror, organized show trials of errant workers. In Moscow's Krasnaia Roza textile factory, a district judge organized a show trial of a woman worker who was late to work. The woman lived twenty miles outside Moscow. Every day, she walked more than a mile with her two small children to the railroad, boarded a train to Moscow, and left the children in a daycare center far from her own shop. She appeared at the trial with her children, and the judge took her case at 11:00 that night. The children and their mother wept through the entire proceedings. She was sentenced to four months of compulsory labor with a deduction of 15 percent of her wage. Unable to return home until well after midnight, she was late for work again the next day. Another woman worker from a textile factory in Iaroslavl was tried for leaving work without permission after she received a letter that her elderly mother was ill. Six hundred workers attended her trial. She, too, cried through the trial. Sentenced to three months, she was placed under guard and taken off to prison. A huge crowd of workers, shouting against the injustice of the sentence, accompanied her to the prison gates. Shvernik wrote a furious letter to the commissar of justice, demanding an end to show trials of absentee workers.[10] But convictions continued. From 1940 to 1952, 17 million people were convicted of violating laws aimed at strengthening labor discipline, of which 3.9 million were sentenced to detention. These errant workers now comprised the majority of people sentenced.[11]

Repression, which began as a series of surgical strikes against "terrorists," had broadened to include former oppositionists, faithful party members, and large social and national groups suspected of political disloyalty. To counter the threat of "terrorists," the Stalinist leadership had eliminated civil liberties, empowered the police, and undermined the rule

---

[9] Filtzer, *Soviet Workers and Stalinist Industrialization*, pp. 233–6; Khlevniuk, *The History of the Gulag*, p. 205.

[10] GARF, f. 5451, o. 43, d. 83, "Narodnomu komissaru iustitsii SSSR tov. Rychkovu, E. M., Prokuroru SSSR tov. Pankrat'evu, M. I.," ll. 216–216ob.

[11] J. Arch Getty, Gabor Rittersporn, and Viktor Zemskov, "Victims of the Soviet Penal System in the Pre-War Years: A First Approach on the Basis of Archival Evidence," *American Historical Review*, 98, 4 (October, 1993), pp. 1033–4; Filtzer, *Soviet Workers and Stalinist Industrialization*, pp. 234–6. On the postwar period, see Filtzer, *Soviet Workers and Late Stalinism* (Cambridge University Press, Cambridge, 2002).

of law. Eventually, methods of repression were applied to workers as well, the very group that the revolution had sought to empower. Ordinary people participated actively in the hunt for hidden "enemies" and "terrorists," and ordinary people filled the prisons and the camps.

This book began with the words of a miner, and perhaps it is fitting that it should end in the same way. In 1940, a young coal miner wrote to Stalin to protest the trials of workers for violations of labor discipline. He raised the question of whether repression was an effective means for building a free and just society. He wrote, "Vyshinskii says that trials are a way to reeducate those who do not understand and are difficult to reason with. They decided to introduce the trial to make the masses self-aware and to introduce wartime discipline. Now we have a population of 193 million. In the future, we will see these horrific trials carried out, and anyone, any random person, will be prosecuted... What will happen, Iosif Vissarionovich, if we prosecute 100 million people? Where will this end?"[12] Stalin did not reply to the young miner's question, although his union and the district party committee, informed of the letter, did. They began gathering evidence against him.

---

[12] GARF, f. 5451, o. 43, d. 91, "G. B. Antratsit. Shakhta no. 15. Obshchezhitie no. 10, kom. no. 2. I. M. Sekarkovskii," "Predsedatel'iu TsK Profsoiuze rabochikh kamennougol'noi prom. Donbassa," ll. 96–98, 103–102. The young miner's letter to Stalin received an extraordinary amount of attention: it was forwarded to the VTsSPS, from the VTsSPS to the head of the Union of Coal Miners, and from the union's head to a union instructor, who undertook an extensive investigation of its author, and sent it on to the district party committee, with a request to organize a lecture on absenteeism for the miners.

Index

Abolin, A. K., 25, 26, 38, 139, 141, 169
abortion decree of 1936, 138, 139
Agranov, Ia. S., 57
Agureev, 219
All Union Central Council of Unions. *See* VTsSPS
Andreev, A. A., 111, 114, 115, 124, 125, 128, 169
Andreev, V. M., 100, 101, 103
Arkus, G. M., 71
Arnol'd, V. V., 100, 105, 106, 109
Artiukhina, A. V., 139, 155–58

Baburkin, 164
Bakaev, I. P., 57, 70
Barkan, B. N., 180, 185
Basin, N. A., 180
Belakovskaia, 181, 182
Beria, L. P., 170, 256
Berman-Iurin, K. B., 71
Birman, S. P., 104
Black Hundreds, 214, 215
Bogdanovich, 74
Bogoliubskii, 75, 76, 233, 242
Boguslavskii, M. S., 100, 105, 106
Boldak, 182
Borisova, 217
Bregman, S. L., 139, 140, 141, 149, 174, 190
Bubnov, 214, 215, 235

Bukharin, N. I., 37, 48, 71, 79, 84, 97, 107, 108, 110, 111, 124, 165, 256
Bundists, 199, 207, 208
bureaucracy, 7, 11, 37, 38, 47, 110, 126, 134, 135, 142, 147, 151, 168
Bykhovskii, M., 71
Bystritskii, 217

canteens, 13, 18, 21, 24, 25, 26, 29, 39, 133
Cheliabinsk, 23, 99, 145
Chislov, 136
Civil War, 45, 60, 82, 119, 181, 199, 207, 208, 216, 224
collective contract, 16, 37, 39, 40, 49
collective farms, 21, 30, 45, 76, 105, 118, 125, 167, 210, 224
collectivization, 7, 13, 23, 29, 30, 44, 45, 48, 49, 62, 78, 85, 108, 210, 253
Comintern (Communist International), 71
Communist Party of the Soviet Union (bolshevik), 6, 7, 8, 13, 14, 16, 17, 28, 35, 36, 41, 47–49, 58, 80, 85, 160, 163, 164, 172, 179, 191, 219, 255
    Central Committee, 16, 25, 37, 38, 57, 60, 63, 65, 69, 70, 72, 79, 80, 85, 86, 88, 89, 92, 99, 104, 115, 135, 166, 179, 199, 201, 212, 256

Communist Party (*cont.*)
  Central Committee plenums, 48,
    63, 64, 69, 95, 96, 109–26, 129,
    133, 134, 149, 161, 166–71, 189,
    192, 196, 197, 200, 201, 204,
    243, 254, 256
  Central Control Commission, 16, 38
  congresses, 39
  democracy, 118–20, 133
  district committees, 44, 59, 86–91,
    92, 95, 120, 152, 216, 238, 241,
    244, 254, 261
  leaders, 5, 6, 7, 10, 12, 13, 14, 16,
    18, 19, 24, 28, 32, 33, 35, 56, 57,
    65, 85, 92, 95, 99, 117, 119, 126,
    128, 129, 148, 151, 158, 179
  Leningrad committee, 1, 55, 58,
    110, 119
  Moscow committee, 60, 73, 86, 87,
    88, 89, 90, 92, 107, 109, 111,
    120, 121, 124, 125, 166, 225,
    244, 258, 259
  party cards, 25, 46, 58, 60, 65, 69,
    87, 113, 123, 127, 208, 230, 238
  party committees, 8, 12, 21, 25, 42,
    47–51, 56, 59, 60, 61, 62, 63, 65,
    66, 69, 71, 72, 74, 86, 90, 91, 92,
    95, 114, 118, 119, 120, 121, 144,
    179, 180, 181, 193, 195, 204–17,
    218, 220, 222, 223, 225, 226,
    228, 234, 235, 236, 237, 244,
    252, 254, 255, 257, 258
  Party Control Commission, 12, 57,
    63, 90, 111, 120, 121, 128, 140,
    166, 173, 174
  Politburo, 15, 57, 59, 69, 97, 98,
    111, 126, 169, 209, 243
  political education, 11, 58, 62, 66,
    117, 123, 221–25
  proverka and *obmen*, 65, 67, 68,
    71, 72, 86–91, 92, 124, 254
  purges, 2, 65
  rank and file, 7, 9, 10, 12, 44–47,
    49, 57, 60, 62, 71, 77, 87, 92, 96,
    111, 117, 118, 119, 120, 126, 127,
    128, 129, 149, 204, 245, 254

  regional committees, 25, 86, 92,
    114, 115, 116, 119, 164, 173, 179,
    180, 185
  shop committees, 206
  Zhenotdel (Women's Department),
    60, 156, 173
communists, 1, 16, 27, 30, 31, 34, 42,
    45, 46, 60, 74, 108, 117, 160,
    209, 228, 234, 235, 237, 244
  foreign, 5, 56, 68, 69, 71
Constitution of 1936, 105, 115–18,
    137, 223
consumption, 14, 19, 20–24, 25, 29,
    31, 142, 258
cooperatives, 14, 21, 22, 42
corruption, 21, 37, 67, 135, 151, 153,
    154, 158, 160, 163, 174, 183, 184,
    186, 187, 195, 197
Council of People's Commissars, 48,
    111, 155, 157, 175
courts, 65, 127, 159, 197, 256
  Military Kollegiia, 68, 100, 105
  Supreme Court, 84, 98

David, F., 71
death penalty, 80, 81, 82, 83, 92
democracy, 8, 11, 35, 37, 47, 96, 110,
    111, 115, 117, 118–24, 127, 128,
    129, 130, 134, 135, 136, 140, 143,
    146, 149, 169, 178, 179, 185,
    186, 187, 188, 189, 190, 191,
    192, 254, 259
directors, 12, 19, 24, 27, 29, 43, 70,
    73, 74, 77, 88, 100, 101, 102,
    104, 138, 143, 145, 147, 150,
    164, 171, 176, 187, 192, 194,
    205, 206, 214–15, 217, 218, 219,
    224, 225, 227, 228, 229, 233,
    234, 235, 236, 237, 238, 239, 240,
    241, 242, 243, 245, 246, 259
Dnepropetrovsk, 25, 30, 104
Donbas, 22, 42, 43, 145
Dorokhov, V. A., 165
Dreitser, E. A., 70
Drobnis, Ia. N., 100, 101, 105, 106,
    107

Egorova, E. N., 141
Eideman, R. P., 175, 177, 216
Eikhe, R. I., 116, 119, 120, 121, 128
elections, 6, 8, 96, 110, 112, 115, 119,
    121, 127, 128, 129, 134, 135, 136,
    141, 158, 160, 161, 168, 188,
    254, 258
  Communist Party, 118–20
  soviets, 115–18, 121, 259
  unions, 126, 142, 146–51, 158, 163,
    188, 189, 190, 258–59
engineers, 9, 11, 18, 83, 96, 98, 99,
    100, 101, 103, 106, 107, 112,
    114, 127, 145, 211, 213, 217,
    218, 224, 227, 228, 229, 232,
    234, 238, 241, 246
enterprises
  1905 factory, 45
  AMO, 59
  Artem mine, 24
  Bolshevik factory, 81
  Bromlei factory, 215
  Bronitskii factory, 22
  Central Urals copper works, 107
  Diat'kovskii Khrustal'nyi factory,
    152
  Dinamo, 59, 141, 204, 206, 213,
    217–19, 222, 223, 224, 225, 226,
    227–28, 236–37, 243–44, 245
  Dzerzhinskii factory, 82
  Dzerzhinskii works, 30
  Elektrosila, 31
  Elektrostal, 211
  Elektrozavod, 137, 144
  Factory No. 2, 91
  Factory No. 24, 91
  Factory No. 4, 91
  Factory No. 45, 30
  Factory No. 46, 80, 84
  Factory No. 95, 82
  Frunze factory, 16, 32
  Izhorskii works, 29, 43
  Kaganovich factory, 71
  Kalibr factory, 82, 121
  Kamenskii factory, 46
  Kauchuk factory, 29

Kolomenskii machine building
    works, 11
Kombin factory, 31
Kommunar factory, 33
Kompressor factory, 45
Kozitskii factory, 47
Krasnaia Roza factory, 260
Krasnaia Talka factory, 20, 21, 33
Krasnoe Sormovo factory, 47
Krasnoural'skii Copper Smelting
    Works, 141
Krasnyi Bogatyr factory, 66, 69
Krasnyi Fakel factory, 42, 152
Krasnyi Proletarii factory, 206, 220,
    224, 225
Krasnyi Putilovets factory, 28, 42,
    43
Krasnyi Tekstil'shchik factory, 144
Krasnyi Tkach factory, 146
Krupskaia factory, 34
Kuznetsstroi, 22
Lezhnevskii factory, 42
Liebknicht mine, 150
Likernovodochnyi factory, 204,
    206, 208–09, 215–17, 226, 239
Linen Factory No. 6, 144
Liuberetskii agricultural machine
    building factory, 32
Liudinovskii factory, 44
Malenkov factory, 42, 83
Marti factory, 40, 45
Metal Factory No. 4, 21
Molotov Motor Vehicle Works,
    170
Nikopol'skii rolling mill, 42
Nogin factory, 34, 84
Paris Commune factory, 46
Petrovskii iron and steel works,
    25–26, 45, 104
Pravda printing factory, 39
Proletarskii Trud factory, 30, 143
Provskii factory, 43
Red October agricultural machine
    building factory, 24
Red October machine building
    plant, 25

enterprises (*cont.*)
  Serp i Molot factory, 59, 66, 72–77,
    205, 206, 210, 211–13, 214–15,
    223, 224, 225, 229–36, 241–43
  Shcherbakova factory, 29
  Sormovo shipyards, 42
  Spetsavtomashina, 121
  Stalin motor vehicle factory, 258
  Stankolit factory, 103
  Trekhgornaia Manufaktura, 60–63,
    205, 206, 210–11, 219, 225, 226,
    227, 241, 246
  Tul'skii factory, 22
  Ural'skii machine building factory,
    194
  Vishkhimzavod, 43
  Voroshilov factory, 34
  Voroshilov factory (Druzhkova), 35
  Zhdanov factory, 160
  Zinoviev factory, 21
  Zlatoustroi, 22
Enukidze, A. S., 64, 65, 91
Esterman, I. S., 70
Evdokimov, G. E., 55, 57, 70, 79
Evdokimov, K. G., 180
Evreinov, N. N., 38, 138, 139, 140,
    141
Ezhov, N. I., 1, 6, 12, 57, 59, 63, 64,
    65, 67, 68, 69, 70, 91, 98, 104,
    120, 122, 124, 125, 172, 196,
    252, 253, 256, 259
Ezhovshchina, 1, 2

factories, 7, 8, 10, 13, 15, 16, 17, 18,
    20, 21, 22, 24, 27, 30, 31, 33, 35,
    36, 42, 45, 47, 49, 50, 56, 57, 59,
    63, 67, 72, 73, 77, 80, 86, 90, 91,
    92, 104, 109, 117, 118, 121, 126,
    135, 137, 143, 144, 145, 148,
    149, 157, 161, 171, 183, 196,
    205, 206, 207, 210, 216, 225,
    226, 236, 245, 246, 252, 253, 254,
    257. *See also* enterprises
factory newspapers, 104, 160, 205,
    223, 230, 234, 240, 243, 244,
    255

famine, 20, 23, 25, 26, 30, 50, 98
fascism, 58, 59, 68, 71, 78, 79, 81, 84,
    101, 102, 106, 108, 109, 123,
    129, 158, 257
Fedotov, I. K., 70
Filatov, 241–43
Fisenko, F. I., 181
five-year plan, 30, 45
  first, 13, 14, 20, 31, 36, 48, 49, 78,
    115, 117, 126, 229
  second, 19, 29, 115
Fokin, 61, 62
Fomin, A. S., 213, 214, 219
food. *See* consumption, shortages
foremen, 7, 19, 28, 35, 66, 73, 74,
    75, 76, 77, 84, 99, 158, 239,
    246

Gamarnik, Ia. B., 121, 167, 170
Geche, 209
Gel'perin, N., 112, 113
Gil'burg, 125, 136, 165, 176
Gorky, 68, 70, 71, 259
"Great Terror," 1, 2, 7
Gringauz, 220
Gul'bis, 208, 209
Gurevich, Kh., 71

Hitler, A., 8, 71, 108
housing, 24–27, 40, 63, 73, 77, 103,
    104, 107, 113, 135, 136, 138, 142,
    145, 146, 152, 158, 161, 183,
    200, 225, 229, 253, 258. *See also*
    living conditions

Iagoda, G. G., 68, 69, 70, 98
Iakovlev, Ia. A., 111, 120, 121, 122,
    128, 166, 174
Iakovlev, M. N., 70, 121
Iarkin, 210, 211
Iaroslavl and province, 24
Iasvoin, 219, 228, 237
industrial accidents, 2, 11, 12, 27–28,
    38, 40, 74, 95, 96, 97, 98, 99,
    103, 104, 107, 113, 127, 133, 134,
    135, 142, 144, 145, 146, 152,

158, 159, 166, 171, 183, 184,
186, 187, 200, 205, 226, 227,
230, 232, 234, 240, 242, 245,
246, 253, 255
industrial sectors
aviation, 195, 232
chemical, 105, 107
construction, 22, 113
garment, 27, 31
lumber, 187
metallurgy, 25, 27, 113, 229, 232
mining, 17, 18, 19, 27, 50–51, 100,
105, 107
oil, 27
porcelain, 27
printing, 27
railroads, 27, 105, 107, 184, 246
textile, 18, 21–22, 27, 35, 42, 44,
155–58, 173
industrialization, 7, 10, 13, 14, 17, 29,
33, 37, 38, 40, 41, 44, 46, 49, 76,
77, 92, 103, 107, 108, 114, 116,
125, 158, 161, 221, 228, 252
industry, 10, 14
heavy, 31, 32, 39, 41, 42, 113,
150
light, 19, 23, 31, 32, 41, 113, 155
Ivanov, 164
Ivanovo and province, 20, 21, 26, 34,
35, 41, 43, 46, 152, 173, 184,
197
Izotov, 73

Kabakov, I. D., 116, 128
Kabarava, K. A., 180
Kaganovich, L. M., 37, 55, 70, 71, 98,
126, 167, 168, 169, 244
Kaganovich, M. L., 193
Kaiurov, 136
Kalygina, A. S., 117, 128
Kamenev, L. B., 47, 48, 57, 60, 61, 64,
65, 68, 70, 71, 72, 78, 79, 81, 82,
83, 85, 97, 107
Kapluna, 60, 61, 62, 63
Karklin, 180
Katyshev, 221

Kemerovo, 28, 95, 96, 97, 98, 99,
100, 102, 107, 112, 254
Khaliavin, I. A., 182
Khorikov, 243
Khrushchev, N. S., 56, 109, 111, 121,
166
Khvedchen, 218
Khvostov, 62
Kiev, 185, 191, 211, 212, 213
Kirdianov, F. F., 180
Kirov, S. M., 1, 6, 55, 57, 58, 59, 62,
63, 79, 253
assassination of, 6, 55–58, 59, 60,
62, 63, 64, 65, 66, 69, 72, 80, 82,
91, 92, 95, 100, 124, 129, 165,
253, 256
Kiselev, A. S., 175
Kliupov, 219
Kniazev, I. A., 106
Kolotilov, N., 136, 173, 174
Komsomol, 46, 83, 84, 114, 193, 197,
204, 211, 212, 218, 233
Konstant, E., 71
kooptatsiia, 118, 119, 120, 129, 135,
140, 160, 164, 172, 255
Korneev, 218
Korneeva, 218
Korostelin, 237–38
Korytnyi, S. Z., 86, 87, 89, 90, 91
Kosior, S. V., 55, 70, 117, 119, 128
Kotliar, S. O., 163, 175–79, 191
Kotov, V. A., 125, 136, 166
Kovalenko, I. E., 100, 101, 103
Kozmin, 196
Krasnovskii, 171
Kreitsberg, 218
Kremlin plot, 63–65, 91
Krivikhin, V. N., 179
Kuibyshev, V. V., 15
Kukuevskii, 164
Kulikov, M. M., 60
Kulikova, 215–16
Kuptsov, A. A., 181
Kurov, M. A., 100, 101
Kuznetsk basin (Kuzbas), 97, 100,
101, 103, 105, 106

labor
  discipline, 37, 38, 40, 76, 85, 237,
    239, 258, 260, 261
  productivity, 14, 15, 17–20, 21, 37,
    39, 40, 85, 99, 258
  safety, 27–28, 96, 104, 127, 135,
    145, 152, 154, 159, 184, 205
  shortage, 15, 107
  turnover, 12, 16, 21, 26, 41, 73,
    107, 143, 158
labor camps, 2, 68, 164, 261
labor legislation, 76, 195, 257, 260
Lagodinskii, M. G., 172
Larkin, P. M., 210, 212
left opposition, 55, 56, 59, 61, 72, 89,
  90, 91, 97, 106, 140, 211, 213,
  221, 253
Lenin, V. I., 28, 31, 79, 83, 84, 221,
  222, 223
Leningrad and province, 1, 18, 19, 20,
  22, 28, 29, 31, 32, 39, 42, 43, 44,
  47, 55, 58, 59, 91, 110, 119, 139,
  145, 171, 172, 176, 177, 182, 190
Leonenko, N. S., 100, 101, 102, 103
Lerner, E. O., 199
Liashchenko, I. T., 100, 101, 102
Liubimov, I. E., 155
Liushkov, G. S., 55
living conditions, 12, 24–27, 76, 113,
  134, 137, 141, 146, 152, 156, 160,
  161
Livshits, P., 71, 106, 107
Lominadze, V. V., 91
Lozovskii, S. A., 183
Lur'e, M. I., 71
Lur'e, N. L., 71

Magnitogorsk, 97
Makints, S. A., 181
malnutrition, 23–34
Mamardashvili, M. N., 181
managers, 3, 5, 10, 14, 15, 16, 17, 18,
  19, 21, 22, 28, 31, 36, 40, 43, 44,
  60, 66, 73, 76, 77, 96, 97, 98, 99,
  101, 102, 103, 104, 106, 112,
  113, 114, 115, 127, 129, 138, 142,
  145, 147, 151, 158, 159, 161, 185,

194, 195, 197, 206, 217, 218,
  221, 225, 227, 228, 229, 230,
  234, 235, 236–39, 241, 245, 246,
  252, 254, 255, 256
Marek, 219
Margolin, 177, 178, 204
Margolina, 219
Margulis, A. Ia., 181
markets, 14, 21, 23, 45, 229
Marmorshtein, L. V., 234
Mashkevich, M. M., 181
mass operations, 5, 6, 9, 209, 256
Mekhonoshina, L. A., 181
Menis, Ia. I., 218, 223
Mensheviks, 44, 64, 98, 169, 215
Meshcheriakov, D. N., 172
Mikhailov, 233
Mikoian, A. I., 116
Minsk, 33, 34, 171
Mironov, 241–43
Molchanov, G. A., 69
Molotov, V. M., 106, 111, 113–14,
  123, 127, 157, 168, 169, 170
Mongert, 239
Moscow and province, 11, 15, 20, 25,
  27, 29, 30, 32, 35, 42, 43, 44, 45,
  46, 58, 59, 60, 66, 73, 77, 82, 83,
  85, 89, 91, 100, 107, 112, 113,
  115, 121, 122, 137, 139, 140,
  141, 142, 143, 144, 153, 154, 155,
  166, 171, 172, 176, 177, 178,
  184, 206, 211, 214, 258, 259,
  260
Moskatov, P. G., 141, 155, 156, 157,
  158, 183, 193
Motorin, M. N., 70
Mrachkovsky, S. V., 70
Muralov, N. I., 100, 105, 106

Nazism, 8
Nifetov, 188, 189, 190, 191
Nikolaev, L. V., 55, 56, 57, 62, 91
Nikolaev, P. S., 180
Nikolaeva, K. I., 141, 173, 174, 175
Nizhnii Novgorod and province, 47
NKVD, 1, 6, 12, 44, 55, 57, 58, 59,
  62, 64, 65, 68, 69, 71, 79, 84, 90,

91, 92, 96, 98, 99, 113, 114, 120,
135, 137, 140, 144, 151, 163, 164,
165, 167, 171, 172, 173, 174,
178, 179, 180, 181, 182, 183,
185, 186, 187, 188, 190, 191,
192, 194, 198, 201, 205, 206,
219, 227, 229, 235, 237, 238,
239, 240, 245, 246, 247, 255,
256, 257
Norkin, B. O., 106
norming and norms, 14, 15, 16, 17,
18, 19–20, 23, 29, 38, 40, 41, 42,
43, 46, 77, 99, 107, 155, 157,
159, 161, 213, 258
Noskov, I. I., 100, 101, 102
Novosibirsk, 99, 100

Odessa and province, 24, 42,
186
Ol'berg, V. P., 68, 71, 91
oppositionism and oppositionists, 5,
8, 13, 44, 47–49, 50, 55, 57, 58,
59–64, 65, 66, 67, 68, 69, 70, 72,
78, 79, 88, 89, 90–92, 95, 96, 99,
100, 101, 106, 108, 111, 119,
122, 124, 126, 127–30, 134, 135,
149, 151, 153, 159, 160, 163, 164,
171, 183, 184, 198, 199, 200,
207, 208, 211–14, 221, 240, 241,
253–54, 260
Ordzhonikidze, G. K., 55, 70, 104,
112–13, 228
Orlov, 75, 76
Osiannikova, 195, 196
Osoaviakhim, 175, 177, 216

Panin, M. A., 50, 51
Pantsulaia, A. A., 181
passports, 26, 50, 84, 100, 209
Pavlov, 210
Pavlova, E. E., 172
peasants, 3, 13, 20, 23, 26, 45, 47, 73,
76, 78, 116, 138, 209, 217, 221,
253, 256
    kulaks, 5, 26, 30, 61, 62, 75, 78,
    115, 116, 117, 180, 209, 210,
    212, 216, 221, 246, 256

migrants, 13, 24, 25, 29, 30, 49, 50,
61, 76, 85, 253, 254
People's Commissariat of Agriculture,
98
People's Commissariat of
Communications, 171, 172
People's Commissariat of Heavy
Industry, 77, 97
People's Commissariat of Heavy
Machine Construction, 108
People's Commissariat of Internal
Affairs. *See* NKVD
People's Commissariat of Justice, 98
People's Commissariat of Labor, 38,
48, 50, 108, 124, 125, 135, 141,
166, 167, 171
People's Commissariat of Light
Industry, 155, 158
People's Commissariat of State Farms,
98
People's Commissariat of Transport,
166, 172
Peshekhonov, I. A., 99, 100, 101
Pestov, 188, 189, 190
Piatakov, G. L., 84, 97, 100, 105,
106–09, 113, 133
Pikel, R. V., 70
Pilinenok, 187
Piterina, M. M., 180
Pivanov, 164
Pogrebnoi, 193, 194
Polonskii, V. I., 38, 111, 128, 139,
166–72
Polozkov, 240
Polukarov, 233
Postyshev, P. P., 55, 70
prices, 14–17, 20–21, 23, 27, 29, 34,
39, 40, 43, 46, 49, 63
procuracy and procurators, 65, 69,
79, 82, 97, 98, 127, 145, 195
production, 13, 16, 112
    plans, 12, 25, 27, 36, 73, 77, 99,
    155, 225, 231, 232
    problems, 8, 72–74, 75, 205, 227,
    229, 233, 234, 235, 245, 246
Prohkorov, 218
Prokof'ev, G. E., 68

purges, 8, 37, 38, 65, 66, 86, 88, 89,
    108, 110, 111, 119, 120–26, 129,
    136, 140, 163, 164, 166, 171,
    172, 179, 185, 198, 199, 201,
    211, 241, 245, 247, 252, 253
Pushin, G. E., 106

Radek, K. B., 80, 105, 106, 107, 108,
    109
Radianskii, 140
Raevskii, G. A., 181
Rataichak, S. A., 106, 176
rationing, 13, 17, 20, 22–23, 25, 27,
    28, 31, 33, 35, 41, 42, 43, 44
Reingold, I. I., 70, 79
revisionism, 3, 6
revolution, 1, 21, 28, 31, 46, 60, 65,
    81, 82, 83, 84, 85, 119, 144, 166,
    183, 208, 211, 214, 215, 218,
    221, 224, 239, 261
Riabov, A. N., 180
rightists, 38, 48, 56, 71, 72, 79, 84,
    90, 107, 108, 119, 124, 125, 136,
    165, 166, 167, 171, 253
Riutin Platform, 48, 108, 124
Riutin, M. N., 48, 124
Romanov, 219, 242
Rostov, 23, 164
Rubel, 188, 189, 190
Rychkov, N. M., 105
Rykov, A. I., 37, 48, 71, 79, 80, 84,
    107, 110, 124, 165, 256

Sagaidak, D., 75, 223, 229–35, 241
Savateev, V. G., 180
Scherbakov, 181
Schetchikova, V. G., 224
Sedov, L., 100, 106, 107
Serebriakov, L. P., 105, 106
Shadabudinov, 11, 12
Sheinin, 219
Shestov, A. A., 100, 101, 105, 106,
    107
Shlykov, M. G., 180
Shmerling, 171
Shmidt, D. A., 71
Shmidt, V. V., 48, 124, 135, 141, 167

shock work, 17–18, 42
shock workers, 17, 34, 37, 40, 42,
    148, 199
Sholmov, A. P., 190, 191
shop
    conflicts, 77, 225, 226, 228–33
    heads, 10, 60, 75, 192, 206, 213,
        218, 225, 227, 228, 233, 235,
        237, 241, 242, 246, 253, 254, 255
shortages, 13, 14, 20, 21, 24, 28–36,
    41, 42, 45, 103, 116, 142, 183,
    184, 200, 225, 253, 259
    food, 20–24
Shtikling, E. P., 100, 101
Shubin, F. I., 100, 101, 102
Shvernik, N. M., 38, 111, 125–26, 128,
    133, 136–37, 138, 139, 141, 151,
    161, 165, 166, 167, 168, 169, 170,
    171, 174, 176, 177, 183, 187,
    192, 194, 195, 258, 259, 260
Sinchuk, I. I., 181
Smilga, I. T., 79
Smirnov, I. N., 48, 70
Socialist Revolutionaries, 44, 169,
    181, 199, 207
Sokol, 241
Sokol, Ia. I., 76, 211–13
Sokolnikov, G. Ia., 79, 84, 105, 108,
    109
Sokolov, D. N., 181
Sokolov, P. P., 181
Somov, A. I., 73, 75, 76, 231, 235, 241
soviets, 8, 110, 115–18, 142, 175
    Central Executive Committee, 64,
        175
    Supreme Soviet, 6
Stakhanov, A., 18, 99
Stakhanovism and Stakhanovites, 18,
    69, 85, 99, 102, 146, 148, 199
Stalin, I. V., 4, 5, 6, 7, 8, 16, 30, 31,
    37, 39, 44, 47–49, 55, 57, 58, 59,
    60, 63, 64, 67–71, 72, 77–81, 82,
    83, 85, 88, 91, 95, 98, 102, 104,
    105, 106, 108–09, 110, 111, 113,
    114, 115, 117, 119, 120, 121–24,
    125, 126, 127–30, 134, 137, 149,
    151, 159, 166, 167, 168, 170,

171, 172, 178, 180, 189, 191,
192, 193, 195, 197, 198, 221,
222, 243, 244, 252, 253, 254, 256,
257, 261
Stalingrad, 23, 25
Stalinsk (Novokuznetsk), 97
Starichkov, 204, 223, 224, 228, 244
state farms, 125, 210
state loans, 36–45, 46, 49, 66
State Planning Commission (Gosplan),
15
state stores, 14, 20, 23
Steklov, M. N., 181
Stepanov, M. P., 155, 156
Stepanov, P. F., 73, 74, 75, 76, 77, 205,
215–35, 236, 237, 242, 243
stoppages, 15, 76, 113, 137, 150, 155,
156, 230, 258
Strievskii, K. K., 180, 193
strikes, 8, 27, 36, 41, 42, 43, 44, 89,
173, 213
Stroilov, M. S., 100, 101, 105, 106,
109
Supreme Council of the National
Economy (VSNKh), 19, 36
Sverdlovsk, 116, 188, 190, 191

Taganrog, 111, 114
Teikovo, 21
Terent'ev, K. K., 180
terrorism and terrorists, 56, 57, 58,
59, 63, 64, 67, 68, 70, 71, 72, 74,
77, 80, 81, 82, 91, 92, 97, 100,
106, 107, 123, 124, 260, 261
Ter-Vaganian, V. A., 70
Tolchinskii, 218
Tomskii, M. P., 36, 37, 38, 48, 71, 79,
80, 84, 85, 107, 108, 124, 125,
135, 136, 141, 166, 167, 173
Toshin, V. A., 179
totalitarianism, 2, 6
trials, 98, 127, 261
    Kemerovo trial, 96–104, 105, 106,
    112, 113, 123, 204
    Shakhty trial, 100, 101, 106
    trial of the anti-soviet bloc of
    rightists and Trotskyists, 110, 256

trial of the anti-soviet parallel
    Trotskyist center, 96, 100,
    104–09, 112, 113, 123, 176, 204,
    254
trial of the anti-soviet united
    Trotskyist-Zinovievite center, 55,
    68–71, 72, 77–80, 86, 91, 95,
    105, 107, 108, 123, 124, 164, 253
of workers, 260, 261
Trotsky, L. D., 47, 48, 60, 62, 64, 68,
    70, 78, 81, 82, 83, 84, 97, 100,
    105, 106, 108, 180, 221, 222,
    223, 224, 253, 254
Trotskyism and Trotskyists, 35, 48,
    57, 58, 59, 62, 67, 68, 70, 71, 72,
    73, 74, 77, 81, 82, 84, 86, 88–91,
    97, 98, 99, 100, 101, 102, 104,
    105, 106, 107, 109, 110, 114,
    115, 121, 122, 123, 124, 125, 136,
    140, 143, 158, 164, 165, 169,
    175, 181, 184, 193, 194, 195,
    196, 197, 200, 211–14, 218, 222,
    223, 224, 227, 228, 232, 233,
    234, 237, 238, 246, 254
Trushin, K. A., 180
Trusov, I. I., 68
Tsbal'skii, 166
Tspaev, A., 180
Tsybal'skii, 168
Turok, I. D., 106
Tynkov, 237–38

Ufa, 187
Ugarov, A. I., 119
Uglanov, N. A., 84, 107, 124, 125,
    135, 141, 167
Ukraine, 23, 25, 35, 106, 107, 117,
    119, 212
Ul'rikh, V. V., 100
Union of Bath, Laundry, and
    Hairdressing Workers, 259
Union of Canning Workers, 164
Union of Cement Workers, 145
Union of Central Cooperative
    Employees (Tsentrosoiuz), 147
Union of Coal and Shale Workers,
    152–54, 160

Union of Coal Miners, 150, 165
Union of Coal Miners and Peat
    Workers, 181
Union of Coke-Oven Workers, 125,
    136, 165, 176
Union of Construction Workers, 150
Union of Construction Workers in
    Heavy Industry, 180
Union of Cooperative Employees, 172,
    185
Union of Cotton Textile Workers, 139,
    155–58, 198
Union of Dairy Workers, 180
Union of Defense Metal Workers, 195
Union of Dining Hall Workers, 181
Union of Drivers, 172
Union of Electric Power Station
    Workers, 145
Union of Electrical Workers, 180
Union of Employees of Economic
    Institutions, 180
Union of Employees of
    Electro-Communications, 180
Union of Employees of State
    Institutions, 163, 172, 175–79
Union of Employees of the Northern
    Sea Lanes, 196
Union of Firemen, 181
Union of Fish Industry Workers, 150,
    180, 181
Union of Garment Workers, 181
Union of Glass Workers, 142, 151–52,
    160
Union of Grain Industry and Elevator
    Workers, 145, 181
Union of Heavy Machine Builders,
    180, 193
Union of Iron and Steel Workers, 37,
    181
Union of Iron Ore Miners, 181, 259
Union of Iron Ore Workers, 150
Union of Leather Workers, 22
Union of Machine Building Workers,
    37
Union of Medical Workers
    (Medsantrud), 150, 181
Union of Metal Workers, 37, 165, 166

Union of Metallurgical Workers, 145
Union of Mine Workers, 166
Union of Miners, 37
Union of Motor Vehicle Workers, 180
Union of Non Ferrous Metal Miners,
    11, 133
Union of Non Ferrous Metal Workers,
    179
Union of Oil Refinery Workers, 136,
    142, 150, 154–55, 160, 165, 180,
    181
Union of Plywood and Matches
    Workers, 187–88
Union of Political Education
    Employees, 172, 173–75, 182
Union of Porcelain Workers, 180
Union of Postal Employees, 164
Union of Press Employees, 196
Union of Primary and Middle School
    Employees, 180, 181
Union of Printers, 194
Union of Railroad and Metro
    Construction Workers, 28,
    183–84
Union of Railroad Construction
    Workers, 147
Union of Railroad Workers, 151, 163,
    181, 182, 198
Union of Retail Clerks, 257
Union of River Transport Workers,
    180
Union of Sawmill and Wood Workers,
    180
Union of Shipbuilders, 180
Union of Shoe Workers, 139, 140, 190
Union of State Farm Beet Workers,
    140
Union of State Farm Grain Workers,
    28, 185–86
Union of State Farm Meat and Dairy
    Workers, 180
Union of Timber Cutters and Floaters,
    165, 180, 188–91
Union of Tractor Industry Workers,
    180
Union of Wool, Silk, and Tricot
    Workers, 23

Union of Woolen Workers, 146
Union of Workers in Heavy Industry, 182
Union of Workers in Municipal Services and Housing Construction, 179
unions, 7, 8, 10, 11, 12, 41, 46, 96, 109, 110, 112, 126, 129, 164, 165, 166, 191, 200, 201, 255. *See also* individual unions
  campaign for *profdemokratiia*, 143, 147, 149, 152, 158, 160–61, 163, 176, 177, 178, 179, 200, 204, 254, 257, 259
  central committees, 37, 139, 141, 142, 147–48, 150, 151, 165, 167, 172
  congresses, 17, 37, 146–47, 149, 155
  democracy, 126, 161
  expulsion and reinstatement, 191–98
  factory committees, 7, 29, 31, 34, 37, 39, 46, 49, 130, 136, 137, 141, 142, 143–44, 145, 146, 147, 160, 194, 197, 214, 258
  leaders, 7, 28, 179–83, 255
  officials, 10, 11, 12, 14, 17, 18, 25, 28, 30, 32, 33, 35, 60, 134, 135, 136, 137, 140–41, 142, 144, 145, 148, 149, 158, 161, 163, 254, 257, 258, 259
  organization of, 37–38, 126
  paid staff, 38, 141, 146, 147, 150–51, 152, 169
  purge of, 37–51, 126, 183–85, 186, 201
  rank and file, 8
  regional committees, 147, 150
  role of, 36–38, 41, 160, 161
  shop committees, 7, 25, 146, 147
Urals, 13, 22, 23, 43, 107, 140, 182

Vardanian, S. Kh., 111, 114
Veinberg, G. D., 38, 39, 40, 141, 168, 169
Vikulov, 216, 239

Voltsit, 180
Voronezh, 117
Voronina, N. V., 137–39, 163, 194, 195, 197
Voroshilov, K. E., 34, 55, 64, 70, 71, 170
VTsSPS, 7, 8, 17, 18, 19, 22, 23, 25, 29, 32, 35, 36, 37, 39, 41, 44, 48, 111, 124, 125, 126, 128, 133, 134, 135, 137, 141, 142, 143, 145, 147, 149, 153, 154, 155, 157, 158, 159, 160, 161, 163, 164, 165–69, 172, 177, 178, 179, 180, 181, 182, 191, 192, 200, 201, 255, 256, 257, 259
  Bureau of Complaints, 194
  Bureau of Social Insurance, 38, 125, 135, 136, 165, 169
  Department of Labor Protection, 165, 166, 168, 171
  investigations, 143–46, 151, 153, 155, 163, 172–73, 175, 179, 183–86, 191, 196, 198–200, 201, 255
  organization, 38
  plenums, 134, 136–41, 142, 143, 147, 176, 189, 192–98, 200
  Presidium, 37, 137, 138, 139, 141
  research institutes, 169, 171–72
  Secretariat, 139, 141, 165, 173, 174, 181, 182, 183, 194
  union press, 23, 134, 137, 142, 143, 165, 185, 188, 198–200
Vyshinskii, A. Ia., 55, 68, 70, 72, 77, 78, 79, 97, 105, 106, 107, 108, 127, 129, 261

wages, 12, 13, 14, 15, 16, 17, 18, 20–51, 74, 99, 137, 144, 155–58, 253, 258
  arrears, 21, 27, 42, 43–44, 113, 142, 161
  differentials, 31, 32, 41
  enterprise funds, 25, 26, 43, 237
  national fund, 14, 15, 16, 18, 19, 38, 40
  overtime, 16, 39, 142

wages (*cont.*)
    piecework, 16, 17, 39, 155, 156
    policy toward, 14–15, 16
    rates, 16, 155–58
    scale, 15, 18, 35, 40, 41, 150
women, 3, 13, 31, 33, 34, 41, 42, 44,
    46, 76, 77, 80, 121, 137, 156, 226
workers, 3, 8, 10, 13, 14, 16, 17, 19,
    21, 22, 23, 24, 25, 27, 44, 50, 69,
    73, 74, 75, 77, 80–92, 99, 114,
    119, 120, 121, 122, 138, 206,
    209, 215, 218, 221, 223, 225,
    226, 229, 230, 233, 235, 245,
    246, 252–61
    and managers, 229, 230, 232, 233,
        236–39, 245
    political attitudes, 11, 27, 31, 35–36,
        39, 40, 44, 45, 46, 48, 50, 51, 62,
        76, 78, 91, 114, 117, 160, 211,
        222, 224, 254, 261
    as political symbols, 95, 197–98,
        201
    and prices, 13, 15–16, 43, 63
    protests, 33–34, 41–44
    resentment against officials, 3, 7, 8,
        12, 28, 32, 136, 183, 234
    response to Kirov assassination, 56,
        59–63, 80–86, 92
    response to loan campaigns, 33–36,
        66
    and unions, 12, 36, 126, 134, 137,
        138, 142, 143, 144, 149, 150–51,
        153, 158, 161, 167, 168, 176, 254,
        257, 259

    and wages, 14, 15–16, 17, 18, 19,
        20, 23, 31, 32, 41, 42, 43, 99,
        158, 191
    and wrecking, 11, 74, 96, 98, 101,
        102–04, 106, 107, 109, 113, 127,
        133, 135, 163, 166, 184, 185, 186,
        200, 223, 226, 230, 231, 232,
        254, 255
Workers' Opposition, 79, 181
wreckers and wrecking, 8, 10, 11, 12,
    27, 28, 51, 56, 57, 66, 72, 73, 74,
    75, 77, 83, 95, 96, 97, 98, 99,
    100, 105–07, 110, 112–15, 122,
    123, 127, 133, 134, 135, 136, 143,
    144, 155, 157, 158, 159, 161,
    200, 205, 207, 210, 214, 219,
    223, 236, 240, 244, 252, 254,
    255, 256, 257, 258

Zdobnov, A. Z., 180
Zhailov, 218
Zharikov, 136, 165, 169
Zhdanov, A. A., 55, 70, 110, 116, 118,
    119, 120, 128, 134, 135, 137, 149,
    161
Zhibrov, S. I., 182
Zhidkova, 234
Zhukov, M. E., 218, 219, 237
Zinoviev, G. E., 21, 47, 48, 55, 57, 60,
    61, 64, 65, 68, 70, 79, 81, 82, 83,
    84, 85, 97, 108, 119, 253
Zinovievites, 57, 58, 59, 67, 68, 69,
    70, 72, 73, 77, 79, 81, 82, 86,
    88–91, 105, 107, 122, 232